The Great Flood of 1993

The Great Flood of 1993

Causes, Impacts, and Responses

EDITED BY

Stanley A. Changnon

WestviewPress

A Division of HarperCollins*Publishers*

*This book is dedicated to all those who
experienced the Great Flood of 1993.
Their unbelievably hard work and courage
in flood-fighting efforts are a credit
to the American Spirit.*

Copyright © 1996 by Westview Press, Inc., A Division of HarperCollins Publishers, Inc.

Published in 1996 in the United States of America by Westview Press, Inc., 5500 Central Avenue,
Boulder, Colorado 80301-2877, and in the United Kingdom by Westview Press, 12 Hid's Copse
Road, Cumnor Hill, Oxford OX2 9JJ

A CIP catalog record for this book is available from the Library of Congress.
ISBN 0-8133-2619-2 (HC) — 0-8133-2620-6 (pbk.)

The paper used in this publication meets the requirements of the American National Standard for
Permanence of Paper for Printed Library Materials Z39.48-1984.

10   9   8   7   6   5   4   3   2   1

Contents

Preface

The inspiration for this book came from several sources. During my 45-year career as a climatologist, I have made extensive studies of the major "climatic aberrations" of the Midwest: floods and droughts. Consequently, an intensive study of the unique flood during 1993 was an inevitable outcome.

My physical proximity to the flood led me to closely observe the day-to-day happenings. In fact, during 1993 I made several trips to the flooded zones in Illinois, Iowa, and Missouri during July, August, September, and October. As a member of the staff of the Midwestern Climate Center, I was engrossed in collecting weather and flood information, and responding to media requests for information about the flood's climatological significance and impacts. All this required the acquisition of much data from various agencies and the systematic collection of newspaper accounts about flood conditions.

I had the good fortune to be asked to serve on the National Flood Disaster Survey Team, a federal enterprise led by the National Oceanic and Atmospheric Administration. As the only nonfederal member of this 16-person team, I got to see first hand many of the flooded areas during an exhaustive ten-day tour of the flood zone--from Minneapolis to northern Illinois, to Des Moines, Omaha, Kansas City, and St. Louis. This event also provided me with unique data and interactions with many of the people affected by the flood.

Soon after the flood, I was asked by two scientific societies, the American Association for the Advancement of Science (AAAS) and the American Meteorological Society (AMS), to plan and organize special symposia on the flood at their annual meetings in early 1994. These exercises gave me the opportunity to seek out a variety of specialists as speakers about all facets of the flood: its atmospheric causes, its hydrologic dimensions, its effects on the environment, and its impacts on society and national policy. In October 1993, I was asked to deliver the keynote address on the flood and its implications at the Illinois Governor's Conference on the Illinois River.

All of these activities, coupled with the writing of six scientific papers about the flood, collectively revealed the enormity of the flood, a once-in-a-lifetime event. The events during and after the flood also revealed the high degree of interest in the flood by the scientific community, by people in and around the flooded zones, by managers in state and federal agencies who must deal with such an event, and by water policymakers at all levels, local to federal. From these many activities and positive interactions, I developed the concept of *The Great Flood of 1993*.

Stanley A. Changnon

Acknowledgments

A book is a wonderful yet difficult undertaking that requires cooperation and exceptional efforts by many people. As editor, I first wish to acknowledge my co-authors who provided timely manuscripts that were excellent and interesting.

Numerous persons provided essential data and information. They included Nora Rotter and Pat Wasson, librarians at the Illinois State Water Survey; Bill Allen, science writer at the *St. Louis Post-Dispatch,* who furnished valuable media information; the staff at the Midwestern Climate Center, who provided data on climate conditions and flood impacts; Ellen Gordon, Director, Iowa Emergency Services Agency; Anne Bennof, Association of American Railroads; D.J. Tisor, Federal Railroad Administration; Mike Demissie, hydrologist at the Illinois State Water Survey, who provided incredible photographs; Mary Fran Myers, Natural Hazards Center, who provided valuable advice; Michael Glantz, National Center for Atmospheric Research, who provided guidance about the handling of the book; and Julia Joun, Westview Press, for her many useful comments.

Certain persons helped prepare materials in individual chapters: Mark Halpert, Gerald Bell, and David Miskus, Climate Analysis Center (Chapter 2); James Angel and Jean Dennison, Midwestern Climate Center (Chapter 4); Mike Demissie, Bill Bogner, and Vern Knapp, Illinois State Water Survey, and Don Vonnahme, Illinois Division of Water Resources (Chapter 5); Robert Maher, John Nelson, Anjela Redmond, and Charles Theiling, at the Long Term Resources Monitoring Program (LTRMP) stations operated by the Illinois Natural History Survey and the Illinois Department of Conservation in Alton, IL, and Douglas Blodgett, Paul Raibley, Camilla Smith, Ruth Sparks, Andrew Spink, and Scott Whitney, Illinois Natural History Survey, Havana, IL (Chapter 6); Adenoir Belshe, Mark Bean, and Steve Monson, National Crop Insurance Services (Chapter 7); Nancy Eiben, National Weather Service (Chapter 8); and Robert Schnorbus, Federal Reserve Bank of Chicago, John Muller, Legislative Fiscal Bureau of Iowa, and Ted Trott, Bureau of Economic Analysis, U.S. Department of Commerce (Chapter 9). Their help is gratefully appreciated. Many unnamed persons working for the U.S. Army Corps of Engineers also helped by providing data.

I am particularly indebted to all those who helped prepare the book. First and foremost is Eva Kingston, who served most admirably as the technical editor for all chapters and made the text very readable. Sarah Hibbeler provided an excellent final edit. Julie Horan, David Cox, and Linda Hascall prepared the excellent illustrations. Debbie Mitchell and Jean Dennison handled the typing, and Charles Mercer prepared the photographic copies. Many photographs presented are those of the editor, and sources are shown for those agencies who graciously gave permission to utilize their photographs or illustrations.

x

Funding to cover the costs of preparing this book came from the University Corporation for Atmospheric Research (UCAR). Funds for the book were provided by the Climate Analysis Center of the National Weather Service, National Oceanic and Atmospheric Administration (NOAA).

The research reported in Chapter 3 was partially supported by NOAA Grant NA46WP0228 and partly by the Illinois State Water Survey. Portions of the research in Chapters 8 and 12 were supported by NOAA cooperative agreement NA47RA0225 and the Illinois State Water Survey. Funding for the measurements taken during and after the flood and used in Chapter 6 was provided by LTRMP, the Illinois Natural History Survey, and by a grant from the National Science Foundation, Division of Environmental Biology (DEB 9413134). The Long Term Resource Monitoring Program (LTRMP), operated jointly by the Environmental Management Technical Center of the National Biological Service and by the five states bordering the Upper Mississippi River, provided most of the information referenced in Chapter 6.

The views expressed herein are those solely of the authors, not those of any state or federal agency, nor the supporting agencies.

SAC

About the Contributors

Nani G. Bhowmik is an internationally recognized river engineer who has published more than 120 articles and reports in the field of hydrology. He is a principal scientist at the Illinois State Water Survey, and for 30 years has conducted and managed multidisciplinary research in the area of large river hydrodynamics, sediment transport, and physical impacts in a river environment. He is a fellow of the American Society of Civil Engineering and co-editor in chief of *Water International*.

Stanley A. Changnon is a professor of geography and atmospheric sciences at the University of Illinois at Urbana-Champaign, and chief emeritus of the Illinois State Water Survey. Many of his climatological investigations have addressed Midwestern droughts, floods, and severe weather. His interdisciplinary interests include the effects of weather and climate on social and physical systems, and government policy and the atmospheric sciences. Five of his papers and a book have won national awards. He is a fellow of three scientific societies and has been president of two professional societies.

Geoffrey J.D. Hewings is an economic geographer involved in modeling research and development and climate investigations. He has served as head of the Geography Department at the University of Illinois at Urbana-Champaign. Recently the University implemented his innovative idea: development of the Regional Economics Applications Laboratory to bring staff and students together with business interests to address real-world problems.

William H. Koellner is a hydrologist who has worked for the U.S. Army Corps of Engineers for more than 30 years. As a professional engineer and hydraulics engineer, he has long been interested in issues related to climate and water. His research includes study of possible changes in the Mississippi River system due to climate change.

Kenneth E. Kunkel is an atmospheric scientist specializing in meteorological studies of floods and droughts, climate change and variability, atmospheric boundary layer processes, and meteorological instrumentation. As director of the Midwestern Climate Center at the Illinois State Water Survey, he has led multi-faceted research projects and developed a computerized climate information system widely used by Midwestern decisionmakers during the 1993 flood and the 1988 drought.

Ramamohan Mahidera is an economist with a background in academia and private business. His major expertise is in developing and using economic models. He was a Senior Research Associate with the Regional Economics Applications Laboratory while on the staff at the University of Illinois, Urbana-Champaign. He is now a senior economist with the Amoco Corporation and he has the responsibility for monitoring economic trends in the United States and overseas.

David R. Rodenhuis is an atmospheric scientist with a career in academia and in government service. He was an associate professor of Meteorology at the University of Maryland for 18 years, and subsequently has served as director of the Climate Analysis Center, National Weather Service. In this position he has led the effort to improve near-real-time monitoring of climate anomalies, both regionally and globally, and directs the research and operations of the group of scientists who provide the nation with long-term climate forecasts.

Richard E. Sparks has directed the large river program of the Illinois State Natural History Survey since 1972. He supervises two field stations that have participated in a joint federal-state monitoring program on the Illinois River and the Mississippi River since 1988. The station located on the Mississippi River near St. Louis was damaged during the 1993 flood and had to be re-located. As a biologist who has long specialized in studies of rivers and floodplain ecosystems, he provided Congressional testimony about the 1993 flood and its environmental impacts.

Lee Wilkins is a professor in the Broadcast News Department at the University of Missouri School of Journalism and a former newspaper reporter who has been teaching journalism and mass communications for 16 years. Her research and teaching interests focus on media ethics, political communication, and media coverage of hazards, disasters, and risk. Her study of media coverage and public response to the Bhopal, India, chemical spill was named a *Choice* outstanding academic book of 1987, and she has been a long-time affiliate of the Natural Hazards Center.

James M. Wright has had extensive experience in planning, developing, and managing floodplain management programs at both the state and federal levels, and has taught university courses on these subjects. He has served on numerous national task forces, panels, and committees established to develop policies, and has managed a five-year federal interagency assessment of the nation's floodplain management program.

Thomas P. Zacharias served on the faculties at Iowa State University and Louisiana State University before becoming vice president of the National Crop Insurance Services in 1990. His wide-ranging economic and statistical studies concern hail and other weather conditions and their implications for the insurance industry, and a recent investigation addressed the use of computer programming in agricultural decisions.

The Great Flood of 1993

1

Defining the Flood:
A Chronology of Key Events

Stanley A. Changnon

INTRODUCTION

The Great Flood of 1993 in the Midwest can safely be labeled as "unprecedented" and the creator of record high financial losses. Damage estimates, which climbed from $5 billion to $25 billion during the course of the flood, are now, with more accurate assessments, $18 billion. And it is the damages that qualify the flood of 1993 as the worst on record for the United States (Zimmerman, 1994). The flood affected a third of the United States and severely tested national, state, and local systems for managing natural resources and for handling emergencies, illuminating both the strengths and weaknesses in existing methods of preparing for and dealing with massive prolonged flooding.

Through detailed case studies and sectoral analyses, this volume diagnoses the social and economic impacts of this monumental disaster, assessing how resource managers, flood forecasters, public institutions, the private sector, and millions of volunteers responded to it. This comprehensive evaluation of the 1993 flood examines ways floods are forecasted and monitored, the effectiveness of existing recovery processes, and how the nation manages its floodplains. The flood taught major lessons for addressing future flood disasters, both to the public and private sectors, and these lessons are identified. The emphasis here is on the flood's many impacts and the policy issues that they raise.

This chapter presents an overview of the flood from a physical and policy standpoint, introduces the impact analyses that are central to the book, and then offers a chronicle of the key events before, during, and after the flood. Chapters 2 through 6 describe various physical aspects of the flood, including the effects on the environment, and Chapters 7 through 11 address the social, economic, and policy impacts. Chapter 12 summarizes the myriad physical, socioeconomic, and political impacts of the flood, and Chapter 13 identifies what we have learned from the 1993 flood: those actions that appear to be necessary if the nation and impacted sectors are to more effectively deal with future floods.

4

Worst Flood Ever?

Some claim that the 1927 flood on the Lower Mississippi River was the worst ever, and others challenge this, claiming the 1993 flood was the worst. The 1927 flood killed many more people (Henry, 1927), but it created less financial loss than the 1993 flood (see Chapter 11). The difference in lives lost (52 in 1993 vs. 313 in 1927) is a reflection of improved flood forecasting and warning systems. The 1993 flood occurred in the Upper Mississippi basin (the area north of Cairo, IL), whereas the 1927 flood occurred in the Lower Mississippi River basin (the area south of Cairo). Both floods led to major federal responses and large expenditures to address restoration of the flooded areas. Remember, the Mississippi River basin is the fifth largest river system in the world and embraces all or portions of 31 of the 48 contiguous states and two Canadian provinces. The 1993 flood ultimately affected 30 percent of this immense area. Figure 1-1 shows where the major flooding occurred.

Debates also continue as to whether the 1993 flood flow in its peak area, St. Louis, MO, ranks second to the massive flood of 1844. Questions over the accuracy of the 1844 measurements of flood flow leave this issue unresolved (Parrett et al., 1993). At some locations, the flood of 1993 ranks as a once-in-100-year event, and at a few others as a once-in-500-year event. Record flooding occurred over 1,800 miles of Midwestern rivers, plus major flooding on another 1,300 miles of rivers (Figure 1-1). In any case, it was a rare and powerful event, a breed apart from other floods.

Defining the 1993 Flood in Space and Time

Pinpointing the beginning and ending of the flood of 1993 is difficult. Some experts would include the spring (April-May) flooding along the Mississippi and Missouri Rivers; others want to confine the Great Flood to the extremes that occurred in June-August; and still others want to include the floods of the fall. Heavy rains across Missouri, Illinois, and Kansas in late September created new flooding on the main rivers and one person drowned. Rains of 3 to 8 inches occurred across southern Illinois and Missouri in mid-November, creating near-instant severe flooding in the Mississippi and its regional tributaries, leading to five deaths. The focus of this book is on the summer flood, a singular geophysical oddity, but attention is given to preceding and ensuing events, which were directly tied to the summer flood.

Defining the flood's spatial dimensions begins with consideration of the summer's 77 large rain areas (each with rains in excess of an inch falling over oblate-shaped areas that were 100 to 200 miles across and 400 to 600 miles long). These rain areas appeared practically every day somewhere in the Midwest during the summer of 1993.

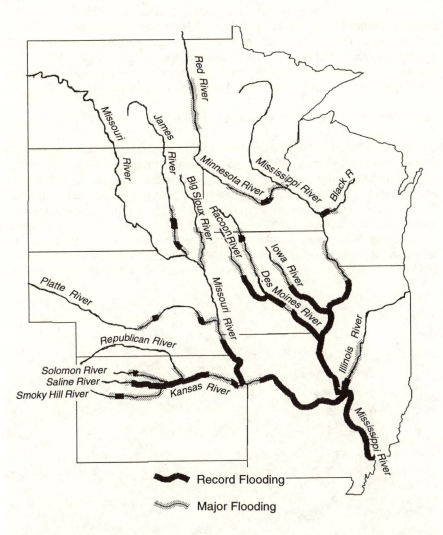

FIGURE 1-1 The reaches of rivers that experienced new record floods and those with nonrecord but major flooding in 1993 (adapted from IFMR Committee, 1994).

Buried within these immense storm systems were at least 175 cores of heavy rain, each producing more than 6 inches of rain in short periods and an untold number of flash floods. These flash floods were an integral part of the flood of 1993 along with the resulting inundation of the floodplains of the major rivers.

6

The extreme wetness in the spring of 1993 continued through the summer and fall with persistent soggy soils and frequent standing water in the flatter upland areas typical of the Midwest. The resulting farm impacts, including delayed crop planting, reduced crop yields, and delayed harvesting, make these wet areas another part of the flood. Thus, the Great Flood included the saturated uplands of the Midwest as well as the flooded streams and rivers and their floodplains, and thus encompassed large portions of nine states. The massive floods on the Mississippi and Missouri Rivers joined at St. Louis (Figure 1-2).

Policy Impacts Extended beyond the Event

The Great Flood of 1993 created monumental impacts in the Midwest but also became a pivotal event nationally by causing major shifts in government policies relating to flood mitigation, weather risks, and natural hazards. The flood was the culmination of a series of climate anomalies in the United States that began in 1976 when three of four winters set records for severe low temperatures and major storms. The early 1980s were the wettest five years on record, resulting in damaging high levels on the Great Lakes and the Great Salt Lake, but conditions abruptly reversed creating a major drought across the nation during the 1987-1989 period. The 1991-1993 period had been marked by major storms: the

FIGURE 1-2 The confluence of the Missouri River (left) and Mississippi River (right) near St. Louis, MO, at the height of the flood, late July 1993. The large floodplain between them was inundated in floodwaters 10 feet deep, and for the first time in recorded history, major flood peaks came down both rivers simultaneously and joined here on August 1, creating a massive flood surge that swept down the Mississippi towards the Ohio River.

High Plains had back-to-back record-high hail losses in 1992 and 1993; Hurricanes Andrew ($30 billion in losses) and Iniki ($5 billion) came in 1992; and the straw that broke the camel's back was the Great Flood of 1993.

The events of these past 18 years proved that our modern society has become ever more sensitive to weather, and in particular to climate aberrations--the prolonged multi-year extremes of weather. Our enhanced vulnerability is tied to many social changes: a growing population at risk, particularly in cities; disaggregated production systems that are highly vulnerable to transportation breakdowns and delays in shipping; an aging infrastructure (highways, drainage and water supply systems, dams, etc.) that is weather sensitive; power utilities facing enhanced economic and regulatory stresses; and ever-enlarging farm sizes, which increase the likelihood of weather losses. Losses from the extremes during the past 18 years also have severely impacted all levels of government, largely through huge relief costs; and the sequence of weather extremes since 1976 culminated in huge costs of the 1993 flood--$6.2 billion from federal coffers and $1 billion from the affected states with 1,000 levees breached (Figure 1-3). The flood finally moved Congress and the Clinton Administration to make fundamental changes in policies and programs involving floodplain insurance, crop insurance, and how the nation handles natural hazards.

Old Man River Takes Back His Flood Plain

FIGURE 1-3   The enormous impact of the flood and the breaking of over 1,000 levees was a major news topic and became a subject of continuing policy debates (Copyright 1993, Engelhardt, in the *St. Louis Post-Dispatch*/reprinted with permission).

Defining the Impacts and Responses to the Flood

The primary emphasis of this book is on the impacts that the flood produced. The impacts of a catastrophic event occur in a three-tiered sequence. The first are the *direct* or initial impacts, such as a measurement that the flooding covered 58 percent of a community's area. The *secondary impacts* evolve from the direct impacts, such as a ruined water treatment system damaged by chemicals released 50 miles upriver by a flood-caused accident at a chemical plant. The *tertiary impacts* are those that occur last, usually months or years after the event. Examples include the collapse of a structure a year after the flood due to unknown undermining of its foundation, or the loss of a family's income because the employer, a manufacturer, had to close due to the flood damage and/or loss of supplies, or an inability to obtain a loan adequate to restore operations, or eventual loss of a market to another competitor without flood problems. This assessment of the flood made in late 1994 indicates that while many of the impacts have occurred and can be identified and quantified with reasonable accuracy, others can not. Notably, we still lack quantification of the serious environmental impacts. There is also considerable difficulty in obtaining highly accurate estimates of the losses and their costs, including the costs of the responses to the flood. This point is illustrated here to alert and caution the reader about the assessment issues. Probably the best data on the flood's effects have been gathered for the state of Iowa.

Analysis of the flood's economic impact in Iowa illustrates widely ranging values, depending on the source of the information and when the loss values were estimated. The *Kansas City Star* provided values in early September 1993 of $3.5 billion and credited these to the Federal Emergency Management Agency (FEMA). Schnorbus et al. (1993) estimated Iowa's direct and indirect losses as $3 billion. The state's own estimates of its losses were "greater than $3.4 billion" (IFMRC, 1994). The National Weather Service estimates (NWS, 1994) were $5.7 billion for Iowa. Which is correct?

Since many damages were found to be greater once the flood had receded and assessment and reconstruction had begun, the larger 1994-issued value, $5.7 billion, is the latest and considered the best estimate of this group. This value does not include considerable damages as yet unquantified, including losses of top soil to erosion (2.4 million Iowa acres suffered "severe erosion"), plus other environmental damages crudely estimated as $0.3 billion, bringing our estimate of Iowa's total loss to $6 billion.

This value is listed as a "loss," but from a broader perspective, many of these losses, or costs to someone, have been or will be recovered. The federal government provided $1.24 billion in federal aid to Iowa, and the state provided an additional $0.2 billion (these costs are losses transferred from those incurring damage to taxpayers). From a broad financial perspective, government funds, insurance payments, and private capital have been spent to rebuild damaged property and the state's infrastructure, and these recovery expenditures represent a benefit to the state's economy. Are they losses or gains? Should these inputs to Iowa's economy be subtracted from the losses? Some of the damaged or destroyed property will not be rebuilt, representing permanent losses. Personal income was lost due to crop failures, lost jobs, and prolonged absences from employment. Some income was recouped from federal aid (crop losses), but much was not. Certain revenue losses due to flood-interrupted sales were deferred and recovered by sales after the flood; other revenue losses were never recouped, at least not in Iowa, and indeed are true losses to the state's economy. These inputs to the state's economy through rebuilding (private and government funds) and recouped revenues have not been subtracted from the $6 billion in losses; however, on the long haul, a sizable amount of the new expenditures have been made and the long-term net effect on the state's economy is much less than $6 billion (probably more nearly $2 billion to $3 billion).

Hopefully, the above dialogue serves as a useful introduction to the area of impact analysis.

CHRONOLOGY OF THE FLOOD

The Great Flood of 1993 on the Upper Mississippi River basin had a unique and seemingly unbelievable evolution for the affected public and most flood experts. Like major droughts, the flood's severity, longevity, and areal extent were not well recognized during its developing stages.

The flood's chronology is an interesting way to tell the story of the "Great Flood of '93" and to assess how key events and issues developed over time. An array of newspaper accounts from the flooded regions was assessed in chronological order to obtain insights into the evolution of the flood. Among the sources were the *Chicago Tribune,* the *St. Louis Post-Dispatch,* the *Des Moines Register*, the *Kansas City Star,* and numerous other regional and national newspapers. Events presented relate to the major *direct* impacts that were occurring, the political actions that developed, the forecasts issued relating to flood conditions, and the relief and restoration activities.

The Formative Period

July 1992-March 1993. Above-normal rainfall occurs throughout the Upper Mississippi basin. Minor winter floods occur after extremely heavy November rainfall along portions of the Mississippi River. On March 3, the NWS *warns* of minor to moderate spring flood potential on the Upper Mississippi.

April-Early May. Snowmelt coupled with an overly wet spring create a typical spring flood along the Upper Mississippi River lasting two to three weeks at most points along the river and a moderate flood lasting 44 days at St. Louis.

Spring (March-May). Copious rains occur across the central United States. Soil moisture values are much above average, and many fields have standing water. Wet soils delay planting of corn and soybeans across the Corn Belt.

The Beginning of Problems

May 6-8. Heavy rains hit the Kansas City area, creating local flash floods, and the Missouri River reaches flood stage.

May 9-10. Heavy rains in Minnesota create floods along the Redwood River in southwestern Minnesota.

May 11. Flooding develops along the Arkansas River in Kansas, and 300 families are evacuated.

May 15-16. Rains totaling 9 inches occur in parts of southern Minnesota and South Dakota.

May 31. Delayed planting of corn and soybeans due to wet soils persists. The NWS outlook calls for above-average summer rainfall in the Midwest.

June 7. At a national agricultural conference, two private sector weather forecasters predict a hot, dry, Midwestern summer with drought developing in July-August, predictions soon shown to be *grossly* inaccurate.

Early-to-mid-June. Moderate to heavy rains occur on eight straight days across much of South Dakota, Iowa, Minnesota, and Wisconsin.

June 10. Concern grows over planting delays of major crops across the Corn Belt now making national news, and the grain market reacts.

Mid-June. Flooding develops along the major tributaries of the Mississippi River in Iowa, Minnesota, and Wisconsin. Damage reports appear for campgrounds, marinas, and birds and wildlife.

June 20. Flooding of the Minnesota River escalates, and the river crests 11 feet above flood stage at Mankato, spreading into the Mississippi River at St. Paul and southward down the Mississippi's main channel. First levee break occurs at Hatfield, WI, and flood stage is reached at the gage at Rock Island, IL, one of the Quad Cities.

Escalation of the Flood

June 23. Port of St. Louis is closed to barges.

June 24. The NWS forecasts a crest of 21.9 feet at Quincy, IL, which is revised upwards to 24.5 feet 24 hours later--the flood is rapidly enlarging southward as heavy rains fall along the river from Quincy to Wisconsin.

June 25. About 250 miles of the Mississippi is closed because of flooded locks and dams with predictions of the Corps of Engineers of the closure lasting two weeks. (*the spring floods closed the river for 12 days*).

June 26. Flood news makes page one of the *St. Louis Post-Dispatch* (first time), with initial predictions of severe flooding in the St. Louis region. The Mississippi rises above flood stage at St. Louis.

June 27. The NWS predicts flood crest of 26.8 feet at Grafton, IL, on July 2. *(Actual value was 28.3 feet and rising rapidly).* Severe flooding begins at Davenport, IA, one of the Quad Cities.

June 28. The Corps closes the Mississippi to barge and pleasure craft above Clarksville, MO, all the way to Minneapolis, MN. About 2,000 grain barges and 50 tugs are reported as stranded along with many other barges containing coal, fertilizer, and cement.

June 29. The Federal Emergency Management Administration (FEMA) denies Missouri's request for $1.5 million for flood relief in eight counties from the spring flood damage. The rash of "last minute" purchases of flood insurance continues, since coverage begins only five days after the date of purchase.

June 30. The flood makes the front page of the *Chicago Tribune* (first time), and is "big news" everywhere (Figure 1-4). The first flood death occurs along the Minnesota River; the governor of South Dakota declares 12 counties as disaster areas; Wisconsin declares 30 counties as disaster areas; and Iowa declares 15 counties as disaster areas. The main line of the Burlington-Northern across Iowa is closed with Amtrak trains re-routed north of the flood. The barge industry spokesmen estimate a loss of $1 million per day to barge operators plus additional losses to shippers. The Corps predicts that it will be two weeks (i.e., July 15) before barges can move again on the navigable rivers.

July 1. Soybean futures began a rapid rise in late June due to excessive wetness. U.S. Department of Agriculture (USDA) Secretary Espy visits the flooded areas in Minnesota, Wisconsin, South Dakota, and Iowa. Senator Dole claims Democrats are playing "politics" with their attention to the flood. The Corps forecasts the flood at St. Louis will last until mid-July but states the crest would not be as high as the spring flood. A few agricultural levees give way along the Mississippi between Quincy, IL, and Davenport, IA. The 90-day outlook issued by the National Weather Service calls for more above-normal precipitation across the Midwest.

July 2. Illinois Governor Edgar declares 17 Illinois counties as disaster areas, and Missouri declares 18 counties as disaster areas. Minnesota Governor Carlson says crop damage in his state exceeds $1 billion. Federal officials say the flood on the Mississippi will be the fifth highest of record. [*The "Wisconsin-Minnesota flood problem" (May to mid-June) has now become an "Illinois-Iowa" problem*].

July 3. Between St. Louis and Keokuk, IA, the only highway bridge across the Mississippi remaining open is at Quincy; all others are closed because their approaches are under water. A 500-mile stretch of the river is closed to barge and pleasure craft, the longest distance closure ever. Estimates of crop losses along the Mississippi are $130 million, and the river level breaks all past records in the Quad Cities area. The National Weather Service issues a forecast stating the flood crest at St. Louis on July 7 will be at 40 feet *(the actual level by July 7 was 42 feet, and the crest came a month later).*

'It's Us Against The River

Shift in weather pattern suggests worse forecast

Bean planting delay flares market scare

DES MOINES, Iowa (AP) — T
weather pattern responsible f
the Midwest floods has chang
for the first time in nearly f
months, but it's not good news.

Davenport's river shows its dark side

Call Goes Out For Sandbagging Volunteers

'They're So Enthusiastic, They're . . . Falling Over One Another Trying To Help'

Mississippi Barges Face Long Wait

Dole blasts Espy's flood visit

Says Democrats are playing politics with disaster

Local guardsmen continue to hold back Mississippi

Rain and floods threaten lives and property in a dozen states; a 12-year-old boy drowns in Wisconsin.

threatened an earthen dam and caused flash floods.

Transportation Snarled
The Midwest's raging rivers were tangling traffic Sunday for planes, trains and automobiles. Truck and

'WERE WE GO AGAIN'

Merciless storms continue assault across Midwest

'It's really hard work, and the conditions aren't the best. They're holding up well, as far as their spirit and morale.'

Clinton splashes into Iowa

President says relief

Worst flooding may not

Firms See Profits Go Down The Drain

Damage estimates still growing

On The Farm

Rain's Damage Goes Beyond Crops In Field

By The New York Times
The Great Flood of 1993 is

Mississippi churning

ECONOMIC STRUGGLES BEGIN

Cities wonder if they'll stay afloat

Floods cripple Des Moines; entire city without water

Downtown may lack electricity for a week

Time and again, the Father of Waters is asserted its authority over mortals

Activist says floods are God's judgments

Flood Pummels Roads, Bridges In Missouri, Illinois

FIGURE 1-4   Headlines of major events during June and July 1993.

July 4. President Clinton tours a flooded area in Davenport, IA, and pledges $1.2 billion in flood relief. Many freedom celebrations in communities along the river are canceled or moved. Flooding on the Upper Mississippi in the

Minnesota-Wisconsin area is the worst since 1960. Between St. Louis and Jefferson City the Missouri River is closed to barge traffic. Secretary Espy says crop disasters will qualify for $297 million in aid, and President Clinton asks Congress to approve an initial $850 million for flood relief.

July 5. Major evacuations occur along the Mississippi: 150 families at East Dubuque, 30 families at Oquaka, and 750 people at Keithsburg, IL; 6,000 people in Madison County, SD; and 400 families near St. Charles, MO. The governor of Iowa estimates state farm losses at $1 billion. Levees crumble in northwestern Missouri, flooding two interstate highways. The Corps predicts a crest of 34 feet on the Missouri River at St.Charles, and comes under media criticism for its flood-protection system (Figure 1-5).

A National Disaster

July 6. Flood news explodes and the flood goes from a regional Midwestern story to a national headline story. The Corps has now placed 440,000 sandbags in the St. Louis area. As a result of the flood scare soybean prices rise to $7 a bushel, the highest price since 1989. The Corps now expects the Mississippi to be open to navigation on July 25. Between the Nebraska border and St. Louis, 16 levees have been breached along the Missouri River. The Illinois River is closed to traffic at Peoria.

FIGURE 1-5 As the flood escalates and moves southward during July, the media targets the flood and often lashes out at the Corps of Engineers and their role in the flood (Reprinted by permission. Tribune Media Services).

July 7. The eighth flood death occurs in Missouri, and the latest NWS forecast of the St. Louis flood crest goes from 40 feet to 43.5 feet set to occur on July 13, which would break the old record. Four riverboat gambling casinos are closed. Flooding has now closed several low-lying railroads in the Midwest, re-routing trains around the Missouri-Iowa area. The Big Sioux River crests 8 feet above flood stage at Sioux Falls, SD. The first of 18 major levee breaks in Illinois occurs at Keithsburg. Iowans accuse the Corps of mismanaging reservoirs, allowing the flooding to become more severe.

July 8. Economists in the *New York Times* indicate that the huge flood loss will have little national effect and will not create any inflation, but losses could raise food prices slightly. The USDA says crop losses nationally will be about $1 billion due to floods and related wetness. The river peaks at Davenport at 22.6 feet, a new record. At St. Louis 2,000 dock workers are laid off, freight terminals are closed, and shipments normally handled by barges have begun to be shifted to rail.

July 9. The flood becomes front page news in *USA Today* and *The Wall Street Journal.* Market values of several agribusiness giants fall due to expected higher grain costs. Agricultural expert investors are baffled as to the flood's potential impact--there are no experiences with a major summer flood of this magnitude. A South Dakota man drowns in his car; Wisconsin increases its disaster area to 31 counties; and 7,800 people are evacuated from Missouri lowlands. Again, the NWS ups its prediction of the flood crest at St. Louis to 45 feet on July 14 (*a 1.5-foot jump in the forecasted level in two days*). Worry grows over potential infections such as hepatitis from floodwaters. Many members of Congress tour flooded areas. Floodwaters retreat somewhat in Minnesota, but half of the state's corn and soybean crops are in extremely poor condition. About 2,500 Iowa families are evacuated. Some businesses are profiting: hotels housing displaced families and flood cleanup and truck rental companies.

July 10. Along the Missouri and Mississippi Rivers, 120 levees have broken and no longer help slow the rise of the rivers: levees north of St. Louis along the Mississippi are now breached and many destroyed. Soybean prices hit a new high, $7.17. The death tally grows to 19: 3 in Minnesota, 4 in Wisconsin, 9 in Missouri, and 1 each in Iowa, Illinois, and South Dakota. Meteorologists debate the causes of the flood-producing rains: effects of the Mt. Pinatubo volcanic explosion, El Niño, global climate change, and plain old "natural" variability. Floodwaters submerge several major east-west rail lines (Santa Fe, Burlington Northern, and Norfolk Southern). Massive re-routing of trains begins with a funneling of rail traffic through St. Louis and Minneapolis. Kansas City experiences "D-Day" as several barges break loose and damage bridge piers.

July 11. *The flood has been widely recognized as truly a "national disaster."* Sudden unexpected flooding of the water treatment plant at Des Moines ends all public water service, and 5,000 people are evacuated. Flooding along the Mississippi River now covers 430 square miles of its floodplains. Crop and property damage estimates are now $2 billion (*a doubling of the estimated loss in just three days)*. Midwestern governors again tour flood regions. Near St. Louis, 4,500 trailer park residents are displaced. Rains will lessen says the head of the NWS.

July 12. Vice President Gore vows "swift aid" after visiting the flood area. In Missouri and Illinois, 4,700 National Guard members are sandbagging, and 49 of 114 Missouri counties have been declared disaster areas. Inactive barge losses are now reported as $2 million per day, and the Mississippi River is closed from Savannah, IL, to Cairo. Some of the 2,900 stranded barges have sunk.

July 13. Major newscasters on ABC, NBC, and CBS all go to St. Louis to do flood stories "raising the national consciousness." *Time* magazine presents a major news story about the flood. Twenty-four more Missouri counties are declared disaster areas, and FEMA opens five Missouri offices to take applications for relief. FEMA Director James Witt tours Missouri and Illinois. Soybean prices finally tumble as the USDA projects a big harvest. In the past week, 1,000 trains have been re-routed around the flood zone, and 550 miles of track on 13 railroads are under water.

July 14. The NWS *forecasts* a flood crest of 45 feet at St. Louis on July 18 *(a correct height for that date, but the crest actually occurs 13 days later on August 1)*. Missouri now reports a total of 14 flood deaths. President Clinton tours Des Moines and proposes $2.48 billion in flood relief, which Illinois senators challenge as being insufficient. Illinois announces flood losses of $1 billion. With major washouts along 34 lines, the flood has affected 25 percent of the nation's rail traffic.

July 15. A new estimate of flood damage is $5 billion (up from $2 billion estimated by experts on July 11). Half of the levees between Omaha, NE, and Jefferson City, MO, have been overtopped or broken. President Clinton flies to Des Moines and then to St. Louis. A major levee break occurs at West Quincy, quickly flooding 34 square miles and causing the closure of the Quincy bridge over the Mississippi, closing the only bridge open between St. Louis and the Quad Cities, a devastating blow to auto and truck traffic.

July 16. Governor Edgar claims the flood is the worst natural disaster ever to occur in Illinois. The Missouri and Mississippi River floods begin to join north of St. Louis, and excessive flooding begins south of St. Louis. Flooding in Fargo, ND, swamps the sewage system. Flood levels at Davenport, IA, begin to recede and cleanup begins. Ecologists blame the record-high flooding on excessive levee construction and the loss of wetlands.

July 17. President Clinton, Vice President Gore, and several cabinet members tour flood areas and meet with the governors of the nine flooded states. Weather experts predict continuing rains. There are now 27 deaths due to the flood, and with 8,000 homes damaged, new loss estimates are at $10 billion.

July 18. Oil, sewage, and chemicals from flooded facilities are polluting the floodwaters, and 500 families are evacuated in St. Louis. An NWS flash-flood warning issued for a large campground near Baraboo, WI, leads to the safe evacuation of hundreds just before floodwaters inundate the area. New York economists claim that the flood will have no measurable effect on the national economy, indicating a projected loss of $15 billion will be about 1 percent of the nation's gross national product.

July 19. Eight million farm acres are under water, and the Mississippi is cresting from Quincy 300 miles south to Cape Girardeau. Deaths due to the flood have jumped to 31, and President Clinton declares disaster areas in eastern parts of North Dakota and South Dakota.

July 21. Water levels in the Missouri River begin to drop, but severe flooding occurs as levees break south of St. Louis. North Dakota has 19 counties flooded and two people killed by the flood. Extensive volunteer efforts with the provision of food, money, and help are occurring across the flooded Midwest (Figure 1-6).

July 22. After 12 days without water, water service is restored at Des Moines. There have been 32 deaths in the Midwest due to the flood. The NWS says a drier weather pattern is being established for the Midwest. Representative Kennedy is drafting a bill to revamp the flood insurance program, as is Senator Kerry in the Senate. Congress has fiery debates over how to raise funds for the $2.98 billion in emergency flood relief requested by President Clinton. Congress is calling for flood studies by the Corps of Engineers.

July 23. Six people are drowned in a cave near St. Louis, caught there by a flash flood. A new NWS forecast at St. Louis calls for the crest to be at 47 feet on July 28 *(the ultimate crest is 49.58 feet on August 1).* The Corps states the

FIGURE 1-6 Thousands of troops, state employees, and volunteers were fighting the flood during June and July. Shown here is one of the many sandbag operational centers with trucks lined up to load sandbags for a nearby levee along the Mississippi (Illinois State Water Survey).

flood could last until September. A major levee breaks south of St. Louis at Kaskaskia, which helps to reduce the river level at St. Louis. The Missouri River crests at 27.2 feet at Nebraska City, 9 feet above flood stage.

July 24. Flood forecasters at St. Louis say the river will go to 48 feet by August 1 *(for the first time the predicted date is correct, but the level is 1.5 feet lower than what occurred).* Flood insurance purchases continue.

July 25. Flood-fighting efforts have created huge debts, in excess of $0.5 million, at several river towns, including Quincy, Hannibal, and Davenport. Cargos worth $1.9 billion are stranded in 7,000 barges on the Mississippi River, costing barge operators $3 million per day. Three days of heavy rains in Kansas bring the crest of the Kansas River at Topeka 9 feet above flood stage.

July 26. Major levee breaks occur south of St. Louis. Continued heavy rains across the Missouri River portion of the basin bring more flash floods to Nebraska and Kansas. Flooding takes out the water treatment plant at St. Joseph, MO, ending service to 77,000 persons, and 10,000 persons are evacuated from flooded areas along the Missouri. *Time* headlines their weekly flood story, "Flood, Sweat and Tears."

July 27. A new flood crest of 48.8 feet occurs at Kansas City: all rail traffic in the Kansas City hub stops, 3,500 persons are evacuated, but major levees hold. After much bickering between Republicans and Democrats, the House of Representatives finally approves $2.98 billion in flood relief, and President Clinton announces he is seeking an additional $1.1 billion after meeting with the governors of six flooded states. Washington economists predict the flood loss will reach $25 billion, claiming the flood of 1993 will be the worst natural disaster ever in the United States. The death toll is 41, and 33 percent of Iowa's soybean crop is failing.

July 28. Flooding along the Illinois River increases rapidly. The Corps strenuously objects after charges by a Des Moines official that they issued false assurances that no flooding would occur in the city. Losses from inoperative barges are now estimated at a rate of $4 million per day.

Late July: in many respects, this was the worst time in terms of flooding extent and damages.

July 29. NWS forecasters again predict weather patterns are changing to a drier regime as heavy rains occur over much of the region. The U.S. Senate considers the $4.3 billion flood relief package. Flooding has driven many tourists away from the Midwest for an estimated 35 percent loss of tourist business. Rail lines remain closed in Kansas City.

July 30. Excessive flooding along the Missouri River "splits" Missouri in two with only one bridge open between St. Louis and Kansas City. A major railroad bridge over the Missouri River collapses. The NWS predicts a 48-foot crest at

St. Louis on August 5. The Senate approves $4.3 billion in flood aid with suggestions that it should become $6 billion.

July 31. The Corps says the St. Louis flood will go to 49.3 feet due to influx of floodwater from the peaking Missouri River.

August 1. The flood takes out the Alton water plant and 70,000 customers lose service. The NWS at St. Louis predicts a crest of 49.7 feet, but the Corps says the flood could go to 50-51 feet.

August 2. A new summary of flood damages for the nine seriously affected states is issued: 40,000 evacuees, $11 billion in crop and property damage, 32,000 homes damaged, 14,000 million acres flooded, and 43 deaths.

August 2-3. A massive flood south of St. Louis breaks several levees putting 70,000 acres under water; three communities are evacuated. This massive break in levees and ensuing flooding is credited with saving St. Louis from the predicted 50-foot crest and potential major flooding as the river begins to fall at St. Louis.

August 3. The flood has been the biggest national disaster to hit the U.S. railroad industry. Spokesmen claim losses are expected to reach $0.5 billion due to damages and re-routing costs.

August 4. Midwestern senators plead for more flood aid, and the Senate approves $5.8 billion along with $1 billion more for farm relief.

August 5. NWS forecasters predict the St. Louis area floods may last until early September or mid-October. Missouri sets aside $10 million to help flood victims move to new housing. Levels of the Mississippi River begin to fall, but the Missouri River rises. A complex of barges at St. Louis breaks loose and threatens bridge piers, and floodwaters lift 100 huge propane tanks, which threaten to break loose. Downstream of St. Louis, a levee is intentionally broken to protect a local community *(and it works)*. Economists predict that the flood's impact in the Midwest will be gone by 1994.

August 6. Many flood victims are experiencing high stress levels and exhibiting great anxiety.

August 7. The U.S. House approves the $5.8 billion flood aid package which includes $2 billion aid to people for homes, $2.4 billion for crop losses, and several million dollars for communities, temporary jobs, flood control works, health and environment assistance, aid for transportation, and restoration of natural resources. Midwestern congressmen seek a major study of the Upper Mississippi River and flood management. Flood cleanup becomes the front page story for many area newspapers.

August 8. The flood crest finally reaches Cape Girardeau, MO. Measurements show that 12,000 pounds of atrazine (a herbicide) pass through the Lower Mississippi every day, as compared to 3,000 pounds in 1992. In St. Louis, 6,000 evacuees return home. Wildlife is experiencing negative and positive impacts, delayed flooding effects.

The Flood Ebbs and Restoration Begins:
New Challenges

August 9. River levels everywhere are falling. Major new concerns are relief and aid for rebuilding (Figure 1-7). A Midwest forecaster predicts high potential for fall, winter, and spring flooding on the Mississippi River.

August 11. Strong odors pervade as the waters retreat. The new question of the day becomes what to do with the millions of used sandbags.

August 12. President Clinton signs the bill for $5.8 billion in flood aid while visiting St. Louis. Flood damage estimates are now $15 billion ($4 billion in Missouri alone). Secretary Espy says crop losses will be $2.5 billion, affecting 2 percent of all U.S. farmers, and that food prices will go up 3 percent in the next six months. USDA estimates call for a much reduced corn crop (down 22 percent from 1992) and a reduced soybean crop (down 13 percent from 1992). *(Final values will show these to be incorrect with corn down 31 percent and soybeans down 16 percent).*

August 13. Major rainstorms across Missouri and Illinois cause flash floods, which raise the Missouri River and the Mississippi River south of St. Louis. The Red Cross in St. Louis reports spending $7.5 million and receiving $4.5 million in donations.

Mid-August: as floodwaters recede, the mess caused by the flooding and the degree of damage are found to be much greater than expected.

August 15. The rampaging Missouri River scours 600 caskets from a cemetery at Hardin, MO.

August 16. Schools throughout the flooded area reopen with difficulty as many routes are closed requiring much bus re-routing. Hydrologists fear that the Mississippi is trying to cut a new channel near Cairo. FEMA, USEPA, the Corps, and USDA debate which levees will be rebuilt: 879 damaged levees are not eligible for federal aid. Soybean prices are now down to $6.45/bushel from the mid-July high of $7.45. Pope John Paul II speaks in Denver but offers no words about the flood.

August 17. Alton water plant reopens. Most National Guard troops assigned to flood duty go home very tired. Governor Edgar convenes a major flood meeting in Illinois to discuss recovery plans.

August 19. Heavy rains in northeastern Iowa cause extensive new regional flooding. Thousands are reported as being despondent over the redevelopment of flooding.

August 22. Time reports that the flood "has produced the greatest network for aid for any flood in the history of the country, from both government and private

If You Have Been Hurt By The Flood, Boatmen's Can Help

If you have lost your home, your job, or your possessions because of the recent flooding, Boatmen's Flood Relief Program is here to help you recover.

HOME IMPROVEMENT LOANS
• Up to $10,000 unsecured

IMPORTANT NOTICE TO FLOOD VICTIMS

If you are a customer of ...1 Group! we want to help. Here's how.
...of The Principal Financial Group
...ntact if you have any

Have a piece of our pie, and a slice goes to ...

BUSINESS BULLETIN

Plan You Disaster Recover

with A Single Phon

Rejoicing, reflecting as water runs

Some begin cleanup; others wonder if they ever can

AFTER THE FLOOD

Getting down and dirty with clean-up projects

Mississippi at St. Louis reaches crest

Neighborhood floods; downtown area remains dry | Area guardsmen's 'valiant effort' can't save levee

Floods knock out water in more towns

Local guardsmen continue to hold back Mississippi

By JULIE WURTH
News-Gazette Staff Writer
and Copley News Service
Dreaded rains were falling again this morning on the Urbana-based National Guard troops shoring up the Say Island levee near Quincy
Anxious volunteers awaited the

'It's really hard wor and the conditions are the best. They're holdi up well, as far as their spirit and morale.'
— Sgt. Brian Albert,

Midwest victims battle the mess, their emotions

Iowa finds a rainbow: Drier days ...een ahead

Flood Victims Grow Weary

FIGURE 1-7   Examples of the key events making headlines during August 1993.

groups." At last the Mississippi is open to barge traffic on 830 river miles from Cairo to Minneapolis.

August 23. Governor Carnahan of Missouri calls a special session of the state legislature to raise funds for flood repairs. *(Federal officials announce that "the 1993 flood was the greatest ever in the Upper Mississippi.")*

August 25. Housing and Urban Development funds available for "buyouts" will influence some flood victims not to rebuild in the floodplain. The White House charges federal agencies with the task of finding "the best way to manage floods," a sign of policy change, and serious policy debate begins on the restoration and question of levees vs. wetlands in floodplains. Flood losses and relief activities are the hot media topics.

Confusion over Relief and More Flooding

August 27. There is much confusion over relief aid: who gets what, when, and how? Many flooded homeowners are unhappy over the lack of action. Recognition grows that cleanup of the gigantic after-flood mess is a massive effort comparable to the flood-fighting effort during June, July, and early August.

August 29. Independent groups call for President Clinton to appoint a special commission to analyze and report what is to be done about floods and floodplain management. The flood tally is now reported as 48 deaths, 50,000 displaced persons, 15,000 square miles flooded, and $12 million in losses.

August 29-31. Rains in excess of 10 inches hit Iowa, and flooding again occurs in Des Moines with a flood crest 9 feet above flood stage.

August 31. Iowa announces flood damages in excess of $5 billion, with all Iowa counties declared as disaster areas.

September 3. Debates rage with FEMA over its use of different relief qualification rules for each state (Missouri vs. Illinois).

September 5. The Corps begins repairing federal levees. Environmental groups complain, asking for a delay in the wholesale rebuilding of other levees.

September 7. Biologists announce that the feared zebra mussel offers a major threat throughout the Mississippi basin due to the flood. Climatologists at the Midwestern Climate Center issue an analysis of soil moisture, revealing that future flooding in the lower portions of the Upper Mississippi River basin are highly likely due to uniquely saturated soils. Illinois decides therefore to hold off on major road repairs and disposal of sandbags until the spring of 1994.

September 8. A St. Louis nuclear engineer claims that the 1993 flood was largely a result of the greenhouse-induced climate change. Others claim the flood was an act of God.

September 9. Residents of flooded Valmeyer, IL, vote to move their town.

September 11. The Corps announces that there were no major changes in the river channels of the Mississippi and the Missouri. Many of the 600 caskets washed away at Hardin, MO, are reburied in a mass grave.

September 12. The NWS announces that its flood forecast problems during the 1993 flood were due to monitoring instruments destroyed by the flood, unmeasured effects due to broken levees, and a computer modeling system that was flawed.

September 13. The river at St. Louis finally goes below flood stage, setting a 79-day record since June 26. Figure 1-8 depicts this event and other headline news during the fall of 1993.

September 14. Congress holds hearings on the flood insurance program and Senator Kerry offers legislation to alter the National Flood Insurance Program. The USDA cancels the rule allowing for the use of federal funds to repair frequently flooded farmlands.

September 15. A St. Louis newspaper starts selling a book about the flood, and the Senate holds hearings on the flood insurance program. The director of the U.S. Flood Insurance Program says "communities" will determine which flood victims move to high ground and which will rebuild, and indicates several towns are apt to rebuild on higher ground.

September 18. NWS meteorologists state that the behavior of El Niño is the primary cause of the flood-producing rains. Department of Defense officials announce that floodwaters swamping the Defense Mapping Agency in south St. Louis in early August have ruined 30,000 maps, many irreplaceable, and caused $20 million in building damages.

September 19. FEMA announces that at least 11 flooded communities want buyout funds to relocate (3 in Illinois, 2 in Missouri, 2 in Wisconsin, 2 in Iowa, 1 in Minnesota, and 1 in Kansas). Congressman Volkmer (MO) offers legislation to provide for these buyouts.

September 20. Frustration levels are high. Most of the 30,000 flood victims in Missouri and the 15,000 in Illinois remain in hotels and temporary apartments, awaiting decisions to rebuild or take buyouts.

September 21. Flooding from ground water emitted at the surface by saturated aquifers along the Illinois River spreads, closing four highways and inundating 38 square miles near Havana, IL.

September 24. President Clinton decides FEMA will pay 90 percent, not 75 percent, of many disaster costs, a great relief to the flooded states who will now pay 10 percent instead of 25 percent of the costs.

September 23-25. Heavy rains fall on still-saturated soils in Kansas, Missouri, and Illinois, creating new flooding on the Missouri, Mississippi, and Illinois Rivers. A St. Louis woman drowns and hundreds who had moved back are once again evacuated.

September 27. Mounting fears over potential crop damage from fall frosts, due to late maturing crops in the Midwest, cause the grain market to rally with an increase in December corn prices of 10 cents a bushel.

October 1. A suspect is charged with purposefully breaking the west Quincy levee on July 16, which flooded a large area and closed the Quincy bridge.

WE RENT AND SELL HIGH PRESSURE WASHERS!

Ideal for cleaning home and businesses
Stop in your loc

BEFORE YOU BORROW MONEY FOR FLOOD RELIEF:

Businesses face 'mess' in payroll after flood
To Bring Iowans Together.

FREE DISASTER RECOVERY TECHNICAL INFORMATION
For Flood Damaged Businesses
Coming to Des Moines...
The leading post-loss disaster recovery
Technical Specialist in the U.S.
PAT MOORE

Wildlife habitats are disrupted

When the floodwaters are gone, what happens to the sandbags?
sand and use it in sandboxes," said
Ron Fournier of the U.S. Army Corps

Officially, It's Almost Over

Gambling On Flood Insurance
Last-Minute Winners' Luck Goes On Taxpayers' Tab

Dams and levees: Can Mother Nature really be fooled?

Flood cleanup slow

Rain just will not go away

COMMENTARY

Don't Remove Farms From River Valleys

FIGURE 1-8 Flood events continued to make headlines from September-November 1993.

October 16. A major agribusiness, Archer-Daniel-Midlands, announces that the flood caused a major decline in their first-quarter earnings (from $125 million in 1992 to $69 million in 1993).

October 18. USDA national corn yield estimates are well down from prior predictions *(revealing more forecast errors)*, with a decrease of 0.5 billion bushels since their August estimate *(a 17 percent error--the September estimate was 7.23 billion bushels)*.

Implications for the Future:
More Floods and Policy Development

October 24. With considerable water still standing in the floodplains, fear grows over winter and spring flooding and over the potential for planting in the floodplains during spring 1994.

October 30. The Corps says flooding in spring 1994 is likely, and climatologists at the Midwestern Climate Center forecast above-average winter wet soils in the Mississippi basin.

November 13-15. Heavy rains across Missouri and Illinois produce new flooding, resulting in five deaths. The flooding subsides in three weeks. Valmeyer residents review plans for their new town on high ground.

December 4. President Clinton signs legislation providing $110 million to help move people to high ground. Major federal aid payments begin to flow.

December 6. Scientists report that, due to the flood on the Mississippi River, the massive outflow of freshwater into the Gulf of Mexico has moved eastward across the Gulf, reached the Gulf Stream of the Atlantic Ocean, and then moved northward along the East Coast, passing Cape Hatteras in early October.

December 17. A survey of 408 Midwestern farms shows 77 percent had crops damaged or destroyed, 17 percent had homes destroyed, 88 percent of the farm families remained under stress, and 62 percent felt positive about prospects for 1994.

December 31. Precipitation during 1993 sets records with the highest values ever experienced in Illinois, Iowa, North Dakota, and South Dakota. Measurements along Missouri bottomlands reveal that 460,000 acres now have between 6 and 30 inches of sand (with costs to remove 24 inches of sand at $3,000 per acre--typically on land valued at $1,800 per acre).

January 1994. Two national scientific conferences conduct special flood symposia with a series of papers explaining flood causes and impacts. As a result of a Congressional Resolution passed in November, the Corps launches an 18-month "Floodplain Management Assessment."

January 10. President Clinton's Floodplain Management Task Force establishes the Interagency Floodplain Management Review Committee. This committee is charged with the task of delineating causes and consequences of the 1993 flood.

January 15. With 60 percent of FEMA's flood aid ($1 billion) spent in nine states, most of the remaining funds are awaiting people to move. FEMA reports 149,000 families received assistance; 40,815 households were affected by the flood; and they received 37,500 requests for funds to repair public buildings, roads, and other infrastructure.

February 22. Flooding develops in northern Illinois and Wisconsin, giving rise to the fear of a major spring flood. Scientists indicate a low probability for a severe spring flood since winter precipitation in the Upper Mississippi basin was much below average.

February 27. Two professors, one at the University of Illinois and another at Iowa State University, predict a 1994 drought in the Midwest *(later shown to be incorrect by near-average summer rainfall).*

March 12. NWS forecasters announce the spring flood danger is over for the Upper Mississippi.

March 27. A museum dedicated to the Great Flood of 1993 is established at Fort Madison, IA.

April 12-16. Extensive heavy rains (7 to 12 inches) cause severe flooding across the southern half of Illinois and Missouri, weakening and destroying some existing and rebuilt levees on the Mississippi River (Figure 1-9).

April 16. Levee repair is lagging: the Corps is working on 200 levees, but only 37 are done--complaints come from many.

May 1. Iowa's Governor reports the state has received $1.2 billion in federal flood aid with more expected.

Spring 1994: Some major trends appear across the flood zone:
- Farmers order record amounts of fertilizers, which railroads and barges are busy delivering.
- Farmers launch extensive planting, with a record high number of acres dedicated to corn and soybeans.
- The Corps frequently has to close the Missouri and Mississippi Rivers to dredge the channels.
- Power utilities, unable to get coal during the flood, are stockpiling coal; rail deliveries of coal are still behind schedule; and the price of coal has increased 25 percent.

June 13. Valmeyer, IL, is in the process of rebuilding its new town. Some 2,600 flood families still live in temporary housing, and 80 communities are planning total or partial relocation.

June 20. The Corps' Floodplain Management Assessment project begins seeking public input (see Figure 1-10).

June 30. The report of the Interagency Floodplain Management Review Committee calls for major changes in U.S. floodplain policy, and the Floodplain

Flood danger from snowmelt in upper Midwest appears over

DES MOINES, Iowa (AP) — The danger of flooding from snow melt in the upper Midwest was ... over Friday although

Bad floods unlikely in state this spring

wa Emergency Management Department's response division, was encouraged but still watchful.

"Compared to what we had last

Renewed flooding takes toll on weary victims

'People just feel ... they can't win'

By Laurie Goering
Staff Writer
COLUMBIA, Ill. (last ...)
Jiohn Keith Nelson ...

The more than 7 inches of rain that has fallen in the last week over a broad band of the Midwest has ...

Many farmers still waiting for levees

By SHARON COHEN
Associated Press Writer

Every spring, Glen Beckmeyer gambles when he plants his crop. This year, the odds are even longer for his farmer facing one big ... It's still waiting for

mmental statements

Fall floods and a severe winter caused more problems. "A lot of the levees had water on them on til late in the year," he said. "There was just a narrow band of time where we could get work done."

THE COST OF RAIN

Impact On The Economy

Year later, flooded town builds higher

'Moment I've been waiting for,' mayor says as town resettles on nearby bluff

By Debbie Howlett
USA TODAY

VALMEYER, Ill. — Over the rumble and roar of massive earth movers, Dennis Knobloch shouts to be heard

"The moment I've been waiting for," yells Knobloch, the mayor and the driving force behind moving his small Mississippi River town to high-

River Control Debate Has Only Begun

FIGURE 1-9   The flood and its aftermath continued to make headlines during spring 1994.

Task Force establishes two working groups to implement the recommendations with deadlines for 1995.

August 1994.   Legislation introduced in the U.S. Senate calls for establishment of a Flood Management Committee to develop a management plan with a balance between ecological and economic interests and the flood control of the Upper Mississippi River.

September 1994.   The National Flood Insurance Program is modified.   The Centers for Disease Control and Prevention announces a program to sample well water (bacteria, nitrates and atrazine) in every flooded county to see if there is any long-term threat to the area's water quality.

ATTENTION !!!

The Rock Island District Corps of Engineers invites you...

...to attend the November Floodplain Management Assessment Public
Meetings. The purpose of these meetings is to discuss the alternatives
developed after the issues and concerns were identified in our June 1994
Open Houses. We want your help in prioritizing land use alternatives so
together we can make wise decisions on floodplain management.

FIGURE 1-10 A part of the Corps of Engineers' announcement of a public meeting held in November 1994 to discuss options for future uses of the floodplains.

October 13, 1994. Congress enacts legislation to reform the Federal Crop Insurance Program.

December 1994. The man who broke the levee at West Quincy is sentenced to life in prison for his act, which resulted in massive flooding.

A Postscript

This assessment of the flood's evolution reveals the confusion and chaos during and immediately after the flood--it defines the flood as it was reported in the media. The evolution revealed a major theme: the continuing escalation of losses, unexpected events, and predicted flood levels. This is true of the forecasts of the flood's magnitude and the continuing extension of the predicted dates of flood crests, and the ever-continuing increases in (a) assessments of flood damages (in each impacted sector and as a total event), (b) political attention, and (c) dimensions of the federal and state relief aid. One would expect the occurrence of frequently changed estimates (upwards) in losses since the flood was an expanding event, at least through late July. However, one is impressed by the large errors in the estimates. It appears that underestimation of losses and hence in aid required were partly due to poor data and inadequate collection of information by government sources.

Flood forecasts of the National Weather Service, which often sizably underestimated future river levels and when the crests would occur, and flood pronouncements of the U.S. Army Corps of Engineers, which included optimistic statements about when the flood would end and navigation would resume, helped lead to the underestimation of the flood damages. These forecasts and pronouncements likely worked to the detriment of the strategies used to fight the flood, shipping alternatives, and other flood-impacted endeavors.

REFERENCES

Henry, A.J., 1927: Frankenfield on the 1927 floods in the Mississippi Valley. *Monthly Weather Review*, vol. 55, 437-452.

Interagency Floodplain Management Review Committee, 1994: *Sharing the Challenge: Floodplain Management into the 21st Century.* Administration Floodplain Management Task Force, Washington, DC, 189 pp.

Kansas City Star, September 4, 1993: Flood losses mount. p.1.

National Weather Service, 1994: *The Great Flood of 1993.* National Disaster Survey Report, National Oceanic and Atmospheric Administration, Washington, DC, 195 pp.

Parrett, C., N.B. Melcher, and R.W. James, 1993: *Flood Discharges in the Upper Mississippi River Basin, 1993.* U.S. Geological Survey Circular 1120-A, Washington, DC, 14 pp.

Schnorbus, R.R., M. Mahidera, and P. Ballew, 1993: The great flood of 1993 and the Midwest economy. *Midwest Economic Report,* Federal Reserve Bank, Chicago, IL, 1-13.

Zimmerman, R., 1994: After the deluge. *The Sciences*, 34(4), 18-23.

2

The Weather that Led to the Flood

David R. Rodenhuis

INTRODUCTION

Changing Sensitivities to Weather and Climate Extremes

During a short span of a few hundred years our national community has grown from a frontier society to an extremely complex, interconnected, and industrialized network of socioeconomic elements. Within this network, the daily needs of dense urban centers are strongly dependent on water resources, agricultural commodities, power generation facilities, and fuel supplies. Our infrastructure of communications, transportation, and resources allows us to maintain a lifestyle usually taken for granted in the United States.

Vulnerability to weather extremes was common in a frontier society. Early settlers were exposed to Midwestern heat and winter cold, the treachery of the dark forests in the east, humidity and insects in the south, High Plains tornadoes, and flash floods on the West Coast--all part of our romantic view of the early struggle to build a national and economically sustaining civilization in this country. Although we accept this vulnerability to nature in our historical past, we are now accustomed to thinking that a truly modern society should somehow be insulated from the vicissitudes of weather and climate fluctuations.

We have, in fact, come a long way in that direction. Most urban settings include air-conditioning in the summer and heating in the winter without having to struggle with a coal shovel or an ax. We take for granted fresh water and indoor toilets existing side-by-side. We travel according to a schedule set weeks in advance, or spontaneously, without thought for weather conditions except possibly the need for an umbrella. Even air transportation, notoriously sensitive to weather, is remarkably routine and safe. Recently, the construction of a new, expensive airport in Denver was advertised as "weatherproof."

Although we are far less sensitive to weather events than were our relatives a hundred years ago, it is ironic that the complex social and economic network we have built has become highly sensitive to climatic variations or persistent weather events. The Great Flood of 1993 is one such aberration revealing our society's enormous sensitivity to such events.

Living with Weather Risks:
The North American Battle Zone

North America is situated between the great polar air masses to the north and the warm, humid tropical air that originates over the equatorial oceans to the south. There are no mountain ranges to separate these contrasting air masses, and along the boundary between them is the path of storms that pass from west to east and give us our weather variability. Consequently, the latitudes from Texas to Montana are a veritable weather battleground throughout the year (Figure 2-1). And, like civilians in a real battle zone, we are constantly at risk from passing armies.

Moreover, a jet stream ten miles overhead moving commonly at speeds of 200 mph guides great waves of alternating cold and warm air across the continent. The west-east jet stream and the circulation of the upper atmosphere influence not only the intensity of the cyclonic storms, but also determine the location and persistence of the storm tracks, and hence any development of a climate anomaly in a region such as the Midwest.

Perhaps the most interesting property of the atmosphere is that it contains a minor fraction of water vapor. The usual source of water vapor in summer is a low-level jet from the Gulf of Mexico. Although the atmosphere typically contains less than 2 percent of this constituent, water vapor coupled with circulation and structural features of the atmosphere is an explosive mixture. First, the good news: water vapor condenses and falls from clouds as rain, replacing the water resources necessary to sustain life on earth. But the bad news is that the process of condensation releases energy, which when organized by weather patterns, can cause extraordinary damage in the form of winter storms, intense flash floods, tornadoes, and hurricanes. Such weather events are all-too familiar to the population of North America.

We have insulated our daily lives from most of these short-term weather events through improved data collection, extended-range weather forecasts, and a rapid warning and communications system. Nevertheless the exceptions are notable, even if they are of short duration, and we continually live at risk of such weather events.

When nature conspires to persistently concentrate weather patterns at one location, even short-term weather events can collectively create a major climate anomaly against which a modern society provides little protection or advance warning. In fact, the concentration of human population, industrial zones, and intensive agriculture makes the interconnected, industrial society more vulnerable and sensitive to climate anomalies. Examples of such geographical risks include the drought of the 1930s, the Mississippi floods of 1927, and most recently, the drought of 1988 and the Great Flood of 1993. In contrast to many short-term weather events, the scope and intensity of occasional persistent climate anomalies are so great that our defensive measures are not very adequate. Like citizens in the weather battle zone mentioned earlier, we are occasionally forced to live on the battlefield itself.

What causes weather events to persist or major climate anomalies to develop? In addition to the natural risks of cold/warm air masses, water vapor, atmospheric waves, and the jet stream, North America lies downstream from two major sources of energy in the Pacific Ocean that affect climate anomalies. First, over the North Pacific near the Aleutian Islands the contrast of polar and maritime air masses over water causes persistent low pressure and creates a natural generation region for cyclonic storms, which subsequently move over North America, one after another, under the guidance of the polar jet stream shown in Figure 2-1.

Second, to the south in the equatorial Pacific the irregular occurrence of very warm ocean surface temperatures significantly strengthens the subtropical jet that subsequently streams from the southern Pacific towards the southwestern United States. Ocean surface temperatures occasionally reach nearly 80°F, and these conditions disrupt the normal tropical ocean circulation as well as the atmosphere;

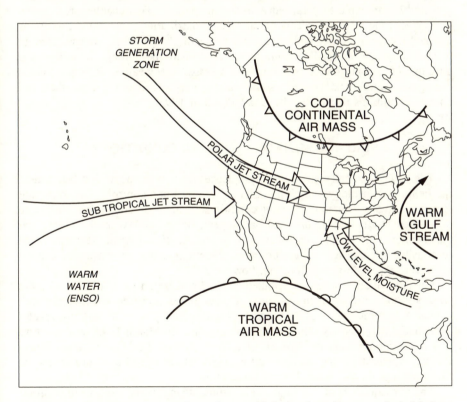

FIGURE 2-1 A schematic diagram of a continent at risk depicts the major meteorological features influencing the weather and climate of North America.

collectively these global anomalies are known as the El Nino-Southern Oscillation (ENSO) effect. The presence or dominance of either of these jets can be critical in establishing a persistent weather pattern over North America.

Finally, the persistence of climate anomalies such as floods or droughts may also depend somewhat on feedback from the land surface itself. For example, to some extent desert conditions persist because their very existence maintains the meteorological drought conditions that cause deserts. More to the point, widespread flooding presents to the atmosphere a large, wet surface area for evaporation and subsequent formation of clouds, condensation, and rainfall, thus maintaining the original conditions until a major change occurs in the atmospheric circulation pattern. In addition, mountain ranges in North America act to affect atmospheric circulation and they cause north-south waves that are sometimes persistent in the atmosphere.

The structure of meteorological features in North America is part of the global climate system that continually places our social and economic structures, even our lives, at risk. Our modern national, social, and economic networks are especially vulnerable to persistent climate anomalies. This chapter provides an overview of the meteorological circumstances contributing to the flood conditions in the Mississippi watershed; examines some of the possible external forcing mechanisms and internal dynamics that controlled the timing, intensity, and duration of the period of precipitation; assesses the weather forecasts issued during the flood; and answers some of the questions about the weather and climate conditions that led to the Great Flood of 1993.

SURFACE METEOROLOGICAL CONDITIONS

The 1993 flood had significant consequences for management of surface water, the fields of hydrology and civil engineering, and flood control. The important elements directly related to flooding conditions include soil conditions, the nature of surface runoff and its physical parameters, design of levees and dams, and management of water resources. Unusual meteorological features were responsible for the heavy and persistent precipitation that served as the critical prelude to the widespread flooding, however.

Surface conditions that contributed to the flood began to unfold in fall 1992 when soil moisture levels in the central United States increased to extremely high values. Accumulations of rain and snow deposited by winter storms further contributed to the nearly saturated soil conditions. By March 1993, soil moisture was at maximum capacity throughout a large area of the Midwest and Central Plains. A map depicting the early spring 1993 pattern of soil moisture across the Midwest appears in Figure 3-7a of Chapter 3.

The consequences of this high soil moisture during spring 1993 were twofold: (1) large surface runoff in response to subsequent spring precipitation and snowmelt, and (2) a large region of potentially high evaporation that contributed to the recirculation of water substance and the persistence of rainfall in the region. The last mechanism, however, requires energy to evaporate surface water and soil moisture, and this is done most effectively through direct solar insolation not often present during a period of cloudy, rainy days such as occurred in 1993.

Major watersheds of the Upper Mississippi and Missouri Rivers were the primary target for the extraordinary and persistent precipitation during the summer months of 1993. The week-by-week rainfall totals from early March through November 1993 are shown in Figure 2-2, along with a cumulative curve of rainfall across the Upper Mississippi River basin. The weekly amounts reveal the continuing wet conditions during the spring and summer. During the summer period (June-August) the net accumulation of rain over the Upper Mississippi River basin was twice the normal value, and the accumulated basin precipitation reached 23 inches. The rapid accumulation of rainfall and its ever-continuing departure above normal are further illustrated in Figure 2-3 which shows the April-August rainfall curves at four widely separated weather stations in the Midwest. They reflect heavy rains at different times with heavy rains beginning in April-May at LaCrosse, WI, compared to July in Salina, KS. At a few sites in Iowa the June-August rainfall exceeded 36 inches.

The immensity of the volume of water deposited can be illustrated by noting that the weekly average rainfall (June-August) was 23 million acre-feet and after 40 weeks, total rainfall was more than twice the volume of water found in Lake

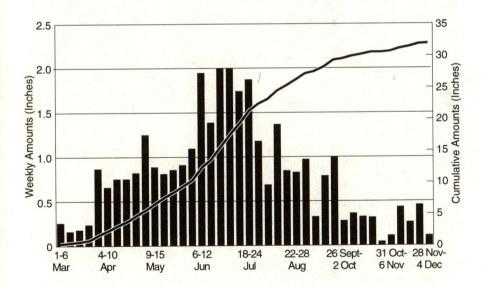

FIGURE 2-2 A weekly account of the precipitation across the Upper Mississippi River basin and Lower Missouri basin from March-November 1993. The curve depicts the accumulated precipitation across this huge area.

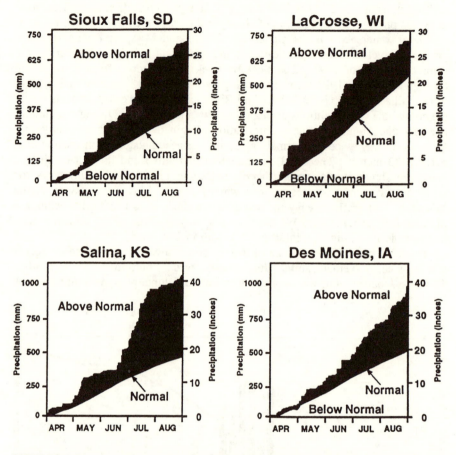

FIGURE 2-3 The temporal accumulation of rainfall during April-August 1993 at four Midwestern weather stations, all showing the excessive departures above normal levels beginning at various times during April or May (Climate Analysis Center, 1993c).

Erie. As a consequence, four Midwestern states (Illinois, Iowa, North Dakota, and South Dakota) recorded the wettest summer in 100 years of record (Richards et al., 1994). Montana and Idaho also recorded their wettest year ever with above-average precipitation in 19 other states, making 1993 one of the top ten wettest years on record in the United States.

The weekly time series of precipitation values, as shown in Figure 2-2, was used to identify rainfall episodes during the flood. A weekly rainfall threshold value (one inch or more) was applied to the data and revealed ten episodes of heavy precipitation beginning the week of May 8 and ending on August 20.

During June and July there were eight consecutive weeks of extreme episodes, a spectacular climatic event as noted by Kunkel et al. (1994). More detailed descriptions of the surface meteorological conditions during summer 1993 are also available (CAC, 1993 a-c), as are climatic summaries (Janowiak et al., 1995; Kunkel et al., 1994) and analyses of physical mechanisms (Mo et al., 1995; Bell and Janowiak, 1995).

Evaluation of the entire period of heavy rainfall allowed identification of five major different rainfall regimes that correspond approximately with six months of spring and summer.

Episode	*Month*
• Buildup phase	April and May
• Transition phase	June
• Sustained precipitation	July
• Extended phase	August
• Intermittent events	September

As if to dramatize the excessive flooding in the central United States, drought and heat-wave conditions developed simultaneously in the southeastern United States beginning in early May 1993. Major temperature anomalies developed in both the southeastern and northwestern United States. Temperatures exceeded 95°F on more than 40 days during June and July in Georgia and South Carolina, while to the west of the Midwestern flood the northwestern United States experienced a very cold summer with record-low temperatures averaging 6°F below normal in Montana, Idaho, and eastern Oregon. Temperature conditions in these two regions were in the extreme 10 percent of the historical temperature distribution (Janowiak et al., 1995).

What caused these extremely persistent precipitation and temperature anomalies across the country? Part of the answer lies in a description of the atmospheric flow conditions extending upwards from the earth's surface to a level approximately ten miles overhead. The surface conditions described are derived from the large-scale, persistent, upper-air flow patterns in the atmosphere.

ATMOSPHERIC CIRCULATION PATTERNS

A review of atmospheric circulation patterns typical during the summer of 1993 (Figure 2-4) reveals that no single description is adequate to explain flooding conditions. These six maps of the height of the 500-millibar (mb) level in the atmosphere reflect conditions typical of the five precipitation periods during April-September 1993. These maps are quite different, illuminating the fact that no single "cause" can be identified with the flooding conditions. Rather, we must search for the background conditions in the atmosphere that supported the sequence of variable circumstances, all of which led to an extraordinary accumulation of precipitation.

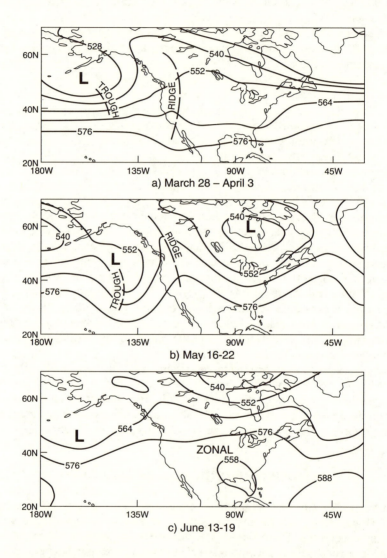

FIGURE 2-4 Typical flow patterns in the middle atmosphere near 18,000 feet (500 mb) during the first two meteorological phases of the flood: the buildup phase and the transition phase, which occurred during March-June 1993.

Buildup Phase (April-May)

The intensification of precipitation during April and May 1993, as noted by Bell and Janowiak (1995), was characterized by a strong Pacific trough and a ridge to the east in western North America (Figure 2-4a). The ridge position at this time (early April) brought westerly flow to the central United States and the first in a series of disturbances that significantly increased the quantity of precipitation (see Figure 2-2). This configuration of a typical planetary wave pattern is recognizable in the spring months as the North Pacific Oscillation (NPO). With an index value of 2.3, the strength of the 1993 pattern was unusual but not unprecedented; this was the first time in the thirty-year record that a sustained period of three months (March, April, and May) maintained a value greater than 1.0, however. Furthermore, a strong NPO index (1.7) also occurred during two spring months in 1992 and again in 1993. The dominance of this planetary mode of atmospheric teleconnection suggests a forcing mechanism beyond the region of North America.

In the subtropics during an ENSO warm phase event, subtropical high pressure patterns are typically enhanced in the upper atmosphere. These circumstances were observed during the buildup phase of rainfall, which was accompanied by an enhancement of the subtropical jet stream that contributed to the kinetic energy and moisture supply of the westerly flow. By late May (Figure 2-4b), the Pacific trough was still sustained.

Transition Phase (June)

The transition phase developed during June and involved a series of rapidly moving spring storms across North America that marked a shift to even higher levels of precipitation. Figure 2-4c defines the weakened Pacific trough and nearly zonal flow pattern, which also defines the path of transient storms.

Sustained Phase (July)

Soon after the end of the transition period, the flow pattern changed to a Pacific ridge where previously there had been a trough (see Figure 2-5a). This change supported the intense precipitation events in the central United States. By late June the transition phase was concluded and a period of sustained precipitation was initiated, as noted by Mo et al. (1995) and Bell and Janowiak (1995). Radically different conditions of the eddy kinetic energy field existed at the jet stream levels in the upper atmosphere (200 mb). A large concentration of energy from transient disturbances (with periods lasting from 2.5 days up to 6 days) was found along the storm path stretching upstream in the westerlies across the Pacific and directed towards the West Coast of North America during June. By way of contrast, the energy was fractionally smaller in quasi-stationary waves over periods of greater than ten days. During July, however, the circumstances were exactly reversed as discussed by Mo et al. (1995).

Thus, the transition phase was characterized by a series of strong transient storms moving quickly underneath an intense jet stream directed towards the West

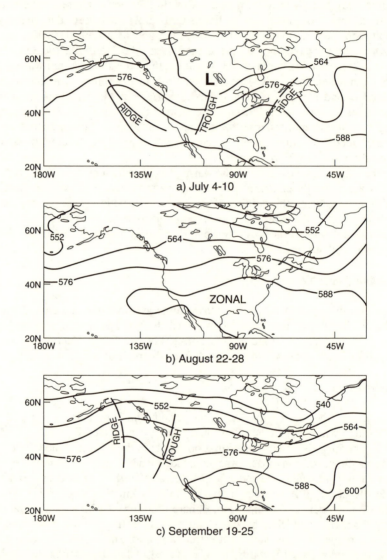

FIGURE 2-5   Typical flow patterns at the 500-mb level during the third (sustained), fourth (extended), and fifth (intermittent) meteorological phases associated with the flooding conditions.

Coast from far upstream in the Pacific. After June 26 in the sustained phase, the atmosphere reversed its earlier configuration and developed a persistent ridge over the Eastern Pacific and a trough pattern in the western United States, as shown in Figure 2-5a. This new configuration supported the sustained period of intense precipitation in the Midwest that was due to persistent meteorological conditions supported by both upper-level and lower-level flow patterns.

Figure 2-6 displays the departure from the average flow (vector winds) in the upper levels (250-mb level) from early June to late July. An unusually strong cyclonic circulation pattern supports sustained vertical motion through a deep level of the atmosphere. Under these conditions moist surface air will condense and fall as precipitation. The net accumulation will depend on both the persistence of the pattern and on the source of low-level moisture.

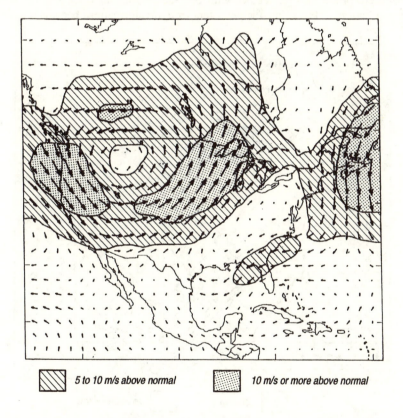

⬚⬚⬚ *5 to 10 m/s above normal*   ⬚⬚⬚ *10 m/s or more above normal*

FIGURE 2-6   Upper-level circulation anomaly (based on difference from mean pattern for 1979-1989) for the period of June 5-July 19, 1993. The pattern is for the 250-mb level which is about 6.5 miles above the surface.

Figure 2-7 emphatically depicts the anomalies in the flow pattern at lower levels (850 mb) for the same June-July period. The anomaly from the climatological average reveals an extraordinary track of moist air originating in the Caribbean and passing northwards directly over the Mississippi valley. With such moisture supplying the traveling summer storms and guided by an intense jet stream and trough position (Figure 2-5a) in the western United States, strong mesoscale convective events were able to deposit the heavy rain over the central United States throughout this period.

Extended Phase (August)

After the widespread flooding in July, an extended phase of decreased but occasionally intense precipitation occurred throughout August followed by an intermittent phase into September with ever-decreasing intensity and frequency of precipitation. At this time the persistent trough-ridge pattern became transient:

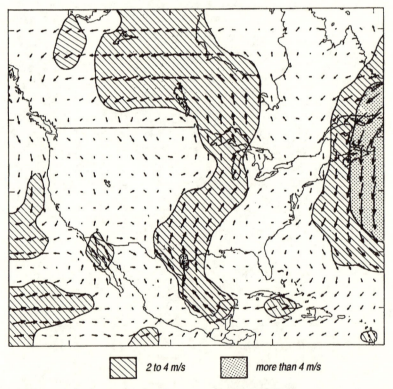

2 to 4 m/s   more than 4 m/s

FIGURE 2-7 The low-level anomaly in the mean circulation pattern for June 5-July 19, 1993. These are vector winds at the 850-mb level (about one mile above the surface) compared with the 1979-1988 average winds.

every week in August the pattern changed. Figure 2-5b shows the zonal flow on which the transient waves developed during the month. Consequently, this change redistributed the rainfall locations and the areas of heavier rainfall did not always coincide with the watersheds of the Midwest floods.

Because of the widespread and extraordinarily high surface moisture conditions in August (see Figure 3-7f for the pattern), and the decreased cloudiness over the flooded area, this period became the summer's best opportunity for recirculation of water vapor to provide self-sustaining conditions for rainfall in August and into September (Janowiak et al., 1995). This idea has been demonstrated in principle with numerical models of the atmosphere (Betts et al., 1994).

Intermittent Events (September)

The concluding period of intermittent rainfall events was supported by a re-intensified jet stream and Pacific Coast ridge pattern during September (Figure 2-5c). The resulting rainfall events were generally weaker, and the trough pattern (with increased support for storm development) was located to the east of the saturated conditions in the Midwest.

Concluding Remarks

The flood-producing rainfall conditions were sustained by a regional configuration of an intense flow of moist air from the Caribbean under the displaced position of an upper-level trough in the west. The trough and the intensity of the jet worked together to support a large number of storms that could concentrate the moisture supply from an intense southerly flow (Figure 2-8).

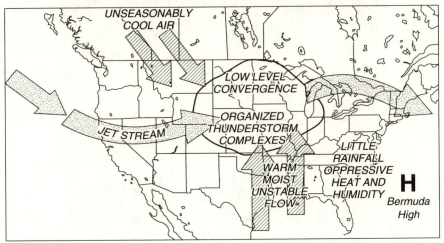

FIGURE 2-8 A schematic weather map illustrating the contrasting summer weather conditions that caused the flood-producing rainfalls in 1993 (NWS, 1994).

Furthermore, we cannot discount the possibility of recirculation of water substance from available surface moisture. Monthly rainfall regimes (buildup, transition, sustained, extended, and intermittent) correspond to changes in the large-scale circulation pattern on a global scale and due to the intensity and location of the western trough position. Consequently, the weather forecasts from late May through August 1993 were for a pattern of repeated rainfall events in the Midwest.

HISTORICAL ASSESSMENT OF 1993 CONDITIONS

Conditions in 1993 were compared with those in prior years to help look for unusual background conditions in the atmosphere. During the three years prior to 1993 (1990-1992) when above-normal oceanic temperatures, the ENSO warm phase, existed in the tropical Pacific, zonally-averaged mid-latitude height anomalies in the Pacific sector (from 120E to 120W longitude) were unusually negative. This is consistent with the Pacific trough-ridge pattern mentioned above, and a stronger jet stream displaced to the south from its normal position, as shown in Figure 2-4a. A more complete analysis by Bell and Janowiak (1995) shows that this spring pattern is a global teleconnection associated with the warm phase of ENSO in 1991-1993. However, the overwhelming impression from study of the time series is one of interannual variability. Simply stated, the global height fields did not respond uniformly to the ongoing ENSO event in the Pacific Ocean area.

FIGURE 2-9   A giant anvil from a mature thunderstorm photographed near St. Louis in early July builds above a new thunderstorm cell developing in the mature storm's flank.

Comparison of mid-level circulation for July 1992 and July 1993 has shown close similarities in atmospheric circulation over the western United States. Nevertheless, the consequences in surface precipitation were quite different for the two years (even though many residents of Kansas, Nebraska, and South Dakota would describe both summers as "wet"). Intense convection existed in both summers, creating massive thunderstorms as shown in Figure 2-9, but the persistence of rainfall in 1993 was extreme.

Comparison of the relatively wet 1992 and the very dry 1988 has also showed an important distinction in the low-level flow (Bell and Janowiak, 1995). A trajectory from the Gulf source region, illustrated in Figure 2-7, also occurred in 1988, but the anomalies from normal conditions indicate a northerly flow in both 1988 and 1992 that cut off the moisture source for heavy precipitation from reaching the Midwest. In 1988, the anomalous flow was actually strongly northeasterly, greatly reducing the normal flow of moist southerly air.

DIAGNOSTICS

The "cause" of many meteorological anomalies is simply the temporary displacement of the atmospheric circulation from its normal state, rather than a response to unusual external forcing such as El Nino or volcanic eruptions (Bell and Janowiak, 1995). External mechanisms are sometimes offered (for example, global climate change, or volcanic aerosols), but after consideration, these seem less plausible and difficult to connect to the 1993 regional event in North America. In particular, during the summer of 1993, surface temperatures in the Northern Hemisphere were not extremely warm (as might be expected if global warming were evident), and the influence of aerosols from the eruption of Mt. Pinatubo should have attained its maximum more than a year earlier.

However, a possible connection between the flood-producing atmospheric conditions and the warm pattern of ENSO in the tropical Pacific has also been studied by Mo et al. (1995). A study of vorticity sources for the Pacific sector investigated a possible connection between the ENSO event and the 1993 anomalies in circulation over North America (Figure 2-4). The dominant vorticity source on the 500-mb weather patterns for June and July 1993 had a zonal orientation of source-to-sinks (Rodenhuis et al., 1994). Analysis revealed that the vorticity sources were not directly connected with the warm sea surface temperatures of the tropics, and the strongest source regions were in the region of the polar jet stream. The subtropical source regions were *indirectly* associated with ENSO via the return flow from deep convection near the equator.

A heuristic model for understanding the influence of ENSO was described in a study of circulation patterns during 1986-1989 (Rasmusson and Mo, 1993). The 1993 conditions were similar to those that existed during 1986-1989 when ENSO had indirectly caused a southward displacement of the storm track in the middle latitudes across North America. The subtropical jet stream was found to be strengthened by the development of anomalous high pressure (anti-cyclones) at 200 mb on either side of the equator.

These atmospheric patterns define a "duct" of westerly winds that penetrate further eastward than normal into North America during ENSO events. This set of conditions is typical in the winter hemisphere during a warm-phase ENSO event but is also similar to conditions during the spring and summer of 1993 when the flood was developing. Hence, ENSO seems to have influenced the development of the jet stream, westerly duct, and resulting storm path that supported the repeated development of spring and summer storms of 1993, especially those early in the season (Bell and Janowiak, 1995). The sources of wave energy in 1993 were found to be an indirect result of ENSO strengthening of the polar jet stream by action of convergence of northward eddy fluxes from the southern part of the westerly wind duct (Mo et al., 1995).

These early (April-June) conditions do not explain the persistence of the flood-producing rains during July, August, and September 1993. Analysis suggests that the late summer intense rains resulted from two conditions. One was the ridge-trough pattern established in strong westerly flow, possibly induced by the perpendicular ridge of the western mountains in the United States (Mo et al., 1995). Second, the precipitation was sustained by the simultaneous, unusually strong moisture supply provided by the low-level southerly flow shown in Figure 2-7.

In summary, the origin of flood-producing rain conditions in 1993 cannot be assigned to any one atmospheric mechanism. Many of the meteorological features found in 1993 appear every year. Results illustrate that the influence of ENSO was very important, but was an indirect mechanism for the flood-producing rains of 1993. Certainly many of the characteristic features of indirect ENSO influence were recognized early in the season: (1) an enhanced subtropical jet stream, (2) a strong pattern of the North Pacific Oscillation, (3) an upper-level duct of westerly winds, and (4) a southward displacement of the storm track. However, the uniqueness of the excessive flood was due to the *intensity* and *persistence* of the rainfall. These two aspects seem to have been controlled by the unusually strong ridge-trough pattern and the synergistic behavior of meteorological features that we see in North America every summer: (1) low-level moisture flow from the Caribbean and (2) summer storms following the wave pattern in the westerly jet aloft.

WEATHER AND CLIMATE PREDICTION

Weather predictions and climate outlooks issued on an operational basis by the National Weather Service (NWS) during the flood have been assessed. Accurate prediction of such extreme precipitation conditions is difficult but of immense practical value to a society under stress, as illustrated in 1993 (Figure 2-10).

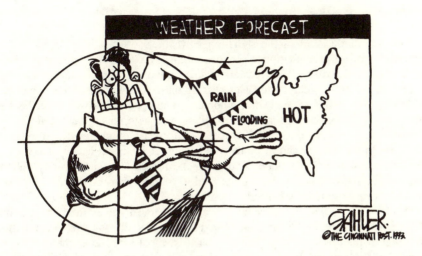

FIGURE 2-10   Persistent rains put pressure on everyone in the Midwest including the weather forecasters who had the thankless duty of reporting the "bad news" (Jeff Stahler, reprinted by permission of NEA, Inc.).

The NWS issues three different types of forecasts, each covering different time periods and each with a different scientific approach: (1) the short-range weather forecast of conditions over the next few hours and days, (2) the extended range forecast for the next 6- to 10-day period with a lead time of 5 days, and (3) the monthly and seasonal climate outlooks for average conditions. Each forecast has important scientific differences related to content and accuracy.

The practical forecast limit of future weather conditions is generally about a week in advance. Beyond a week it is possible to predict only the average conditions created by the weather events. A climate forecast seeks to predict the average of the weather fluctuations, as well as the difference of this average from the long-term mean value. Thus, for prediction purposes "climate" begins beyond the forecast limit of weather prediction. Global numerical weather forecast models are also used to predict average conditions in the "extended range" (6 to 10 days). The 6-to 10-day forecasts are made by running the weather forecast model repeatedly to obtain a range of possible solutions from which the probability of wetter or drier, warmer or cooler conditions is identified.

Beyond two weeks ahead, the weather forecast model is of more limited value. The results of extended model runs are combined with other empirical methods to reach the final forecast of the probability of monthly mean temperature and precipitation. Beyond one month ahead, the seasonal outlook is constructed mainly employing empirical methods and the experience of the forecaster. Often analogues from previous years are used to develop a regionally consistent probability forecast of climatic anomalies.*

Short-Range Weather Forecasts

The test of the skill of the short-range weather forecast is its capability to accurately predict precipitation, as to location, areal extent, and intensity. Every day a small group of NWS forecasters makes a quantitative precipitation forecast (QPF) for multiple precipitation patterns for the next two days. Their work is guided by the output from several complex computer models that describe and interpret the atmosphere on a global scale as well as on a regional scale in the United States. However, a highly detailed forecast of summer precipitation requires skillful interpretation of the model output by experienced forecasters. During the summer 1993 flood conditions, the forecasters were usually able to identify the areas of heavy daily precipitation (greater than one inch), and their forecasts often located these events correctly.

A statistical basis for assessing forecast accuracy involves the Threat Score (TS), which compares the magnitude and location of the forecast precipitation with that of the observed precipitation. That is, the TS measures the fraction of overlap of the magnitude of the forecast and observed rain areas. For example, a TS of 0.4 corresponds to 60 percent overlap, assuming the area of the precipitation forecasted and observed are about the same. The score can range from zero (a "miss") to 1.0 (perfect overlap). The average TS for the QPFs issued during the warm season of 1993 was 0.15, and many forecasts issued had a TS between 0.3 and 0.45 (NWS, 1994). These scores for 1993 indicate that between a quarter and a half of the heavy rain areas were overlapping. This indicates impressive skill, and the forecasters often correctly identified the most intense cores in rain areas.

On a very short time scale, however, the local forecast office interprets the QPF using local observations. A notable example of a successful short-term flash-flood warning occurred in Wisconsin on July 18. A Limited Automatic Remote Collection device located along the Baraboo River in Wisconsin signaled at 2 a.m. that very heavy rains were beginning. The NWS forecaster at Milwaukee noted the report, analyzed the QPF situation, and issued a heavy rain and local flood warning before dawn (NWS, 1994). Local authorities moved through a large public campground along the river warning the campers to leave as soon as possible, leading to the evacuation of hundreds of campers just before floodwaters swept through the area. No lives were lost in what could have been a major disaster.

---

*Early in 1995 the monthly and seasonal forecasts were changed to include objective methods, and empirical methods and results from an ocean-atmosphere model are now used to make climate outlooks for up to a year in advance.

The NWS investigated several forecast examples during the summer of 1993 (NWS, 1994). Although the precipitation forecasts are not designed to predict isolated extreme rainfall rates, analysis revealed that the area-integrated volumetric rainfall rate forecasted correlated reasonably well with the observed rainfall at a value of 0.43. Although the extreme, site-specific rainfall rates could not always be accurately forecast, analysis showed that the volumetric forecasts were almost always overestimated, with a typical ratio of 1.6 (observed/forecast). Importantly, the QPF forecasts were "conservative" in the sense of rarely underestimating the danger of extreme rainfall conditions.

In summary, the short-term forecasts of the location and intensity of rainfall issued in 1993 gave adequate warning one to two days in advance. Although the weather conditions during the flood were the most unusual ever experienced by the QPF forecasters, their level of skill maintained the standards of more normal conditions. This performance was far superior to the objective output from numerical models.

Medium-Range Forecasts

Medium-range forecasts are issued three times a week and address conditions in five-day periods that begin five days (days 6 to 10) after the forecast is issued. Since these conditions are beyond the range of usual weather prediction, the forecasts are based on interpretation of repeated runs of a weather forecast model and study of the mid-level flow as primary guidance. The numerical model is run repeatedly with 13 slightly different initial weather conditions to obtain an ensemble of values from which the forecaster defines the average values and the

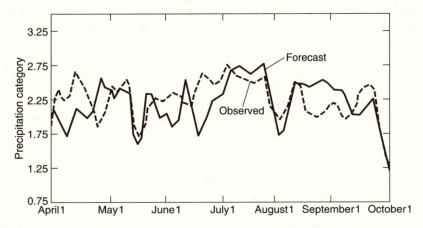

FIGURE 2-11 Comparison of the 5-day rainfall observed during 1993 with that forecasted five days in advance (based on forecasts issued at 16 Midwestern weather stations). The precipitation categories indicate: dry or low rain conditions (value of 1), the median level of rain (value of 2), or very wet conditions (a value of 3) (O'Lenic, 1994).

ranges of outcomes over the five-day period. The forecast has a three-category outcome for above-normal, normal, or below-normal conditions of temperature and precipitation in the future.

The prediction of precipitation expected 6-10 days in advance is a severe test of model performance, and skilled forecasters must interpret the model outputs to derive the final forecast. A comparison of the 1993 precipitation amounts from the official forecasts and those actually observed was based on the forecasts from 16 Midwestern weather stations (O'Lenic, 1994). Results (Figure 2-11) show that the official forecasts continued wet conditions (a mean of categorical values of approximately 2.5) and closely followed the observed precipitation amounts for many weeks. Disagreement occurred during late June when the forecasts were underestimating the heavy rain conditions (forecast values ranged from 1.75 to 2.25, as compared to about 2.5 for the observed rainfall). From July 1 through mid-August (the height of the flood), the forecasts for the area closely followed observed conditions.

When model results were used without the benefit of an experienced forecaster (values not depicted in Figure 2-11), a systematic departure occurred after May 1 below the observed precipitation rates. The official forecast was much better than the model guidance. In summary, although this is a limited analysis of the accuracy of the 1993 medium-range forecasts, there is substantial evidence that the wet conditions were forecast rather accurately five days in advance.

Monthly and Seasonal Outlooks

The prediction of average conditions for the next month or for the season (next three months) is beyond the range of numerical weather forecasting or the techniques used for the medium-range predictions. For a climatic outlook covering this time scale, only empirical techniques and analogues can be used. The experience of the forecaster can be an especially important factor.

These outlooks are scored by comparing them with observations in three categories at stations around the nation. The national scale of the evaluation of the monthly and seasonal outlooks is far larger than the size of the Midwestern flood. Several of the monthly outlooks issued during May-August 1993 correctly forecast the above-normal precipitation conditions in the Midwest. However, their overall skill was typically about 40 percent, indicating the fraction of national verification sites that scored correctly. The forecast for the beginning of the heaviest precipitation in April was more skillful (50 percent), and the highest skill was 67 percent for the month of July.

The outlook issued in May for the entire summer season of 1993 showed little skill for the nation as a whole. Although this result is disappointing, it is quite understandable, since such extreme conditions had not been encountered in the recent historical past. However, the three-month outlooks issued on June 1, 1993 (for June-August), and on July 1 (for July-September) correctly called for an increased chance of above-average precipitation in the Midwest.

There have been some ambitious efforts to predict extreme conditions such as the flood of 1993 using ocean-atmosphere coupled models. Although an experimental forecast conducted after the event indicated heavy precipitation conditions, we cannot announce complete success.   There is also some encouragement with studies conducted with the numerical model using historical data. In a number of comparison studies using the model of Ji et al. (1994), predictions of patterns of major seasonal precipitation events over an 11-year period show general agreement with observations. This topic is one of intense current research interest.

LESSONS LEARNED

The causal link to antecedent features of the flood-related atmospheric circulation in 1993 and the influence of the warm phase of the ENSO event in the tropical Pacific have been clearly identified: background conditions of a strong, southward-displaced jet stream and a direct strengthening of the subtropical jet stream (Bell and Janowiak, 1995). Furthermore, there seems to be good evidence for a specific, but indirect influence through the strengthening of the Pacific jet stream by action of eddy fluxes (Mo et al., 1995). A structural interaction with the mid-latitude trough-ridge position is necessary to explain the persistence of the precipitation pattern in the Mississippi basin.   Therefore, it has been suggested that the topographic influence of the Rocky Mountains and the Sierras contributed to the development of the characteristic trough pattern in the western United States in June and July. The sustained pattern of precipitation critically depended upon on a reliable source of low-level moisture transported from the Caribbean.

Issues of global warming, aerosols from volcanic eruptions, and positive feedback from surface moisture excess have not been fully examined. Factors such as these are considered to be of secondary importance, or less, in explaining the flood-producing rains during 1993.

Monitoring and Diagnostics

The capability to monitor major climate anomalies such as the 1993 flood as they develop has been demonstrated. To make this happen, however, we must routinely bring together, on a weekly basis, (1) quantitative measures of precipitation (magnitude, ranking, area, event-counting, and soil moisture), (2) circulation (jet stream and anomalies, teleconnection indices, moisture transport, and anomalies), and (3) global sea-surface temperature.

Causal Relationships

There are periods of several years in duration in which major global-scale climate anomalies, following the phasing of southern oscillation events, influence the flow in the middle latitudes of the Northern and Southern Hemispheres. These circulation anomalies are associated with an increase in strength of the direct circulation of the tropics, and these anomalies can be simulated in simplified atmospheric models, as well as in global climate prediction models. Further, tropical forcing may induce a wave train of anomalous circulation; for example, by inducing changes in the intensity and orientation of the subtropical jet.

The exact phase of the wave train is critical to the climate in North America and is influenced by several factors (topography, natural variability, surface feedback from topography and even recirculation of water substance, as well as extratropical forcing).

The transport of water vapor by the low-level, southerly flow from the Caribbean was a critical difference in the drought conditions of 1988 and between the location and intensity of wet conditions in 1992 and those that created the flood conditions of 1993.

Prediction

A description of the evolution of the atmospheric circulation leading to major floods and an understanding of the role of ENSO forcing holds promise for forecasting these events before they develop. There is a subtle interaction between the strengthening of the subtropical jet, the location of the Pacific jet, the trough/ridge position, the pattern of circulation in mid-latitudes, the forcing of topography, and the source of moisture transport. As a result, the capability to predict extreme climate anomalies in North America with physical models has not yet been established.

Existing techniques for short-term and medium-range forecasting were found to be successful if not superior in forecasting the unusually heavy rain during May-September 1993. However, these forecasts relied on the interpretative skill of experienced forecasters, not just the output of atmospheric models which were less accurate than the official forecasts.

Many potential losses during the 1993 flood were prevented by adequate weather and climate forecasts. This demonstrates the extreme value of accuracy and lead time in precipitation forecasts. New objective techniques hold the promise for outlooks with longer lead times.

REFERENCES

Bell, G.D. and J.E. Janowiak, 1995: Atmospheric circulation associated with the Midwest floods of 1993. *Bulletin American Meteorological Society*, 76, 681-696.

Betts, A.K., J.H. Ball, A.C.M. Beljaars, M.J. Miller, and P. Viterbo, 1994: Coupling between land-surface, boundary-layer parameterizations and rainfall on local and regional scales: Lessons from the wet summer of 1993. *Preprints Fifth Conference on Global Change Studies,* American Meteorological Society, Boston, 8 pp.

Climate Analysis Center, 1993a: *Special Climate Summary 93/1: Midwestern Floods; Heat and Drought in the East, July 12, 1993.* National Weather Service, Washington, DC, 14 pp.

Climate Analysis Center, 1993b: *Special Climate Summary 93/2: Update on Midwestern Floods; Heat and Drought in the East, August 9, 1993.* National Weather Service, Washington, DC, 19 pp.

Climate Analysis Center, 1993c: *Special Climate Summary 93/3: Growing Season Summary: Midwestern Floods, Heat and Drought in the East; Cool in the Pacific Northwest, September 14, 1993.* National Weather Service, Washington, DC, 24 pp.

Janowiak, J.E., G.D. Bell, and R. Tinker, 1995: The global climate for June-August 1993: The great Midwest U.S. flood. *Journal of Climate,* 8, in press.

Ji, M., A. Kumar, and A. Leetmaa, 1994: A multi-season climate forecast system at the National Meteorological Center. *Bulletin American Meteorological Society,* 76, 569-577.

Kunkel, K.E., S.A. Changnon, and J.R. Angel, 1994: Climatic aspects of the 1993 Mississippi River Basin flood. *Bulletin American Meteorological Society,* 75, 811-822.

Mo, K.C., J. Nogues-Paegle, and J. Paegle, 1995: Physical mechanisms of the 1993 Summer floods. *Journal of Atmospheric Sciences,* 52, 879-895.

National Weather Service, 1994: *The Great Flood of 1993.* Natural Disaster Survey Report, Department of Commerce, National Oceanic and Atmospheric Administration, Washington, DC, 194 pp.

O'Lenic, E.A., 1994: Summer 1993 medium range forecasts for the United States: A period of flood and drought. *Proceedings Fourth Workshop on Meteorological Operational Systems (22-26 November 1993),* European Centre for Medium-Range Weather Forecasts, Shinfield Park, United Kingdom, 87-91.

Rasmusson, E.M. and K. Mo, 1993: Linkages between 200-mb tropical and extratropical circulation anomalies during the 1986-1989 ENSO cycle. *Journal of Climate,* 6, 596-616.

Richards, F., D. Miskus, and S. Changnon, 1994: Hydrometeorological setting. *Coastal Oceanographic Effects of Summer 1993 Mississippi River Flooding,* Special Report of National Oceanic and Atmospheric Administration, Washington, DC, 3-26.

Rodenhuis, D.R., D. Miskus, G. Bell, and K. Mo, 1994: Meteorological flood--origins, description and causes of the great flood of 1993. *Preprints Symposium on the Flood of 1993,* American Meteorological Society, Boston, 1-13.

3

A Hydroclimatological Assessment of the Rainfall

Kenneth E. Kunkel

INTRODUCTION

Highly unusual and persistent weather patterns persisted across the central United States (described in Chapter 2) for most of the summer of 1993 and brought copious rainfall almost daily to the Midwest. By nearly every conceivable measure, the rainfall was unique and record-breaking. Unprecedented heavy daily rainfalls, very rare events and newsworthy in a normal summer, became commonplace and deposited several inches of rain over large areas of 10,000 square miles or more. June-August rain totals were double and even triple the normal amounts as a result of the barrage of heavy rains. For example, Webster City, IA, received 37.5 inches of rain, nearly three times its normal June-August total (13 inches) and more than central Iowa usually receives in an entire year.

The entire Upper Mississippi River basin, an area covering 300,000 square miles, received an average of nearly 20 inches during June-August, 2.5 inches more than during any previous three-month period dating back to 1895. The sheer magnitude by which this and other rainfall amounts broke previous records places the flood of 1993 in a select group of unique climatic anomalies, such as the heat wave in July 1936 (the hottest month on record in the Midwest). Heavy rains during 1993 have made this rainfall event the yardstick by which future extended heavy rain periods will be measured.

This chapter examines the unique hydroclimatic factors that created the circumstances responsible for the excessive flooding--including the rainfall that fell in the months prior to the flood. After analyzing the rainfall totals in an historical context, the conclusion is that rainfall of such magnitude and areal extent is likely to occur less than once every 200 years. Furthermore, when these record-breaking rains began in June 1993, they fell upon the Midwest's previously saturated soils, the result of a persistent, wet pattern beginning in July 1992 that had already caused minor flooding and high streamflows in the previous winter and spring. When the saturated soils could not absorb further rainfall at the end of May, the stage was set for the prolonged heavy rains and catastrophic flooding that followed.

This hydroclimatic assessment of the 1993 flood was based primarily on daily and monthly precipitation data sets. The daily Summary-of-the-Day (SOD) data set was provided by National Weather Service (NWS) cooperative observers from the archives at the National Climatic Data Center. It includes daily precipitation values at a relatively dense spatial resolution (approximately one raingage per 400 square miles) in digital form for many stations from 1948 to the present. The second precipitation data set consists of monthly precipitation values calculated using all stations in climate divisions (CDs) within the Midwest. For each state there are approximately eight or nine homogeneous subregions (CDs), each encompassing an area of about 8,000 square miles. Division values are averages of observations from 10 to 20 raingage stations within each CD. Although the CD data set is limited in both temporal (monthly) and spatial resolution, digital values are available from 1895 to the present, which allows a more extended period for historical comparisons.

Soil moisture conditions played a significant role in the development of the flood. Since in-field soil moisture measurements in the Midwest were not widely available, the assessment used an operational soil moisture model calibrated successfully against actual field data (Kunkel, 1990). This model uses observed meteorological variables (maximum and minimum temperature, and precipitation) and potential evapotranspiration (PET). Using the Penman-Monteith formula (Monteith, 1965), PET was estimated from hourly surface observations. The procedure is explained in Kunkel et al. (1994). The hydroclimatic analyses focused on the Upper Mississippi River basin upstream of Cairo, IL, including the lower portion of the Missouri River basin but excluding the upper reaches of the Missouri River basin largely controlled by dams and reservoirs.

TEMPORAL DISTRIBUTION
OF MONTHLY AND SUMMER RAINFALL

Monthly basin precipitation amounts were calculated by averaging the monthly precipitation values for all available raingage stations located within the basin. An analysis of the monthly values for 1992-1993 (Figure 3-1) indicates that the flood was preceded by a persistent wet pattern beginning in mid-1992, 12 months before the flood. Precipitation in July 1992 was 75 percent above the long-term basin average (3.7 inches). Excessively heavy precipitation again occurred in November 1992--precipitation more than twice the normal 1.8 inches was followed by flooding along the Mississippi River. Near to slightly above average precipitation fell during January and February. After near-normal rainfall in March, wet conditions returned in April and May with above-normal rainfall, leading to more flooding on the Upper Mississippi and delaying planting of grain and vegetable crops. The accumulation of the above-normal rainfall over time across the basin is illustrated by conditions at four weather stations (Figure 2-3).

From June through September 1993 precipitation was excessive. Rainfall amounts were more than 60 percent above normal in June, more than twice the normal in July, and above average in August and September. Drier conditions developed during the last three months of 1993.

Several key factors become evident from the assessment of the daily average basin rainfall values for summer 1993 (Figure 3-2). First, the most significant rainfall episodes occurred on June 6-8, June 16-19, June 23-24, June 29-July 10, July 16-17, July 21-24, August 14-15, and August 28-30. Note that the time intervals between the first five episodes varied from three to seven days, allowing no time for drying out. Second, the most significant rain period of the summer was June 29-July 10 during which excessive rains fell in the region every day. Basinwide rainfall during this 12-day period was 4.93 inches, well above the 1.2 inches normally experienced and more than the normal rainfall for an entire summer month. Third, during the 92-day period from June 1 through August 31, rainfall less than 0.05 inch fell on only 17 days, and there was more than 0.25 inch across this huge basin on 36 days. Both values set new records for the 1948-1993 period.

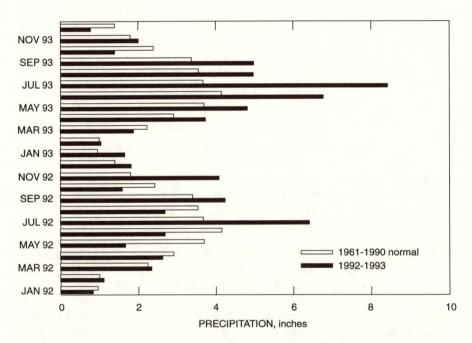

FIGURE 3-1 A comparison of monthly average precipitation for the Upper Mississippi River basin (solid bars) and the 1961-1990 normal values (open bars) for January 1992-December 1993. The 1993 monthly values exceeded the normals from April to October.

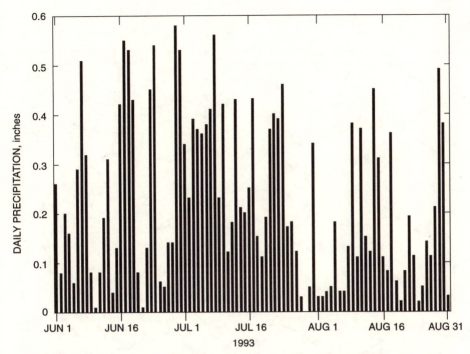

FIGURE 3-2   Daily average rainfall amounts for the Upper Mississippi River basin show almost continuous moderate to heavy rains from June 1 through August 31, 1993.

SPATIAL DISTRIBUTION OF RAINFALL

Normal summer rainfall (based on 1961-1990 data) across the Upper Mississippi River basin varies from roughly 8 inches in the extreme northwestern part of the basin to 13 inches in the southwestern part of the basin. During the summer of 1993, however, nearly the entire basin received precipitation well above normal (Figure 3-3). More than 20 inches fell over a large area that included southern Minnesota, southwestern Wisconsin, northwestern Illinois, northern Missouri, most of Iowa, southeastern Nebraska, and northeastern Kansas, covering most of the Upper Mississippi and Lower Missouri basins.

Interestingly, this was the area that experienced the most severe flooding. More than 28 inches fell over parts of Iowa, Missouri, and Nebraska, an area of 38,000 square miles. Rainfall exceeded 35 inches at a few locations in central and eastern Iowa and central Missouri, representing three times the normal summer rainfall.

Examination of Figure 3-3 illustrates a key factor relating to the flood. The heavy rainfall pattern coincided rather closely with the boundary of the Upper Mississippi River drainage basin. Nearly all of the basin upstream of St. Louis

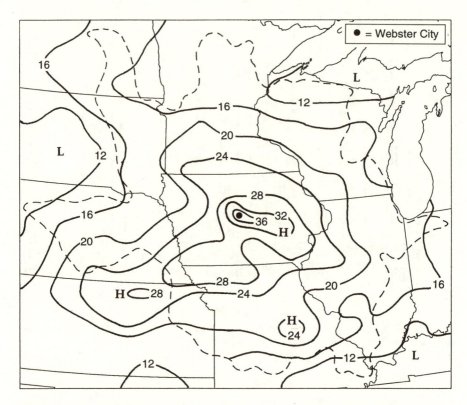

Figure 3-3   Rainfall pattern (in inches) for June 1-August 31, 1993. Isohyetal lines have been smoothed to simplify the presentation.   The dashed line denotes the outline of the Upper Mississippi River basin but excludes the controlled upper reaches of the Missouri River.

experienced excessive rainfall, more than 16 inches, which created record-breaking flood levels in the lower reaches of the Mississippi and Missouri Rivers and their tributaries (see Figure 1-1).

The rainfall patterns during three significant rain episodes are also revealing. One such episode on June 16-19 (Figure 3-4a) resulted in heavy rains in the northern portion of the basin.   More than 3 inches fell over much of southern Minnesota and northern Wisconsin, with 5 inches or more at several locations.

The major rainfall episode of the summer was from June 29 to July 10 (Figure 3-4b).   Daily rains during this 12-day period averaged more than 0.2 inch across this huge basin (see Figure 3-2).   Precipitation totals for this 12-day period exceeded 4 inches over much of the basin: rainfall in excess of 8 inches fell across large portions of central and southern Iowa, in northern Missouri, and in northeastern Kansas. Several individual stations received in excess of 12 inches,

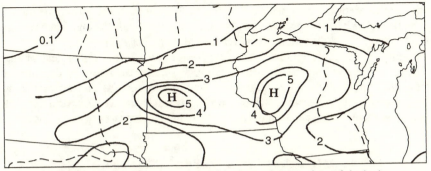

a. Rainfall during June 16-19 was concentrated in the northern portions of the basin.

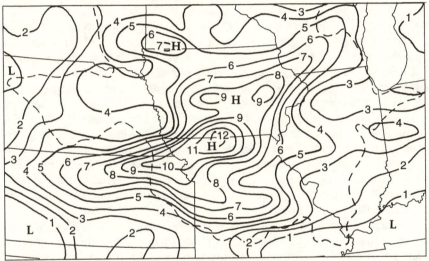

b. Rainfall during June 29-July 10, the summer's wettest period.

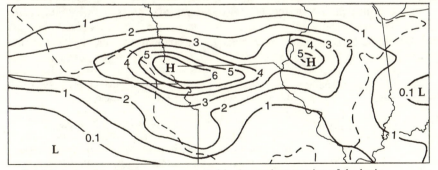

c. Rainfall during July 21-24 was concentrated in the southern portion of the basin.

FIGURE 3-4   Spatial patterns of three heavy rain periods during the summer of 1993. Rain amounts (isohyetals) are in inches.

equivalent to a normal summer's total. Figure 3-5 captures the growth of major convective clouds over Iowa on July 9, the last day of this second intense rain period. Such cloud development was a typical sight during 1993.

A third major rainy episode on July 21-24 (Figure 3-4c) was typical of the frequent heavy rains across the basin's southern sections in July. Amounts in excess of 3 inches fell over significant parts of this region, and an east-west oriented band 700 miles long, from eastern Nebraska to western Illinois, had certain raingage stations with more than 10 inches over this four-day period.

COMPARISON OF 1993 PRECIPITATION
WITH HISTORICAL RECORDS

Precipitation totals during the 1993 flood were compared with past heavy precipitation events from monthly CD data for 1895-1993 (99 years), and the comparison was restricted to totals for whole months ranging from one month up to 12 months. The 99 values of each monthly duration across the basin were then ranked from high to low. The top five precipitation events for each duration (Table 3-1) demonstrate the magnitude of the 1993 event. For each duration, the 1993 value ranks as the largest in the historical record dating back to 1895. For example, the wettest month of 1993 (July 1993 with a basinwide average of 8.03 inches) also ranks as the wettest single month in the past 99 years. It is also noteworthy that the 1993 values for all four durations exceed the second-ranked episode by a significant margin. For example, the 14.76 inches that fell in June and July 1993 is 26 percent larger than the second-ranked event (11.7 inches in May-June 1908).

Standard hydrometeorological techniques (Huff and Angel, 1992) were used to estimate the frequency of occurrence or return period for the 1993 precipitation amounts shown in Table 3-1. The estimated return period for the July 1993 total of 8.03 inches is 80 years. For periods from 2 months up to 12 months, the estimated return period of the 1993 values exceeds 200 years (Kunkel et al., 1994). The statistically based estimate of greater than 200 years results because the 1993 value is not only the top-ranked value, but also substantially greater than

TABLE 3-1   Rank, Magnitude (inches), and Date (month/year) of the Five Largest Precipitation Events Recorded on the Upper Mississippi River Basin for Selected Durations

Rank	1 month	2 months	3 months	12 months
1	8.03 (7/93)	14.76 (6-7/93)	19.62 (6-8/93)	45.00 (10/92-9/93)
2	7.30 (6/47)	11.70 (5-6/08)	17.20 (5-7/15)	39.38 (11/85-10/86)
3	7.24 (9/65)	11.52 (5-6/90)	16.10 (5-7/02)	38.98 (2/51-1/52)
4	7.05 (9/26)	11.35 (6-7/15)	15.91 (6-8/51)	38.83 (7/72-6/73)
5	7.01 (6/67)	11.28 (8-9/65)	15.70 (5-7/90)	38.51 (6/02-5/03)

FIGURE 3-5   Across an Iowa prairie darkened by heavy rain from a nearby thunderstorm, several cumulus congestus clouds are developing into new storms under highly unstable weather conditions on July 9, 1993.

the second-ranked value. Rainfall amounts in 1993 were indeed excessive and unprecedented in the historical record. And the precipitation during the summer and in the preceding eight months (October 1992-May 1993) was the primary hydroclimatic factor causing the flood.

FLOOD-CAUSING HYDROCLIMATIC CONDITIONS

A hydroclimatic analysis of the rainfall characteristics reveals that five key rain conditions combined to create record rain totals and a flood that was unprecedented (a) for its summer season occurrence, (b) for its areal size, and (c) for its long duration. These five factors (high frequency of heavy multi-day events, high number of extreme flash-flood-producing rainstorms, high number of large-sized rain areas, persistent high soil moisture, and low evapotranspiration) greatly influenced the severity and nature of the floods.

Large Number of Heavy Rain Events

Kunkel et al. (1993) identified heavy rainfall events that resulted in flooding in the Midwest during the period 1921-1985 and found that flooding events on streams and rivers were often related to heavy precipitation accumulations occurring over a period of a few days. Particularly strong correlations existed for precipitation events of 7-day duration. At any given point in the Upper Mississippi River basin, 7-day events producing 4 inches or greater are expected to occur about once per year. All 7-day periods with precipitation amounts exceeding 4 inches were identified for each raingage station in the basin and then the total number of 4-inch events occurring each month within the basin was counted. (This analysis was limited to the data for the 1948-1993 period.) The number of events occurring during 1-, 2-, 3-, and 12-month periods were ranked, and the top four events are listed in Table 3-2. For example, in July 1993, there were 57 heavy rain events for every 100 stations, the second highest single-month total in the past 46 years. For longer durations, the 1993 values ranked as the highest on record and they were much higher than the second-ranked values. For

TABLE 3-2 Ranking of the Number (per 100 stations) and Date (month/year) of Heavy 7-day Precipitation Events Exceeding 4 Inches, Based on Data for 1948-1993

Rank	1 month	2 months	3 months	12 Months
1	66 (9/86)	99 (6-7/93)	122 (6-8/93)	187 (10/92-9/93)
2	57 (7/93)	71 (8-9/86)	93 (7-9/86)	151 (10/85-9/86)
3	49 (6/67)	67 (8-9/65)	78 (5-7/81)	134 (8/80-7/81)
4	49 (9/65)	60 (5-6/90)	75 (7-9/65)	128 (8/89-7/90)

example, during the period of June-August 1993, there were 99 heavy rain events for each 100 stations; the second highest total was 71 events per 100 stations during 1986.

Twenty-four stations received 7-day rainfall in excess of 10 inches during June-July 1993 compared to six 7-day events of 10 inches or greater received in an average year. Most of these 24 stations from the summer of 1993 were located in northwestern and south-central Missouri, central Iowa, and southeastern Nebraska. This was an area where the summer total rainfall amounts exceeded 28 inches (Figure 3-3): 13 events occurred during the very wet episode in the first half of July (Figure 3-4b), 5 events occurred in northwestern Missouri and southeastern Nebraska during the third week of July, 5 events occurred in Missouri during the third week of September, and 1 event occurred in Illinois during mid-November. The last six episodes caused recurrences of flooding in Missouri and south-central Illinois.

High Number of Extreme
Flash-Flood-Producing Rainstorms

The incidence of short duration (6 to 24 hours) heavy rainstorms producing from 6 to 12 inches of rain during 1993 was critical because they often caused flash floods on small to moderate-sized basins. In much of the basin, the 6-inch threshold corresponds to an event expected to occur about once every 50 years, but the number of reports in the basin during summer 1993 was actually double the number of events expected to occur during an entire year. Unofficial reports indicate that 175 such storms occurred in the basin between late May and August 1993 (NWS, 1994), but most of these storms missed official raingage sites. However, there were 28 official reports of 24-hour rainfall totals in excess of 6 inches throughout the summer and fall in many parts of the basin (Figure 3-6). These storms were highly concentrated during the most significant heavy rainfall period (June 29-July 10, Figure 3-4b). Also shown on Figure 3-6 is the rainfall pattern for a flash-flood storm on July 6-7, just one of the many flash-flood storms that occurred. Not shown on the map are six small areas where weather radar indicated 10 inches of rain fell (NWS, 1994). The heavy rains indicated by the four dots in west-central Iowa (Figure 3-6) occurred on July 9 in the drainage basins of the Raccoon and Des Moines Rivers. These rains were the immediate cause of the flooding in Des Moines, IA, that disabled the water treatment plant on July 12 (as described in Chapter 4).

Extreme Number of Large-Sized Rain Areas

A critical requirement for producing heavy summer rainfall over a large area such as the Upper Mississippi River basin is large rain areas. Past studies have demonstrated the importance of mesoscale convective complexes (MCCs) as a major source of large-area rainfall in the central United States during the warm

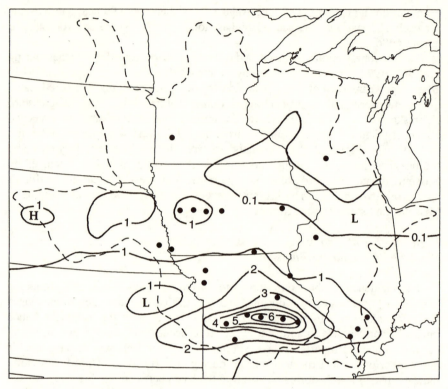

FIGURE 3-6 The rain pattern (in inches) for July 6-7, one of the many flash-flood-producing rainstorms in Missouri during July. Dots denote the locations of raingage stations experiencing one-day rains in excess of 6 inches during 1993.

season (e.g., Kane et al., 1987). Inspection of daily rainfall maps for 1993 indicates that on many days one or two large-sized rainfall areas in the region were of a scale and shape appropriate to MCCs. There were 80 distinct, large-sized rain areas during the 1993 summer months, each covering 50,000-square-mile areas that were 100 to 200 miles wide and 400 to 600 miles long. Most included large areas with 1 to 2 inches of rain over 5,000 to 15,000 square miles (NWS, 1994). Often these rain areas aligned themselves along a major river basin creating rapid runoff and rapid rises in the river levels. Figure 3-6 illustrates one such area that was aligned along the main stem of the Missouri River, which extends from west to east across central Missouri.

Persistent High Soil Moisture

A series of soil moisture maps (Figure 3-7) denote the shifting soil moisture conditions across the Midwest from March through August 1993. These were

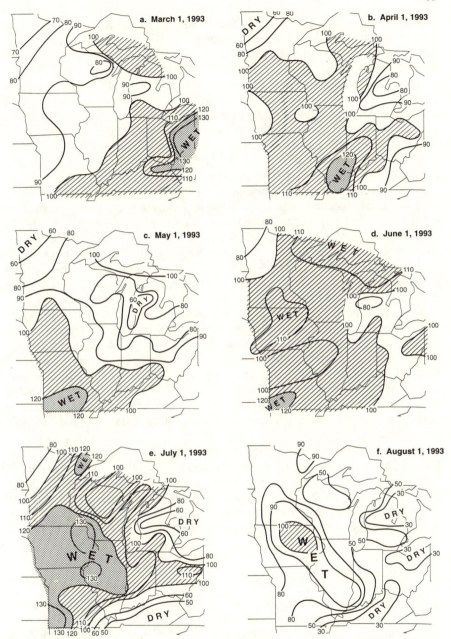

FIGURE 3-7   Percent of soil moisture at selected dates during 1993 for the top 12 inches of soil, with values expressed as percent of plant available water.   A value of 0 represents no plant available water, 100 represents field capacity, and 120 represents fields with some standing water.

developed using the operational soil moisture model of the Midwestern Climate Center (Kunkel, 1990). They illustrate the soil moisture in the top 12 inches of the soil expressed as percent of potential plant available water. Values of 100 percent represent field capacity and values in excess of 100 percent represent muddy field conditions. Values in excess of 120 percent identify areas with some standing water. Normally, values approaching 100 percent are experienced during the early spring months. Then during the latter part of spring (May) and through the summer, soil moisture decreases to 50 percent or less as plants use the stored soil water for growth. Such was not the case in 1993.

During the early spring of 1993 (Figures 3-7a and 3-7b), soil moisture was high in much of the Midwest with values exceeding 100 percent by April 1. The western part of the basin was somewhat drier in March, which is quite typical. Above-normal precipitation in May caused soil moisture values to increase, and by June 1, virtually the entire region had values above 100 percent (Figure 3-7d). Normally, a rapid decease of soil moisture begins during May. The excessive wetness of the soils on June 1 set the stage for the flood: there was little capacity for the soils to absorb the heavy summer rains that began in June. This resulted in high runoff rates. There was also no opportunity for soils to dry as they normally do during June.

On July 1, nearly the entire Midwest was still experiencing values in excess of 100 percent with values of 120 percent or higher indicating saturation across large areas of Iowa, Illinois, and Missouri (Figure 3-7e). Heavy rains that fell in early July resulted in very high runoff rates into streams and rivers. The latter part of July was somewhat drier. Thus, by August 1 there had been some drying with values in much of the basin falling slightly below 100 percent (Figure 3-7f). A significant portion of the flooded area was still experiencing values above 90 percent compared to normal values at this time of the summer, which are less than 50 percent, however.

The change in the amount of soil moisture over time in the heavy rain area of Iowa is illustrative of what happened. Normally, the amount of plant available water in the top 42 inches of the soil is between 5 and 6 inches during the spring, and then drops to about 2 inches by late summer. In contrast, values in excess of 6 inches persisted throughout the spring and summer 1993. At several times during the summer, the 1993 soil moisture values exceeded the previous highest value of record.

Low Evapotranspiration

Below-average evapotranspiration was the fifth hydroclimatic factor contributing to the floods of 1993. The very heavy, frequent rains were accompanied by much-above-normal cloud cover for the June-August period. In addition, temperatures were below normal over much of the basin, particularly the northwest portion. Together, these two factors resulted in a significant reduction in potential evapotranspiration (PET). For the three-month summer period the estimated PET value was 15.2 inches, compared with a long-term average value of 17.4 inches.

POST-FLOOD CONDITIONS

Although the rains remained high in August, the floodwaters began to recede in late August. Soil moisture amounts remained high throughout the basin, leaving the area very vulnerable to recurrences of flooding during the following fall, winter, and spring. Four episodes of heavy rain indeed occurred and resulted in significant flooding. More than 2 inches of rain fell over a large area including much of Missouri, Illinois, and southern Wisconsin from September 12 to 14 (see Figure 2-2 in Chapter 2). A second episode occurred shortly thereafter on September 18-25 with more than 3 inches of rain over Missouri, southern Illinois, and eastern Kansas. Many locations in Missouri received more than 6 inches, and Waco (in southwestern Missouri) received 12.5 inches. Both episodes again caused waters to rise in the tributaries and main stem of the Mississippi. The third episode occurred from November 12-15 with rainfall amounts of 3 to 9 inches over southern Illinois and southeastern Missouri. Many tributaries flooded and river levels along the Mississippi River main stem rose again, particularly from St. Louis southward.

After a relatively dry winter, a fourth heavy rain episode occurred from April 9-12, 1994. Rainfall amounts of greater than 5 inches fell over a 50,000-square-mile area that was up to 150 miles wide and extended from eastern Kansas into west-central Indiana. This is more rain than typically falls during an entire month in Kansas, Missouri, Illinois, or Indiana. Nevada (in western Missouri) received 14.4 inches during these four days. Major flooding occurred on many streams and rivers in Missouri, Kansas, and Illinois. However, basin-wide flooding due to snowmelt did not occur in 1994 since the winter precipitation across the upper Midwest was well below average. In each of the fall, winter, and spring flood episodes, the severity of the flooding was exacerbated by the very wet soils that were a legacy of the summer 1993 heavy rains.

The longer-term future may hold ever more floods for the Upper Mississippi River basin. A study of past floods and associated heavy precipitation at 149 basins scattered across the Midwest, based on high quality data for the 1921-1990 period, found statistically significant increases in flood occurrences in the warm season (May-September) across Minnesota, Iowa, western Wisconsin, and northern Illinois (Changnon and Kunkel, 1995). The period of increase began about 1940 and persisted through 1990. The upward trend was explained largely by increases in the frequency and magnitude of heavy precipitation events in this same area, signifying a progressive 50-year shift in regional precipitation conditions, which may or may not end in the future.

SUMMARY

During the flood there was much controversy about the effects of levees and other human influences on the severity of the flooding. Although these effects cannot be discounted, it is clear that the primary influence on the flooding was Mother Nature and the extreme rainfall. Analysis of the rainfall shows that the magnitude of the precipitation conditions was unprecedented in this century.

Hydroclimatological assessment indicated that the following five conditions were of most relevance to the flooding. These include:

- Heavy rains throughout the summer covered vast areas of the Upper Mississippi River basin. Total rainfall during the summer months (June-August) was greater, by a large margin, than that during any previous three-month period since records began in 1895, and the estimated return period exceeds 200 years.
- Flood-producing conditions had developed over many months prior to the flood: wet soils and high river flows at the beginning of the summer were created by a persistently rainy pattern that began in late July 1992, leading to high soil moisture levels and setting the stage for the heavy summer rains.
- The major summer rainfall episode occurred June 29-July 10 with heavy rains over the basin each day, resulting in massive accumulations of rainfall at many points. However, there were several other heavy rain episodes throughout the summer, and this high frequency of large-area heavy rain episodes was the key feature of this flood.
- The heavy rain pattern was centered over the Upper Mississippi River basin, rather than straddling two or more basins. Thus, almost all sub-basins received excessive rainfall and experienced very high runoff, together producing the huge and destructive flows on the main stem of the Mississippi and the Missouri Rivers.
- Low summertime evapotranspiration further exacerbated the situation by keeping soil moisture values high throughout the summer. (A primary factor in reducing evapotranspiration was the unusually high number of cloudy days.)

The major lesson learned is that these highly unusual and unique natural circumstances all helped to shape the flood of 1993. Consequently, they should be kept in mind when considering governmental responses to the flood.

REFERENCES

Changnon, S.A., and K.E. Kunkel, 1995: Trends in floods and precipitation across the Midwest. *Journal of Water Resources Planning and Management*, American Society of Civil Engineers, in press.

Huff, F.A., and J.R. Angel, 1992: *Rainfall Frequency Atlas of the Midwest.* Illinois State Water Survey Bulletin 71, Champaign, IL, 141 pp.

Kane, R.J., Jr., C.R. Chelius, and J.M. Fritsch, 1987: Precipitation characteristics of mesoscale convective weather systems. *Journal of Climate Applied Meteorology*, 26, 1345-1357.

Kunkel, K.E., 1990: Operational soil moisture estimation for the Midwestern United States. *Journal of Applied Meteorology,* 29, 1158-1166.

Kunkel, K.E., S.A. Changnon, and R.T. Shealy, 1993: Spatial and temporal characteristics of extreme precipitation events in the Midwest. *Monthly Weather Review*, 121, 858-866.

Kunkel, K.E., S.A. Changnon, and J.R. Angel, 1994: Climatic aspects of the 1993 Upper Mississippi River basin flood. *Bulletin American Meteorological Society*, 75, 811-822.

Monteith, J.L., 1965: Evaporation and environment. *Symposium Society Experimental Biology*, 19, 205-234.

National Weather Service (NWS), 1994: *The Great Flood of 1993.* National Oceanic and Atmospheric Administration, Natural Disaster Survey Report, Washington, DC, pp. 3-22 to 3-23.

4

The Flood's Hydrology

William H. Koellner

INTRODUCTION

Floods such as that in 1993 are unprecedented in modern history. The hydrologic enormity and severity of this particular flood are not subject to dispute. In all, 1,800 miles of rivers experienced record high flows, including 520 miles on the Mississippi, 415 miles on the Missouri, 190 miles on the Des Moines, 185 miles on the Kansas, 165 miles on the Iowa River, and shorter portions of eight other Midwestern rivers. Another 1,300 miles of rivers were listed as experiencing "major floods," those with flows rated above five-year return intervals but less than the record. These rivers and their major tributaries are shown in Figure 1-1.

Several floods of large magnitude have occurred in the Mississippi River basin since humans first began keeping records of this type of data 160 years ago. When compared to all other past floods, the 1993 flood differs by being larger in areal extent, larger in magnitude, longer in duration, greater in volume of floodwater, greater in amount of damage produced, and also by occurring at a different time of the year (summer rather than winter or spring). Weather conditions that caused the flood events were uncommonly persistent (Chapter 2) and the rains produced were exceptional in their magnitude and areal extent (Chapter 3). As floodwaters spread across large parts of nine states, isolating and paralyzing communities, public service utilities, and transportation systems, the impact was catastrophic.

Large Mississippi River floods previously occurred in 1965, 1969, and 1973. When one of these floods was over, floodplain inhabitants typically called it the "greatest flood" in their lifetimes. After each of these floods, floodplain inhabitants also wanted better flood protection, and states and communities called for adequate floodplain delineation and zoning. Unfortunately, the floodplains have been developed by private landowners, industries, communities, and states, often for widely varying and conflicting purposes, all challenging each waterway's primary function--drainage.

Initially, this chapter describes how floods are defined and addresses the effects of the 1993 flood on major reservoir operations and commercial navigation. The next section treats the antecedent conditions that helped set the stage for the flood, followed by a description of the significant rain events during the flood. A discussion of the flooding on the Mississippi River includes an analysis of the floods on its tributaries in Minnesota, Wisconsin, Illinois, and Iowa. There is also an assessment of the flooding on the Missouri River and its flooded tributaries in Nebraska, Kansas, and Missouri. The chapter concludes with a summary and an assessment of lessons learned from the 1993 flood.

Flood Definitions

Engineers and scientists have defined floods by studying historic floods and comparing them regionally against all past floods. Discharge-frequency relationships have been established at stream locations for which good hydrologic records exist by using statistical methods. Scientists have created synthetic floods for varying recurrence intervals ranging from 2-year up to 500-year return intervals. Subsequently, high-water stream profiles were computed, and these values were used in planning for community development and in designing flood protection projects.

Older levees in the Upper Mississippi River basin, some dating back to the 1850s, were designed and constructed to withstand 25-year or 50-year floods. Unfortunately, many early hydrologic designers had to define floods at a time when only short streamflow records existed for 20 years or less, but today we have much longer hydrologic records (up to 80 years of record). Several flood control projects on the Mississippi River were designed and constructed as a direct result of the 1965, 1969, and 1973 floods, depending on available funds. In other cases, levee systems existed as products of emergency construction, such as those of "Operation Foresight" done just before the 1969 flood. While the majority of the agricultural flood control projects are earthen walls, urban communities have constructed wall levees using both earth and concrete.

Effects of Reservoirs

The magnitude of the 1993 flood and resultant damages would have been greater had large volumes of floodwaters not been stored in the Midwestern reservoirs of the Corps of Engineers and the Bureau of Reclamation and, to some extent, those of the Soil Conservation Service. These flood control projects worked in tandem with downstream local flood control projects to reduce damages to agricultural lands and urban areas, as well as to prevent the loss of human lives. Many of these reservoirs stored large volumes of floodwater, thus attaining record stage levels. At some of the reservoirs, the spillways were used for the very first time to pass excessive floodwater. The volume of runoff from the 1993 flood was so large that the equivalent volume was equal to as much as 12 times the storage capacity of each reservoir. Even though large volumes were released through outlet works and over spillways, the inflows to those reservoirs were higher than the outflows. These operations reduced the peak flow of the Mississippi River at Quincy, IL, by 2 feet and by 1.5 feet at Hannibal, MO (U.S. Army Corps of Engineers, Rock Island District, 1994).

Effects on Commercial Navigation

Most of the locks and dams on the Mississippi River were closed during the high water period. At many of the facilities, the entire lock was under water. Consequently, navigation on the Mississippi River had to be halted, and traffic operations were closed from Canton, MO, north to Bellevue, IA, by the U.S. Coast Guard on June 25, 1993. All 27 locks and dams were closed by July 8 except the Melvin Price Lock at Alton, IL. The Missouri River was closed from July 2 to August 20, and by July 10, the lower 63 miles of the Illinois River Waterway were closed. During a 30-day period in July, navigation losses due to suspended traffic movement were estimated as $111 million (U.S. Army Corps of Engineers, St. Louis District, 1994). Navigation on the Mississippi and Illinois Rivers was allowed to resume on August 27. More than 200 towboats were stalled on the Upper Mississippi River at a cost of $750,000 per day. More than 7,000 barges were stranded across the Midwest, and this value did not include the barges amassed near St. Louis and Cairo, IL, awaiting resumption of navigation (Hines, 1993).

RELEVANT ANTECEDENT CONDITIONS

Antecedent moisture conditions contribute to the potential for a spring or a summer flood. In the Upper Mississippi River basin these conditions include: above-normal rainfall in the fall season, above-normal snow depth during winter, high water content in the snowpack, high ground-water levels, high soil moisture levels, warm temperatures during the spring snowmelt period, high river flows, and above-normal seasonal rainfall during spring, summer, or both. For example, the spring floods of 1965 and 1969 were preceded by very large water contents in the basin's winter snowpack in conjunction with early spring warm temperatures and heavy rainfall. As a result, significant spring flooding occurred. In contrast, the 1973 flood was due to excessive spring rainfall across Iowa, Illinois, and Missouri.

Prior to the snowmelt runoff in February 1993, the flows of the Mississippi River and its tributaries between Dubuque, IA, and Hannibal, MO, were between 160 and 170 percent of long-term normal flows (U.S. Army Corps of Engineers,

Rock Island District, 1993). And although drought conditions existed in much of the western Missouri River basin, heavy fall precipitation had improved the soil moisture conditions basinwide. Soil moisture for the Upper Mississippi River basin in winter ranged between 75 percent and 85 percent of normal (Wendland and Dennison, 1993). The water equivalent of the 1992-1993 snowpack for Minnesota, Wisconsin, Iowa, Illinois, and Missouri ranged between 0.5 and 5.1 inches (Newmann, 1993). Basin ground-water levels were above normal in March 1993 (USGS, 1993a). Abnormally cold temperatures from November 1992-February 1993 created heavy ice thickness on lakes and rivers in the basin (U.S. Army Corps of Engineers, Rock Island District, 1993). These factors caused spring snowmelt flooding in the Upper Mississippi basin followed by much-above normal rainfall beginning in April and persisting through the summer, as described in Chapter 3.

HYDROLOGICALLY SIGNIFICANT RAINFALL EVENTS

A sequence of six rain events occurred in the upper Midwest during June, July, and August 1993, and these were the major factors in producing and sustaining the summer flood. Some of the rain systems covered large areas and resulted in significant runoff, leading to the crests on the Mississippi and Missouri Rivers. Other smaller-scale storms caused local flash flooding on the tributaries, as discussed in Chapter 3. A listing of the most significant flood-producing rain systems and the primary areas of flooding resulting from them follows.

June 16-19

Heavy rains fell on saturated soils throughout southern Minnesota, northern Iowa, and southwestern Wisconsin (see Figure 3-4a). The Minnesota River basin and its tributaries in Minnesota plus the Chippewa and Black River basins in Wisconsin were affected. This three-day storm event initiated the Great Flood of 1993 on the Upper Mississippi River basin. The resulting flood crest reached Clinton, IA, on July 5 (see Figure 4-1). Additional heavy rainfall on June 19-20 enhanced the flooding on the Chippewa, Trempealeau, Black, and Wisconsin Rivers, resulting in the partial failure of a dam on the Black River.

June 25-29

The alignment of the surface fronts and the jet stream was favorable for the production of repeated thunderstorms for five days in the same area: Iowa and eastern Nebraska. Several of the storms created flash floods (Maddox et al., 1979), but the heaviest rainfall occurred on the Des Moines, Skunk, and Iowa River basins in Iowa, and on Papillion Creek basin near Omaha, NE. More than

7 inches fell over the Iowa Great Lakes region in northwestern Iowa (U.S. Army Corps of Engineers, Omaha District, 1994).

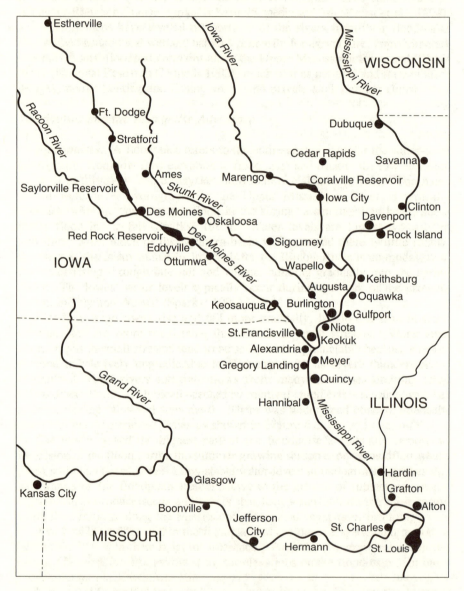

FIGURE 4-1 Rivers, reservoirs, and locations where extreme flooding occurred in Iowa, Illinois, and Missouri during June, July, and August 1993.

July 1-9

Rainfall exceeding 5 inches fell in southeastern Iowa and western Illinois on July 1. The Mississippi River continued to rise with a second crest developing at Dubuque, IA (see Figure 4-1) on July 6. This crest with additional inflow from tributary streams established record crests from Rock Island, IL, downstream to St. Louis. As the crest moved downstream, a number of agricultural levees were overtopped. Runoff from the rainstorms on July 4 and July 8 caused record peak discharges in the basins of the Iowa, Skunk, Raccoon, and Des Moines Rivers in Iowa. Flood peaks from these tributaries all entered the Mississippi River at about the same time the flood peak on the Mississippi (from the late-June storms in Minnesota and Wisconsin) reached the point at which these Iowa rivers emptied into the main stem. The resulting massive crest approached St. Louis from the north where it was joined by high water entering from the Missouri River. *Such a conjunction of major crests had never occurred since the Corps of Engineers has been keeping records* (U.S. Army Corps of Engineers, St. Louis District, 1994). The final storm event in this nine-day period (see Figure 3-4b) produced 8.5 inches of rain on July 9 (recorded at Jefferson, IA, in the basin of Iowa's Raccoon River). The resultant record flood overtopped the levees protecting the water treatment plant in Des Moines, IA (U.S. Army Corps of Engineers, Rock Island District, 1994).

July 17-18

Intense rains producing 2 to 5 inches fell in one-hour periods over the Mill Creek basin near Cherokee, IA (U.S. Army Corps of Engineers, Omaha District, 1994). The two-day rain event produced an additional 5 inches of rain over the upper Cedar River basin in Iowa. Heavy rains in Wisconsin caused flash flooding on the Baraboo River.

July 22-25

Rains from 4 to 13 inches fell from a huge area covering parts of Nebraska, Kansas, Missouri, Iowa, and Illinois on July 22-23. Then on July 24, an additional 4 inches fell on southern portions of Iowa and Illinois. The four-day totals are shown on Figure 3-4c. Again, the Missouri and Mississippi Rivers began to climb, and the Illinois River went above flood stage (U.S. Army Corps of Engineers, Rock Island District, 1994). There were reports of up to 16 inches of rainfall in southeastern Nebraska, and the Kansas River crested.

August 10-11

Initially, 4 inches of rain fell near Iowa City, IA, on August 10, causing flooding. Then 5 inches of rain fell on the Iowa River and Cedar River basins.

Flash floods occurred near Marshalltown and Tama, IA (U.S. Army Corps of Engineers, Rock Island District, 1994).

FLOODING ON THE MISSISSIPPI RIVER BASIN

Flooding along the Mississippi River from the 1993 rainstorms was the most devastating in the history of the United States in terms of property loss and disrupted lives and business activities. Millions of acres of farmland were under water for weeks during the growing season. Damaged highways and roads disrupted overland transportation throughout the flooded region (see Chapter 8). The Mississippi River was closed to navigation for eight weeks. The banks and channels of the Mississippi River and its tributaries were severely eroded in many reaches (see Chapter 5). In addition to the erosion by the rivers, erosion of valuable topsoil occurred. The extent and duration of the flooding caused more than 1,000 levees to fail. Tremendous efforts were extended in the resulting fight to save homes, farms, livestock, industries, and communities from the flood. Every gaging station on the Mississippi below Rock Island experienced a new flood of record, and to the north the 1993 flood was surpassed by only one other event: that of April 1965. A summary of the top two floods of record for the gaging stations along the Upper Mississippi River's main stem from Dubuque, IA (Lock and Dam 11) downstream to Hannibal, MO (Lock and Dam 22) is shown in Table 4-1 (U.S. Army Corps of Engineers, Rock Island District, 1994).

The following major section describes the floods on the Mississippi River above Cairo, IL, and on the river's principal tributaries that experienced flooding. The presentation is divided into three sections: (1) floods on the tributaries in Minnesota and Wisconsin, (2) floods on the tributaries in Iowa and Illinois, and (3) flooding along the Mississippi's main stem from Minneapolis, MN, to St. Louis. All the flow values assigned a recurrence interval are based on an evaluation using U.S. Geological Survey Circular 1120-A (1993a).

The slope of the Mississippi River between St. Anthony Falls at Minneapolis, MN, downstream to its confluence with the Missouri River averages approximately 6 inches per mile except at the Rock Island-LeClaire Rapids in Pools 14-15 and in the Des Moines Rapids in Pool 19 where the low water slope prior to construction of these navigation pools was approximately 1.5 feet per mile. During the 1930s, 27 major locks and dams were built along the Mississippi River between Alton, IL, (near St. Louis, see Figure 4-1) and Minneapolis to allow operation of commercial navigation. As shown in Figure 5-1 (in Chapter 5) each lock and dam is numbered, and each has developed a "pool" of water behind it. Topography near the navigation pools is generally characterized by high bluffs and rolling hills. The mean annual runoff of the Mississippi River is 7 inches at Lock and Dam 20 near Canton, MO. This is equivalent to 49,279,000 acre-feet of water from 134,300 square miles of drainage area. The infiltration rate over the watershed is approximately 0.1 inch

TABLE 4-1 Top-Ranked Floods on the Mississippi River between Hannibal, MO, and Dubuque, IA. The 1993 Values Ranked First South of Rock Island and Second at Sites North of Rock Island

Station	Date	First stage, ft	Date	Second stage, ft
Dubuque	4/26/65	26.81	7/01/93	23.84
Sabula	4/27/65	22.90	7/07/93	21.30
Clinton	4/28/65	24.85	7/08/93	22.98
Rock Island	7/09/93	22.63	4/28/65	22.48
Muscatine	7/09/93	25.61	4/29/65	24.81
Keithsburg	7/09/93	24.15	4/27/65	20.36
Burlington	7/10/93	24.98	4/25/73	21.50
Keokuk	7/10/93	27.58	4/23/73	27.58
Quincy	7/13/93	32.13	4/23/73	28.90
Hannibal	7/16/93	31.80	4/25/73	28.59

per hour. The mean annual runoff fluctuates from year to year with extremes of 0.3 to 21.7 inches.

Floods on Tributaries in Minnesota and Wisconsin

Redwood River Basin. Heavy rainfall on two successive days (May 6 and 7) in southern Minnesota caused major flooding on the Redwood River at Marshall, MN. A 5.1-inch amount was recorded at Florence, MN, in a six-hour period. The Redwood River crested 3 feet above flood stage, and the rise in the river required the city of Marshall to construct a half-mile emergency levee and a second emergency levee to protect a trailer park (U.S. Army Corps of Engineers, St. Paul District, 1994). The greatest flood on record at Marshall was in 1969 from snowmelt with a flow of 8,090 cubic feet per second (cfs). The May 9 flood had a provisional instantaneous peak discharge of 6,380 cfs, and ranks second in the 54 years of river record. The 1993 value has a recurrence interval of once in 50 years.

A second significant flood occurred about a month later, after a rainstorm on June 16-17 in southwestern Minnesota (see Figure 3-4a). The average basin rainfall was 4.9 inches, with point rainfall of 8 inches at some locations. Several industries had to close due to high water in Marshall and the wastewater treatment plant was inundated. On June 17, the peak flow was 16.25 feet with an instantaneous peak discharge of 4,800 cfs, representing a recurrence interval of 25 years. This peak became the fourth largest flood of record.

Heavy rains associated with a third storm occurring on July 3 centered over the Redwood River basin, again causing flooding at Marshall, its third flood in nine weeks. An upstream basin average rain of 3.5 inches caused a peak discharge of 4,050 cfs, a recurrence interval of 20 years, and the fifth largest flood at Marshall.

Minnesota River Basin. The Minnesota River drains the southern third of Minnesota and experienced severe flooding during late May and June 1993. The river at Mankato crested at 30.11 feet with a discharge of 75,600 cfs on June 21, which exceeded the record in 1881 (29.9 feet set with a discharge of 110,000 cfs). The 1993 flood was rated greater than a 50-year flood but less than a 100-year flood. Table 4-2 summarizes the 1993 floods on the Minnesota River.

Black River Basin. During a five-day period, June 16-20, rainfall totals between 5.7 inches and 7.3 inches fell over this basin in western Wisconsin (see Figure 3-4a). Fifteen roads were closed due to flooding, and erosion and damage were reported at many small dams. Levels of Lake Arbutus had been rising during the prior week, and flooding began in the Hatfield area on June 19. The advancing floodwaters threatened Hatfield Dam, which impounds Lake Arbutus. Ultimate structural damage to the dam was a hole 8 feet deep and 6 feet across. Operational failures included three tainter gates on the dam that were not operating and about half of the dam's flashboards. No continuous streamflow record exists immediately downstream of Hatfield Dam, but the Wisconsin Geological Survey documented the peak flow at 80,000 cfs (2.4 feet above the 100-year flood level). Downstream at Galesville, WI, the instantaneous peak discharge was 64,000 cfs, a once-in-75-year event.

Baraboo River. A highly localized rainstorm on July 17-18 produced a 12.7-inch rain near Baraboo, WI. Flash floods occurred on the Baraboo River in western Wisconsin (NWS, 1994). Wisconsin hydrologists analyzed the flood event and concluded that the flooding around Devils Lake State Park was at or greater than a 500-year flood (Wisconsin Department of Natural Resources, 1993).

Floods on Tributaries in Iowa and Illinois

Rock River Basin. The flooding that occurred in the Rock River basin, which drains northwestern Illinois and southern Wisconsin, was not as severe or long-lived as floods in some nearby basins. Most of the flooding was related to ice jams in March. The small communities of Hillsdale, Erie, and Green Rock, IL, fought the flood and prevented the inundation of their communities. As the crest water attempted to pass through the Joslin, IL area, the ice jam surged and eventually overtopped some small agricultural levees that allowed the peak to be stored inside the levee districts. The failure immediately caused the crest to occur from Joslin to Moline, IL. Other than the Joslin area, the lower Rock River below Green Rock again flooded in June from a combination of high Rock

TABLE 4-2 Comparison of the 1993 Flood with Record Past Floods on the Minnesota River

Location	Flood stage, ft	1993 stage, ft	1993 discharge, cfs	Record discharge, cfs	Date
Montevideo	14	16.46	11,500	35,100	4/12/69
Mankato	19	30.11	75,600	110,000	4/18/81
Jordan	20	33.52	92,200	117,000	4/11/65

River flows and the excessive backwater caused by the high floodwaters on the Mississippi River.

Only two of the gaging stations on the Rock River recorded 1993 flood stages that were in the top five floods of record: Joslin's 18.35 feet on March 26, 1993, was a record, and the June 12, 1993, value at Moline, IL, ranked as the fifth highest on record. No other streamgage stations on the Rock River or its tributaries had stages approaching record floods.

Iowa River Basin. During spring and summer 1993, the Iowa River experienced severe flooding. The hydrograph for the Iowa River gaging station at Marengo, IA, which is in east-central Iowa, is shown on Figure 4-2 to illustrate the Iowa River's behavior. The river was above flood stage (14 feet) for the entire summer, as well as during April and early May. The peak on July 19 was the second flood of record, reaching a peak stage of 20.31 feet. A peak on August 19, the fourth highest flood of record, reached a peak stage of 19.61 feet. From April-September 1993, the runoff depth at Marengo was 28.2 inches. In contrast, the mean runoff depth for these months, based on the 36-year period of record is only 5.5 inches (U.S. Army Corps of Engineers, Rock Island District, 1994).

The gage hydrograph for the Iowa River at Iowa City, IA (Figure 4-2), which is downstream of Marengo and the Coralville Reservoir, reflects the river's regulation at Coralville Dam. The flood stage of 26 feet was not exceeded until July, but then remained above flood stage until early September (U.S. Army Corps of Engineers, Rock Island District, 1994). Table 4-3 compares the top three floods at stations in the Iowa River basin.

Flooding on the main stem of the Iowa River from Iowa City and downstream was reduced due to the operation of the Coralville Dam. By June 4, outflows from Coralville Reservoir were down to the maximum release allowed during the growing season when not in Major Flood Operation (6,000 cfs). Intense rain raised the inflows to 17,000 cfs on June 21, causing the reservoir to go over elevation 707 feet early on June 20, thus shifting the reservoir regulation to the category of Major Flood Operation. Some 1.3 inches of rain occurred on June 25, but although the rain was not widespread, it did keep inflows high as the pool went above 711 feet late on June 25. Coralville's regulation plan provided for rapid increase in release rates between 711 and 712 feet (full flood control pool)

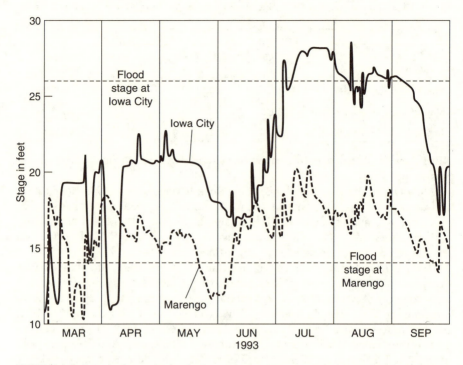

FIGURE 4-2 Stage hydrographs for the Iowa River at Marengo and at Iowa City for 1993.

from 10,000 cfs to 20,000 cfs. Another heavy rain was centered near the reservoir early on June 27. By the end of June, the pool was at 711.5 feet with an outflow of 12,000 cfs and an inflow of 11,400 cfs (U.S. Army Corps of Engineers, Rock Island District, 1994).

Coralville Dam's spillway overtopped for the first time in history on July 5. Resulting high flows in Iowa City and downstream of Wapello caused great concern for downstream residents. Reservoir inflows averaged 35,700 cfs on July 5, and outflows increased to 17,400 cfs during July 5 (the historical maximum release had been 13,000 cfs in 1969). On July 6, the inflow fell to 22,800 cfs, and the outflow remained at 17,400 cfs. Outflows increased on July 7 to 18,100 cfs, and after reaching a peak pool elevation of 713.4 feet, the pool slowly fell.

Additional rainfall occurred in the Iowa River basin above Coralville Dam during the wet July 1-9 period with up to 9 inches over central Iowa (see Figure 3-4b). High inflows predicted for the already full reservoir raised concerns about flooding of the water treatment plants at Iowa City and at the University of Iowa, both downstream of the dam. It was determined that the water treatment plants would not be inundated if the stage at Iowa City remained below 28.5 feet. The dam was operated to maintain 28 feet at Iowa City. The outflow regulation goal was intended to get as much water out of the reservoir as possible but still save

TABLE 4-3 Top Floods of Record on the Iowa and Cedar Rivers in Iowa

Station	Date	First stage, ft	Date	Second stage, ft	Date	Third stage, ft
Iowa River at Marshalltown	8/17/93	20.77	6/18/90	20.47	3/31/93	20.26
Iowa River at Belle Plaine	7/11/93	19.59	6/5/18	17.86	4/2/93	17.48
Iowa River at Marengo	7/19/93	20.31	7/12/69	19.79	8/19/93	19.61
Iowa River at Iowa City	1851	34.1	7/18/81	31.10	6/8/18	29.60
Cedar River at Cedar Rapids	1851	20.00	3/18/29	20.00	3/31/61	19.66
Iowa River at Wapello	7/7/93	29.53	6/18/90	28.91	4/22/73	28.63

the water treatment plants. Reservoir operations were modified to limit the opening of the conduit. A flash-flood regulation was added to the criteria for flow regulation such that flow reductions would be made at Coralville Dam if significant runoff was forecast.

The Coralville Pool reached its peak for the summer at 716.7 feet on July 24, being 129 percent of total flood control storage and representing 3.5 inches of runoff. On this basin the flood of 1993 had consisted of a series of storms over many months without enough time to evacuate stored water between events. Full conduit outflow was reached for the first time on July 30 with the pool at 713.3 feet. Total runoff entering the pool between March 1 and September 30 was 30.3 inches, more than 11 times the total flood storage available at the dam. The peak one-day inflow for 1993 had a frequency of once in 20 years (5 percent probability), the 30-day peak inflow had a frequency of once in 200 years (0.5 percent), and both the 90-day and 120-day inflows were estimated to be greater than the once-in-1,000-year event (0.1 percent) (U.S. Army Corps of Engineers, Rock Island District, 1993). Given these extremes, damage reduction was still accomplished downstream by Coralville Dam. Table 4-4 compares the observed and reconstituted stages and flows at three downstream locations: Iowa City, Lone Tree, and Wapello, IA. (U.S. Army Corps of Engineers, Rock Island District, 1993). Reductions ranged from 0.7 to 1.6 feet.

Skunk River Basin. Flooding in the Skunk River basin, which lies across central Iowa, caused catastrophic losses in Ames, IA. Squaw Creek, a tributary to the Skunk River, reached record heights and flooded Iowa State University's Hilton Coliseum with 14 feet of water and several other buildings. Squaw Creek rose from a stage of 5 feet to a stage of 18.5 feet in eight hours. Table 4-5 lists the top three floods of record at five locations from central Iowa (Ames) to the

80

TABLE 4-4   Stage Reductions on the Iowa River from Operations of Coralville Dam

Station	Observed Stage, ft	Observed Flow, cfs	Reconstituted Stage, ft	Reconstituted Flow, cfs	Reduction, ft
Iowa City	28.5	28,000	30.1	39,000	1.6
Lone Tree	22.9	57,000	23.9	65,000	1.0
Wapello	29.5	111,000	NA	NA	0.7

Note: NA = not available

river's mouth at the Mississippi near Augusta. Peaks on June 17, July 6, July 9, July 15, and August 15 reflected the excessive and continuing floods.

Des Moines River. The 1993 flooding on the Des Moines River was the most severe in hydrologic history and created major impacts on Des Moines. As shown in Figure 4-1, the Des Moines River extends from southeastern Iowa to northwestern Iowa. Record rainfalls across the basin resulted in floods that ultimately overtopped several levees and inundated Des Moines' water treatment plant on July 12, leaving residents without drinking water for three weeks. The storm primarily responsible for this event lasted five hours, adding 6.5 inches of rain on July 8 to an already swollen Des Moines River basin. Flash flooding occurred on the Raccoon River, a tributary that joins the Des Moines River in that city. Their combined flows compounded the severity of the flooding in Des Moines. Figure 4-3 reveals the Des Moines River was well above 30 feet for several days during early July (flood stage is 23 feet).

TABLE 4-5 Top-Ranked Floods at Five Locations on the Skunk River Basin

Station	First Date	First stage, ft	Second Date	Second stage, ft	Third Date	Third stage, ft
South Skunk River at Ames	8/16/93	14.23	5/20/84	13.90	6/10/54	13.66
Squaw Creek at Ames	7/9/93	18.54	6/17/90	15.97	6/4/18	14.50
South Skunk River at Oskaloosa	1944	25.80	7/15/93	24.78	6/23/90	22.98
N. Skunk River at Sigourney	6/20/90	25.37	3/31/60	25.33	7/6/93	24.68
Skunk River at Augusta	4/23/73	27.05	4/3/60	25.00	9/24/65	24.90

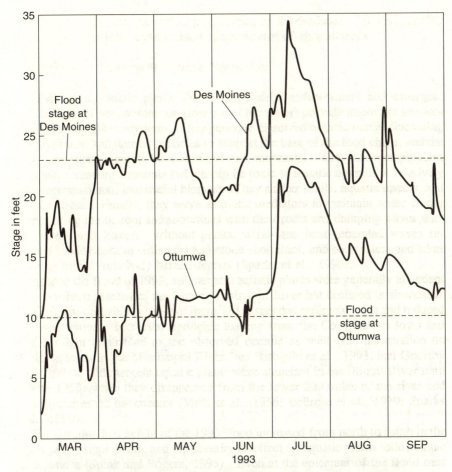

FIGURE 4-3 Stage hydrographs for the Des Moines River at Des Moines and Ottumwa.

The top floods of record on the Des Moines River are listed in Table 4-6. In the basin's upper reaches (Estherville), floods in May and June 1993 were high ranked; further downstream, the July 1993 stages ranked first or second highest on record. The hydrograph for the Des Moines River at Ottumwa, IA (Figure 4-3) reveals the river was above flood stage (10 feet) from late April through September. Ottumwa fought the flood to prevent overtopping of the levee that protects the water treatment plant. In early July, the river rose dramatically, and on July 12 a new flood of record occurred (22.15 ft) (U.S. Army Corps of Engineers, Rock Island District, 1993).

The Raccoon River basin in west central Iowa covers 3,629 square miles. The flood of record over most of this basin occurred on July 9-10, 1993. At Van Meter, IA, the river crested at 26.34 feet, 13.34 feet above flood stage. The Van

TABLE 4-6 Top Three Floods at Locations along the Des Moines River

Station	Date	First stage, ft	Date	Second stage, ft	Date	Third stage, ft
Estherville	4/12/69	17.68	4/10/65	15.61	6/8/53	15.53
Fort Dodge	6/23/47	19.62	6/21/65	19.28	4/8/65	17.79
Stratford	4/2/93	25.68	7/11/93	25.64	6/19/64	24.08
Des Moines	7/11/93	34.29	4/10/65	29.72	6/19/84	28.46
Ottumwa	7/12/93	22.15	5/31/03	22.00	6/7/47	20.20
Keosauqua	6/1/03	37.85	6/10/05	33.80	7/13/93	32.66
St Francisville	8/19/86	35.03	7/15/93	32.02	3/14/79	30.15

Meter streamgage recorded a peak flow of 70,200 cfs on July 10, which greatly exceeded the previous record flood of 41,200 cfs (based on 79 years of record). The 1993 storm responsible for the flood of record on the Raccoon River was also responsible for the flooding in Des Moines. The National Weather Service (NWS) raingage at Coon Rapids, IA, recorded 4 inches of rain on July 8, an amount exceeding the 100-year rainfall frequency (Hershfield, 1961).

FIGURE 4-4 Floodwaters surround the water plant at Quincy, IL. The plant is protected by temporary steel walls erected as the Mississippi River continued to rise on July 3.

Saylorville Reservoir. This large reservoir on the Des Moines River is located just above Des Moines. Heavy spring rains produced excessive floods in April and May (see Stratford values in Table 4-6), and then heavy rains in June brought enormous inflows to this reservoir. On June 17, water flowed over the reservoir's emergency spillway for the second time in 1993. The peak inflow during June 1993 was 35,900 cfs on June 18. Releases were increased to 21,000 cfs and maintained there until the reservoir climbed to an elevation of 889.0 feet on June 21. At this level, rules call for reservoir releases to be increased so that at full flood control pool the reservoir's conduit is fully open. As a result, releases were increased to a maximum discharge of 28,500 cfs, causing the reservoir to peak at elevation 889.35 feet at noon on June 21. Subsequently, discharges gradually receded to 21,000 cfs as the pool fell below 889.0 feet (U.S. Army Corps of Engineer, Rock Island District, 1993).

On June 30, slow-moving storms again produced widespread rainfall over the basin above Saylorville Reservoir. With the pool already between elevation 887 and 888 feet, inflow forecasts indicated that the pool would exceed 890 feet. The pool reached 889.4 feet on July 5, and the combined conduit and spillway discharge totaled 31,400 cfs. During the next few days, the pool fell slowly as reservoir outflows exceeded inflows. Outflows tapered off slowly until July 9 when up to 4 inches of rain covered a broad area above the reservoir. By midnight on July 9, the reservoir had exceeded 890 feet and reservoir releases were increased from 34,500 cfs to 37,900 cfs. No further increases in discharge were made to minimize flood damage in Des Moines (U.S. Army Corps of Engineers, Rock Island District, 1993). However, by 6 a.m. on July 11, the total discharge from the reservoir had climbed to 39,200 cfs due to increased head on the spillway. Earlier that same morning, the levee protecting the Des Moines Waterworks was overtopped as the Raccoon River reached its record levels. In order to aid flood-fighting efforts, discharges from Saylorville Reservoir were decreased to 34,800 cfs.

Over the next few days, a constant discharge of 11,500 cfs through the conduit was maintained as flow over the spillway increased as the pool level rose. On July 13, the pool climbed to a peak elevation of 892.03 feet, 107.6 percent of flood control capacity. The corresponding outflow from the reservoir was 43,500 cfs, while inflow was 47,100 cfs. Following the peak, discharges slowly decreased as the pool fell. As the Raccoon River flood receded, reservoir releases were gradually increased to reduce pool levels without causing additional flooding downstream. A peak outflow of 44,500 cfs was recorded on July 18. A comparison of runoff into Saylorville Lake versus the volume of runoff that was stored or evacuated between March and September 1993 is given in Table 4-7 (U.S. Army Corps of Engineers, Rock Island District, 1993). At full flood control pool elevation (890 feet), the reservoir has the capacity to store 1.89 inches of runoff. For this seven-month period, runoff to Saylorville Lake totaled 23.9 inches (eleven times the storage capacity available at full flood control pool and more than six times the normal cumulative inflow of 3.88 inches of runoff).

TABLE 4-7 Comparison of Runoff vs. Storage Used in Saylorville Reservoir (in inches)

Date	Total runoff	Storage utilized	Incremental change in storage
March 31	1.28	0.36	+0.35
April 30	4.60	1.56	+1.20
May 31	2.80	0.80	-0.76
June 30	4.25	1.78	+0.98
July 31	6.37	1.46	-0.32
August 31	2.99	1.22	- 0.24
September 30	1.58	0.17	-1.05

The Des Moines River flood of 1993 was the result of successive precipitation events that occurred over a period of six months. The one-day peak inflow had a frequency of once in 20 years (5 percent), the 30-day and 90-day peak inflows approached once in 140 years (0.7 percent), and the 120-day peak inflow was a 200-year (0.5 percent) event (U.S. Army Corps of Engineers, Rock Island District, 1993).

Red Rock Reservoir. About 30 miles downstream of Des Moines is Red Rock Reservoir (see Figure 4-1) where upstream flooding became a serious operational problem in July. Releases were held at 30,000 cfs, the maximum seasonal release, until July 1. Then all of the sluice gates controlling the low-level conduits were closed because the gated spillway would have to be used to pass the expected outflow from the dam (capacity of the conduits is limited to 38,000 cfs). Outflow was increased to 35,000 cfs on July 1, and 24 hours later the outflows were increased to 45,000 cfs as the pool had risen above elevation 779 feet. (The record previous maximum release was 40,000 cfs.) An elevation of 780 feet is full flood control pool. Releases were held near 45,000 cfs until July 5. Inflow to the reservoir increased from a daily average of 51,800 cfs to 100,400 cfs on July 5 and remained above 100,000 cfs on July 6 due to rains above the reservoir. On July 7, the outflow was increased to 70,000 cfs as rain continued to fall, keeping inflow high. As the pool rose, outflow from the dam continued to be increased. However, releases were below those prescribed in the regulation plan to aid flood-fighting efforts in downstream communities of Eddyville and Ottumwa.

A peak inflow of 134,900 cfs occurred July 11, and the pool rose to 782 feet. As a result, the release dam was increased to 100,000 cfs, still well below the release called for in the regulation plan, which calls for the outflow to be increased to 130,000 cfs when the pool reaches an elevation of 782 feet. However, levees downstream were saturated and in danger of being breached or overtopped. The peak elevation reached on July 13 was 782.68 feet. At this elevation, the reservoir was at 112 percent of flood control capacity. Although no further gate openings were made, the release from the reservoir peaked at 104,500 cfs as a result of increased head on the spillway.

From March 1 to September 30, the runoff into Lake Red Rock totaled 22.38 inches, nearly ten times the storage capacity available at full flood control pool and more than five times the normal cumulative runoff of 4.3 inches for this period. The 10-day and 30-day peak inflows for 1993 had an estimated frequency of once in 1,000 years (a 0.1 percent chance). Yet, Saylorville and Red Rock Dams reduced downstream damage.

Flooding on the Mississippi River

The prior two sections described excessive flooding events in May, June, and July on the Mississippi's main tributaries located in Minnesota, Wisconsin, Illinois, and Iowa. These swollen rivers disgorged their flows into the main stem of the big river, creating a massive volume of water. These inputs plus the heavy rains falling directly over the main stem created a record flood, and a chronology of the key events from mid-June through early-August follows.

Iowa experienced very heavy rains on June 18-19 and again on June 25-27. More than 90 percent of the storage on the three large reservoirs on Iowa rivers was used by June 27, and all locks and dams on the Mississippi River had been closed except Lock and Dam 15 at Rock Island. Additional rainfall on June 28

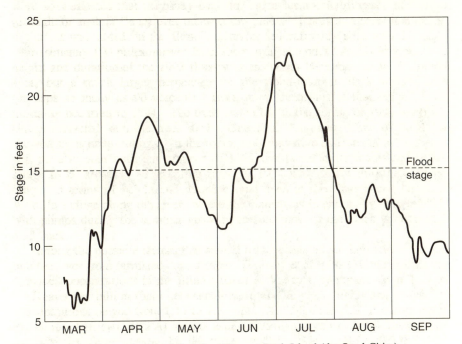

FIGURE 4-5 Hydrograph of the Mississippi River at Rock Island (the Quad Cities).

in the Upper Mississippi basin near Dubuque, IA (see Figure 4-1), provided additional runoff, producing a record crest on the Mississippi River below Rock Island, IL. This crest had formed above La Crosse, WI, and was moving downstream. The very rapid late-June rise in the Mississippi River at Rock Island, IL, is shown on Figure 4-5. An additional 2 inches of rain fell on June 29 in central and eastern Iowa, and the water in the three large reservoirs rose higher. Some Davenport residents evacuated their homes on June 29 due to a lack of adequate flood protection.

Near Quincy, IL, 170 miles downstream, an additional 2 to 5 inches of rain fell on July 1, helping to fill the river's main stem. Seepage through the levee systems in Oquawka, Keithsburg, and Bay Island, IL, became a major problem, but local residents continued to strengthen their flood protection systems. On July 3, homes were evacuated at Andalusia and Keithsburg, IL, 70 miles south of Rock Island. New flood records were forecast for Keithsburg, IL, and Burlington, IA. The Quad Cities continued to experience flooding throughout this period. A levee north of Canton, MO, was overtopped, inundating 8,000 acres of farmland. As seepage through the levees accumulated, residents in low-lying areas of Oquawka, IL, were evacuated on July 4-5.

On July 6, the Mississippi River crested for a second time at Dubuque, IA. This second crest continued downstream to the Quad Cities, as shown in Figure 4-5, and went on to Burlington and Keokuk, IA (by July 10). There was simply too much water, and a new series of levee failures began. On July 8, a nonfederal levee at Union Township, MO, was overtopped, flooding 5,000 acres of agricultural lands. Figure 4-6 provides a typical view of the flooding.

At Ottumwa, IA, a private levee broke, and some residents evacuated their homes. At Keithsburg, IL, a nonfederal levee was overtopped, and the town was

FIGURE 4-6 Waters covering the Mississippi River floodplain near Meyer, IL, seen through the dense haze caused by high humidity following heavy July rains (Illinois State Water Survey).

inundated. Another nonfederal levee was overtopped at Louisa, IA, flooding 5,700 acres of farmland and many residences (some of these agricultural acres will be bought in the federal buyout program). The Mississippi was at crest stage along 40 miles of river north of Rock Island. The Gregory Drainage District levee in Missouri, a federal levee, was overtopped and breached, and the floodwaters inundated 8,000 acres. At the Des Moines-Mississippi Drainage District in Iowa, the federal levee was overtopped and Alexandria went under 6 feet of water. The governor of Iowa declared 45 counties as disaster areas.

On July 9, the Mississippi crested for a third time at Clinton, IA, and also crested again at Rock Island (Figure 4-5). Federal levees north of Quincy, IL, were overtopped, inundating 28,000 acres of farmland and Meyer, IL (see Figure 4-6). On July 11, there was heavy rainfall across central Illinois and flash-flood conditions on the Raccoon River in Iowa. The resulting high water on the Des Moines River caused a federal levee T-wall below the confluence with the Raccoon River to fail, and an older industrial section of the town was flooded. Flash flooding along Deer Creek in Iowa inundated Tama, IA. When a non-federal levee was overtopped in Niota, IL,, homes and the Atchison, Topeka & Santa Fe (AT&SF) rail line went under water. A federal levee was overtopped at the Green Bay Drainage District near Burlington, IA, flooding about 13,500 acres, a fertilizer plant, and a grain elevator (U.S. Army Corps of Engineers, Rock Island District, 1994).

On July 12, the Mississippi River was at crest from near Dubuque to Keokuk, IA, as shown in Figure 4-7. Work to restore the operation of the Des Moines water treatment plant continued; however, high river levels resulted in limited effectiveness of pumping. The lower section of the Indian Graves Drainage District (a federal levee) located south of Warsaw, IL, was overtopped, and 8,000 acres of farmland and 12 farms were inundated.

On July 13, the Mississippi River began to drop very slowly as heavy rains fell across central Iowa. The South River Drainage District federal levee was overtopped at Willings Crossing, MO, flooding approximately 10,000 acres. The upper end of the Indian Graves federal levee was overtopped, and 10,000 additional acres were flooded.

On July 15, the Fabius Drainage District federal levee across the river from Quincy, IL, experienced two problems: (1) the clay portion of the levee system began to slide and the resulting seepage area required continuous attention, and (2) the levee was overtopped (with some human intervention), drawing a barge and tow into the breach, and the errant tow then hit a fuel supply station. The levee overtopping also caused the closing of the U.S. Highway 36 bridge at Quincy, the only remaining open bridge between St. Louis and the Quad Cities. Approximately 24,300 acres were then flooded along with 400 homes and several businesses. A section of a private levee in Des Moines experienced some sloughing, and residents were evacuated from their homes. The numerous levee failures occurring during mid-July upstream from Hannibal caused the "jagged" ups and downs of the river at Hannibal (see Figure 4-7).

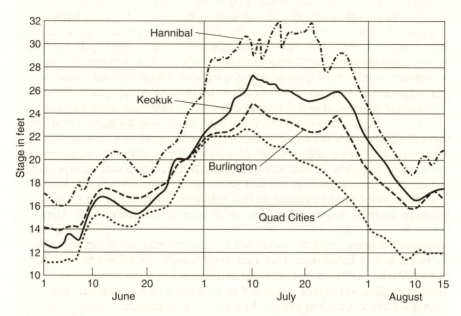

FIGURE 4-7 Stage hydrographs at four sites along the Mississippi River revealing the multiple crests experienced during the summer.

A second crest developed on the Mississippi in the Burlington and Quincy area in late July (see Figure 4-7) as crests from the Iowa, Skunk, and Des Moines Rivers entered the main stem. On July 24, an additional 4 inches of rain fell across the river's middle section, and the Mississippi River began to climb again, as the Illinois River also went above flood stage. The upper third of the Sny Island Drainage District levee system was overtopped on July 25, and 44,000 acres were flooded including 200 homes (Figure 4-8). On July 26, the Mississippi River began to gradually drop at the upper end of the record flooding (above Burlington). However, as shown on Figure 4-7, the river's lower end continued to rise at and below Hannibal, MO (U.S. Army Corps of Engineers, Rock Island District, 1994), as the peak flood flows on the Iowa and Des Moines Rivers entered the Mississippi. Fortunately, stage and damage reduction on the Mississippi River occurred because of the careful regulation of the three reservoirs in Iowa. The Corps calculated these operations had lowered the crest by 2.0 feet at Quincy.

Concurrent flooding from the Upper Mississippi and Missouri Rivers created higher crests at downstream locations on the Mississippi River near St. Louis, MO. The Missouri River crested 50 miles west of St. Louis on July 31 and at St. Louis on August 2. The Mississippi River crested at Grafton, IL, and St. Louis on August 1.

TABLE 4-8 Flood Crest along the Mississippi River from Louisiana, MO, to Thebes, IL

Gage station	*1993 stage, ft*	*Date*	*Highest previous stage, ft*	*Date*
Louisiana	28.40	07/28	27.0	4/24/73
Lock & Dam 24	37.70	07/29	36.8	4/24/73
Lock & Dam 25	39.60	08/01	36.9	4/27/73
Grafton	38.15	08/01	33.2	4/28/73
Price Lock & Dam	42.72	08/01	36.7	4/28/73
St. Louis	49.58	08/01	43.3	4/28/73
Chester	46.69	08/07	43.3	4/30/73
Cape Girardeau	48.49	08/08	44.2	5/01/73
Thebes	45.50	08/07	44.2	5/06/83

The peak flow at Hermann, MO (see Figure 4-1), was 750,000 cfs, and that at St. Louis was 1,070,000 cfs at a crest stage of 49.58 feet, as shown in Figure 4-9. The peak flow at St. Louis rated somewhere between a 150-year and 200-year flood. The Mississippi River at St. Louis first exceeded flood stage (30 feet) on June 26 and fell below flood stage on September 13 (Figure 4-9). Table 4-8 lists the 1993 flood crest from Louisiana, MO, to Thebes, IL. The river was above flood stage for 80 days (U.S. Army Corps of Engineers, St. Louis District, 1994).

FIGURE 4-8 A hydrologist surveys the condition of the Sny Levee prior to its overtopping on July 24 (Illinois State Water Survey).

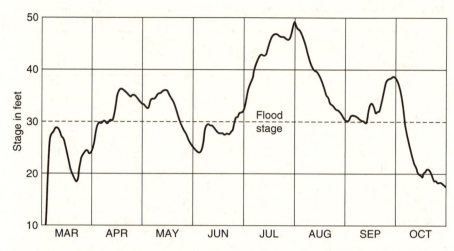

FIGURE 4-9 Stage hydrograph for the Mississippi River at St. Louis shows the spring flood, the major summer flood, and the fall flood.

MISSOURI RIVER BASIN AND ITS TRIBUTARIES

Other major floods of 1993 occurred along the lower Missouri River from its juncture with the Mississippi at St. Louis upstream to Omaha. The flooding in this large area included several major tributaries to the Missouri River in Kansas, Nebraska, Iowa, and Missouri.

Flooded Tributaries to the Missouri River

Iowa Great Lakes. During late June and early July, 7 inches of rain fell on the drainage area of the Iowa "Great Lakes" (Spirit Lake, Lake Okobojii, and Lower Gar) located in northwestern Iowa. The lakes reached record highs, and emergency assistance was required to evacuate people living along the lakes, as well as to provide protective measures for local communities. Water from the Iowa Great Lakes was discharged into the Little Sioux River to lower the lakes. The absence of long-term records precludes the assessing of a recurrence interval for the flood conditions (U.S. Army Corps of Engineers, Omaha District, 1994).

Papillion Creek. On July 24, Papillion Creek at Fort Crook, NE, was being affected by backwater from the high Missouri River, which reached a record stage of 32 feet. The stage was 3 feet above flood stage and 1.3 feet higher than the previous flood of record (1982). The peak flow was 12,000 cfs, which has a recurrence interval of five years. A higher discharge occurred on June 28 with a peak of 32.3 feet, and a third flood occurred on August 28, flooding Papillion.

TABLE 4-9   1993 Flood Data for the Missouri River and Selected Tributaries

| | Peak record | | 1993 Peak | | |
| | | | | | |
Station	Date	Gage height	Date	Gage height	Frequency, years
Missouri River at Omaha	4/18/52	40.20	Jul 10	30.26	2 - 5
Platte River at North Bend	3/29/60	10.04	Mar 9	10.56	50 - 100
Platte River at Ashland	6/12/44	8.10	Jul 25	21.63	25- 50
Platte River at Louisville	6/14/84	11.34	Jul 25	11.90	25 - 50
Missouri River at Nebraska City	4/19/52	27.66	Jul 23	27.19	10 - 25
Little Nemaha River at Auburn	5/9/50	27.65	Jul 24	26.49	25 - 50
Missouri River at Rulo	4/22/52	25.61	Jul 24	25.37	50 - 100

Platte River.   Flooding in July 1993 on the Platte River was caused by excessive rainfall (more than 14 inches) over many of its lower basin tributaries. The peak discharge at Ashland, NE, was 107,000 cfs on July 25 (Table 4-9), compared to the previous peak discharge of 114,000 cfs in 1984. Flooding was confined to the lower 28 miles of the Platte River. The 1993 discharge was greater than a 50-year event.

Kansas River.   The Kansas River and its tributaries experienced severe flooding and in turn contributed to the major flooding at Kansas City and the crest along the Missouri River. Significant flooding began on July 19 from a two-day storm on the Kansas River basin, and the river exceeded flood stage downstream from Fort Riley, KS. A second rainstorm on July 24 contributed to flooding conditions that persisted until August 7. All along the Kansas River the 1993 flood was exceeded in stage only by the 1951 flood. The stage at Topeka on July 25 was 34.9 feet and corresponded to a discharge of 170,000 cfs, which rates between a 10-year and 50-year flood. The stage at Lecompton, KS, on July 27 was 30.23 feet and corresponded to a discharge of 190,000 cfs, an event greater than a 50-year flood but less than a 100-year flood.

A 5-inch storm on July 16 produced excessive runoff on the Republican River, a tributary to the Kansas River. This caused Milord Lake to exceed the top of the flood control pool (elevation 1176.2 feet) on July 19, and the flood crest set a new record elevation of 1181.9 feet on July 25. Evacuation notices were issued by the state of Kansas for areas below Milford and Tuttle Creek Lakes. An additional 6 inches of rain fell in central Kansas on July 21 (Figure 3-4c). The maximum daily inflows to Milford Lake exceeded 40,000 cfs on July 9 and again on July 24. The maximum outflow was 35,000 cfs on July 25 and July 26 (outlet flow was 15,000 cfs and uncontrolled spillway flow was 20,000 cfs). The maximum flood level was 5.7 feet above the top of flood control pool.

The same two July rains that affected the Republican River also caused flooding on the Little Blue and Big Blue Rivers, which drain southeastern Nebraska and northeastern Kansas. The resulting flood caused Tuttle Creek Lake to exceed the top of the flood control pool at an elevation of 1136 feet on July 20 and to reach a new record elevation of 1137.7 feet on July 23. The maximum daily inflow to Tuttle Creek Lake exceeded 90,000 cfs on July 6, and the maximum outflow was 60,000 cfs on July 23 and 26. The entire town of Elwood, KS, was evacuated on July 23. The combination of the flow reduction by all the reservoirs in the Kansas River basin contributed to a significant stage reduction in the Missouri River, and reduced the flood crest entering the Missouri River by about 85,000 cfs (U.S. Army Corps of Engineers, Kansas City District, 1994).

Missouri River

The 1993 flooding on the Missouri River was the worst since 1952 from Omaha downstream. Flooding on this river is reduced by several reservoirs built along the Missouri River basin to serve different interests including flood control, irrigation, power production, recreation, and water supply. The most significant reservoirs are created by six main stem Missouri River dams that control runoff from 279,000 square miles of Upper Missouri River basin. During the 12-month period ending July 31, 1993, a total of 10,143,000 acre-feet of floodwater was stored in the six Missouri River main stem reservoirs (U.S. Army Corps of Engineers, Omaha District, 1994).

Table 4-9 lists the peak discharge and gage height summary in an upstream-downstream order for Missouri River drainage in Iowa, South Dakota, and Nebraska (USGS, 1993b). Note that the 1993 values were not the flood of record but became most extreme at Rulo in the extreme southeastern corner of Nebraska. The flood on the Missouri increased southward with the recurrence interval for Omaha being 2 to 5 years, Nebraska City 10 to 25 years, and Rulo 50 to 100 years.

Strong thunderstorms occurred on July 5 over northeastern Kansas and northwestern Missouri with rainfall amounts of 4 to 7 inches. Evacuation of 20 families in Nemaha County, MO, was due to flooding of the South Fork of the Big Nemaha River. Rainfall amounts of 7 and 8 inches fell across central Missouri on July 6-7 (see Figure 3-6, Chapter 3). Resulting excessive runoff contributed to widespread flooding on the Lower Missouri River basin in Missouri, central and eastern Kansas, southeastern Nebraska, and southwestern Iowa. The intense and repetitive storms in July contributed to flood crests that eventually inundated levee systems on the Missouri River. On July 7-8 near-record flooding occurred over a large area centered 80 miles northwest of Kansas City and affected the Tarkio River near Fairfax, MO, Turkey Creek near Seneca, KS, and Big Nemaha River near Falls City, NE. Damaged bridges and submerged highways disrupted transportation (Chapter 8). Commercial navigation on the Missouri River was suspended for 49 days from July 2-August 20 (U.S. Army Corps of Engineers, Omaha District, 1994).

The Missouri River at St. Joseph, MO, was above flood stage for 43 days, (June 26-August 6). The river crested at 32.07 feet on July 26 with a flow of 335,000 cfs. On July 24, the St. Joseph Airport Levee was overtopped, and St. Joseph lost its water supply for a week as a result of flooding. The local airport was flooded and breaches of levees became common (see Figure 4-10). Severe flooding occurred near Glasgow, MO, which washed out the Gateway Western Railroad embankment on July 15, and the river threatened to change its course. Army Reserve helicopters moved 750 tons of rock to the breach, thereby preventing failure of the levee and a shift in the Missouri's course.

The behavior of the Missouri River at Kansas City is depicted in Figure 4-11. The river had an initial crest on July 11, rose to another peak on July 24, and after receding went to its final major crest on July 27 of 48.87 feet which is 541,000 cfs (flood stage is 32 feet). The Missouri crested at 37.1 feet at Boonville, MO (about halfway between Kansas City and St. Louis), and at 36.97 feet at Hermann, MO, 65 miles west of St. Louis. The Missouri River stages at Hermann (Figure 4-12) reveal four floods in 1993: one in May, one in early June, the major flood from July 2 to August 25, and one from September 13 to October 5. Note that the summer flood had four peaks as the surges came from the various upstream tributaries. Table 4-10 ranks the top two floods on the Missouri River from St. Joseph to Boonville, MO. The 1993 flood rated first at all sites. The Corps of Engineers conducted a flow frequency study for the Missouri River in 1962, which included consideration of the effects of reservoirs. Comparison of the 1993 river values against these frequencies reveals the Kansas City and Boonville flows (Table 4-10) rated as 500-year events, whereas the flow at other locations was between a 100-year and a 500-year event (U.S. Army Corps of Engineers, Kansas City District, 1994).

Record stages were experienced all along the Grand River, a tributary located in north-central Missouri (see Figure 4-1), washing out the main line of the AT&SF railroad near Marceline, MO (Chapter 8). Levee failures created short-

TABLE 4-10   Top-Ranked Floods of Record on the Lower Missouri River

Streamgage	Date	First flow, cfs	Stage, ft	Date	Second flow, cfs	Stage, ft
St. Joseph	7/26/93	335,000	32.07	4/22/52	397,000	26.82
Kansas City	7/27/93	541,000	48.87	7/14/51	573,000	46.20
Waverly	7/27/93	633,755	31.15	6/23/84	245,000	29.22
Boonville	7/29/93	755,000	37.10	7/17/51	550,000	32.82

94

FIGURE 4-10 A breached levee along the Mississippi River south of St. Louis with water from the river (left) pouring into the floodplain (right) (Illinois State Water Survey).

lasting declines on the Missouri River at Hermann (see Figure 4-12) and St. Charles, MO. These events allowed for additional sandbagging in preparation of higher crests. Jefferson City, MO, was one of the worst damaged cities on the

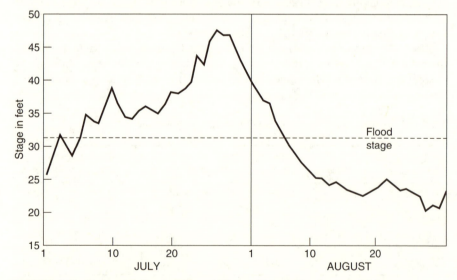

FIGURE 4-11 Hydrograph for the Missouri River at Kansas City shows multiple crests.

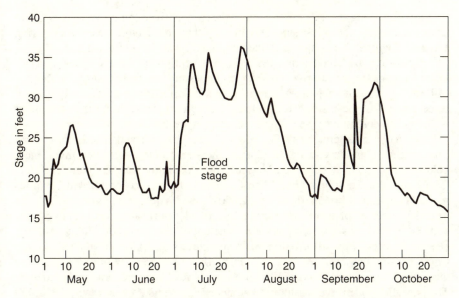

FIGURE 4-12 Hydrograph for the Missouri River at Hermann, MO, shows multiple floods.

Missouri River, with many homes and businesses inundated and a correctional center essentially destroyed (see Chapter 10). When the Monarch-Chesterfield private levee failed on July 30, 250 businesses were inundated in the area of Chesterfield, MO, located just west of St. Louis, and the Spirit of St. Louis Airport was flooded as were several highways. The flood crest moved rather rapidly across Missouri. It took only four days to travel from Rulo, NE, to Hermann, MO, and then only one day to travel 99 miles from Boonville to Hermann. The river was moving rapidly.

The second major area lost to inundating floodwaters was due to a levee breach in St. Charles County, MO, on July 16. The river cut across the peninsula separating the Missouri and Mississippi Rivers in the vicinity of Portage des Sioux, 13 miles upstream from the confluence of both rivers. Floodwaters were 20 feet deep in the area and buried three Missouri towns (Portage des Sioux, Orchard Farm, and West Alton), making 800 homes uninhabitable (U.S. Army Corps of Engineers, Kansas City District, 1994).

Flood control reservoirs on the Missouri River basin had a significant effect on reducing flood discharges on the Lower Missouri main channel, and in turn on the Mississippi River downstream from the confluence of the Missouri River. This reduced the flow on the Lower Missouri River by about 80,000 cfs. The peak flows were 755,000 cfs and 750,000 cfs, respectively (USGS, 1993a).

BEYOND ST. LOUIS

Flooding along the 180 miles of the Mississippi River south from St. Louis to Cairo, IL, where the Mississippi is joined by the Ohio River, was severe during July and August 1993, ultimately matching the severity found north of St. Louis. The first levee breached along this 180-mile section of the river "beyond St. Louis" was near Cairo at river mile 24 (24 miles upriver from Cairo). It flooded Miller City, IL, and began a scouring action described below. On July 22, the levee protecting the historic Kaskaskia Island broke, flooding 14,000 acres and isolating the community (see Chapter 5 and Figure 5-8).

The major crest created at St. Louis as the Missouri and Mississippi crests came together at the end of July, a unique event unto itself, became a huge volume of water that began pushing inexorably southward, threatening all the levees south of St. Louis. On August 1, the Columbia Levee located 30 miles south of St. Louis broke, flooding 13,000 farmed acres (see Figure 5-7). The next day a series of levees protecting five flood control districts crumbled and 43,000 more acres went underwater, including the town of Valmeyer, IL. Desperate to save the historic floodplain community of Prairie du Rocher, IL, the Corps broke a nearby levee in a conscious effort to reduce the pressure and save the town. This action flooded 13,000 nearby acres but saved Prairie du Rocher. The peak flow of the Mississippi at Chester occurred on August 6 when 950,000 cfs passed, and the peak came at Thebes (river mile 34) on August 7. The flow at Thebes was 975,000 cfs, the greatest ever measured. The peak stages easily broke prior records below St. Louis (Table 4-8).

The Len Small Levee, breached on July 15 near Cairo, continued to widen, becoming an opening 1550 feet wide by July 27 as floodwaters poured into nearby Horseshoe Lake (see Figure 5-11). By July 28, 20 percent of the Mississippi's flow was moving into the breach, traveling overland, and re-entering the river's main stem several miles downstream. This potential by-pass began scouring a new channel, which had reached a depth of 70 feet at the breach by August 8 when the breach had widened to 2,500 feet. Fears that this new channel would cut off the river's 10-mile-long meander named Dogtooth Bend led to massive efforts during late August to fill the breach and stem the tide. The Soil Conservation Service built a loop-shaped levee and the river was contained in its age-old course. (By April 1994 this special levee broke in spring floods, and the Corps rebuilt it.) The flood crest dissipated as it joined the Ohio River, which fortunately was at normal flow. The Great Flood of 1993 disappeared as the waters entered the much wider river course south of Cairo.

SUMMARY AND CONCLUSIONS

The 1993 flood differs from other floods in its areal extent, magnitude, duration, volume of floodwater, severity, extent of damage, and the time of the year in which the flood occurred. The rainfall causing the flood events was uncommonly persistent and excessive over a huge drainage area embracing most of nine states. This scenario caused many tributaries to crest at about the same time and to synchronize with crests on the main stem of the Mississippi and Missouri Rivers, producing record large crests on both rivers and very high recurrence intervals.

The floodplains of these rivers have been changed over the past 150 years to serve many masters and varying purposes that often conflict. The flooding of the Mississippi and Missouri Rivers resulted in 52 deaths and $18 billion in damages, largely as a result of the conflicting uses of the floodplains. In some communities, properties were inundated and people were displaced in many areas classified by flood insurance as within the 100-year floodplain (National Flood Insurance Act, 1968).

Reservoirs in both the Mississippi and Missouri River basins proved to be effective in reducing river stages and downstream damages. Flood control reservoirs on the upper Mississippi River tributaries had to contend with a large volume of runoff from the 1993 flood, such that the equivalent volume was equal to as much as 12 times the storage capacity of each reservoir. However, the aggregate reduction in peak stage was 2 feet at Quincy, IL, and 1.5 feet at Hannibal, MO. Flood control reservoirs on the Missouri River basin had a significant effect on reducing flood discharges on the lower Missouri's main channel and on the Mississippi River downstream from the confluence of the Missouri River. Reservoirs reduced the flow on the lower Missouri River by about 80,000 cfs. Reservoirs on the Kansas River reduced the flood crest entering the Missouri River by about 85,000 cfs. The aggregate effect of the reservoir systems reduced the flow to about 211,000 cfs at Hermann, MO. The value of the levees, reservoirs, and other existing flood control measures was high. In the St. Louis District of the Corps the federal flood reduction components reduced damages by an estimated $5.4 billion compared to actual damages estimated as $1.4 billion (Dyhouse, 1994). A federal flood assessment group reported that the flood control structures in the nine-state flood area saved $19.1 billion in damages (IFMR Committee, 1994), slightly more than the current estimate of $18 billion in total losses from the flood.

Residents of areas along the flooded rivers and National Guard troops assigned to help performed magnificent flood-fighting efforts to protect endangered farms and property. As during 1965 and 1973, the flood crest forecasts by the National Weather Service frequently changed as conditions changed, raising near-record crest forecasts from about 50-year flood levels to above 500-year flood levels (NWS, 1994). People in farms and communities behind levee districts did not give up but built temporary protective dikes using sandbags, polyethylene, and plywood to prevent flooding of their properties. In many locations, the fight was successful, but at many others the levees were overtopped. In those locations, the stage of the river dropped for a few hours while the levee district filled with floodwater and the river resumed rising to the forecasted crest. Levee failures due to the 1993 floods were extensive, as shown by the numbers in Table 5-2 (Chapter 5). Nearly 80 percent of all nonfederal levees failed.

Will a similar flood happen again? Yes, if meteorological conditions similar to the 1993 conditions recur. A future flood could be worse than the 1993 flood, in that many streams in states east of the Mississippi River did not flood to the same extent as did those in Iowa, Nebraska, Missouri, and Kansas. It is not too late to obtain as much information from the 1993 flood as possible to use in planning for a similar event in the future. Planning and designing the use of the floodplains have been and remain of paramount importance to lawmakers, public officials, and landowners. The future of the floodplains will be a significant factor in determining whether devastation such as occurred during 1993 will be repeated with future floods.

Lessons Learned

Rainfall and streamflow data are absolutely priceless information during floods. In the last 20 years, many rainfall and streamgaging stations in the flooded area and elsewhere in the nation have been closed. Many closures were due to lack of sponsorship or provision of the funds required to operate and maintain a river or raingage site. There are very few champions for such data, except when a flood occurs. All levels of government have a responsibility to support the operation and maintenance of data collection sites, but often this multiagency responsibility becomes a hindrance. Future measurements need to employ new and highly technical equipment to minimize annual costs and to allow operations during severe flood events with the highest level of accuracy.

Field data need to be collected hourly during floods using space-age technology such as data collection platforms, satellites, and the information superhighway. When weather and river stage forecasts are produced, faster dissemination to primary users is necessary. Information such as quantitative precipitation forecasts (QPFs) and their effects on river stages, needs to be evaluated and provided for planning purposes to federal, state, and local governments, which can also be accomplished through the information superhighways.

Collection of flood information during flood events is essential. The projections of crest forecasts are only as good as the information in the river models. During the 1993 flood, stages were at levels that have never been measured by the U.S. Geological Survey. Therefore, stage-discharge relationships were not available for the higher flows. Furthermore the channel characteristics have been changed where scour and erosion have changed the cross sections of the river. This has changed the rating relationships, and the modified relationships need to be established after the flood.

System models for the Mississippi and Missouri Rivers need to be developed and applied to use. The present models historically do not have adequate mathematical routines to address flood routing when a levee is overtopped or fails. The addition of a model similar to the UNET model (Barkau, 1994) would greatly improve the accuracy of flood forecasting. Long-term modeling of the entire floodplain should be considered. Since the hydraulic roughness, (Manning's "n" value) is not well understood for certain flow regimes, research is needed.

A multiagency task force should be examining the flood records for all the major streams and determine if any adjustments in frequency relationships are required. In addition, the National Oceanic and Atmospheric Administration should examine the frequency relationships of short-term rainfall that were last published in 1961 (Hershfield, 1961). Fortunately, the Midwestern Climate Center has updated the rainfall frequencies for the Midwest, and the new values are quite different than those of 1961 (Huff and Angel, 1992). There need to be similar studies for other regions.

REFERENCES

Barkau, R.L., 1994: *UNET Model Study of Five Levee Scenarios on the Middle Mississippi River.* Preliminary Report to the Scientific Assessment and Strategy Team.

Dyhouse, G. R., 1994: The hydrologic effects of the 1993 flood-myths and misconceptions. *Preprints of Symposium on The Great Flood of 1993,* American Meteorological Society, Boston, 3 pp.

Hershfield, D.M., 1961: *Rainfall Frequency Atlas of the United States.* Technical Paper No. 40, U.S. Weather Bureau, Washington, DC, 115 pp.

Hines, M., 1993: Personal communication. Chief, Project Operations Branch, Rock Island District, U.S. Army Corps of Engineers.

Huff, F.A., and J. Angel, 1992: *Rainfall Frequency Atlas of the Midwest.* Research Report 92-03, Midwestern Climate Center, Champaign, IL, 141 pp.

Interagency Floodplain Management Review Committee, 1994: *Sharing the Challenge: Floodplain Management Into the 21st Century.* Administration Floodplain Management Task Force, Washington, DC, 191 pp.

Maddox, R., A. Chappell, and L.R. Hoxit, 1979: Synoptic and mesoscale aspects of flash flood events. *Bulletin, American Meteorological Society,* 60, 115-123.

National Flood Insurance Act. P.L. 90-488 (Section 1302 (c)), 1968.

National Weather Service, 1994: *The Great Flood of 1993.* National Disaster Survey Report, Washington, DC, 210 pp.

Newmann, P., North Central River Forecast Center, 1993: Personal communication.

U.S. Army Corps of Engineers, Kansas City District, 1994: *The Great Flood of 1993 Post-Flood Report.* Appendix E.

U.S. Army Corps of Engineers, Omaha District, 1994: *The Great Flood of 1993 Post-Flood Report.* Appendix D.

U.S. Army Corps of Engineers, Rock Island District, 1993: State Records in Water Control Section files.

U.S. Army Corps of Engineers, Rock Island District, 1994: *The Great Flood of 1993 Post-Flood Report.* Appendix B.

U.S. Army Corps of Engineers, St. Louis District, 1994: *The Great Flood of 1993 Post-*

Flood Report. Appendix C.

U.S. Army Corps of Engineers, St. Paul District, 1994: *The Great Flood of 1993 Post-Flood Report*. Appendix A.

U.S. Geological Survey, 1993a: *Flood Discharges in the Upper Mississippi River Basin, January 1 through July 31, 1993*. Circular 1120-A, Washington, DC.

U.S. Geological Survey, 1993b: *Water resources data for Kansas, Missouri, Nebraska, Iowa, Minnesota, Wisconsin, and Illinois, Water Year 1993*. Washington, DC.

Wendland, W., and J. Dennison, 1993: *Weather and Climate Impacts in the Midwest January-September*. 3(2-10).

Wisconsin Department of Natural Resources, 1993: *The Floods of 1993. The Wisconsin Experience*. Madison, 39 pp.

5

Physical Effects: A Changed Landscape

Nani G. Bhowmik

INTRODUCTION

This chapter focuses on the general physical and morphometric changes associated with the 1993 flood, including soil erosion, channel scours, bank erosion, and the movement and deposition of eroded sediments and chemicals. As part of this physical assessment of the hydraulic and hydrologic impacts in the Upper Mississippi basin, the changes produced in the river courses, floodplains and levees, and ground water are documented. Effects on river water quality extending down the lower reaches of the Mississippi River and into the Gulf of Mexico are also documented.

Physiographical Features and Human Alterations in the Upper Mississippi River Basin

The Upper Mississippi River Basin (UMRB) drains about 23 percent of the conterminous United States and includes the Missouri River above its confluence with the Ohio River at Cairo, IL. (see Figure 1-1). The drainage area of this huge basin is about 700,000 square miles, and although the Missouri drains 73 percent of the total basin, it contributes only 36 percent of the total streamflow passing Cairo. Seasonal flow of the Missouri River is heavily regulated for navigation, power generation, and flood control. The flow of the Mississippi River above St. Louis is also managed to maintain navigation.

Physiographically, the UMRB lies in the nation's Central Lowlands area with some land in the Ozark Plateaus and Superior Upland provinces. The region's topography has been shaped primarily by repeated glaciation, except for unglaciated regions in southwestern Wisconsin and extreme southern Missouri, which have been extensively dissected by streams creating numerous escarpments and bluffs. The remainder of the basin is gently rolling terrain, with no sharply contrasting orthographic features and many natural lakes. Land elevations range from 280 to 1,940 feet above mean sea level (msl).

Soils and their slopes play an important role in the erosion and sedimentation of a basin during extremely heavy precipitation and ensuing flooding events. The region's slopes vary from level to rolling plains (SAST, 1994). Prairie origin soils, or Mollisols, cover more than 50 percent of the UMRB and are the dominant soils in seven of the nine flooded states (North Dakota, South Dakota, Nebraska, Kansas, Minnesota, Iowa, and Illinois). Alfisols are the dominant soil types in Wisconsin and Missouri. Hydric soils reflect the presence of wetlands and are common in the eastern Dakotas, a third of Minnesota, and in the floodplains of the Missouri and Mississippi Rivers. The UMRB has two distinct kinds of landscapes: open systems in which the drainage grades from small streams to larger trunk streams, and closed systems where the drainage is trapped within a common depository and where surface flow, if it occurs, is mostly in ill-defined drainageways to trunk streams (Ruhe and Walker, 1968).

A river requires a floodplain to convey the floodwater and will capture a floodplain whenever needed. Human intervention is not always sufficient to avoid such flooding. The floodplains of the Mississippi and Missouri Rivers appear similar but are quite different and responded differently during the 1993 flood.

Even though the Missouri River drains a larger area than the Mississippi River, the annual water discharge for both the rivers is comparable. The average annual sediment yield of the Missouri River is about five times that of the Upper Mississippi River; hence, the slopes of the floodplains of the Lower Missouri River have adjusted to this increased sediment load, being almost twice the slope of the Middle Mississippi River below the confluence of these two rivers. The floodplain of the Missouri River ranges from 2 to 10 miles in width over an area of about 2 million acres (SAST, 1994). The river widths also differ, the Lower Missouri River being about half the river width of the Middle Mississippi.

During the 1993 flood, the Missouri River's velocity remained quite high, even with numerous levee breaches, due to the existence of narrow floodplains. This created large deep scour and heavy sediment deposition on the bottomlands. Levee breaches on the Middle Mississippi River did not create comparable scour or sedimentation although they led to flooding of large expanses of land. The Missouri River is quite narrow between Glasgow and St. Charles, MO (see Figure 5-1), and this area was flooded bluff to bluff, with very deep scours in the meanders, followed by thick deposits of sediment.

Human Changes. Since 1824, the UMRB has been subjected to numerous alterations for navigational purposes. Navigation channel projects were authorized by Congress in the 1930s to ensure a 9-foot depth for both the Mississippi and Illinois Rivers. About 700 miles of navigable channel was created using locks and dams, wing dikes, and occasional dredging (Figure 5-1). The locks and dams created a "stairway of water" consisting of a series of pools from St. Louis to Minneapolis.

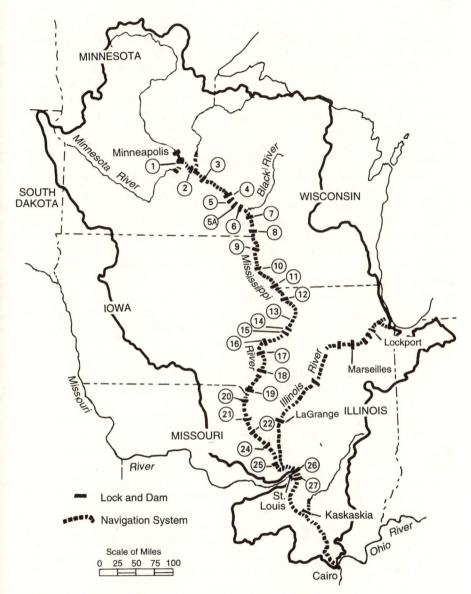

FIGURE 5-1 The navigation system of the Upper Mississippi River system.

The modification of the Mississippi north of St. Louis has created three distinctly different reaches, and each reacted quite differently to the 1993 flood. The river from its headwaters to Lock and Dam (L&D) 10 is "island braided" with many islands, bars, and side channels. There are 13 locks and dams on the main stem and tributaries to the river, as well as numerous wing dams, closing dams, and annual dredging activities, all necessary to maintain the commercial navigation system in this reach. The next reach of the river, from L&D 10 to L&D 19, is an area of considerable physical transition: braided islands give way gradually to a well-defined main channel structure. This reach includes several pools and more than 100 miles of agricultural levees. The lower (southernmost) reach of the controlled section, from L&D 19 to L&D 26, has six pools that are maintained for navigation. This area has a wide floodplain extensively altered by more than 117 miles of levees protecting vast agricultural lands. The navigation channel has significantly reduced the cross-sectional area of this reach.

The Middle Mississippi River extends 202 miles from L&D 26 at Alton, IL, to the mouth of the Ohio River at Cairo, IL, includes only one lock and dam (L&D 27) that cannot be regulated, and its pool is essentially free flowing. Construction on this segment has included dikes that first constricted the river's channel to a width of 2,500 feet, then to 1,800 feet, and then to 1,500 feet. Extensive wing dams, revetments (bank protection), and levees have been constructed to maintain the navigation channel and to protect agricultural and urban lands in the floodplain.

All these changes to the river between 1888 and 1968 have reduced the river's surface area by one-third, the island area by one-half, and the riverbed by nearly one-fourth. Most side channels have been blocked off with closing structures.

EROSION, SCOUR, AND SEDIMENT TRANSPORT AND DEPOSITION DURING THE 1993 FLOOD

The floods in spring, summer, and fall 1993 on the UMRB were historic events in terms of the time of the year, flood magnitude and duration, and physical effects on the river and its floodplains. The Mississippi, the Missouri, and the lower reaches of the Illinois Rivers reached unprecedented levels of flood inundation (see Chapter 4). Never in recorded history has such an event occurred in this part of the river where the floodplains are so extensively used for agricultural, recreational, and urban purposes. Data available on the transport and movement of suspended sediments, bed loads, bank erosion rates, and sediment deposition rates due to the flood are extremely scarce, and in many cases not available, not yet analyzed, or not yet published. Information from several case studies has recently become available, however.

Soil Erosion

High-intensity rainfall across the UMRB in 1993 (see Figure 3-2) greatly increased the rate of soil erosion, producing an increase in sediment transport rates and deposition within the slackwater areas, even though aggradation (build-up of sediments) occurred on parts of the river's main channel. Most of the erosion took the form of sheet and rill erosion, an effect not normally visible to the naked eye. Even though specific estimates of the agricultural erosion rates are not available across the Midwest, it is estimated that about 4 million acres of tillable land were severely eroded in the 1993 flood. Some agricultural fields in Iowa lost as much as 20 tons of top soil from each acre. (This rate of soil loss is approximately four times the soil tolerance value of 5 tons per acre per year, the rate at which soil is normally regenerated.) Extensive conservation practices in Iowa have helped to reduce soil erosion in about 10 percent of the cropland, but estimates indicate that 2.4 million acres of Iowa lost 20 tons or more of top soil.

Streambank Erosion

Very little information is available about the amount of streambank erosion due to the 1993 flood, but visual inspections by river experts indicate that a significant amount of streambank erosion indeed occurred. Damages surveyed at archaeological sites within the Midwest were mostly related to streambank erosion. This type of erosion included the scour of the toe of the vertical banks (cutbanks), and erosion at high water marks due to the wave action and erosive forces of the flowing water. The U.S. Army Corps of Engineers in a post-flood report (1994a) indicated that damage to riprap due to wave action in Mississippi River Pools 7-10 may require repairs costing $145,000.

Chrzastowski et al. (1994) reported on bank erosion at the Kaskaskia Island levee along the Mississippi River south of St. Louis where an erosion cut of 5 feet was observed as a result of wave action. They also measured erosion along abandoned railroad buildings where crushed rock up to a depth of 4 feet was scoured, including lifting and transporting sections of asphalt pavement.

Impacts and Responses of the Rivers to Scour, Sediment Transport, Channel Alteration, and Sedimentation

The 1993 flood created extensive scouring, transported and deposited huge volumes of sediments, and severely altered channels. However, each condition exhibited sizable spatial variations across the UMRB. To help assess this variability, conditions found in each of the Corps districts are presented.

St. Paul District. This district includes the Upper Mississippi River from its headwaters south through L&D 10 in Wisconsin (see Figure 5-1 for lock and dam locations). The Corps' preliminary investigation to determine the impacts of the 1993 flood on the channel morphometry revealed that Pools 2, 5, 7, and 8 had net deposition, whereas Pool 5A showed net scour during the flood. The net effect on these pools is shown in Table 5-1, which reveals that both erosion and deposition occurred in all the pools. In most places, normal flood-induced scour

TABLE 5-1   Net Deposition or Net Scour in Pools 2, 5, 5A, 7, and 8 on the Upper Mississippi River Due to the 1993 Flood

Pool	Deposition (cubic yards)	Scour (cubic yards)	Net depth change (feet)
2	284,000		-0.5
5	107,600		-0.2
5A		59,000	+1.2
7	148,000		-0.2
8	123,000		-0.3

(occurring on the outside bank of a curved reach of the river) and deposition (which normally occurs on the inside bank of the river channel between a straight reach and a curved reach) occurred in 1993, but it was not the case where the main river flow was divided among the main channel and a major side channel, or a series of side channels.

The measurements (Table 5-1) show a net deposition in all pools except Pool 5A. In Pools 7 and 8, less than 50 percent of the river flow was conveyed through the navigation channel during the 1993 flood. The Corps had to increase their dredging activities during the 1994 navigation season to maintain the channels in this section of the river. The total dredging required in these pools doubled from 146,111 cubic yards in 1992 to 310,056 cubic yards in 1993. The Mississippi's headwater reservoirs (north of the section modified for navigation) are naturally occurring lakes, and they showed no increase in sedimentation rates due to the flood.

The flood also caused a significant amount of scour and deposition on the Minnesota River. A cross section of the Minnesota River near Le Sueur, MN (Figure 5-2), reveals the riverbed was 8 to 10 feet lower in 1993 than when measured in 1986. The high sediment load during the 1993 flood forced the city of Le Sueur to dredge 4,000 cubic yards from their wastewater ponds. A similar problem occurred at the intake of a power plant near Mankato, MN, which experienced near record-high river flows (see Table 4-3).

The 1993 flood also affected the river's navigation channels by depositing sediments at numerous locations, and a total of 31 individual channels and two small boat harbors had to be dredged. Portions of the Minnesota River and every pool along the Mississippi in the St. Paul District (except Pool 1) required dredging to remove 900,000 cubic yards of sediment in 1993. Dredging was postponed at 17 other locations until 1994 when 500,000 cubic yards of materials were removed.

Rock Island District.   This district covers the main stem of the Upper Mississippi River between L&D 11 through L&D 24 and the Illinois River from the LaGrange Lock through the Marseilles Lock (Figure 5-1). The Corps evaluated the channel stability and the sediment deposition rates in the district's

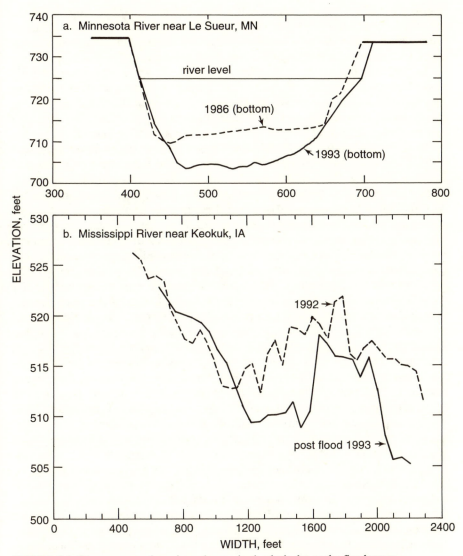

FIGURE 5-2 River cross sections show changes in riverbeds due to the floodwaters.

portion of the Mississippi River. The slow recession of the flood hydrographs in the 1993 flood was associated with a lower sedimentation rate within the 14 pools in this district. Changes in channel morphometry due to the 1993 flood were measured by depth soundings at 26 cross sections of the channel where data had been collected in 1992. Thirteen cross sections showed sediment deposition, four had scour across the entire width of the channel, and the other nine were approximately the same as they were in 1992. The most extreme scour (Pool 11) measured 5 feet across the entire channel bottom, and Figure 5-2 indicates sediment deposition of about 9 feet at this cross section on Pool 18, representing the most extreme cases among the 26 cross sections.

In 1993, the Corps collected and analyzed data on suspended sediment loads near Dubuque and Keokuk, IA (see Figure 4-1 for locations), where measurements had been made since 1968. The suspended sediment loads measured for most months in 1993 exceeded any observed before with very high values in May-August at Dubuque and in May-September at Keokuk.

From March to November 1993, the Mississippi River at Dubuque transported about 6.7 million tons of suspended sediment. The long-term average annual sediment load for these months is 3.74 million tons, indicating that the river carried 180 percent of the average load in 1993. At Keokuk the river transported 33.7 million tons of suspended sediment load in 1993 compared to an average annual transport rate (based on previous 22 years) of 10.9 million tons, an increase of 308 percent. Comparison of the suspended sediment loads transported in 1973, the last major flood on the Upper Mississippi River, reveals that the 1993 annual suspended sediment load at Dubuque was 90 percent of the 1973 sediment load, but at Keokuk the suspended sediment load transported by the river in 1993 was about 120 percent of that in 1973. Chapter 4 illustrates that the flow at Dubuque was high but not a new record, whereas the flow at Keokuk was a record-high value. Possible effects of sedimentation on reservoirs within this district could not be assessed because of the lack of data.

Omaha District. This district embraces the upper reaches of the Missouri River above Rulo, NE. Twelve major tributaries of the Missouri River were flooded in 1993 (see Chapter 4), and the most severe flooding on the main stem of the Missouri River within this area extended from Omaha to Rulo (Figure 1-1).

The large dams and reservoirs built 40 years ago on the main stem of the Missouri River have had significant impacts on the downstream sediment loads since completion in 1955. For example, before the construction of the Gavins Point Dam (about 150 river miles north of Omaha), the average sediment load of the Missouri River was 135 million tons per year at the dam site, but all incoming sediment loads were trapped by the dam after construction. As a result, the river tries to recover its bed load from the riverbed downstream of the dam. Data on suspended sediment loads during the flood were collected at three sites: Sioux City, IA, Omaha, and Nebraska City, NE. The monthly sediment loads at Sioux City, IA, were lower than most values before 1993, except for July when the river transported 2.3 million tons of sediment, more than double the average load since construction of the Gavins Point Dam and the largest monthly sediment load since 1955. The suspended sediment load at Omaha during the 1993 flooding never approached the values measured before construction of the Gavins Point Dam. However, in July 1993, the river carried 5.89 million tons of suspended sediment, the second largest monthly value in the post-dam era. The monthly suspended sediment load at Nebraska City, NE, where river flow reached an all-time record (see Figure 1-1) from March-July 1993, exceeded the measured loads in the post-dam era. In July 1993, the river carried 11.87 million tons of suspended sediment, the largest monthly sediment load since post-dam measurements began. Hydrologists observed that tall grasses growing on levees in this district were effective in controlling erosion.

Kansas City District. This district extends 498 miles from the Missouri River at Rulo, NE, to its mouth near St. Louis, MO. This entire segment of the Missouri had record-high flows, as did several tributaries in Kansas and Missouri. The 1993 flood inflicted major damages on the floodplains, on bank stabilization, and on navigation structures (COE, 1994e), and caused numerous blowouts (the eruption of a levee after it starts to fail) and some channel cutoffs. The major navigation channel remained intact, however. Most damages to channel structures were confined to the private levees built close to the bankline. Failures of these private levees were mostly confined (1) to areas crossing old meanders or oxbows, and (2) to the upstream end of the levees, which indicated that insufficient heights had been provided at these flanking areas.

Along this 498-mile reach, the flood resulted in 14 channel changes and the development of chutes with an average length of 11.6 miles, a maximum length of 43.8 miles, and a minimum length of 2.5 miles. Chutes are backwater areas that had been closed from the river but that were opened by the flood. Another 70 blowouts occurred on both sides of the river, of which 14 varied from 1,000 to 2,000 feet, and the others were several hundred feet across. Other less significant breaches occurred, and these too ultimately contributed to larger blowouts (COE, 1994e).

Flows "trained" and/or directed by the interior levees, terraces, or roadways caused most of the blowouts and channel changes in 1993. In several instances, the "domino effect" greatly extended the chute development by breaching tributary tieback levees and the main stem of private levees in the narrows downstream of Glasgow, MO. Most blowouts were associated with the development of scour holes and the deposition of sediment somewhere away from the scour holes.

An evaluation of the bed scour of the Missouri River at several locations (based on the bed level measurements made by the U.S. Geological Survey, or USGS) revealed five key points along the river's main stem (COE, 1994e). First, in 1993 about 8 to 10 feet of scouring occurred from St. Joseph to Hermann, MO. At Lexington and Jefferson City, MO, in early 1994 the riverbed was 8 feet below the level measured in 1987. Between July 12 and July 28, 1993, the deepest part of the river at Kansas City developed a scour zone of 14.7 feet, but the river recovered its scoured area and by August 12, the scouring of the bed was only about 6.3 feet. At Boonville, the river initially scoured out 4 feet, then sediment deposition elevated the bed by 10 feet, followed by a scour of 12 feet, that left the river 2 feet below its level before the flood. In the St. Charles area,

FIGURE 5-3   A view of the elongated sand deposits on the floodplain near St. Charles, MO, as the floodwaters recede in early September 1993.

the bed was lowered by 4.3 feet between July 24 and August 5, 1993. During this time, measured velocities near St. Charles were about 17 feet per second.

Large amounts of sediments were transported by the Lower Missouri River during the flood, and significant amounts of sediment were also scoured away and redeposited within this reach of the river. Sand deposits and scouring damaged 455,000 acres or 60 percent of the cropland in the Missouri River floodplain (see Figure 5-3). The sand deposits totaled more than 546 million cubic yards: 237,000 acres (52 percent of the damaged acreage) were covered with up to 6 inches of sand, 77,500 acres (17 percent) were covered with 6 to 24 inches of sand, and 59,000 acres (13 percent) were covered with more than 24 inches of sand. Furthermore, scouring had damaged 81,500 acres (18 percent of the damaged acreage).

The USGS estimated that between June 26 and September 14, 1993, 76.8 million tons of sediment consisting of 21.8 million tons of sand and 55 million tons of silt and clay passed the Hermann Gaging Site in Missouri (see Figures 4-1 and 4-12). Reconnaissance sedimentation surveys conducted in 1993 for seven lakes within this district revealed minor storage losses between 1 and 2 percent due to the flood.

St. Louis District. This district includes the Mississippi River from just below L&D 22 (Figure 5-1) to the confluence of the Mississippi River with the Ohio River. Most of the data on suspended sediments and levee breaches have not yet been available in the published literature (COE, 1994d).

Cross sections of the river at three locations revealed widespread deposition at the St. Louis Harbor from a maximum of 20 feet compared to only a few feet at Chester, IL. There was also some minor scour at Chester and Thebes, IL (near Cairo). From June 26 to September 14, 1993, about 60 million tons of suspended sediment passed St. Louis, but no increased sedimentation rates were observed within the Lower Mississippi River. At all sites with breached levees, rushing water created large scour holes with associated sediment deposition. The average length of the breaches in the federal levees within this district was about 1,000 feet, with a maximum opening of 3,500 feet. Along this 212-mile reach, 111 nonfederal levee breaches occurred, with an average length of 200 feet. The consolidated North County, MO, levee system had 51 breaches 12,000 feet long.

Impacts at Archaeologic Sites

The 1993 flood eroded, scoured, and left sediment at many archaeological sites located close to the rivers, and numerous field surveys of these sites offer useful data on the small-scale effects largely unmeasured elsewhere. Most native settlements in the United States and throughout the world were originally located close to a water body that provided some of the basic necessities of life: water, food, and transportation. The proximity of ancient settlements along the Mississippi and Missouri Rivers and their tributaries meant that several of these sites incurred damage during the flood.

A special report on flood damages at various archaeological sites was based on data from archaeological surveys throughout the Midwest (Green and Lillie, 1994). A survey of 28 archaeological sites in North Dakota during October 1993 showed that ten sites experienced significant erosion damage. All sites had accelerated cutbank (vertical bank) erosion due to sustained high water levels, and bank erosion rates were from 3 to 6 feet. Damage assessments at 23 archaeological sites in eastern South Dakota indicated no accelerated stream erosion due to the flood, however.

Flood damage assessments at 76 sites across Iowa revealed that only 23 sites sustained significant damage in 1993. All the sites suffered from erosion, deposition, or some combination thereof. The most serious threats came from streambank erosion, including many uprooted trees lodged at downstream locations. Some typical flood damages noted at various Iowa sites were: 0.3 to 0.6 foot of sediment deposition, bank erosion at a site along the Des Moines River, erosion of 5 to 10 feet of bankline, and erosion of an estimated 16,300 square feet of bankline.

Flood damage assessments at 82 sites in Wisconsin found ten sites that were significantly affected. Most damages were due to gulleying and streambank erosion, but none of the sites were along major rivers.

Damage surveys at eight sites from Pools 11, 13, 14, 16, 17, and 18 on the Mississippi River (shown in Figure 5-1) revealed that the flood induced two types of bank erosion (Benn, 1994): erosion of the vertical bank, and scouring and deflation of the surface of the floodplain. All the erosion occurred at the vertical bank sites. At one site the floodwater was halfway up the 15- to 21-foot cutbank and scoured the lower half of the bank. This scouring started a new cycle of slumping from the crest of the bank for a distance of about 250 feet.

The results obtained to date indicate that the main mode of impact was the accelerated bank erosion that often cut into these sites. At several locations, sediment deposition and removal of vegetation were also important factors. Another significant impact was the widespread destruction of vegetation. Loss of trees at the archeological sites has resulted in further erosion since the riverbank lost its stabilizing force. Moreover, sustained high water at many sites killed many trees already stressed by rising water levels (see Chapter 6).

IMPACTS ON LEVEES, FLOODPLAINS, AND CHANNELS

Levee Breaches

The 1993 flood caused numerous levee failures on the Upper Mississippi and Missouri Rivers (Bhowmik et al., 1994) which are illustrated in Figure 5-4. One reason for levee failure is the saturation of levee materials and resulting loss of soil stability. As the floodwaters rise, so does the saturation level in the levee. Levee cross section size and materials, relief wells, ditches, or levee toe filters on the land side, generally determine whether the line of saturation remains well within the levee near the land-side toe, as shown in Figure 5-4. When the line

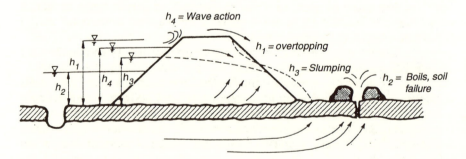

FIGURE 5-4 A schematic shows various ways water induces levee failures to occur (adapted from Bogardi and Mathe, 1968).

of saturation exceeds the ground level at the land toe, seepage and sloughing result in loss of slope stability.

A second major reason for levee failure is wave action caused by wind or by commercial or recreational vessels. These waves impact the river-side slope of the levee, especially if the levees are close to the main channel and the river is in flood stage. To allow for water-level fluctuations caused by waves, levees are designed with about 2 feet of freeboard above the design flood level. Waves caused by high-speed winds traversing broad rivers, such as on the Mississippi during the high flood stages of 1993, adversely impact the river side of the levee. If the upper portion of the levee is not adequately compacted (and maintained) or if the freeboard is not adequate for water levels, the levee top gradually wears down, water spills over the top, and the levee can fail. Bogardi and Mathe (1968) identified these and other reasons for levee failure, including overtopping, sand boils, and hydraulic soil failure, as illustrated in Figure 5-4. Levee design and construction must consider mitigation of all these factors.

Several studies assessed levee failures during the 1993 flood. Almost all the sand levee projects experienced some kind of sand boils (Figure 5-5) on the landward side of the levee, and boils occurred at the toes, insides of curves, or at groves of trees. Traffic on the levees also aggravated the boils. Sinkholes, a major problem as the flooding continued, were generally interconnected with the boils. For example, at the Sny Island Levee and Drainage District Reach 1 (in

FIGURE 5-5   Illinois Guard troops work to stave off a developing sand boil behind a levee along the Mississippi River near Meyer, IL (Illinois State Water Survey).

Illinois), "most sinkholes developed on berms at distances of 10 to 75 feet riverward of berm toe boils" (COE, 1994c). Most sinkholes were about 5 feet in diameter with a depth of 1 to 8 feet.

A common problem on all sand levees was erosion initiated by seepage. Emergency levee repairs with bulldozers and removal of toe materials by vehicular traffic contributed to levee failures. Sloughing was a major cause of levee failures, and, of course, some levees failed due to overtopping.

On the Missouri River, more than 90 percent of the area affected by erosion and sedimentation is generally associated with breached levees in active high-energy floodplain zones. A historical review of the levee failures on the Missouri River revealed most failures occurred "at sites of natural river cutoff or chutes in the past three decades. Construction of levees across these high energy channels is a risky investment which has required repetitive repair" (IFMR Committee, 1994). After assessing levee breaches on the Missouri River, the Scientific Assessment and Strategy Team (1994) found that most levee breaks occurred in one of the four floodplain settings listed below (percentages shown are for the total area along the 225-mile reach between Glasgow, MO, and St. Louis).

Locations of Most Levee Breaks

- Areas occupied by one or more active channels within the past 20 years (72 percent)
- Areas along downstream channel banks between the initiation and inflection points of meanders (17 percent)
- Areas along tributary channels subjected to significant cross flow conditions during flooding (17 percent)
- Areas along chutes or minor subsidiary channels (8 percent)

Preliminary geomorphic mapping of the Missouri River floodplain, coupled with analysis of the spatial distribution of levee failures, indicate that many existing reaches are particularly susceptible to catastrophic levee failure, extensive deep scour, thick sand deposition, or all three. Some of the factors contributing to these failures were areas of high-amplitude, short wavelength meanders (loop bottoms), long-bottom areas where remnants of historic channels intersect the upstream end and extend along much of the length of the long bottom, and areas with significant floodplain constrictions (artificial structures, such as bridges, power plants, etc.). Along the Lower Missouri River between Kansas City and St. Louis where more than 500 scour holes developed as a result of levee breaches, cobbles deposited within some holes indicated that the depth of scour penetrated "the entire thickness of Holocene-age alluvial deposits into the underlying glacial outwash sediments" (SAST, 1994).

A total of 1,082 levees in the Midwest were damaged in 1993. Table 5-2 displays the incidence of damages by type of levee: 17 percent of the federally

TABLE 5-2 Preliminary Estimates of Damage to Levees in the Mississippi River Basin in 1993 (Myers and White, 1993)

Designation	Eligible for federal assistance	Total number of levees	Number of levees damaged	Percentage of levees damaged
Federally constructed and maintained	Yes	15	3	20
Federally constructed and locally maintained	Yes	214	36	16.8
Subtotal for federally constructed		229	39	17
Not federally constructed and locally maintained	Yes	268	164	61.2
	No	1,079	879	81.5
Subtotal for not federally constructed		1,347	1,043	77.4
Total		1,576	1,082	68.7

constructed levees were damaged compared to 81.5 percent of the nonfederally constructed, locally maintained levees. Most of the nonfederal levees protected agricultural lands, and 1,079 of these levees are ineligible for future federal assistance for rebuilding.

Typical Scour Hole Development and Sedimentation. At numerous levee breaches, there was a common pattern: scour and sediment deposition with the development of a scour hole at the breach. Scouring of the floodplain continued until the water surface elevations on both sides of the levee became equal. Before most levee failures occurred, differences between the heights of water surfaces were as much as 20 feet or more. With this kind of head differential, the velocity of water at the breach could attain 20 to 25 feet per second. Most levees were constructed of locally available sand, silt, and clay materials that obviously could not withstand flow velocities of a few feet per second; hence, they were swept away. Scour holes of 20 to 50 feet or deeper developed once levees failed.

Initially, scour holes developed near the levee breach. However, as the rushing water spread over the land behind the failed levee, its velocity decreased. This process was thus associated with a slowly decreasing erosion rate and increasing sedimentation rate away from the failed levee. Chrzastowski et al. (1994) observed that at several breaches, erosion scars 1 to 2 feet deep developed about half a mile from the breach. In agricultural land and where the plowing had been perpendicular to the levee alignments, the erosion scar followed the plow furrows, thus enhancing erosion. Whenever the floodwater moved through stream channels perpendicular to the levee alignment, scour and erosion were generally very high. Other structures such as roads and highways also increased the scour of the land by channeling high-velocity water. As the floodwaters spread across the floodplains, sediment deposition began in a radial fashion similar to an alluvial fan at a river's mouth. Then several minor tributary type flow channels developed away from the scour hole as the floodwater dispersed.

Case Studies of Levee Breaches. Detailed information on most levee failures is not yet available. However, some useful case studies were completed, and those for levees at Columbia and at Kaskaskia Island are presented to illustrate the spatial conditions associated with levee failures.

The Columbia Levee is on the east side of the Mississippi River about 30 miles south of St. Louis. This levee was built by a levee and drainage district organized in 1882 to protect agricultural land. When this levee was breached on August 1, 1993, approximately 13,000 acres were flooded (Figure 5-6). Failure of the levee produced a scour hole and the associated deposition of sediments on the floodplain. The deposition pattern was similar to that expected from such a failure (Chrzastowski et al., 1994): the deposited sand fanned out with the maximum deposition occurring close to the

breached area, and then extending out and away from the scour hole with decreasing depositional height. As expected, the areal extent of the deposited sediment went further downstream (south) where the water from the breached area was flowing. Sand covered about 760 acres of floodplain and extended about 1.5 miles beyond the breached levee. These sand deposits resembled "snow drifts or a desert landscape" (Chrzastowski et al., 1994). The thickness of sand deposits varied, but the maximum depth of deposition was 8 feet, and the highest deposition of sand, above 3 feet, looked like large sand dunes.

Kaskaskia Island Drainage and Levee District was organized in 1916 to protect approximately 9,362 acres of land. The levee protecting Kaskaskia Island along the Mississippi River broke on July 22, 1993, flooding 14,000 acres of land. The breach was associated with typical scour hole development and movement of significant amounts of sediment. The scour hole became 50 feet deep and 400 feet wide at the levee breach (Chrzastowski et al., 1994). The scour hole was typical of those found at other levee breaches. Scour holes typically took about a day to fully develop. Scouring at the Kaskaskia Levee removed about one million cubic yards of materials which is equivalent to a six-story high block of sediment over a football field.

Review of these and other case studies indicates that whenever a levee failed due to overtopping, seepage, or combination of the two, the initial impact was the failure of the levee and the development of a scour hole near the axis of the levee. This was followed by deposition of the scoured sediments in down-valley reaches. Sediment deposition away from the scour hole ranged from mere inches up to 10 feet in depth and occurred in a fan-shaped area. More than 90 percent of the erosion and sediment deposition on the Missouri River was associated with levee failures.

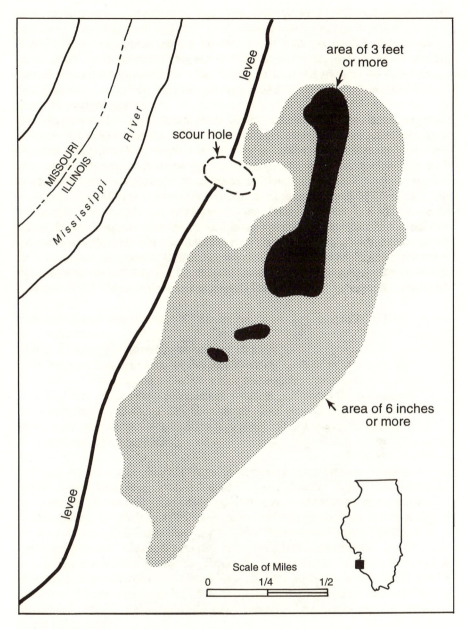

FIGURE 5-6   The scour hole and sediment deposited at the breach in the Columbia Levee south of St. Louis (adapted from Chrzastowski et al., 1994).

Floodplain Flow and River Cutoffs

Floodplain Flow. The 1993 flood reinforced the concept that the floodplains are meant to carry the floodwaters (Figure 5-7). It also demonstrated that rivers can and will try to alter their course in response to extreme flows (Bhowmik and Stall, 1979; Bhowmik et al., 1980).

The movement of water within a river and its floodplain changes over the duration of a flood (Bhowmik and Stall, 1979; Bhowmik and Demissie, 1982). A flood having a duration of 2.33 years will normally flow within the banks of the river. As the flood volume increases, the water will start to invade the floodplain where it will either be stored or carried away downstream. The volume of water stored or carried by floodplains depends upon the quantity of water that has to be moved, the condition of the floodplain, and the amount of resistance in the form of vegetation and structures.

The relative magnitudes of the floodflow on the floodplain increases as the flow duration increases. It has been postulated that when the return period of a flood approaches a value of about 40 years, the main channel and the floodplain behave like a single conveyance channel, carrying a proportional amount of water relative to their cross-sectional areas (Bhowmik and Demissie, 1982). Data were

FIGURE 5-7   The meandering course of the flooded Lower Illinois River with an inundated floodplain in the foreground. Note the darker (cleaner) water behind the levee where the sediment has settled from the still waters. The moving river appears to be lighter because it is carrying a large volume of suspended sediments (Illinois State Water Survey).

collected during the 1993 flood and show this to be the case at many locations. For example, the Missouri River at the Hermann, MO, gaging station (see Figure 4-12 for stage levels) had significant changes in its "stages" as the discharge increased. As the floodflow increased, the river cleared off most obstructions and vegetation and scoured away a substantial amount of bed sediment. The Corps (1994e) indicated that about 8 to 10 feet of the Missouri River bed from St. Joseph to Hermann was scoured away.

The river stage at Hermann dropped by 4.29 feet between July 8 and August 6, 1993, but the flow remained nearly the same. At least two factors may have been responsible for this drop in stage. During this period, the river essentially reclaimed its floodplains by clearing off all obstructions so the floodplains were forced to carry water proportionate to their areas. Moreover, some of the bed was also scoured away, increasing its cross-sectional area. Both factors helped increase the river's carrying capacity. Similar types of flow distributions occurred at many locations where the floodplain was forced to carry a substantial amount of water. During this process the river also created some side channels.

River Confluences. The hydrodynamics of flow at or near river confluences, or within a reach of the river where oxbows are present, change dramatically during large flooding events. Two case studies reveal what happened during the 1993 flood and why these forces could have altered the courses of the Missouri and Mississippi Rivers.

Missouri River at St. Charles. During the height of the flood in mid-July 1993, the Missouri River downstream of St. Charles overtopped the nonfederal levee on the left descending bank and started to flow across the St. Charles peninsula towards the Mississippi River. Figure 5-8 depicts the approximate path followed by this "crossover flow" in late July, which entered the Mississippi River approximately 18 miles upstream of the confluence of the two rivers near Portage des Sioux, MO. The elevation difference between the Missouri River at St. Charles and the Mississippi River at Portage des Sioux is about 12 feet. Thus, this crossover flow had a significant amount of head differential, forcing the scour and erosion of the floodplain between the two big rivers. By this action, the Missouri River was trying to increase its slope, and if left alone, the river would try to attain a new dynamic equilibrium. During the height of the flood, approximately 50 percent of the Missouri River flow (approximately 350,000 cfs) flowed over this peninsula and discharged directly to the Mississippi River. Similar types of crossover flow occurred at this location during floods in 1986 and 1973. Fortunately, this crossover flow did not fully capture the Missouri River flow. Had the Missouri River been successful in cutting a new channel at this location with more than 50 percent of its parent flow, then this area would have witnessed a tremendous amount of scour, erosion, meandering, and instability. In turn, the Mississippi River reach below the Portage des Sioux entry point would also have become unstable due to the significant increase in flows. The river would have scoured its bed and banks to establish a dynamic balance between the flow and sediment loads. There would also have been severe

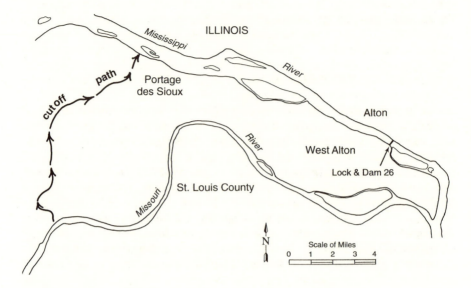

FIGURE 5-8 Crossover flow developed in July 1993 between the Missouri and Mississippi Rivers north of St. Louis.

impacts on the operation of the new L&D 26 located between the present confluence and the entry point (see Figure 5-8 for its location).

Mississippi River near Miller City. The Mississippi River levee breach near Miller City, IL, differed from that near St. Louis (Bhowmik et al., 1994). In a few cases, a levee breach leads to a separate path for the conveyance of floodwaters downriver. On July 15, 1993, the Len Small Levee was breached by the Mississippi (Figure 5-9), and a portion of the entering water started flowing northwest toward the lowland area at Horseshoe Lake in the ensuing days. Floodwaters moved through the lake, over its dam, and along Lake Creek to the Cache River diversion outlet, and into the Mississippi River. As shown in Figure 5-9, another path of water developed, moving southeast of the breach and into the Mississippi downstream. By July 27, the breach had expanded to 1,550 feet and was accepting a significant portion of the Mississippi River's flood flow, which amounted to 20 percent of the total flow (178,000 cfs). Within a few days, the flow increased to 200,000 cfs and was scouring a channel into the levee district and along the farmland side of the levee. By August 8, the breach had expanded to 2,429 feet with the depth of flow along the breach varying from 30 to 70 feet.

By August 25, 1993, much of the water moving through the breach bypassed the Horseshoe Lake area, spreading out along the former farmland and moving more directly toward the downstream portion of the Mississippi River. This excessive diversion could have been a precursor to a new cutoff, eliminating the 20-mile reach of river called Dogtooth Bend. This levee breach ultimately created

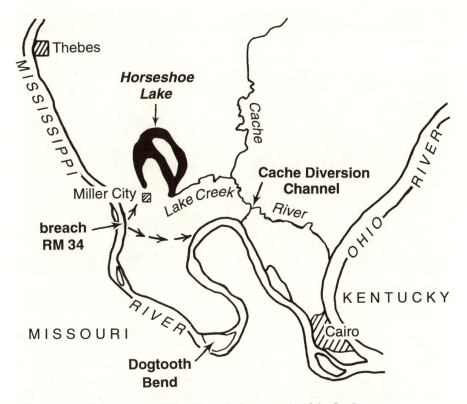

FIGURE 5-9 The breach near Miller City and alternate paths of the floodwaters.

a scour hole one mile long and a quarter mile wide with a depth of about 100 feet at a few locations. Fortunately, however, the river flow decreased and the river did not create a permanent channel. Over time the Mississippi River has occupied various channels at this location including the present Horseshoe Lake area. The cutoff with a river length decreasing from about 20 miles to 6 miles and with a local slope increase by about 370 percent would have tremendously increased the velocity, making it very difficult for normal navigation to pass through this reach.

Missouri River at Glasgow. A breach of a levee at a sharp curve in the Missouri River near Glasgow, MO, was the site of a third potential cutoff. The river broke through the levee on July 14 and the force tore out 2,000 feet of the major railroad embankment serving as the levee. The Corps reacted quickly and brought in 800 tons of boulders and rock to fill the gap over a three-day period. Four Army helicopters were used and at times hauled boulders weighing 7 tons. Their efforts succeeded, saving a cutoff of 14 miles of the river.

Conclusions. These three cases of crossover flows and impending cutoffs with a shortening of the river's length show that rivers can and will try to adjust their planform characteristics when external forces develop. The normal behavior of any river faced with extreme events only reinforces age-old principles: a river needs its floodplain (1) to convey the excess water, and (2) to scour its bed and banks to expend its energy, thus creating meanders and cutting oxbows. The Mississippi and Missouri Rivers will eventually scour or erode the cutoff areas, recreate new meanders, and start this process all over again. The only uncertainty is the timeframe for these processes: normally this complete reworking of the rivers takes centuries. The Mississippi and Missouri Rivers in 1993 showed that they are indeed capable of major changes. Scientific knowledge of river mechanics helps us understand these processes, and at least we can now predict them qualitatively, if not quantitatively.

EFFECTS ON GROUND WATER

In general, floodwater on the floodplains led to increased infiltration of the ground water. The prolonged 1993 flooding fully recharged many aquifers underlying floodplains, and the impact on selected aquifers was sizable (Bhowmik et al., 1994).

Large supplies of ground water for domestic, municipal, and industrial development are withdrawn from permeable sand and gravel in unconsolidated valley fill in the bottomlands adjacent to the Mississippi and Missouri Rivers. Valley fill is composed of recent alluvium and glacial valley-train material and typically ranges in thickness from near zero close to the bluff boundaries to more than 175 feet near the river. The thickness is generally greatest and exceeds the average near the centers of any buried bedrock valleys that may bisect some of these low-lying areas. In addition, these sand-and-gravel deposits commonly become progressively coarser with depth, and the coarsest deposits (those most favorable for development of a water well) are commonly encountered near the bedrock surface.

Ground water in the bottomland areas commonly occurs under leaky artesian and water-table conditions. The water level measured in a well at a particular time reflects not only seasonal variation, but also factors such as recent climatic conditions, nearby pumpage, and the water levels of nearby surface water bodies. Figure 5-10 shows the observed monthly ground-water elevations since 1954 at an observation well in the floodplain east of St. Louis. Ground-water levels fluctuate in this sand-and-gravel aquifer system from near record lows during the drought of 1988-1989 to record-setting highs during the flood of 1993. Monthly water levels during 1993 were at record highs from April-December 1993 in this same well. Under normal hydrological conditions, ground water usually discharges from the aquifers into the rivers. Until late 1993, ground-water levels measured at a "nest" of observation wells east of St. Louis indicated this to be the

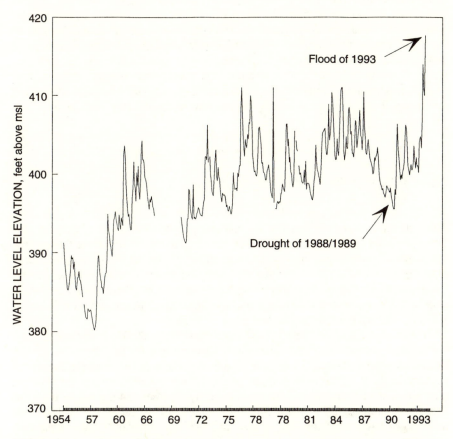

FIGURE 5-10   Ground-water levels in an observation well in the floodplain east of St. Louis reveal that record high levels were achieved as a result of the 1993 flood.

case in that region.   Their ground-water levels correlated well with the nearby stages of the Mississippi River, revealing the hydraulic connection between the river and the sand-and-gravel aquifer.   Prolonged flooding along the Mississippi River valley may have reversed the ground-water flow gradient in certain other areas, however.   This could shift ground-water flow patterns, thus changing concentrations and characteristics of plumes of contamination in polluted aquifers.

Bacterial contamination of individual domestic and municipal wells can be a problem where surface water has entered a well.   Additional ground-water contamination problems can exist where floodwater entering a well contains materials that may have washed off or out of areas such as landfills and storage areas for road salt and hazardous materials (for example, petroleum and pesticides).   The true extent of this problem depends on the kind and amount of contaminated material in the floodwaters, the proximity of these waters to flooded wells, and the length of time these wells remained underwater. Some ground-water quality impacts documented in 1993 include bacterial contamination of wells and contamination of aquifer systems with nitrates, pesticides, herbicides, and other hazardous materials. The increase in ground-water levels in 1993 also led to damage of buried utility systems (and particularly sewage systems) and flooded basements. Along the Illinois River, flooding due to high ground-water levels was a major problem in 1993 in the lowlands area near Havana, IL.

EFFECTS ON WATER QUALITY

Upper Mississippi River Basin

The flood moved tremendous amounts of water to the Gulf of Mexico. Through erosion and flooding of agricultural soils throughout the Midwest, the floodwaters picked up vast quantities of various chemicals, including those from flooded industries along the rivers. Substantial quantities of these agricultural (and other) chemicals were transported into the streams and rivers, either as dissolved matter or in suspension. Extensive data on these chemicals were collected at six selected locations along the Mississippi River and its tributaries and analyzed by the USGS (Goolsby et al., 1993).

Estimates suggest that during 1987-1989 more than 100,000 tons of pesticides (herbicides, insecticides, and fungicides) were applied on the croplands of the Mississippi River basin in addition to 6.3 million tons of nitrogen fertilizers applied in 1991 alone. The three principal herbicides used in the UMRB (atrazine, alachlor, and metolachlor) collectively represent 54 percent of the total herbicides applied. Concentrations of atrazine from the upper end of the Mississippi River to Baton Rouge, LA, in 1993 were similar to those measured in 1991, a non-flood year. For example, the concentrations of atrazine at Thebes (see Figure 5-11) during July 1993 varied from about 2.2 to about 3.0 milligrams per liter (μg/l), which is identical to values in 1991 and 1992. Since 1993 had record flooding, early forecasts were for lower concentrations of all herbicides in water due to expected dilution, but the concentrations actually remained about the same as in non-flood years. Given the much higher volume of water in 1993, the total amount of herbicides transported was much higher than in previous years. This is illustrated in Table 5-3 which shows the highest loadings at three measuring stations for 1991, 1992, and 1993. For example, the highest daily loading of atrazine at Thebes was about 13,728 pounds during 1993 compared to a maximum loading of 7,964 pounds in 1991.

The total amount of atrazine delivered to the Gulf of Mexico by the Mississippi River from April-August 1993 was 1,185,800 pounds. This was 85 and 235 percent higher than loads delivered during the same period in 1991 and 1992, respectively. About 909,700 tons of nitrate-nitrogen were discharged to

TABLE 5-3 Largest Daily Load Estimates for Herbicides at Three Sampling Sites on the Mississippi River (after Goolsby et al., 1993)

Herbicide	Clinton, IA			Thebes, IL			Baton Rouge, LA[1]		
	1991	1992	1993	1991	1992	1993	1991	1992	1993
Atrazine	530	96	780	3,620	1,780	6,240	6,060	2,330	7,110
Alachlor	260	27	180	780	160	780	840	210	760
Cyanazine	310	100	750	2,980	890	4,180	2,930	980	3,130
Metolachlor	190	46	380	1,830	430	2,400	2,280	1,080	2,250

Notes:

Estimates are in kilograms per day (1 kg = 2.2 pounds).

[1] Measurements at Baton Rouge include the amounts of herbicides diverted from the Mississippi River into the Atchafalaya River.

the Gulf of Mexico from April-August 1993, a value 37 and 11 percent greater than loads for 1991 and 1992, respectively (Goolsby et al., 1993). Of course, there was an immense discharge of freshwater to the Gulf of Mexico during the summer of 1993.

Water quality and sediment samples were collected during August, October, and December 1993 flooding in the Horseshoe Lake area (Figure 5-11). This area was flooded extensively from a major breach in the Mississippi River (Klubek et al., 1994). To some extent their findings show what happened on the floodplains during the 1993 flood. Suspended solids were highest in August and decreased thereafter. Herbicide concentrations for alachlor, atrazine, and cyanazine were less than 3 parts per billion, and significant amounts of coliform bacteria were not detected in the floodwater. The study concluded that the 1993 flood did not contaminate the Horseshoe Lake area with imported herbicides.

Lower Mississippi River and Gulf of Mexico

The 1993 flood carried tremendous amounts of water and increased loads of herbicides through the Lower Mississippi River and into the Gulf of Mexico. Analyses have shown that the delivery of this water and its dissolved and suspended materials affected the ecosystem of the Gulf of Mexico (Dowgiallo, 1994). The question is how severe were these impacts, many of which have yet to be determined. Flow records from Tarbert Landing in Mississippi indicate that the river's flow at this location was higher than the long-term average maximum daily records for 37 consecutive days (from August 5-September 10, 1993). The river again exceeded the long-term average maximum flows at this location from October 1-14, 1993. During the rest of the year, however, the daily flows were lower than the long-term maximum flows.

Discharges of herbicides and nitrate to the Gulf of Mexico were substantially higher in 1993 than in prior years. About 405 tons of atrazine (the most widely used herbicide in the basin) were discharged to the Gulf of Mexico during July-September 1993. The plume of water from the Mississippi River entering the Gulf produced very turbid waters that spread across the northern Gulf. This water was relatively warmer than Gulf waters: as much as 3°C higher at the mouth of the river during August. This plume of warm, turbid water moved east toward Florida because of abnormal easterly winds during July and August. Satellite imagery indicated that the freshwater reached the western shores of Florida, and local measurements confirmed its presence. This increased discharge of freshwater also decreased the saline concentration in the Gulf, especially near Atchafalaya Bay. Salinity data collected July 13-23, 1993, in the Gulf between Timbalier Bay, LA, and Galveston, TX, indicated a significant drop in the salinity from 20-25 practical salinity units (psu) to 6 psu. Ebbesmeyer and Weeks (Dowgiallo, 1994) indicated that this is the lowest salinity ever observed in this area (the basis for comparison was data collected on four previous trips in 1992 and April and July 1993). Chapter 6 describes the ecosystem effects of these chemicals.

Low salinity water from the floodflows intruded in the coastal waters west of Florida and persisted below the surface through October 1993 (Dowgiallo, 1994). Low salinity water was observed from a depth of about 80 feet to the north shelf to less than 60 feet in the southern shelf region. Similar observations of low salinity water along the western Florida shelf were made in 1949-1950 and again during the 1973 flood on the Mississippi River. Low salinity water originating from the flood discharges was also observed in the Straits of Florida during September 9-13, 1993 (Dowgiallo, 1994). The plume of low salinity water was found near Cape Lookout, NC, in September between 53 and 122 miles offshore and in the Gulf Stream, and scientists concluded that the only source was the freshwater from the Mississippi (Dowgiallo, 1994).

The huge amount of freshwater discharged from the Mississippi River had a significant impact on water quality in the Gulf, but its ultimate influence on the Gulf's ecosystem has yet to be defined. Discharges of freshwater with high turbidity and elevated nutrients and temperatures certainly can temporarily alter the oceanic ecosystem in this area. These impacts could include increased turbidity enhancing net productivity, increased carbon production, decreased oxygens level near the bed (hypoxic conditions), a decrease or elimination of shellfish, and increased densities of phytoplankton. It is also quite remarkable that some of these effects were detected so far away from the river's mouth.

SUMMARY

The physical effects of the 1993 flood were many and varied on river processes (erosion, sediment and pollutant transport, and sedimentation) and on river responses to increased water and sediment loads. These effects are still sketchy because data collected by many agencies have yet to be analyzed.

Soil erosion from the heavy rains during 1993 was excessive: for example, Iowa lost 20 tons per acre over more than 25 percent of the state compared to a normal soil tolerance value of 5 tons per acre per year. Most of the streambank erosion occurred in high-energy areas where old meander loops existed, and bank erosion occurred on the outside banks of the rivers. Wave erosion was also a problem during the prolonged flooding. Narrow valleys in the lower reaches of the Missouri River experienced significant amounts of erosion and sedimentation during the 1993 flood.

Many upstream pools on the Upper Mississippi River experienced both erosion and sedimentation. Deposition of as much as 284,000 cubic yards of sediment occurred in Pool 2, and this coupled with deposition in other pools forced the Corps to increase dredging efforts in 1993 and into 1994. Some tributary streams have experienced bed scour of as much as 10 feet; within some river pools, the Mississippi scoured beds by as much as 5 feet and deposited up to 9 feet of sediment in other locations.

The Mississippi River at Dubuque transported 6.7 million tons of sediment during a nine-month period in 1993, 180 percent of the long-term average. Farther south at Keokuk, IA, the river transported 33.7 million tons of sediment in 1993, or 308 percent of the long-term average. Sediment transport in the flooded sections of the Lower Missouri River during July 1993 was also sizable: at Sioux City, IA, the river carried about 2.3 million tons of sediment (the highest monthly amount since construction of the Gavins Point Dam in 1955), and the river carried 11.87 million tons of sediment past Nebraska City, NE.

Within the lower 498-mile reach of the Missouri River, the raging floodwaters led to 14 channel changes, many chute developments, plus 70 blowouts. The maximum length of the new chutes was 43.8 miles and the minimum length was 2.5 miles. The river also scoured its bed by up to 10 feet over more than 400 river miles between St. Joseph and Hermann, MO, with some scouring as much as 14.7 feet.

About 455,000 floodplain acres on the Missouri River were damaged, and sand deposits totaled 546 million cubic yards, with 77,500 acres experiencing sand deposits between 6 and 24 inches deep. Between June 26 and September 14, 1993, the total amount of sediment moving past St. Louis was 76.8 million tons. Some lakes within Kansas and Missouri lost 1.6 percent of their capacities to sediment deposited in 1993. In the St. Louis area, as much as 20 feet of sediment was deposited in the Mississippi River. Surveys of many archaeological sites located on riverbanks revealed damages from both streambank erosion and sediment deposition. Removal of vegetation by floodwaters produced additional erosion. The immense physical force of the floodwaters affected thousands of levees and floodplains, and 1,062 levees were damaged. The average length of breaches in federal levees in the St. Louis District was 1,000 feet with some up to 3,500 feet long. Most levees failed due to overflow or seepage, and sand boils on the landward side were often followed by levee failures. Most levee failures were also related to old active channels. Inadequate levee design and insufficient flanking heights (connecting levee to the bluff) also contributed.

Levee breaches were associated with scour hole development followed by deposition of sediment in a fan-shaped area extending in the downstream/down valley direction. The pattern of sediment deposition mimicked that of a snow drift or desert environment. On the Missouri River, between Kansas City and St. Louis, more than 500 scour holes developed in the breaches. These scour holes varied in size, shape, and depth: some were 100 feet deep and up to one mile long.

The river recaptured its floodplains to help convey the floodwaters. For example, on the Missouri River at Hermann, MO, the river stage dropped by 4.29 feet during July and August 1993 for the same flow (about 411,000 cfs). The Missouri tried to carve a new channel across the floodplain at Glasgow, MO, and at the St. Charles (MO) Peninsula, and for a time about 50 percent of the river's entire flow (350,000 cfs) was flowing to the Mississippi River 18 miles upstream of the confluence of the two rivers. Similarly, along the Mississippi River north of Cairo, IL (the confluence with the Ohio River), floodwaters pouring through a large breach (200,000 cfs) for several weeks cut cross country and almost created a new cutoff that could have reduced the river's length from 19 miles to 6 miles. Fortunately, none of these potential cutoffs became permanent, largely due to efforts to fill the breaches.

High water levels in the floodplains and rivers recharged the connecting aquifers, but the effects of the flood were no different than effects during other previous floods. Observation wells near St. Louis had the highest ground-water levels since record keeping began in the 1950s. Ground water seeping to the surface in large quantities was responsible for widespread flooding in the Havana Lowland area along the Illinois River.

The Mississippi River eroded and carried significant amounts of herbicides during the flood. For example, the atrazine load exceeded 13,700 pounds near Thebes, IL, compared to 7,900 pounds in 1991. There were no significant sedimentation problems on the Lower Mississippi River. However, large volumes of turbid, fresh, and relatively warmer water entered the Gulf of Mexico and spread east to Florida and into the Gulf Stream.

Long-Term Impacts

Knowledge of river behavior makes it possible to estimate the flood's long-lasting effects on the morphometry of the Upper Mississippi River basin, including rivers, floodplains, and levee breach areas. Some certain and likely effects are now listed.

- Increased soil erosion (20 tons per acre compared to normal annual values of 5 tons per year) at many locations due to increased intensities and duration of rainfall has had a significant impact on the landscape. It will take many years before the landscape is able to regenerate this topsoil.

- Increased streambank erosion may have initiated long-term changes of the channel bankline, including the loss or impending loss of some archaeological sites.
- More than 500 scour holes on the Missouri River and 1,062 levee breaches serve as permanent scars on the landscape, scars that will probably never be filled. These scour holes may have increased the number of aquatic habitats in addition to creating new wetlands.
- Recapture of many floodplains by the Missouri River and some by the Mississippi River may have permanent impacts on future floodplain use and management.
- New chutes, or reestablishment of old chutes, by the Missouri River may be a permanent feature on this basin, especially in the lower reaches of the river.
- Levee breaches that go unrepaired may help the river floodplain to act as a single conveyance unit.
- Impacts on the river due to the increased transport of chemicals during the flood are likely to be high but have not yet been fully evaluated.
- Even though the river was not successful in shortening its length or in creating new cutoff channels at several locations, those areas may again experience similar impacts when another major flood occurs.
- Sand deposits, especially those close to the levee breaches and on very fertile agricultural lands, may render some lands less productive and less useful for years to come.

Lessons Learned and Reaffirmed

The flood taught, or reaffirmed, a series of lessons about the effects of a massive flood on river behavior and clearly illustrated that levees should not be built on old meander loops or cutoff areas. Events on the Missouri River demonstrated that these areas are the most unstable zone in the river floodplain system. Data also demonstrate that levees and river protection works should not be placed too close to the rivers. As was suspected during the flood, most erosion occurred on the outside bank of the river, and deposition occurred within the slack water areas or crossings.

New information about the causes of levee failures was gathered. For example, levee breaches occur when the seepage is too high and washes away the fine sediments from the levees.

Exceptionally large amounts of farm chemicals were eroded from fields and transported during the 1993 flood. Further, record floods such as the 1993 flood may impact the Gulf of Mexico by increasing the turbidity of the water, enhancing the temperature regime, decreasing the salinity, causing the Gulf bed

130

to be hypoxic by decreasing the dissolved oxygen content (because of increased production of carbons), and changing the water environment from Texas on the west to Florida on the east. Finally, the summer flood illustrated that ground-water levels close to the rivers, especially those in the broad floodplain east of St. Louis, experienced significant impacts. During the latter part of the flood, ground-water levels essentially mimicked river water levels, and high ground-water levels can be responsible for extensive flooding in lowlands adjacent to the rivers. *The main lesson from this event is that it is environmentally and economically better to work with a river than to work against it. The river can and will reclaim its floodplains whenever conditions are just right.*

REFERENCES

Benn, D.W., 1994: Reconnoitering Archaeological sites after the flood in the Rock Island District, Upper Mississippi River Valley. In W. Green and R.M. Lillie, ed., *Archaeology and the Great Midwestern Flood of 1993*, Research Reports, Office of State Climatologist, University of Iowa, Iowa City, IA, 19(4), 153-168.

Bhowmik, N.G. and J.B. Stall, 1979: *Hydraulic Geometry and Carrying Capacity of Floodplains*. University of Illinois Water Resources Center, Research Report No.145, Urbana, IL, 147 pp.

Bhowmik, N.G., A.P. Bonini, W.C. Bogner, and R. P. Byrne, 1980: *Hydraulics of Flow and Sediment Transport in the Kankakee River in Illinois*. Illinois State Water Survey Report of Investigation 98, Champaign, IL, 39 pp.

Bhowmik, N.G., and M. Demissie, 1982: Carrying capacity of floodplains. *ASCE Journal of Hydraulics,* 108(HY3), 67-76.

Bhowmik, N.G., A.G. Buck, S.A. Changnon, R.H. Dalton, A. Durgunoglu, M. Demissie, A.R. Juhl, H.V. Knapp, K.E. Kunkel, S.A. McConkey, R.W. Scott, K.P. Singh, T.-W.D. Soong, R.E. Sparks, A.P. Visocky, D.R. Vonnahme, and W.M. Wendland, 1994: *The 1993 Flood on the Mississippi River in Illinois*. Miscellaneous Publication 151, Illinois State Water Survey, Champaign, IL, 149 pp.

Bogardi, I. and C. Mathe, 1968: *Determination of the Degree of Protection Offered by Flood Levees and the Economic Improvement Thereof*. National Water Authority Publication, Dept. of Flood Control and River Training, Budapest, Hungary, 77 pp.

Chrzastowski, M.J., M.M. Killey, R.A. Bauer, P.B. DuMontelle, A.L. Erdmann, B.L. Herzog, J.M. Masters, and L.R. Smith, 1994: *The Great Flood of 1993: Geologic Perspectives on the Flooding along the Mississippi River and its Tributaries in Illinois*. Illinois State Geological Survey Special Report 2, Champaign, IL, 45 pp.

Corps of Engineers, 1994a: *The Great Flood of 1993 Post Flood Report, Upper Mississippi River Basin, Appendix A*, St. Paul District, 192 pp.

Corps of Engineers, 1994b: *The Great Flood of 1993: Post Flood Report Upper Mississippi River and Lower Missouri River Basins, Main Report*. North Central Division, 60 pp.

Corps of Engineers, 1994c: *The Great Flood of 1993: Post Flood Report, Upper Mississippi River Basin, Appendix B*. Rock Island District, 95 pp.

Corps of Engineers, 1994d: *The Great Flood of 1993: Post Flood Report,Lower Missouri River Basin, Appendix D*. Omaha District, 90 pp.

Corps of Engineers, 1994e: *The Great Flood of 1993: Post Flood Report, Lower Missouri River Basin, Appendix E*. Kansas City District, 110 pp.

Dowgiallo, M.J., ed., 1994: *Coastal Oceanographic Effects of Summer 1993 Mississippi River Flooding*. National Oceanic and Atmospheric Administration Special Report, Washington, DC, 77 pp.

Goolsby, D.A., W.A. Battaglin, and E.M. Thurman, 1993: *Occurrence and Transport of Agricultural Chemicals in the Mississippi River Basin. July Through August 1993*. U.S. Geological Survey Circular 1120-C, U. S. Government Printing Office, Denver, CO, 22 pp.

Green, W., and R.M. Lillie, (ed.), 1994: *Archaeology and the Great Midwestern Flood of 1993*. Research Reports, Office of State Climatologist, University of Iowa, Iowa City, IA, 19(4), 1-4.

Interagency Floodplain Management Review Committee, 1994: *Sharing the Challenge: Floodplain Management into the 21st Century*. Report to the Administration Floodplain Management Task Force, Washington, DC, 191 pp.

Klubek, B.P., S.-K. Chong, and J.T. Weber, 1994: Herbicide and coliform monitoring of the Mississippi floodplain. *Proceedings of the Illinois Groundwater Consortium*, Makanda, IL, March 23-24, 143-153.

Myers, M.F., and G.F. White, 1993: The Mississippi flood. *Environment*, 35(10), 7-35.

Ruhe, R.V., and P.H. Walker, 1968: Hillslope models and soil formation. I. Open systems. *Ninth International Congress of Soil Science,* [Translations 4], 551-560.

Scientific Assessment and Strategy Team (SAST), 1994: *Science for Floodplain Management into the 21st Century*. Preliminary Report of the Interagency Floodplain Management Review Committee to the Administration Floodplain Management Task Force, Washington, DC, 171 pp.

6

Ecosystem Effects:
Positive and Negative Outcomes

Richard E. Sparks

INTRODUCTION

Many people find it surprising that the flood of 1993 had both positive and negative effects on the Upper Mississippi, the Illinois, and the Lower Missouri River-floodplain ecosystems. Many mobile organisms have adapted to exploit seasonal floods. For example, the flood benefitted fishes that spawned on the inundated floodplain, and wading birds, in turn, exploited the huge crop of young fish. On the other hand, long-lived, stationary organisms, such as trees, were severely stressed or died as a result of the exceptionally long period of inundation. And yet, the news is not all bad. In fact, many seedlings cannot germinate or grow in the shade of mature trees, so old forests are rejuvenated when mature trees die of old age or due to a major disturbance such as fire or flood.

This chapter defines rivers and their floodplains as ecosystems that are created and maintained by floodpulses, and then describes the effects of the 1993 flood on selected biota and biological processes in these flood-adapted ecosystems. The flood also had long-range impacts: excessive nutrients washed from the Midwest lowered dissolved oxygen levels and adversely affected biota in the Gulf of Mexico. Flood data are interpreted in the light of current theories (floodpulse concept, floodpulse advantage, and the moving littoral) regarding large river-floodplain ecosystems. Chapter 5 addressed the physical effects of the flood on erosion, on levees, and on the transport and deposition of sediments including the quality of surface water and ground water.

Because it was an exceptionally strong environmental stimulus that evoked strong responses, the 1993 flood provided a unique opportunity to test these theories. It would probably require years of data to distinguish weaker responses to more moderate, seasonal floods.

In addition, the flood height and duration increased from north to south (Figure 6-1), so the flood was like a set of graduated dose-response experiments-- only the doses were prescribed by nature and the responses were measured, not

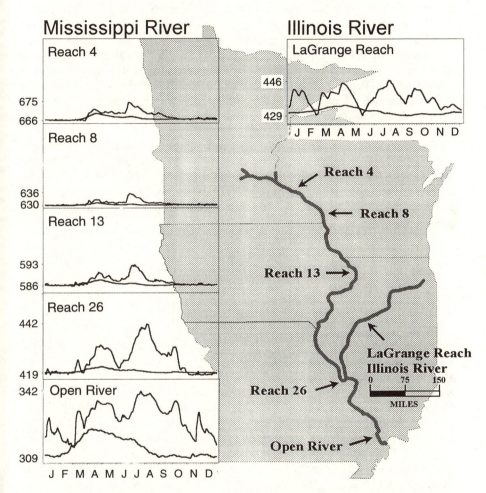

FIGURE 6-1   Water-level hydrographs in six river reaches (defined by navigation dams) monitored by the National Biological Service and the five states bordering the Upper Mississippi River. The lower lines on each hydrograph are the average daily water levels since the navigation dams were built in the late 1930s. The spring floodpulse is apparent. The upper lines are the daily water elevations in 1993. The mean low water elevation and the peak elevation in 1993 are shown on the vertical axis, in feet above mean sea level (Prepared by John Nelson, Long Term Resource Monitoring Program (LTRMP), Alton, IL from data supplied by the St. Louis, MO, Rock Island, IL, and St. Paul, MN, districts of U.S. Army Corps of Engineers).

under carefully controlled laboratory conditions, but in the field, under inconvenient sometimes hazardous conditions by the staff at six field stations who had been monitoring 20- to 40-mile reaches of river since 1988 (Figure 6-1). Five of the stations are on the Upper Mississippi River and one is on the Illinois River. The stations are operated jointly by the National Biological Service and the five states bordering the Upper Mississippi River.

Most of the flood data reported herein were obtained at one study reach at the confluence of the Lower Illinois River and the Mississippi River in the vicinity of Alton, IL (Figure 6-2). This area was the epicenter of the 1993 flood, just upstream of St. Louis, where the Missouri, the Illinois, and the Upper Mississippi Rivers converge. Although it was fortuitous that the station was located here, much more could have been learned had there been advance preparations for sampling during a flood.

Finally, this chapter summarizes the key findings, identifies lessons learned, and recommends research (including flood-triggered sampling) to improve our understanding of river-floodplain ecosystems and policies that will maintain and restore the valuable ecological services (water purification, nutrient recycling, maintenance of biodiversity, and fish and wildlife habitat and production) these ecosystems provide.

RIVER-FLOODPLAIN ECOSYSTEMS

Floodplains

Ecologists hyphenate river-floodplain to emphasize that rivers and their flood-plains are interdependent parts of one ecosystem (Junk et al., 1989; National Research Council, 1992:184-186). Floodplains in the upper Midwest were created by alluvial rivers that deposited sediments during seasonal floods in broad valleys several miles wide. The valleys were carved when sea levels were lower and river gradients were consequently steeper and the erosive power of huge volumes of meltwater from continental glaciers peaked. When the Great Lakes and many northern rivers in North America and Europe disappeared under ice sheets or became too cold for warmwater species during the ice ages, the mainstem Mississippi (which runs north-south) conserved species by providing an escape route to southern freshwater refuges (Moyle and Herbold, 1987).

In the post-glacial period, flows and gradients lessened and the rivers deposited and reworked sediments, creating a complex system of flowing channels and lateral floodplains within the bedrock valleys (Hajic, 1990). The floodplains include natural levees, floodplain lakes, backwaters, and shallow wetlands. Aquatic species recolonized these habitats from the southern refuges they had occupied during the glaciations. As a result of the southern refuges and the great variety of habitats for a variety of species provided by the river-floodplain ecosystems, the Mississippi and its major tributaries are now home to one third

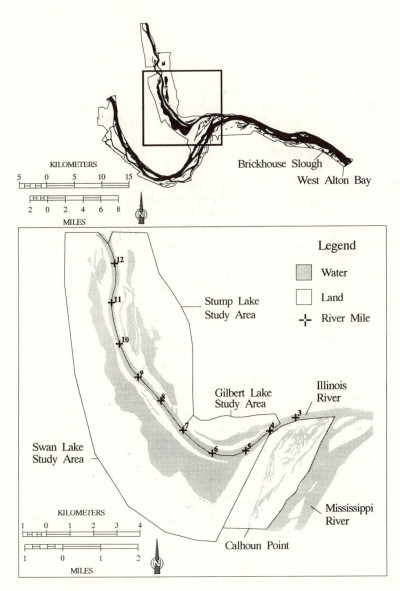

FIGURE 6-2   Study areas at the confluence of the Illinois River and Upper Mississippi River, Reach 26. Numbers refer to distance in miles upstream from the confluence (Prepared by Anjela Redmond, LTRMP, Alton, IL).

of the 600 freshwater fishes in North America and most of the 297 species of freshwater mussels in the United States (Fremling et al., 1989; Neves, 1993; Turgeon et al., 1988). In contrast, western Europe has only 15 species of freshwater mussels (Neves, 1993), and its river-floodplain ecosystems, such as the upper Rhone in France, typically have 25 species of fish (Persat et al., 1994). Although humans have leveled off portions of the rivers from their floodplains and drained aquatic and wetland habitats primarily for agriculture, approximately half the original floodplain remains along the Upper Mississippi River and Illinois River (National Research Council, 1992), much of it as national and state wildlife refuges, public hunting and fishing areas, and private duck hunting clubs.

Floodpulses and the Floodpulse Advantage

Floodpulses. A floodpulse refers to the entire annual cycle of the water-level hydrograph, from low flow elevation to flood crest and back to the low elevation (Junk et al., 1989). There may be more than one flood per year. The mean annual water-level hydrograph for the Upper Mississippi River is typically bimodal, with the year's major flood in the spring, a summer low level, and a minor flood in the fall (Sparks, 1995). Water levels are lowest typically in midwinter when much of the northern basin is frozen and there is little runoff. In contrast, the mean annual hydrograph for the Illinois River is unimodal, with the water rising through late fall and winter, building gradually into the spring flood. The lowest water levels typically occur during the peak of the growing season in July and August (Sparks, 1995).

Floods in large rivers rise and fall more gradually, last longer than in small streams, and are more predictable than floods in small streams. Water-level hydrographs in small streams tend to be spiky and unpredictable because streams respond to relatively unpredictable local events, such as severe thunderstorms. In contrast, large rivers integrate flows from many tributaries draining large basins where floods are typically caused by relatively predictable seasonal weather patterns (spring rains and snowmelt). There was widespread concern about the flood's effect on various species as shown in Figure 6-3.

The low part and the highest part of the floodpulse are equally important. Recession of the flood during the summer growing season exposes mudflats where moist soil plants germinate. Low, stable water levels in the permanent lakes and backwaters on the floodplain are conducive to the growth of submersed aquatic plants, which produce seeds and tubers that feed waterfowl during their spring and fall migrations along the Mississippi. Perennial vegetation, including trees, grow at land elevations within the floodplain where the average annual period of inundation is within their range of tolerance. Pin oaks (*Quercus palustris*) and pecans (*Carya illinoensis*) grow at higher elevations on the floodplain than more water-tolerant black willows (*Salix niger*).

Although floodpulses in large rivers are smoother and more predictable than in small streams, floodplains exert an additional smoothing effect by acting as hydraulic capacitors, storing water on the rising stages of major annual floods and releasing it gradually back to the river on the falling stages. During the summer growing season, normally the period of low flow, floodplains also buffer plant communities from the minor floods caused by local thunderstorms. Floodplain vegetation can withstand prolonged flooding during the dormant season, and even some moderate flooding during the summer growing season, but excessive water fluctuations or prolonged flooding during the summer can be detrimental. Isolated summer thunderstorms may cause extreme variations in tributary water levels over the span of a few hours, but the amount of water delivered to an intact river-floodplain ecosystem is usually small in relation to storage capacity. A portion of the floodplain may be flooded while vegetation elsewhere on the floodplain is protected. The larger the floodplain and the more gradual the slope (from upstream to downstream and laterally from river to bluff), the greater the flood's smoothing and buffering effects.

The Moving Littoral. The shallow zone (littoral zone) along the margins of lakes and rivers is usually more biologically productive than deeper areas because the shallows are well oxygenated, the water is usually warmer, and light can penetrate to the bottom and support green plants. In a river-floodplain ecosystem, the advancing margin of the flood creates a littoral zone that traverses the width of the floodplain: a moving littoral, as defined by Junk et al. (1989). The same authors suggest that nutrients are released from the newly flooded soils, thereby stimulating primary production (growth of green plants, including algae) and secondary production (growth of animals, including aquatic insects and microscopic zooplankton that consume plants or plant products).

The Floodpulse Advantage. The stimulatory effect of the moving littoral travels up the food chain to fish and is partly responsible for the observed increase in fish yield in rivers with floodpulses compared to rivers without them (Welcomme, 1979)--a phenomenon Bayley (1991) termed the "floodpulse advantage." Riverine fish use the flood to access floodplain resources, including spawning sites, nurseries, and feeding areas. Fish that hatch when the littoral is moving across the floodplain can find zooplankton on which to feed. As the fish grow, they graduate to aquatic insects; still later, the fish-eaters among them begin to eat their smaller brethren. When the waters recede, the summer's production of small fish is concentrated and forced into the jaws of predators waiting in deeper water. Humans view this winnowing process as advantageous because biomass produced on the floodplain moves up the food chain into larger fish sought by both commercial and sport fishers. More static bodies of water, however, become dominated by large populations of stunted fish that grow very slowly, a phenomenon known to fisheries managers as the aging reservoir syndrome. New reservoirs act like the rising floodpulse, releasing nutrients from flooded soils, expanding the aquatic habitat, and fish populations often expand. Once water levels stabilize, however, nutrient release may decline. Moreover, small fish are not forced out of the weedy shallows by falling water levels. The populations become too large for the available food resources, so they grow very slowly. Large fish that occupy deeper water cannot prey on the well-protected small fish, so they also grow very slowly, and eventually die of old age or get caught. The end result is a large population of small fish of little use to sport or recreational fishers.

Desirable flooding characteristics, from a fish's point of view, include a spring flood when water temperatures are rising and the fish is ready to spawn. The flood should last through part of the summer, so fish eggs have a chance to hatch and the young have time to feed in the moving littoral and to find shelter in flooded terrestrial vegetation. The flood should fall slowly, so that young fish are not prematurely washed out of the floodplain into the river channel or stranded on drying mudflats. In temperate climates like the Midwest, the extent to which the water-level hydrograph coincides with the annual temperature graph is critical (Figure 6-4). A midwinter flood does little to boost fish production because fish are not ready to spawn or grow rapidly. Of course, different species spawn at different times, so the timing and duration of the flood may favor some species one year and others the next year.

FIGURE 6-3 During the flood there was concern about the plight of the animals, and the problems experienced by gambling casinos in boats along the river were a subject of some ridicule (Reprinted by permission, Tribune Media Services).

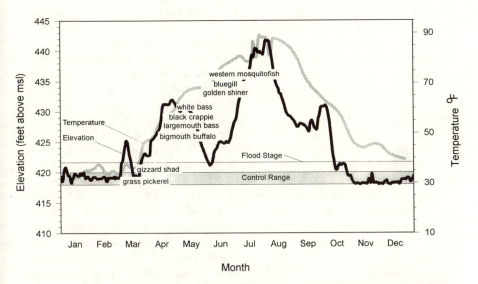

FIGURE 6-4   Temperature and water surface elevation at Grafton, IL, in 1993. Approximate fish spawning dates and spawning temperatures are indicated by the position of the fish names on the graph. Nine of the 52 species of fish found on the floodplain during the flood are shown to indicate the maximum range of spawning dates and preferred temperatures. The 1993 floodpulse was closely coupled with the annual temperature pulse, a condition that favors fish that use the floodplain for spawning, nurseries, and feeding. Although fishes differ in the timing of spawning, the 1993 flood had multiple peaks that bracketed the favored spawning periods of virtually all species. Control range refers to the range of water elevations that can be controlled by the operation of the downstream navigation dam at Alton, IL. Normally the dam is operated to maintain the water elevation at the middle of the control range, to maintain water depths for navigation (e.g., in February). However, in 1993, when water levels finally dropped within the control range in October, the levels were further lowered to the bottom of the control range to facilitate drainage of water from flooded levee districts (Prepared by Robert Maher, LTRMP, Alton, IL, with temperature and water elevation data from the St. Louis District, U.S. Army Corps of Engineers).

EFFECTS OF THE 1993 FLOOD

Nutrients, Chlorophyll, Invertebrates, and the Moving Littoral

Chlorophyll and Nutrients. Water samples were taken along the border of the main channel, in backwater lakes, and in the moving littoral on the floodplain at the confluence of the Illinois and Mississippi Rivers during the 1993 flood (Figure 6-2, Ratcliff and Theiling, 1995). The quantity of microscopic aquatic plants (phytoplankton) in the water column before and during the flood was assessed indirectly, by measuring chlorophyll-a, a plant pigment essential in photosynthesis. Chlorophyll-a concentrations at the time of the flood crest in July were significantly lower in the channel borders and backwater lakes (probability < 0.05) than in the two summers preceding the flood (Table 6-1). However, there was roughly six times more chlorophyll-a in the moving littoral (29.3 milligrams per cubic meter or mg/m^3) than in deeper areas, including portions of Swan Lake. Although chlorophyll-a concentrations in Swan Lake had averaged 87.1 mg/m^3 in years prior to the 1993 flood, concentrations in the lake averaged only 4.9 mg/m^3 during the flood. Maximum chlorophyll-a concentrations in the moving littoral (301.6 mg/m^3) exceeded the previous highs in Swan Lake by 25 percent. Samples were taken near the time of the crest (July 19-26, 1993) and as the flood receded (August 28-September 3, 1993), so no information is available on chlorophyll-a or nutrient concentrations during most of the rising part of the floodpulse.

Increased chlorophyll-a in the moving littoral, relative to the other habitats during the flood, is probably related to the availability of phosphorus, an important plant nutrient. During the flood, the concentration of phosphorous was higher in the littoral zone than in the other habitats, although not as high as in the open waters of Swan Lake prior to the flood (Table 6-2, Ratcliff and Theiling, 1995). Nitrogen concentrations did not differ significantly among habitats during the flood nor among years (p < 0.05), so nitrogen alone cannot explain the increased chlorophyll concentration. Phosphorus concentrations were lower in the border of the main channel and in Swan Lake in 1993 than in previous years, indicating that there may have been dilution or uptake of nutrients during this long-duration flood (Table 6-2). While these results are not conclusive, they are

TABLE 6-1 Chlorophyll-a Concentrations (means and ranges, mg/m^3) in Four Habitats of the Illinois River before and during the Flood of 1993 (Preflood Measurements Were Made from 1991 to 1992. All Measurements Were Made from July 15 to September 15, Roughly the Period Covered by the 1993 Flood)

Habitat	Preflood	During flood
Border of main channel	46.5 (16.0-120.3)	2.9 (1.8-4.1)
Swan Lake open water	87.1 (20.0-240.6)	4.9 (1.0-12.7)
27 open water sites, including Swan Lake		5.6 (1.0-18.1)
15 shoreline sites on the floodplain		29.3 (2.6-301.6)

TABLE 6-2   Total Phosphorus Concentrations (means and ranges, mg/l) in Four Habitats of the Illinois River before and during the Flood of 1993   (Preflood Measurements Were Made from 1991 to 1992. All Measurements Were Made from July 15 to September 15, Roughly the Period Covered by the 1993 Flood)

Habitat	Preflood	During flood
Border of main channel	0.28 (0.23-0.31)	0.21 (0.20-0.22)
Swan Lake open water	0.55 (0.22-1.71)	0.22 (0.19-0.26)
27 open water sites, including Swan Lake		0.21 (0.18-0.27)
15 shoreline sites on the floodplain		0.26 (0.19-0.67)

consistent with the moving littoral concept. Phosphorus concentrations may have been higher in the moving littoral than elsewhere, because phosphorus was released from newly flooded soil. The relatively high chlorophyll concentrations in the moving littoral, compared to other habitats, indicated that phytoplankton may have been stimulated by the phosphorus.

Invertebrates.   As expected, invertebrates were relatively abundant in the moving littoral, particularly where decaying terrestrial grasses provided shelter and perhaps food (Figure 6-5, Theiling et al., 1995). Aquatic insects dominated the shoreline invertebrate communities, with water boatmen (Corixidae) and bloodworms (Chironomidae) being most common (Theiling et al., 1995).

Fish and the Floodpulse Advantage

The annual floodpulse and annual temperature pulse were closely coupled in 1993, and fishes that spawn on the floodplain should have had an exceptionally good year (Figure 6-4, from Maher, 1995). The flood lasted an unusually long time, cresting four times and falling very slowly, so it bracketed the preferred spawning seasons of virtually all fish species found in the river-floodplain ecosystem.   The flood allowed adult fish to find firm terrestrial soils and terrestrial vegetation for spawning sites, whereas only unsuitable, flocculent bottom sediments are available in permanent lakes and backwaters during nonflood years. Not only was the quality of spawning sites better, but the total area suitable for spawning was greatly expanded as well.

Sampling Problems.   Although conditions were favorable for floodplain spawning in 1993, it is very difficult to quantify how many adult fish used the floodplain and how many young they produced, even if the sampling effort is

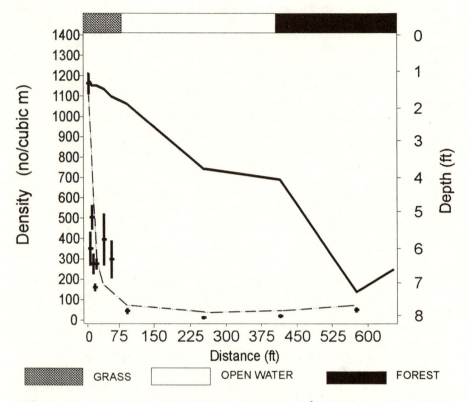

FIGURE 6-5   Population densities (number of organisms/m³=about one cubic yard) of invertebrates (mostly aquatic insects and microcrustaceans) in open water and shoreline habitats on the floodplain of the lower Illinois River during the flood of 1993. Most of the invertebrates were in very shallow water in flooded grass. Samples were taken with paired plankton nets in July and August 1993. (Prepared by Charles Theiling, LTRMP, Alton, IL).

standardized among sampling sites and years to facilitate comparisons. Fish catch was standardized to a unit of fishing effort (the more time spent fishing or the more nets used, the higher the total catch). For example, a net day is a standard unit of fishing effort equal to one net deployed for 24 hours. If five nets are set for one day, the total fish catch is divided by 5 so that comparisons can be made among sites and years in terms of catch per net per day, analogous to measuring human effort in man-days. During a flood, fish scatter throughout the expanded aquatic habitat, so the average density of fish per acre may drop, even if the total number of fish in the study areas increases due to immigration and reproduction. Worse yet, conditions during a flood make it difficult to use the sampling gear. For example, standard fyke nets may have to be moved frequently to maintain them at optimum sampling depths as water levels change, and flooded terrestrial vegetation may hamper placement of these large, heavy trap nets.

Boat electroshockers that are used to temporarily stun fish so they can be collected with dip nets are most efficient when the fish are herded or crowded toward the shoreline. During a flood, it may be impossible to reach the shoreline or even maneuver the boat around flooded trees and brush. Standardized sampling protocols and gear that can be used on floodplains during floods, such as small fyke nets (also called minnow fyke nets) and nets that can be triggered to drop down from poles or pop up from the bottom, should be developed and tested before the next major flood. These techniques should be calibrated so that fish population (number of individuals) and fish biomass (total weight) densities can be calculated from catch rates (Bayley and Dowling, 1990).

Occurrence of Juvenile Fishes on the Floodplain in 1993. As expected, juveniles from 52 species and 15 families were collected during the flood on the floodplain near Grafton, IL (Maher, 1995). While the presence of juveniles in the late summer and early fall indicates that adults had spawned on the floodplain in spring and early summer, it is impossible to quantify how many juveniles were produced in the area.

Relative Abundance of Juvenile Fishes after Floods. Until methods for sampling fishes during floods are developed, the only reliable method for assessing the effects of floods on fish populations is to compare catch rates under comparable low water conditions in years before and after the flood. An example is provided by the catch rates of juvenile black crappie (*Pomoxis nigromaculatus*, an important sport fish) on the Illinois River at Havana, from 1990 to 1994 (Table 6-3, Raibley, 1995). Sampling was conducted at fixed sites during 1990-

TABLE 6-3 Catch of Juvenile Black Crappie in the Illinois River near Havana, 1990-1994

	Summer water height				
	1990 *high*	*1991* *low*	*1992* *variable*	*1993* *high*	*1994* *low*
Standard sampling gear					
Day electrofishing (fish/hour)	5.53	8.81	8.45	0.18	17.90
Night electrofishing (fish/hour)	4.53	12.96	8.46	0.19	22.30
Fyke netting (fish/net day)	21.21	74.52	8.48	0.43	84.60
Experimental sampling gear					
Minnow fyke netting (fish/net day)	0.00	2.11	0.57	1.85	1.53

1992, and at sites randomly selected within habitat types (main channel border, backwater contiguous to the main channel, etc.) in 1993 and 1994. The black crappie is representative of nest-building fishes from the centrarchid family that use the floodplain: crappies, sunfish, and several bass. Juveniles are less than 8 inches long and less than two years old.

The standard sampling included electrofishing during the day and at night and trapping with full-size fyke nets. A smaller minnow fyke net was used experimentally. Considering the standard methods first, the catch rates of juvenile black crappie were low when summer water levels were high in 1990 and 1993, mainly because fish dispersed throughout the expanded aquatic areas, and sampling efficiency was low, as explained above. The catch rates were higher in 1991, following the summer of high water in 1990, and highest after the 1993 flood, indicating that juveniles had been produced during floods. The results from the experimental minnow fyke nets are mixed and reflect year-to-year modifications in the nets themselves and where (habitat types) and when (season of the year) they were deployed. Of interest, however, is that catch rates of black crappie with minnow fyke nets were greater than with other types of gear during the 1993 flood. Total catch rate for all species averaged 106.5 fish/net-day between June 15 and October 31, 1993, indicating that the minnow fyke nets can be developed as a good sampling technique to use during floods.

Post-Flood Stress. In order to reach a catchable size, the young-of-the-year fish must survive and grow for several years, including the first critical winter of their lives. Fish prefer wintering areas with adequate dissolved oxygen levels (5 parts per million, ppm, or higher), water temperatures above freezing (preferably 39°F, the temperature at which water reaches its maximum density and consequently pools on the bottom of floodplain lakes), and low current velocity, so they do not have to expend energy swimming at a time when both their metabolism and food supplies are low. These conditions are usually met in backwater areas or floodplain lakes. If water levels drop too low, however, the fish may become trapped in shallow backwaters where oxygen levels may decline or the water may freeze to the bottom.

Unfortunately for the fish, the St. Louis District of the Corps of Engineers took the unusual step of lowering the river in November and December 1993 below the level they normally maintain for navigation. To assist with drainage of agricultural levee districts that remained flooded in November and December, the water level was lowered to the bottom of the authorized operating range, whereas it is normally maintained at the midpoint of the range (Figure 6-3). Even though the flood had retreated, some land within the broken levees remained flooded because it was actually below the river's low water level. In other words, without levees and pumps these areas would be permanent backwaters or floodplain lakes. An important policy issue is whether government should subsidize dryland agriculture in former lakes and floodplains through price supports, disaster assistance, and maintenance and rebuilding of levees and pumping stations rather than subsidizing aquaculture, flood-adapted fish and wildlife production, or at least a more flood-adapted form of agriculture.

Submergent and Emergent Aquatic Vegetation

Submergent aquatic plants (grow completely under water) and emergent aquatic plants (float on water or grow out of the water) provide important services in river-floodplain ecosystems. They generate dissolved organic matter (including carbohydrates) and detrital particles to support the base of the food chain, and the plants are eaten directly by waterfowl and muskrats. They convert problem nutrients, including ammonia (which can be toxic to aquatic animals at relatively low concentrations), into useful biomass. They shelter snails, aquatic insects, and juvenile fishes. Finally, they serve as biotic mediators to maintain water clarity by anchoring the bottom and shorelines with their roots and damping waves with their stems and leaves. Without plants, wind- and boat-generated waves re-suspend muddy bottom sediments and erode shorelines, and backwaters and lakes turn into turbid, relatively barren deserts (Sparks et al., 1990).

Prior to the flood of 1993, submergent aquatic plants were generally abundant in the northern reaches of the Upper Mississippi River but declined in abundance downstream, probably because of increased suspended sediment loads and reduced light penetration. Increased herbicide loading from the Corn Belt in Iowa and Illinois might contribute to the observed decline as well (for information on herbicide loads in the Mississippi River, see Battaglin et al., 1993, and Goolsby et al., 1993). Submergent aquatic plants were abundant in the Illinois River until the late 1950s when they disappeared from the lower 200 miles of the river and its well-connected backwaters (Mills et al., 1966; Bellrose et al., 1979; Sparks et al., 1990).

The duration and height of the 1993 flood increased from north to south in the Upper Mississippi River, and the severity of effect on aquatic plants followed the same pattern (Spink and Rogers, 1995). Even at the epicenter of the flood near St. Louis, aquatic plants began to grow during the early stages of the flood in April and May. In the north, as the water levels rose, some plants were able to cope by rapid stem growth that enabled them to reach the light. For example, stems of the introduced Eurasian water milfoil, *Myriophyllum spicatum*, grew to lengths of 11 feet in Reach 8 (see Figure 6-1 for location) as the water rose. Despite this capacity for compensatory growth, former stands of Eurasian milfoil were replaced by July 1994 with two native species, wild celery (*Vallisneria americana*) and water-stargrass (*Zosterella dubia*) in portions of Lake Onalaska, WI, just upstream of Reach 8.

As the flood rose higher late in the growing season in the southern portion of the Upper Mississippi River, aquatic plants were virtually eliminated from backwaters where they had been abundant prior to 1993 (Figure 6-6). By the summer of 1994, however, most populations were regenerating from propagules. For example, the submergent species sago pondweed (*Potamogeton pectinatus*),

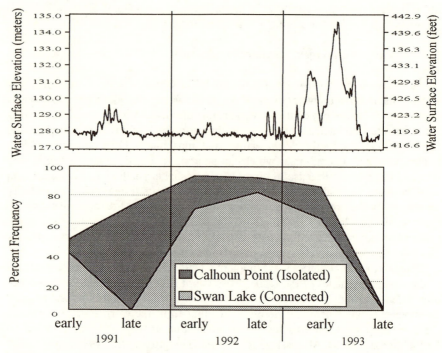

FIGURE 6-6 Relationship between water levels (feet above mean sea level) and submergent aquatic vegetation (percent frequency of occurrence at sampling sites) at the confluence of the Illinois River and Upper Mississippi River, Reach 26 (see Figures 6-1 and 6-2 for location). Calhoun Point contains many small water bodies, ranging from 0.03 to 46.39 acres in size, that are isolated from the main rivers during low river stages by low natural and man-made levees. Swan Lake is approximately 2,410 acres of open water, permanently connected to the Illinois River at the downstream end of the lake (Figure 6-2). Moderate flooding in 1991 decreased submergent vegetation in Swan Lake, but the vegetation rebounded in 1992--a period of relatively low, stable water levels. Vegetation at Calhoun Point was relatively unaffected by the 1991 flood. Although vegetation was abundant in both study areas at the beginning of 1993, it virtually disappeared as flooding continued throughout the summer growing season.

an important waterfowl food, was regrowing from tubers; the lotus (*Nelumbo lutea*), whose leaves float early in the growing season and emerge from the water later, was sprouting from seeds; and the river bulrush (*Scirpus fluviatilis*) was regrowing on shorelines from buried rhizomes (Spink and Rogers, 1995). The submergent and emergent aquatic plants seem to have recovered quickly because they have strategies for coping with and surviving floods.

Death and Regeneration in Floodplain Forests

Role of Droughts and Floods in Maintaining Forest Biodiversity. To the average human observer, floodplain forests appear to change scarcely at all from

year to year, and therefore the death of trees during or after a major flood seems catastrophic. In actuality, the diversity of vegetation on the floodplain is a product of disturbances, such as major fires, droughts, and floods that occur very infrequently, in terms of a human life span. Without droughts, the floodplains would not get dry enough to burn, and fire-intolerant species such as silver maple (*Acer saccharinum*) would crowd out the wet prairies and trees such as bur oak (*Quercus macrocarpa*). Without great floods, cottonwoods (*Populus deltoides*) would gradually be replaced by hackberry (*Celtis occidentalis*) and American elm (*Ulmus americana*), because cottonwood seeds only germinate on moist mud and the seedlings cannot grow in the shade of taller plants. Elm and hackberry, however, can grow in shade and eventually reach through the low canopy to form a higher canopy of their own.

Critical factors in maintaining species diversity are the frequency, intensity, and extent of disturbance (Connell, 1978; Stanford and Ward, 1983). If disturbances occur too frequently and over an entire area, then only pioneering, short-lived, and opportunistic species survive. If disturbances occur too infrequently, then slower growing, superior competitors for light, water, and nutrients replace the pioneers. Maximum diversity is maintained by an intermediate level of disturbance, so that patches of pioneers and superior competitors both occur within the landscape (Connell, 1978).

In many rivers, including the western Amazon, the Lower Missouri, and the Mississippi downstream from the mouth of the Missouri, erosion and sedimentation during floods were the main disturbance processes (Kalliola et al., 1991; Salo et al., 1986; Saucier, 1974). Even though humans have attempted to stabilize the rivers with riprap, wing dikes, and lateral levees, the Middle Mississippi and Lower Missouri opened new channels or reoccupied old ones during the 1993 flood (see the next section). Prior to human alteration of the Missouri and Middle and Lower Mississippi Rivers, floods eroded the outside banks of meander bends and washed away mature, late-successional vegetation. After floods, seedlings sprouted on the inside of the meander bends, where sediments were freshly deposited. From the air, the history of channel movement in these rivers can be read from the arrangement of vegetation on the floodplain by age and type. In the Illinois River and the Mississippi River north of the Missouri, however, the position of the channel has been relatively stable for 2,500 years (Hajic, 1990). Biodiversity on these river reaches must be maintained, not by flood-induced channel migration, but by other effects of floods and by other disturbances, such as droughts and fires.

The 1993 flood presented a rare opportunity to test theories regarding the role of disturbance in maintaining the vegetative diversity of floodplains. It will take years of monitoring to follow the long-term effects of the flood, to unravel all the interactions among the hardy pioneering species and the superior competitors, and to better understand and manage the floodplain forests. Consequently, the remainder of this section reports on the early effects of the 1993 flood, based largely on Yin et al. (1995) and personal communication (Nelson, 1994).

Tree Death. One year after the flood, in the summer of 1994, the health of floodplain forests was surveyed in seven reaches of the Upper Mississippi River from Lake City, MN, to Cape Girardeau, MO (Yin et al., 1995). The recurrence frequency of the flood in the upper reaches of the river in Minnesota and Wisconsin was estimated to be once in 10 to 50 years (1:10 to 1:50), and scarcely any mortality could be attributed to the flooding. Downriver, however, the flood was of much greater magnitude, with an estimated recurrence of once in more than 100 years, and the percentage of trees that had died within the year increased from 3.7 percent near Bellevue, IA, to 37.1 percent near St. Louis, MO, and 32.2 percent at Cape Girardeau, MO. Mortality of saplings was even higher, increasing from 1.8 percent in Minnesota to 80 percent near St. Louis. The mortality rate was related to the stature (height) and species of tree, and flood height and duration. Saplings are more vulnerable than adult trees because saplings are shorter, and more of the plant (often including the crown of leaves) is submerged at a given flood elevation. Both flood height and duration increased in the downstream direction, toward St. Louis. There seemed to be critical thresholds for both factors, and the data are currently being analyzed to determine the lethal thresholds of immersion period and depth for common species of floodplain trees.

There were marked differences in mortality among species. Trees are sorted by land elevation in the floodplain with the most flood-tolerant species (for example, black willow, *Salix nigra*) growing at lower elevations that may be flooded nearly every year, often for weeks at a time. Trees that can stand relatively brief inundation (for example, hackberry) grow at higher elevations, often on natural levees and terraces. In the vicinity of St. Louis, where the flood rose higher and lasted longer than anywhere else, the tree mortality rate was 33.3 percent of the black willow and 99.4 percent of the hackberry trees (the highest mortality rate of any tree species).

The flood of 1993 lasted the entire growing season near St. Louis, and even though surface water may have drained from higher elevations by fall, the soils may have remained waterlogged and deoxygenated. Without oxygen, roots do not move water upward in the tree where it is needed in the leaves, and the tree dries out and dies. One of the strangest phenomena during the 1993 flood was the sight of trees standing in water with their leaves shriveling up and turning brown as though in a severe drought!

Regeneration. Because very large trees often survived, there will be a source of seeds to regenerate the forests. In fact, regeneration is likely to be accelerated in some areas where the competing understory vegetation was temporarily eliminated, where sunlight can reach the forest floor because of the death of some of the canopy trees, and where nutrient-rich sediments were deposited. Regeneration may not have to wait for the seeds produced in post-flood years; viable bur oak acorns and shellbark hickory (*Carya laciniosa*) nuts were found on the floodplain in 1994, even in the St. Louis vicinity, where flood duration and flood heights had been greatest. At least some nuts had not been carried away from the parent oak-hickory stands, perhaps because water current velocities had been relatively low deep in forests and because the forest litter of twigs and leaves had helped retain these heavy seeds.   The thick shells of the hickory nuts, in particular, seemed to have protected the inner seeds from water and rot. These observations suggest that oak-hickory forests will regenerate directly without passing through a pioneer willow-cottonwood stage that might be succeeded by hackberry-elm-silver maple, rather than oaks and hickories. Oak-hickory forests are valuable not only because of the hardwood lumber they can provide, but also because they provide nuts for squirrels, mallard ducks, and other wildlife.

In other types of forest near St. Louis, first-year seedlings of black willow, eastern cottonwood, and sycamore (*Platanus occidentalis*) were observed in 1994. These species ordinarily do not germinate and grow within forests where there is too much shade, but on mud flats along shorelines that are exposed as annual floods recede. Most of these shoreline seedlings are usually drowned or swept away by the next seasonal flood or scoured away by ice in winter. Occasional great floods are therefore necessary for cottonwoods, sycamores, and many other species to regenerate on ground high enough for them to reach maturity. Cottonwoods and sycamores are among the tallest (100-foot) trees to grow in the floodplain forest, and consequently they often provide rookery sites for herons and egrets and roosting sites for hawks and eagles.

Delayed mortality. Some of the mature trees that survived the 1993 flood were so weakened that they may succumb to insect attack, disease, and stress (drought or another flood) over the next few years. However, a more disturbing lag effect was noted on the Illinois River at several study sites near Havana, approximately 100 miles upriver from the confluence with the Mississippi. The height and duration of the 1993 flood was much less here than in the St. Louis area, but a much larger percentage of the flood-tolerant black willow died (perhaps as many as 90 percent). Even more disturbing is that much of the mortality occurred in 1994. The trees leafed out in the spring of 1994, then the leaves shriveled, and the trees died. Late in the summer, some of the trees showed signs of sprouting from the roots, so quantitative assessment of mortality will have to wait until the summer of 1995. A factor other than flood stress seems to be at work. The spring flood of 1994 was well within the average range, in terms of height and duration, and even at the Chautauqua National Wildlife Refuge along the river, where the water was intentionally drawn down with pumps during the summer growing season, most of the black willows still died back.

Among the possible factors that should be investigated are herbicides flushed into the river from farmland during rains. Goolsby et al. (1993) reported that the atrazine concentrations in the Illinois River at Valley City ranged from 1.97 to 2.87 parts per billion (ppb) between July 16 and July 26, 1993, and cyanazine concentrations ranged from 1.17 to 1.51 ppb. Although the U.S. Environmental Protection Agency (USEPA) has not established standards or criteria for most of the current generation of herbicides, the Canadian government has (Pauli et al.,

1991a, 1991b; Trotter et al., 1990). The Canadian aquatic life guidelines for atrazine and cyanazine are 2 ppb for each, and three of the four samples taken from the Illinois River during the flood exceeded the criterion for atrazine.

The dose of a toxicant depends not only on the concentration, but also on duration and repetition of exposure. Of all the floodplain trees, willows tend to be exposed to floodwaters the longest, because they grow at the lowest elevations. If the concentrations of atrazine in the Illinois River in July 1993 were typical of the rest of the flood period, then the willows were exposed to these levels throughout the entire growing season. Goolsby et al. (1993:3) point out that although the current generation of herbicides is biodegradable, they last "much longer in surface water than in the soil because surface water contains much less organic matter and fewer microorganisms to degrade the herbicides." If the herbicide concentrations in the Illinois River follow the same patterns observed downstream in the Mississippi and in other tributaries, then it is quite likely that the willows were dosed not only during much of the 1993 growing season, but again in the spring flood of 1994 (see Chapter 1). At Baton Rouge, LA, atrazine concentrations were 3.23 ppb when sampling began on July 7, 1993, remained above 2 ppb until July 26, and then declined slowly to 1.5 ppb on August 12, when sampling stopped (Goolsby et al., 1993). Even during years without great floods, covering the period 1978-1989, maximum atrazine levels during summer in the Mississippi River at Vicksburg, MS, generally ranged from 1.5 to 3 ppb, with a few values that ranged from 4 to 6 ppb (Tierney, 1992). In 1991, the four highest atrazine concentrations in the Mississippi River at Thebes, IL, ranged from 3.3 to 4.2 ppb, and from 1.3 to 2.6 ppb in 1992 (Goolsby et al., 1993:10).

Aquatic life standards are normally based on laboratory tests of single toxicants. However, plants in the river and its floodplain are exposed not just to one herbicide, but to several herbicides simultaneously. If the effects of individual herbicides are additive, then toxic effects could occur even if the individual herbicide concentrations do not exceed the criteria. The total concentration of the triazine family of herbicides (including atrazine, simazine, and propazine) reached peaks of 4 to 8 ppm from May to July in a tributary of the Illinois River (Sangamon River) during a study conducted in 1990 (Goolsby and Battaglin, 1993). In summary, some factor that interacted with the flooding in 1993 seems to be implicated in the die-back of most of the flood-tolerant black willows in the central reach of the Illinois River in 1994. Data from the Mississippi River and its tributaries suggest that herbicides should be investigated as a possible contributory factor that could be affecting aquatic and floodplain plant populations under more typical hydrologic regimes, not just during floods.

Pests and Introduced Species

Mosquitoes. The flood proved beneficial for several pest species, including some mosquitoes that are vectors of human disease (for example, the Asian tiger mosquito, *Aedes albopictus*, carries both St. Louis and La Crosse encephalitis).

The larvae of several species of mosquitoes thrive in temporary pools, water-filled containers, abandoned tires, and tree holes where their predators (primarily other insects and fish) cannot enter or survive. After the flood receded, there were water-filled scour holes at the bases of the trees in some of the forested floodplains. These may well have been good mosquito nurseries.

Facilitation of the Zebra Mussel Invasion. The European zebra mussel (Figure 6-7) was carried into the St. Lawrence-Great Lakes drainage system in the freshwater ballast of ocean-going ships in 1985 or 1986 (Marsden et al., 1991). The Great Lakes are connected to the Illinois River by man-made canals at Chicago, and the Illinois River is a tributary of the Mississippi. It was only a matter of time until zebra mussel larvae were carried downstream from Lake Michigan into the Illinois River and zebra mussel adults, which attach to boat hulls, were transported throughout the inland navigation system. Although scattered, low-density populations were reported from both the Upper Mississippi River and the Illinois River as early as 1991 (Marsden et al., 1991), the first population explosion, with densities approaching 100,000 mussels per square yard of river bottom, was reported in the Lower Illinois River during the flood of 1993 (Sparks, 1994).

Since population densities 160-180 miles upriver on the Illinois only ranged from 1 to 1,800 per square yard, it appeared that a pulse of mussel larvae had been carried from southern Lake Michigan or the Upper Illinois River far downstream by the high current velocity of the 1993 flood. This hypothesis was supported by the uniform, small size of the mussels found near the confluence with the Mississippi, which indicated that they had come from a larval settlement.

FIGURE 6-7 A group of zebra mussels attached to a native mussel extracted from the Illinois River near Havana, IL, in July 1993 (Illinois Natural History Survey).

Further upstream, the range of sizes among adults indicated they had settled out in different years. Larvae were carried far into the floodplain, where, in the autumn, duck hunters found adult mussels attached to trees and in the crops of waterfowl they shot. When the Mississippi rose and backed water far up tributary streams and rivers, it may have transported zebra mussels much farther up the tributaries than they would have gotten on their own. Zebra mussels do not spread readily upstream unaided, because the larvae drift downstream, and adults cannot move more than a few feet upstream unless they attach to boat hulls or are accidentally transported in bilge water or bait buckets.

Zebra mussels will have serious environmental and economic effects because they overgrow and kill native clams and mussels (Figure 6-7), plug engine cooling systems and municipal and industrial water intakes, and increase the water resistance of boat hulls, thereby increasing fuel and maintenance costs. Estimated annual costs for the chlorine alone that will be required to kill zebra mussels in industrial plants along the Illinois River are up to several hundred thousand dollars per plant.

The respiratory oxygen demands of the carpet of zebra mussels (averaging $61,000/yd^2$) in the Lower Illinois River may have contributed to low dissolved oxygen concentrations (1.7-3.0 ppm) in the summers of 1993 and 1994--well below the state water quality standard of 5.0 ppm. Rough calculations indicate that the mussels could consume 2.4 ppm of oxygen per mile of main channel. The low dissolved oxygen levels, coupled with warm summer temperatures, probably stressed native aquatic organisms, including native mollusks and fish, which were floating dead in substantial numbers during the summer of 1994. Zebra mussels evidently stressed themselves too because their populations at the confluence with the Mississippi fell to 657 per square yard by October 1994. Zebra mussel populations are likely to oscillate during the next few years, building up when oxygen levels recover and new larvae settle out, and then plummeting when the mussels become so dense that the oxygen levels drop. These next years will prove difficult for native aquatic organisms.

Release of Black Carp. In 1993, aquaculturists in Missouri imported the Asian black carp (*Mylopharyngodon piceus*), a mollusk-eating fish touted as a possible biological control for the zebra mussel (Trosclair, 1993), even though fishery biologists recommended that the fish not be introduced (French, 1993). Unfortunately, the aquaculture ponds were on a floodplain of the Osage River-- one of the rivers that flooded in 1993--and the black carp escaped into this Mississippi River tributary (UMRCC, 1994). Such introductions are unwise without careful evaluation because the introduced species may introduce its own parasites and diseases, compete with native fishes, and consume native mollusks already under siege by the zebra mussel. In this case, the introduction of the black carp was completely unnecessary because the native freshwater drum (*Aplodinotus grunniens*) and at least two other native fishes consume mollusks, as do native diving ducks.

Long-Range Effects: Nutrient Loads
and Hypoxic Zones in the Gulf of Mexico

Not only did low oxygen levels occur in the Lower Illinois River and in the waterlogged floodplain soils of Illinois and Missouri in 1993, but also 700 miles due south, off the coast of Louisiana, where the floodwaters of the Mississippi mixed with the saltwater of the Gulf. Nitrogen washed from the flooded agricultural fields in the Midwest stimulated plankton blooms along the Louisiana coast. When the blooms of algae died and sank, the decaying organic matter used up oxygen in the bottom layer of water, thereby lowering oxygen levels to less than 2 ppm over an area of about 6,000 square miles and threatening valuable fisheries (Turner and Rabalais, 1991, 1994). Where the Mississippi River exited the flood-affected region of the Upper Midwest at Thebes, IL, it was transporting approximately 22,000 tons of nitrate downstream to the Gulf every day during July 1993 compared with about 4,400 tons per day during more typical river flows in July 1991 (Taylor et al., 1994). Excessive nitrogen loading of the Gulf had been a problem in the past, and the dead zone averaged 3,000 to 4,000 square miles, but the size of this zone increased dramatically during the 1993 flood. Even worse, the dead zone remained larger in 1994 than in years prior to 1993, perhaps because some of the extra nitrogen delivered by the flood or some of the extra organic matter produced in the Gulf was stored over winter in bottom sediments and remobilized during the summer of 1994.

The 1993 flood did not initiate the dead zone, but did exacerbate and bring to public attention a river management, land use problem that has been building for decades. Delivery of nutrients to rivers has increased because of increasing use of fertilizers in upland watersheds and continual improvements in a man-made land drainage system of subsoil pipes in fields, storm sewers in urban and suburban areas, and channelized tributaries and rivers. During and after a rainstorm on a typical Corn Belt farm, some rain runs off into nearby drainage ditches while the rest percolates through the topsoil, picking up dissolved nutrients on its way to a network of subsurface perforated pipes that deliver both water and nutrients to the ditches. Although municipal waste treatment is improving, some cities still flush nutrient-laden sewage into rivers during rainstorms when overloaded sewers discharge storm drainage as well as sewage. More nutrients are added if nutrient-rich soil is added directly to the water by erosion of topsoil, streambeds, and banks. Simulation models using data on soil types, farming practices, and fertilizer application indicate that the nitrogen load at the mouth of the Mississippi has doubled or tripled over the presettlement load (Vorosmarty et al., 1986). In the flood-affected region, approximately 90 percent of the presettlement wetlands that would have removed some of the nutrients have been drained (National Research Council, 1992:276). Levees now isolate at least half the former floodplains along the Upper Mississippi River, the Illinois River, and the Missouri River that could have absorbed nutrients during floods and turned them into useful biomass (floodplain forests, fish, and wildlife). Even though these ecosystems have been altered, the remnants (and reservoir storage) still remove approximately 35 percent of the total nitrogen entering the Mississippi from its watershed (Vorosmarty et al., 1986), so nutrient loading of the Gulf probably will get worse if draining of wetlands and leveeing continue. At the last stop on the journey to the sea, the Mississippi Delta, levees no longer permit the nutrient-laden waters to spread over and nourish the wetlands that are the nurseries for fish and shellfish (Davis, 1995) Instead, the nutrients are piped between levees directly into the Gulf (as depicted in the political cartoon in Figure 12-8 in Chapter 12).

A nutrient asset has been turned into a nutrient liability by hundreds of thousands of seemingly beneficial independent actions over the last century. These actions culminate in a system that now leaches nutrients out of the Midwest and mainlines them directly into the Gulf of Mexico. It makes no sense economically or ecologically for the same river to simultaneously carry so many millions of tons of valuable nutrients in two opposite directions: upstream on fertilizer barges and downstream in the water. Perhaps by bringing this problem to public attention in such a spectacular way, the 1993 flood has sounded an alarm and thereby served to educate the public.

SUMMARY AND RECOMMENDATIONS

The flood of 1993 in the Upper Midwest was an economic disaster, but it was a boon to many plants and animals that live in the Missouri, Illinois, and Upper Mississippi Rivers. Even the few species that appear to have been harmed by the flood, such as some trees, may benefit in the long term. Any harm that did occur may have been more the result of human factors rather than the flood itself including: catastrophic failure of man-made levees, excessive loading of rivers with herbicides and of the Gulf of Mexico with agricultural fertilizers, widespread dispersal of introduced pests, and the excessive drawdown of the Mississippi River after the flood.

Floodplains are creations of alluvial rivers that regularly overflow their banks and deposit sediments in broad lateral valleys. During periods of low flow, typically in midsummer, the rivers occupy channels. During rainy seasons, the rivers rise onto their floodplains, recharging the floodplain wetlands, forests, and lakes with fresh supplies of water, nutrients, and sediments. During great floods, the floodplains do not merely store water, they become part of the flowing river itself, conveying water slowly downstream through the forests and marshes (see next part of this chapter for further information). Plant and animal species have adapted over time to exploit, tolerate, or escape seasonal floodpulses and exceptional great floods. The combination of the flood-adapted animals and plants, the seasonal floodpulses and great floods, the river and its channels, and the complex patchwork of floodplain habitats constitute the dynamic and phenomenonally productive river-floodplain ecosystem.

Every component of the river-floodplain ecosystem, from the bottom to the top of the food chain, responded to the exceptional flood of 1993. At the shallow margins of the flood, nutrients were apparently released from newly flooded soils, stimulating phytoplankton. Aquatic insects likewise concentrated in the shallow water, perhaps consuming either the plankton or the remains of flooded terrestrial vegetation. As the water rose along the Upper Mississippi River in Minnesota and Wisconsin, submergent aquatic plants grew so they could reach sunlight. Some native species, such as wild celery and water-stargrass, were evidently better adapted than an introduced pest, the Eurasian water milfoil; by the following summer, the native species had replaced the interloper in some back-waters. Farther downstream, where the flood rose higher and lasted longer, submersed aquatic plants virtually disappeared in deep areas in 1993, but regrew in most areas from tubers, rhizomes, and seeds in 1994. About 52 species of fishes representing 15 families evidently spawned on the floodplain during the flood. The abundant juvenile fish, in turn, became food for larger fish and fish-eating birds, such as herons and egrets.

The flood also took a toll of the longest-living organisms in the floodplain: trees. The average mortality among all species of trees along the Upper Mississippi ranged from undetectable in Minnesota to a high of 37 percent near St. Louis. Even in the case of the trees, however, the story is not over, nor is it all bad. Many seeds cannot germinate and grow in the shade of mature trees, so old trees must die before new ones can grow. Major natural disturbances, such as fires or floods, rejuvenate old forests.

More than natural forces were at work during the 1993 flood, however. Flood-tolerant black willows along the Illinois River leafed out in the spring of 1994, but the leaves subsequently shriveled and the trees died back to the roots. No one knows yet whether this is a delayed effect of the flood; perhaps the trees absorbed too much herbicide during the protracted inundation. A serious economic and environmental pest, the zebra mussel, washed from the Upper Illinois River downstream into the Lower Illinois and the Mississippi. The flood carried zebra mussel larvae far back into the floodplain and upstream into tributaries that were backed up by the mainstem rivers. Still another potential pest was introduced when a fish farm on a tributary of the Mississippi flooded out and Asian black carp escaped. It is ironic that sterile black carp were to be developed and tested as a zebra mussel control. Now fertile adult Asian black carp are free to consume endangered native mussels and clams and to compete with the native fishes and ducks that already consume zebra mussels.

The benefits of a slow-rising, natural floodpulse did not occur where levees failed catastrophically, sending a rush of water onto the floodplain that may have swept up terrestrial animals that would normally migrate out of the floodplain ahead of the flood. The full erosive power of the river was concentrated at the levee breaks, scouring out holes (often acres in size on the Lower Missouri River) that may subsequently serve as refuges for fish during low flow periods. Although fish will probably benefit from the scour holes along the Missouri, they did not benefit from another human-mediated action.

After the flood retreated in October, the U.S. Army Corps of Engineers opened gates in the navigation dam at St. Louis and kept the river lower than the normal level during November and December 1993. The purpose was to assist pumping and drainage of former floodplain lakes that had been surrounded by agricultural levees in the 1920s and subsequently drained, but had refilled when the levees broke in 1993. In order for the abundant 1993 crop of juvenile fish to survive the first critical winter of their lives, they needed wintering areas in backwaters and floodplain lakes. The lowered water levels may have stranded fish or trapped them in shallow backwaters where oxygen levels declined or the water froze from top to bottom.

The flood affected distant ecosystems. About 700 miles south of the rain-soaked Midwest, approximately 22,000 tons of nitrate passed into the Gulf every day in July, stimulating plankton blooms. When the plankton died and sank, the decaying organic matter used up oxygen in the bottom layer of water, lowering oxygen levels over an area of 6,000 square miles and threatening valuable fisheries. This "dead zone" remained larger in the summer of 1994 than it had been prior to 1993, perhaps because some of the extra nitrogen delivered by the flood or the extra organic matter produced in the Gulf was stored over winter in bottom sediments and remobilized in 1994. Additional information about other effects created by the enormous flow of floodwaters into the Gulf is presented in Chapter 5.

Lessons Learned

The flood taught a number of valuable lessons. Lesson one is that it is a bad idea to quarantine introduced aquatic species on floodplains. Lesson two is that floods can facilitate pest invasions. A plan to prevent the introduction of aquatic pests and to limit the dispersal of pests already here should be formulated and implemented. The aquatic pest prevention and containment plan should be part of a much more comprehensive plan to reduce future flood damages and to protect, maintain, and recover valuable natural services and functions of the large river-floodplain ecosystems. Data collected during the flood of 1993 indicated what these functions are and how they are maintained by seasonal floods and occasional great floods. Much more could have been learned had the sampling been planned in advance and then triggered by the flood. There is still much that can be learned if measurements continue to document the rejuvenation of the floodplain forests, the fate of the 1993 year class of fishes produced on the floodplain, the relationship between river-borne nutrients and the dead zone in the Gulf, and the unexpected legacies and lag effects that are sure to turn up. Events such as the 1993 flood happen rarely but are extremely important in the behavior of river-floodplain ecosystems, which is why plans should be formulated now for opportunistic sampling during the next great flood or drought that is sure to occur. It's just a matter of time. But exactly how much time remains to be seen.

Recommendations

Large river-floodplain ecosystems provide valuable hydrological and ecological services and functions, including flood storage and conveyance; maintenance of biodiversity; retention, recycling, and conversion of potentially polluting nutrients into useful biomass; production of fish, wildlife, and forests; and corridors for migratory fish and wildlife. The master variables that regulate and maintain these ecosystems are annual floodpulses that promote exchanges of water, sediment, nutrients, and organisms between the rivers and their floodplains, and infrequent great floods and droughts that maintain habitat and species diversity through disturbance. *The 1993 flood illuminated the fact that a careful balance should be struck between controlling variation for navigation and flood protection and capitalizing on natural variation to sustain and recover beneficial services.* Otherwise, increasing human resources will be required to mitigate impacts and maintain a valuable ecosystem that could maintain itself, and the risk of ecosystem degradation or even collapse will increase.

First and foremost, *a comprehensive ecosystem management plan should be developed to reduce future flood damages, accommodate navigation, and to maintain and recover the valuable natural services and functions of the large river-floodplain ecosystems in the region affected by the 1993 flood.* One objective of such a comprehensive plan should be to restore the seasonal connection between the rivers and their floodplains by lowering or breaching levees that are economically unjustifiable and where landowners are willing to sell out or accept a more flood-adapted use of the land (grazing, floodplain forest, recreational use, biomass crops for energy production, etc.). The system of subsidized levee construction and repair, disaster assistance, flood insurance, set-aside payments, conservation reserve payments, and commodity price supports should be restructured to support this objective. For example, landowners who agree to flood-adapted land uses or lower levees (e.g., that protect against a 10-year flood) might be compensated for income loss when their land is used for flood storage and conveyance.

A second objective would be to operate the navigation dams for environmental benefits, as well as for navigation. In years with typical seasonal water regimes, dams should be operated to maintain the floodpulse advantage (the flood-induced boost in fish yield) and other natural benefits subject to constraints imposed by the need to maintain navigation. In years with exceptional floods, such as 1973, 1982, and 1993, the navigation dams should not be used after the flood to lower water levels so quickly and to such an extreme that the floodpulse advantage is lost. Environmental rehabilitation and lock and dam rehabilitation should be jointly and opportunistically planned to take advantage of droughts so river reaches can be drawn down to expose mud flats, to dry and compact sediments, and to stimulate regeneration of vegetation. These recommendations should be developed as part of the Corps of Engineers' ongoing navigation expansion plan.

The flood of 1993 exacerbated several pre-existing environmental problems in need of attention.

1. It facilitated the spread of a serious economic and environmental pest, the European zebra mussel, that was accidentally introduced to the St. Lawrence-Great Lakes drainage by transoceanic ships and may well have facilitated other introduced pests, such as the Asian tiger mosquito.
2. Nutrient loading of the Gulf of Mexico was exceptionally high because of the 1993 flood, and the summer dead zone in the Gulf consequently expanded, with potential detrimental impacts on the largest fishery in the lower 48 states. The effect persisted into the summer of 1994.
3. Maximum atrazine concentrations in the Mississippi River and several tributaries exceeded the Canadian guidelines for aquatic life both during the 1993 flood and in previous years (the USEPA has not established its own guidelines). Delayed die-back of flood-tolerant black willows (in the spring of 1994) and failure of submergent aquatic plants to recolonize a 200-mile reach of the Illinois River where they died out in the late 1950s may be related to more than just water fluctuations and turbidity that collectively reduces light penetration.

The upstream source population of zebra mussels that seeded the lower Illinois River and the Mississippi River needs to be identified. Then, a dispersal barrier for the zebra mussels and the other introduced pests that are now in the Great Lakes, might be created by using chemical, ultrasound, or thermal treatment in the lock chambers or other constricted points within the man-made connection between the Great Lakes-St. Lawrence Drainage and the Mississippi Drainage.

Congress should extend the law requiring ocean-going ships to exchange freshwater ballast with seawater to all ports, (the law currently applies just to the St. Lawrence Seaway, even though pests can enter the United States through many ports, including New Orleans). Border protection against biological invasions is a federal responsibility. Also, GATT and NAFTA, by increasing world trade, will increase the rate of introduction of new pests. The planned expansion of the federal inland navigation system will increase the dispersal of the pests once they are in the United States.

Another necessary action relates to aquatic species. *Congress should regulate the intentional introduction of certain aquatic species (common carp, grass carp, bighead carp, black carp, Asiatic clams, and their associated parasites and diseases).* Again, border protection, import regulation, and regulation of inter-state commerce are federal responsibilities.

Government incentives, programs, and authorizations should be restructured to reduce the leaching of nutrients from the Midwest and the resulting excessive nutrient loading of the Louisiana coastal zone. Methods should be developed to reduce nutrient losses from soils while maintaining crop yields. Riparian zones, floodplains, and the Mississippi Delta should be used to remove nutrients from rivers and convert them to useful biomass before the nutrients reach the sea.

The U.S. Environmental Protection Agency should establish aquatic life criteria for modern herbicides that are in common use. The causes of delayed mortality in black willow in the Illinois River following the flood of 1993 and the factors that still prevent submergent aquatic plants from recolonizing a 200-mile reach of the river following a die-off in the late 1950s should be identified and controlled before the problem expands elsewhere in the Mississippi system.

The river-floodplain ecosystems we observe and manage today are products of disturbances that occurred before our time. Terrible as the destruction of the 1993 flood was, it was also an opportunity to learn much more about an ecosystem that sustains thousands of species, ranging from migratory waterfowl that breed in the far north, to the valuable fish and shellfish in the Gulf of Mexico that depend upon the supply of fresh water, sediment, and nutrients to the productive wetlands and coastal zone of the Mississippi Delta. A flood as big as the one that occurred in 1993 may not occur again in the lifetime of the current generation of river scientists. It is important to capitalize on this opportunity with long-term, follow-up measurements, and to prepare for the next opportunity.

Responsible federal agencies (the National Science Foundation, the U.S. Geological Survey, and the National Biological Service), universities, and state agencies should track the long-term effects of the 1993 flood on the Mississippi River system and the Gulf of Mexico. They can sponsor or undertake long-term measurements and analysis as part of a coordinated, cooperative program. The resulting data should be kept in a computerized, readily accessible form, and made available to all investigators. The data collected by the Scientific Assessment and Strategy Team of the Interagency Floodplain Management Review Committee should also be maintained on the same system. The same cooperators should plan a comprehensive sampling program to be triggered by the next major natural or human disturbance (flood, drought, repeat of the New Madrid, MO, earthquake, or catastrophic spill) in the Mississippi system.

REFERENCES

Battaglin, W.A., D.A. Goolsby, and R.H. Coupe, 1993: Annual use and transport of agricultural chemicals in the Mississippi River, 1991-92. In D.A. Goolsby et al. (eds.), *Selected Papers on Agricultural Chemicals in Water Resources of the Midcontinental United States.* U.S. Geological Survey Open-File Report 93-418: 26-38.

Bayley, P.B., and D.C. Dowling, 1990: *Gear Efficiency Calibrations for Stream and River Sampling.* Illinois Natural History Survey Aquatic Ecology Technical Report 90/8, Champaign, IL, 51 pp.

Bayley, P.B., 1991: The flood pulse advantage and the restoration of river-floodplain systems. *Regulated Rivers Research and Management,* 6, 75-86.

Bellrose, F.C., S.P. Havera, F.R. Paveglio, and D.W. Steffeck, 1979: *The Fate of Lakes in the Illinois River Valley.* Illinois Natural History Survey Biological Notes 119.

Connell, J.H., 1978: Diversity in tropical rain forests and coral reefs. *Science,* 199, 1302-1309.

Davis, M., 1995: Personal Communication, Coalition to Restore Coastal Louisiana, Baton Rouge, LA.

Fremling, C.R., J.L.Rasmussen, R.E. Sparks, S.P. Cobb, C.F. Bryan, and T.O. Claflin, 1989: Mississippi River fisheries: a case history. *Proceedings of the International Large River Symposium (LARS),* Canadian Special Publication of Fisheries and Aquatic Sciences, 106, 309-351.

French, J.R.P., III, 1993: How well can fishes prey on zebra mussels in Eastern North America? *Fisheries,* 18, 13-19.

Goolsby, D.A., and W.A. Battaglin, 1993: Occurrence, distribution, and transport of agricultural chemicals in surface waters of the Midwestern United States. In D.A. Goolsby et al. (eds.), *Selected papers on Agricultural Chemicals in Water Resources of the Midcontinental United States,* U.S.Geological Survey Open-File Report 93-418, 1-24.

Goolsby, D.A., W.A. Battaglin, and E.M. Thurman, 1993: *Occurrence and Transport of Agricultural Chemicals in the Mississippi River Basin. July through August 1993.* U.S. Geological Survey Circular 1120-C, U.S. Government Printing Office, Denver, CO, 22 pp.

Hajic, E.R., 1990: *Late Pleistocene and Holocene Landscape Evolution, Depositional Subsystems, and Stratigraphy in the Lower Illinois River Valley and Adjacent Central Mississippi River Valley.* Ph.D. thesis, University of Illinois, Champaign, 301 pp.

Junk, W., P.B. Bayley, and R.E. Sparks, 1989: The flood pulse concept in river-flood plain systems. *Proceedings of the International Large River Symposium (LARS),* Canadian Special Publication of Fisheries and Aquatic Sciences, 106, 110-127.

Kalliola, R., J. Salo, M. Puhakka, and M. Rajasilta, 1991: New site formation and colonizing vegetation in primary succession on the western Amazon floodplains. *Journal of Ecology,* 79, 877-901.

Maher, R.J., 1995: *Observations of Fish Community Structure and Reproductive Success in Flooded Terrestrial Habitats During an Extreme Flood Event on the Lower Illinois River.* National Biological Survey, Environmental Management Technical Center, Onalaska, WI, Long Term Resource Monitoring Program Technical Report, LTRMP 95-T (in press).

Marsden, J.E., R.E. Sparks, and K.D.Blodgett, 1991: Overview of the Zebra Mussel invasion: Biology, impacts and projected spread. *Proceedings of the 1991 Governor's Conference on Management of the Illinois River System,* October 22-23, 1991, Peoria, IL, 88-95.

Mills, H.B., W.C. Starrett, and F.C. Bellrose, 1966: *Man's Effect on the Fish and Wildlife of the Illinois River.* Illinois Natural History Survey Biological Notes No. 57, Urbana, IL, 24 pp.

Moyle, P.B., and B. Herbold, 1987: Life-history patterns and community structure in stream fishes of western North America: comparisons with eastern North America and Europe. In W. J. Matthews, and D. C. Heins (eds), *Community and Evolutionary Ecology of North American Stream Fishes*. University of Oklahoma Press, Norman, OK, 25-32.

National Research Council, 1992: Restoration of Aquatic Ecosystems. *Science, technology, and public policy,* National Academy Press, Washington, DC, 552 pp.

Nelson, J., 1994: Personal communication, Long Term Resource Monitoring Program-Reach 26, Alton, IL.

Neves, R.J., 1993: A state-of-the-unionids address. In K.S. Cummings, A.C.Buchanan, and L.M. Koch (eds.), *Proceedings of An Upper Mississippi River Conservation Committee Symposium, Conservation and Management of Freshwater Mussels*, October 12-14, 1992, St. Louis, MO, 1-10.

Pauli, B.D., R.A. Kent, and M.P. Wong, 1991a: *Canadian Water Quality Guidelines for Cyanazine: Ottawa.* Environment Canada, Scientific Series 180, 26 pp.

Pauli, B.D., R.A. Kent, and M.P. Wong, 1991b: *Canadian Water Quality Guidelines for Simazine: Ottawa.* Environment Canada, Scientific Series 187, 29 pp.

Persat, H., H.M. Olivier, and D. Pont, 1994: Theoretical habitat templets, species traits, and species richness: fish in the Upper Rhone River and its floodplain. *Freshwater Biology,* 31, 439-454.

Raibley, P.T., 1995: Personal communication, Long Term Resource Monitoring Program, Havana, IL.

Ratcliff, E.N., and C.H. Theiling, 1995: *Water Quality Characteristics during and prior to an Extreme Flood on the Lower Illinois River.* National Biological Survey, Environmental Management Technical Center, Onalaska, WI, Long Term Resource Monitoring Program Technical Report, LTRMP 95-T (in press).

Salo, J., R. Kalliola, I. Hakkinen, Y. Makinen, P. Niemela, M. Puhakka, and P.D. Coley, 1986: River dynamics and the diversity of Amazon lowland forest. *Nature,* 322, 254-258.

Saucier, R.T. 1974: *Quaternary geology of the Lower Mississippi Valley.* Arkansas Archeological Survey Research Series, No. 6, 1-23.

Sparks, R.E., 1994: *Zebra Mussels in Rivers.* Illinois Natural History Survey Reports, No. 3225, Champaign, IL, 3-4.

Sparks, R.E., 1995: Need for ecosystem management of large rivers and their floodplains. *BioScience,* 45 (in press).

Sparks, R.E., P.B. Bayley, S.L. Kohler, and L.L. Osborne, 1990: Disturbance and recovery of large floodplain rivers. *Environmental Management,* 14, 699-709.

Spink, A., and S. Rogers, 1995: The effects of the flood of 1993 on the vegetation of the Upper Mississippi River System: some preliminary findings.

Stanford, J.A., and J.V. Ward, 1983: Insect species diversity as a function of environmental variability and disturbance in stream systems. In J.R. Barnes, and G.W. Minshall (eds.), *Stream Ecology: Application and Testing of General Ecological Theory,* Plenum Press, NY, 265-268.

Taylor, H.E., R.C. Antweiler, T.I. Brinton, D.A. Roth, and J.A. Moody, 1994: *Major Ions Nutrients and Trace Elements in the Upper Mississippi River Basin July through September 1993.* U.S. Geological Survey Circular 1120-D, U.S. Government Printing Office, Denver, CO, 21 pp.

Theiling, C.T., J.K. Tucker, and P.A. Gannon, 1995: *Nektonic Invertebrate Distribution and Abundance during Prolonged Summer Flooding on the Lower Illinois River*. National Biological Survey, Environmental Management Technical Center, Onalaska, WI, Long Term Resource Monitoring Program Technical Report, LTRMP 95-T (in press).

Tierney, D.P., 1992: *A Review of Historical Surface Water Monitoring for Atrazine in the Mississippi, Missouri, and Ohio rivers, 1975-1991*. Ciba Geigy Corporation, Technical Report 6-92, Greensboro, NC, 69 pp.

Trosclair, C., 1993: Three U.S. fish farms preparing to spawn black carp for use against zebra mussels. *Water Farming Journal*, May, p.3.

Trotter, D.M., A. Baril, M.P. Wong, and R.A. Kent, 1990: *Canadian Water Quality Guidelines for Atrazine: Ottawa*. Environment Canada, Scientific Series 168, 106 pp.

Turgeon, D.D., A.E. Bogan, E.V. Coan, W. Emerson, W.G. Lyons, W.L. Pratt, C.E. Roper, A. Scheltema, F.G. Thompson, and J.D. Williams, 1988: Common and Scientific Names of Aquatic Invertebrates from the United States and Canada: Mollusks. *American Fisheries Society Special Publication 16*, 1-277.

Turner, R.E., and N.N. Rabalais, 1991: Changes in Mississippi River water quality this century. Implications for coastal food webs. *BioScience,* 41, 140-147.

Turner, R.E., and N.N. Rabalais, 1994: Coastal eutrophication near the Mississippi River Delta. *Nature,* 368, 619-621.

Upper Mississippi River Conservation Committee (UMRCC), 1994: Black carp escapes to Missouri waters. *Upper Mississippi River Conservation Committee Newsletter*, March/April, Rock Island, IL, p.11.

Vorosmarty, C.J., M.P. Gildea, B.C. Moore, B.J. Peterson, B. Bergquist, and J.M. Melillo, 1986: A global model of nutrient cycling: II. Aquatic processing, retention and distribution of nutrients in large drainage basins." In D. L. Correll, ed., *Watershed Research Perspectives*. Smithsonian Environmental Research Center, Washington, DC, 32-53.

Welcomme, R.L., 1979: *Fisheries Ecology of Floodplain Rivers*. Longman, Inc., NY, NY, 317 pp.

Yin, Y., J.C. Nelson, and G.V. Swenson, 1995: *Tree Mortality and Flooding During 1993 in the Upper Mississippi River Valley*. National Biological Survey, Environmental Management Technical Center, Onalaska, WI, Long Term Resource Monitoring Program Tech. Report, LTRMP 95-T (in press).

7

Impacts on Agricultural Production: Huge Financial Losses Lead to New Policies

Thomas P. Zacharias

INTRODUCTION

The Great Flood of 1993 had tremendous impacts on Midwestern agriculture, and financial losses exceeded those of all other sectors (see Chapter 9). The impacts flowed through every facet of agriculture beginning with sizable erosion of soils, fertilizers, and herbicides (as discussed in Chapter 5). Extreme wetness and flooding severely reduced crop yields, and this affected farmers and their families (as discussed in Chapter 10). The ensuing impacts hampered Midwestern agribusinesses and shippers (discussed in Chapters 8 and 9), affected the grain market, and ultimately influenced federal agricultural policies. This assessment focuses on the farming activities and the corn and soybean crops in the Midwest (Illinois, Iowa, Minnesota, Missouri, and Wisconsin), and the chapter begins with a chronology of events that affected agricultural practices and crop development during the growing season, followed by a discussion of the resulting effects on crop yields, the crop insurance industry, the commodity market, total grain production, and losses suffered by the agricultural sector. Finally, there is a discussion of a major outcome of the flood: its effect on U.S. policy addressing weather-induced losses to agriculture.

THE 1993 GROWING SEASON

April: Wet Field Conditions

April precipitation across the Upper Mississippi basin was about 4 inches (1 inch above average). Soil moisture conditions prior to April 1 were reported as surplus (see Figure 3-7), and this excess coupled with above average precipitation resulted in planting delays in corn across the five-state region. The *Weekly Weather and Crop Bulletin* reported on April 7, 1993, that early tillage and fertilizer applications "were behind normal for all areas." Fertilizer applications and seedbed preparations in Iowa were 50 percent behind schedule.

By late April, spring tillage and planting activities throughout the Midwest were falling behind schedule. Field preparation normally 75 percent complete in Iowa was 25 percent complete on April 30. Spring tillage in Wisconsin was 9 percent complete compared to the norm of 26 percent. Minnesota reported completion of only 5 percent field preparation for corn compared to 28 percent under average conditions. For the week ending April 25, farmers across Illinois, Iowa, Minnesota, and Wisconsin reported no corn planting activity for the month even though 25 percent of the corn in Illinois and 8 percent of the corn in Iowa is usually planted by this date. Missouri reported 3 percent of its corn crop planted by April 30, compared to an average of 34 percent.

May: Wet Planting Conditions Followed by Drier Weather

Midwest tillage operations and planting were substantially behind schedule according to the May 4, 1993, *Weekly Weather and Crop Bulletin* covering conditions during the week ending May 2. Fertilizer applications and preparation for Iowa should have been 85 percent complete, but reports indicated completion of only 30 percent. Minnesota's ground preparation for corn was only 16 percent complete compared to a normal of 50 percent, and the state's soybean tillage was 4 percent complete, much behind the average of 15 percent. Wisconsin farmers reported completion of 10 percent of intended tillage (normally about 50 percent) on May 2.

The majority of the corn crop in Iowa, southern Minnesota, southwestern Wisconsin, and the northern two-thirds of Illinois is typically planted during the first two weeks of May. Corn in the lower tier of Missouri and southern Illinois is planted during the last half of April and after mid-May in the remaining portions of Minnesota and Wisconsin. Soybeans are planted after corn, beginning before May 5 (southern Illinois and most of Missouri), between May 5-15 (southern Minnesota, Iowa, and the upper tier of Missouri), and after mid-May (southern Wisconsin)

The majority of corn grown in the Midwest is planted by the middle of May, but this was not the case in 1993: Illinois, Iowa, Minnesota, and Wisconsin reported less than 5 percent of their corn acres planted by mid-May. Normal mid-May conditions range from 20 percent (Minnesota) to 50 percent complete (Illinois and Missouri). Some soybean planting also usually occurs during mid-May. Table 7-1 contains the 1993 corn and soybean planting activity reports for the middle two weeks of May as compared to average conditions. The Corn Belt was far behind. Only 40 percent of the nation's corn crop, rather than the normal 80 percent, had been planted by mid-May, with the delay largely due to conditions in the Midwest.

TABLE 7-1 State Percentages of Acreage Planted for May 9 and 16, 1993 (Source: *Weekly Weather and Crop Bulletins*, May 11 and May 18, 1993)

	Crop	1993 percent	Average percent
May 9	*Corn planted*		
Illinois		4	73
Iowa		7	65
Minnesota		18	54
Missouri		13	67
Wisconsin		8	30
	Soybeans planted		
Illinois		0	20
Iowa		0	11
Minnesota		3	14
Missouri		0	10
May 16			
	Corn planted		
Illinois		41	86
Iowa		20	84
Minnesota		34	76
Missouri		16	76
Wisconsin		21	60
	Soybeans planted		
Illinois		5	44
Iowa		5	33
Minnesota		9	37
Missouri		1	20

In the five-state region, less than 20 percent of the corn crop had been planted by May 9, whereas well over 50 percent of the region is normally planted. Soybean planting was also experiencing similar delays. Generally, one-third of the soybean crop is planted by mid-May, but reports indicated that approximately 5 percent of the crop was planted. In general, the corn crop was estimated as two weeks behind average conditions. However, crops in the eastern Corn Belt (Indiana and Ohio) were making favorable progress.

When weather conditions improved during the last two weeks of May, there was a rapid increase in tillage operations, fertilizer applications, and planting. Iowa reported seedbed preparation and fertilizer application as 75 percent complete on May 31 compared to 100 percent under normal conditions. For the week ending May 30, 1993, the U.S. corn crop was one week behind schedule. Planting in the five-state region was now 80 percent complete compared to more than 90 percent under typical conditions.

Crop rating and crop progress reports became available for corn in late May. Corn height in Illinois fields was reported at 2 inches compared to an average growth of 7 inches. Normally 80 percent of corn in Iowa and Minnesota has emerged by May 30, but only 40 percent had appeared. Early crop ratings for Illinois, Iowa, and Wisconsin reported the majority of the corn crop in "good" condition with about 30 percent listed as "fair."

June: Planting Completed under Cool, Very Wet Weather

Corn planting in the Midwest is normally completed by the end of May or early June. Rapid planting in late May meant that 90 percent of the corn crop was planted by June 6 (*Weekly Weather and Crop Bulletin*, June 8). Soybeans are typically 85 percent planted by early June in Illinois, Iowa, and Minnesota; but by June 6, 1993, 71 percent of the soybeans in Illinois were planted, 45 percent in Iowa, and 61 percent in Minnesota. Iowa reported no first-time cultivations of planted fields compared to 33 percent under normal conditions. Crop emergence in Minnesota was well behind its normal pace: 59 percent emergence of corn (89 percent is average) and 23 percent emergence of soybeans (67 percent is average).

The first official corn crop condition report (issued June 8) for all major corn producing states revealed that the impact of the Great Flood of 1993, and its accompanying excessive moisture conditions, were not being uniformly felt across the Corn Belt. For example, 76 percent of the Illinois corn crop was rated "good to excellent," whereas more than 60 percent of the crops in Iowa, Minnesota, Missouri, and Wisconsin were rated "fair to poor."

Things got worse when excessive rain fell across the five-state study region during mid-June (see Figure 3-4a in Chapter 3). Ultimately the region's June 1993 rainfall amounted to 7.9 inches, double the normal amount. Soil moisture values across the entire region remained excessive by July 1 (see Figure 3-7e).

Temperatures were somewhat below normal, making the cumulative growing degree-day index well below average for much of the region. For example, Mason City in north-central Iowa reported 664 growing degree-days by June 30, 200 days below normal. The corn crop was not progressing as fast as usual. Missouri was 10 percent behind in growing degree-day accumulation, Wisconsin was 15 percent behind, and Illinois was 5 to 10 percent behind.

Extreme moisture conditions in June coupled with the progressive decline in cumulative growing degree-days resulted in two problems: poor crop conditions and the inability to manage the crops in the field. Iowa reported only 1 percent first-time cultivations of cornfields compared to an average of 54 percent. Similar cultivation reports for Minnesota and Wisconsin indicated field operations were roughly 70 percent behind schedule. Normal corn plant height in late June for Minnesota and Wisconsin is about 15 inches, but heights ranged from 5 to 7 inches. Flooding had become a major problem at lowland farms in river valleys

FIGURE 7-1 Flooded farmland along the Illinois River (Illinois State Water Survey).

along the rivers in Minnesota, North Dakota, Wisconsin, Iowa, and Illinois (Figure 7-1).

The soybean crop was also suffering. Under normal conditions for mid- to late-June, soybeans should be 80 to 90 percent emerged, but emergence was only 40 to 50 percent in Iowa and Minnesota in late June. Both Illinois and Iowa were reporting large acreages of soybean replants during this period, necessitated by overly wet field conditions. Interestingly, the June 29 *Weekly Weather and Crop Bulletin* rated the majority of the corn and soybean crops for the five-state region "fair to good." The most pessimistic crop condition report was for Minnesota: only 16 percent of the corn crop was in "good" condition, with 79 percent "fair to poor." Farm flooding had become a major issue in the Midwest (Figure 7-2).

July: Weather and Crop Conditions Worsen

As was the case for June, all-time record-high rainfall occurred again in July (see Table 3-1). July precipitation for the Upper Mississippi basin averages about 4 inches compared with 8.03 inches in July 1993, and July mean temperatures were generally cooler than average. However, the below-normal departures of the cumulative corn growing degree-days improved relative to their status in June. Corn growing degree-days in Illinois and Missouri were nearly normal by July 31, but the corn crop was still behind schedule in Iowa, Minnesota, and Wisconsin. The July 7 *Weekly Weather and Crop Bulletin* pronounced the majority of the Midwest's corn and soybeans were "fair to good," but things were

FIGURE 7-2 The plight of Midwestern farmers was a subject of the cartoonists in major news-papers (reprinted by permission: Tribune Media Services).

worse in some areas. For example, 45 percent of Minnesota's crops were "poor to very poor."

As July progressed and heavy rainfall continued across the Corn Belt, crop conditions deteriorated across most of the five-state region, except for the eastern half of Illinois where rainfall was not as heavy. Virtually every crop status report published during mid-July indicated that most of the corn and soybean crops experienced negative weather impacts. Minnesota and Wisconsin reported crop height for both corn and soybeans at 50 percent of normal.

Corn silking is generally well underway by mid-July across the Corn Belt, but for the week ending July 18, silking was only 20 percent complete for Illinois and Missouri, versus 60 percent under normal conditions (*Weekly Weather and Crop Bulletin,* July 20). Minnesota, Wisconsin, and Iowa reported less than 1 percent silking. Typically these states report 15 to 30 percent silking during this period.

Soybean status reports for mid-July indicated that less than 3 percent of the region's soybean crop had set pods compared to 10 to 15 percent in an average year. The July 20 *Weekly Weather and Crop Bulletin* rated overall soybean progress at 30 percent below normal.

By July 31, wide spatial differences in crop progress were becoming very apparent across the region. Almost 80 percent of the Illinois corn crop was rated "good to excellent," with 65 percent of the soybean crop comparably rated. In contrast, 80 percent of the corn and soybean crops in Missouri and Wisconsin were rated only "fair to good," and 85 percent of the corn and soybean crops in Iowa and Minnesota were rated "fair to very poor." Late July reports for Iowa and Minnesota indicated that only 20 percent of the corn crop had achieved normal tasseling compared to 60 percent in Missouri, which was farther along because of warmer temperatures. The conditions were well expressed in the following story from the *Wall Street Journal* (Taylor, July 28, 1993a).

As farmers in such flood-ravaged states as Iowa and Kansas bemoan their stunted plants and muddy fields, many in Illinois, Indiana, and Ohio are raising bumper crops. And western farmers have taken additional beatings at the Board of Trade, while their eastern counterparts have used the market to make big profits.

'The only real problem I'll have is the Internal Revenue Service--I'll make too much,' says Mike Wells, who farms 1,200 acres near Morris, IL. Mr. Wills estimates that his positions at the CBOT will add as much as $54,000 to what he earns selling his big crop of soybeans this year.

Galen Isley, a farmer who raises corn and soybeans near rain-drenched Cedar Falls, IA, isn't as lucky. Mr. Isley has been using a CBOT investing strategy that reaped big profits in the past. But this year, he says, his positions in corn and soybean options have produced thousands of dollars in losses. 'If it had been a normal year, I'd have been in good shape,' he lamented.

August: Crop and Weather Conditions Improve

Precipitation was above average in August, but the big impacts on the region's two major crops were soggy conditions and below-normal growing degree-days during June and July, which would have a lasting impact on the region's crops for the remainder of the growing season. Crop moisture indices in August were well above "standard" levels, indicating excessive moisture. For example, the Palmer moisture value of "4" is considered to define an "extreme moist spell," and most areas in Iowa had higher Palmer values of "6." In early August, most crop reporting districts in the five-state region were well above a Palmer index of "3" indicative of a "very moist spell." Figure 3-7 (in Chapter 3) shows that on August 1, many Midwestern soils were nearly at field capacity at a time when they are normally quite dry due to the evapotranspiration from the growing crops. Interestingly, cumulative corn growing degree-days by the end of August were close to normal: Illinois and Missouri were slightly above average in growing degree-day accumulations, Minnesota was just below average, and Iowa and Wisconsin were 5 to 10 percent behind schedule.

In early August, progress of corn silking was "favorable" for Illinois and Missouri, but corn tasseling was considerably behind schedule in Iowa and Minnesota. The dough stage of corn was behind schedule in all five states. Progress of soybean blooming was favorable across the region, but pod-setting was well behind normal. In general, crop conditions indicated that corn and soybeans had stabilized during August and were showing some improvement. Corn crop conditions remained stable in Illinois and Missouri, with slight improvements reported in Iowa and Minnesota. Essentially, less corn in the Midwest was rated as "very poor" and "poor," shifting to more ratings of "fair and good" as August ended.

August soybean reports indicated more favorable progress. All five states reported soybean shifts from "fair" to "good" and shifts from "poor" to "fair." For example, 58 percent of Wisconsin soybeans were rated "good to excellent" in early August, 83 percent by late August. By the end of the month, the corn crop was a week or two behind average, and soybeans were just over a week behind in development.

September: Cool, Wet Conditions Affect Harvest

September 1993 was generally cooler than normal. Although growing degree-day accumulations stabilized across the region during August, September growing degree-day accumulations declined markedly in relative terms. Precipitation levels varied across the region in contrast to the overall cooler-than-normal conditions. Illinois and Missouri both experienced above-normal rainfall, whereas normal amounts were recorded in Wisconsin and Minnesota. Rainfall across Iowa varied from much below to above average.

September weather conditions also caused crop conditions to vary across the region: crops in certain states tended to stabilize, while conditions in other areas either improved or deteriorated. Wisconsin's corn and soybean conditions remained very stable during September, with 90 percent of both crops rated "fair to good." For Illinois, 77 percent of both crops were rated "good" by the end of September, an increase of 7 percent from the start of the month. Conditions in Iowa were stable through September with just under 70 percent of the corn crop rated "fair to good," but soybean conditions declined somewhat from early to late September. Beginning and ending reports for Minnesota revealed crop condition shifts: there were notable increases in the percentages of corn and soybeans rated "poor to very poor." For example, 63 percent of the corn was rated "poor to very poor" on September 30 compared to 55 percent on September 1. Early September reports in Missouri rated 38 percent of the corn crop "good to excellent" with 42 percent rated "fair." By late September, these values had shifted dramatically, with only 26 percent rated "good to excellent" and 54 percent rated "fair." Missouri soybeans remained reasonably stable.

September marks the start of the harvest period in the Corn Belt. The corn and soybean harvest moves northward across the five-state region, and except for southern Missouri, the soybean harvest[1] generally begins and is completed before the corn harvest. As farmers formulate their harvest expectations, fear of an early killing frost becomes a major concern. Due to delayed crop growth and maturity in 1993, this concern had been recognized by market participants and reactions realized in higher grain prices had occurred (Taylor, *Wall Street Journal,* August 27, 1993; Long, *Kansas City Star*, September 28, 1993). First fall freeze dates normally occur in early to mid-October for most of the Corn Belt, but no frost damage occurs once both crops have reached maturity.

With respect to the schedule for soybean harvesting, roughly 1 percent of the crop was harvested for the five-state study region during September, compared to 15 percent under typical conditions. Cold air brought below-normal temperatures into the Upper Midwest during late September. Widespread damaging frosts were reported on September 30 and October 2 in Wisconsin and Minnesota, respectively (*Weekly Weather and Crop Bulletin*, October 5), ending the growing season in these states. According to one Minnesota farmer with 1,500 acres of corn and soybeans, "We had a frost here about two weeks ago, maybe 50 percent of a killing frost. The tops got burned off the beans" (Taylor, *Wall Street Journal,* October 4, 1993). The grain market reacted with corn prices increasing ten cents per bushel. Crop insurance losses due to the frosts in Minnesota were 36 percent of the total crop insurance indemnities, and those in Wisconsin were 67 percent of the state's total. Nationwide, the 1993 insurance-paid losses due to frost were 17 percent of the total crop insurance indemnities. (These losses were in addition to the losses required to trigger deductibles of 25 to 35 percent losses in yields.)

October and November: Delayed Harvests

Only 5 percent of the soybean harvest in Illinois, Iowa, and Minnesota had been completed by early October when normal soybean harvesting is well underway and roughly 40 percent complete. During the weeks ending on October 17 and 24, considerable progress had been made in soybean harvesting in all three states, Missouri was somewhat behind schedule, and Wisconsin was ahead of schedule. By October 31, the 1993 soybean harvest was virtually complete for the region.

---

[1] Soybean harvesting begins in mid-September (most of Missouri and southern Illinois), late September (northern Missouri, upper two-thirds of Illinois, Iowa, and southern Minnesota), or early October (Wisconsin). Some corn harvesting typically occurs in early September (southern Missouri), by mid-September (central Missouri and southern Illinois), early October (northern Missouri and the majority of Illinois and Iowa), or mid-October (northern sections of the Corn Belt: Wisconsin and Minnesota).

As the soybean harvest progressed, the Corn Belt farmers awaited the final maturity of the corn crop and its subsequent harvest. For early October, corn maturity was very close to normal in Illinois and Missouri (Illinois' crop was 82 percent mature compared to an average of 89 percent, and Missouri was at 90 percent compared to an average of 95). Iowa and Wisconsin reported corn maturities as 50 percent behind normal, while Minnesota was 80 percent behind normal for early October. Through mid-October, the corn crop in Iowa made excellent progress, and crops reached maturity there and in Illinois and Missouri. Less than 20 percent of the region's corn crop had been harvested, however. At the same time, major frosts ended the growing season for most of the Midwest (*Weekly Weather and Crop Bulletin*, October 12). Normally, harvest is about 50 percent complete. There was good progress during the latter part of the month, and the harvest was approaching its normal pace.

The late October report for corn (*Weekly Weather and Crop Bulletin*, October 26) rated 85 percent of the Illinois crop as "good to excellent" while 87 percent of the Iowa crop was rated "fair to poor." Almost 75 percent of the Minnesota crop was rated "fair to poor," with 23 percent rated "very poor." Nearly two-thirds of Missouri's corn was considered "fair" with 19 percent rated as "good." The Wisconsin corn crop was rated 80 percent "fair to good" with the rest rated as "poor." By mid-November, the Midwest's corn harvest was on schedule and nearing completion, with only Minnesota and Wisconsin marginally behind.

IMPACTS AND RESPONSES

Corn and Soybean Yields

Given the perilous journey of corn and soybean crops through the excessively wet, cool 1993 growing season and early frosts, coupled with millions of floodplain acres with flooded-out crops, many wondered just how low the crop yields would be. More than 70 percent of the crop losses were due to the overly wet uplands where conditions prevented planting or harvesting. Farmers and agribusiness leaders feared the worst, and most of these negative expectations were realized. Table 7-2 presents the final yield estimates derived by the U.S. Department of Agriculture (USDA) for the five states. Also presented are average yields for the previous five-year period, 1988-1992. Corn yields in 1993 were dramatically lower than the previous five-year average for all states but Illinois. The average corn yield for Iowa was only 80 bushels per acre compared to a five-year average of 118 bushels per acre, a 31 percent reduction. Similarly, the average corn yield for Minnesota was 70 bushels per acre compared to a five-year average of 115 bushels per acre. The 1993 corn yield for Wisconsin was 13 percent below the average, and that for Missouri was down 11 percent.

Soybean yields in 1993 were also reduced relative to the average for the previous five-year period: Iowa down 9.1 bushels or 25 percent, Minnesota down

TABLE 7-2   Corn and Soybean Yields (bushels per planted acre) for 1993 and 1988-1992

Crop	State	1988-1992	1993
Corn			
	Illinois	116.0	130.0
	Iowa	118.0	80.0
	Minnesota	115.0	70.0
	Missouri	101.0	90.0
	Wisconsin	106.0	92.0
Soybeans			
	Illinois	37.1	43.0
	Iowa	39.1	30.0
	Minnesota	34.5	22.0
	Missouri	30.5	33.0
	Wisconsin	35.7	35.0

36 percent, and Wisconsin down 2 percent. However, the soybean yields in Missouri were slightly above the 1988-1992 average, and the soybean yield in Illinois was 6 bushels per acre above the average.

Effects on Crop Insurance

The flood and extremely wet conditions in the Midwest had profound effects on the crop insurance industry as a result of crop losses and their associated payments, as well as existing problems in government policies relating to crop insurance and relief payments. Under the Multiple Peril Crop Insurance (MPCI) program, crops are insurable against damage due to flood, drought, and other weather perils. The program is regulated by USDA as part of its Federal Crop Insurance Corporation (FCIC). MPCI is primarily sold and serviced through private sector insurance companies, but policy provisions and premium rates are set by the FCIC. Private sector insurance companies bear a portion of the risk of losses and can "reinsure" the remaining risk with FCIC. Federal involvement in terms of government subsidy is required due to the highly correlated nature of agricultural risks across a region (that is, "if it rains too much on you, then it rains too much on me too"). This regional spread of risk is in sharp contrast to other conventional lines of private insurance that deal with individual items.

As one would expect, 1993 crop insurance losses were catastrophic over large portions of the Midwest, with heaviest losses experienced in Iowa, Minnesota, northern Wisconsin, and counties along the Missouri and Mississippi Rivers in Illinois and Missouri.

TABLE 7-3   Corn and Soybean Insurance Loss Ratios (indemnities divided by premiums) for 1993 and for Prior Years (Source: Federal Crop Insurance Corporation)

Crop State	1993	1988	1981-1992
Corn			
Illinois	57.0	569.8	121.4
Iowa	496.1	462.6	76.6
Minnesota	827.5	306.6	58.5
Missouri	199.0	268.2	90.5
Wisconsin	441.8	641.1	110.1
Soybeans			
Illinois	61.9	350.0	100.0
Iowa	381.8	193.3	68.0
Minnesota	549.3	219.9	67.9
Missouri	210.9	178.5	136.5
Wisconsin	162.9	437.2	118.5

Insurance profitability is generally measured by the ratio of indemnities to premiums, referred to as the "loss ratio." With the federal subsidy, the FCIC national "target" loss ratio for the MPCI program is about 90 percent. Table 7-3 summarizes crop insurance loss ratios for five states for 1993, for 1988 (a major Midwestern drought), and for 1981-1992 based on the industry's cumulative experience. Together, these loss ratios allow assessment of the 1993 values.

Comparison of the loss ratios for the five states listed reveals catastrophic state-level impacts associated with the flood of 1993 and the 1988 drought. Corn and soybean loss ratios for 1993 approximate 200 percent or higher in all states except Illinois. In past years (1981-1992), most states in the Corn Belt have had industry "tolerable" experience; that is, approximating FCIC's target loss ratio of 90 percent. Note that the values for 1981-1992 are at or below 90 percent for Iowa, Minnesota, and Missouri. Interestingly, these three states were hardest hit by the 1993 flood. Obviously, 1988 and 1993 were both catastrophic years; however, the 1993 loss experience for Illinois was good, being well below 90 percent for both crops.

Figure 7-3 provides a county-by-county depiction of crop insurance results for 1993. Most counties in Iowa, Minnesota, and Wisconsin had corn loss ratios exceeding 300 percent. The pattern of soybean loss ratios shows values greater than 100 percent over most of the five-state area where soybeans are grown. Loss ratios in counties along the Missouri River in Missouri are notable and reflect floodplain losses. Industry insurance payments across the nine-state region with excessive flooding (Illinois, Iowa, Kansas, Missouri, Minnesota, Nebraska, North Dakota, South Dakota, and Wisconsin) amounted to $1,017 billion. The

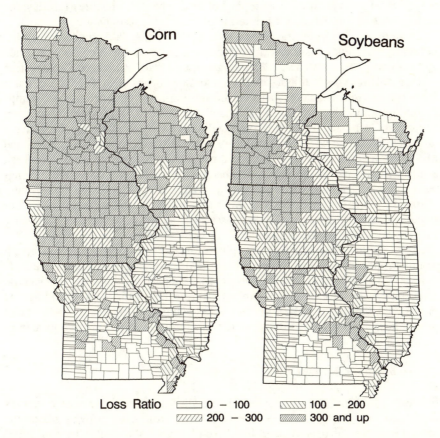

FIGURE 7-3 Patterns of insurance loss ratios for corn and soybeans based on county values in 1993. High loss ratios for corn occurred in most of Iowa, Minnesota, and Wisconsin, whereas the highest ratios for soybeans were found in northern Iowa and southern Minnesota. Much of the high loss was in upland areas of the Iowa-Minnesota region.

largest payments were $353 million to Minnesota, $281 million to Iowa, and $139 million to North Dakota.

The nation's crop insurance MPCI loss ratio for 1993 was 219 percent, second only to that recorded in 1988 (240 percent). Total losses for 1993 were in excess of $1.65 billion. Losses totaled $1.03 billion for all nine states impacted by the flood. Losses for the five-state study region were $740 million. Although these insurance outcomes were excessive, adequate federal and private reinsurance capacity existed and was able to handle the region's losses. There were no reported insolvencies for companies writing crop insurance as a direct result of the 1993 flood losses. The flood losses caused the industry's surplus to be drawn down considerably, and these losses and other competitive pressures forced some realignment within the industry in terms of company consolidation.

In addition to crop insurance indemnities, the USDA paid an additional $1.7 billion in emergency assistance for agricultural losses in the nine states affected by the flood. This assistance included Agricultural Stabilization and Conservation Service of USDA disaster assistance (crop loss) payments of $1.463 billion, Farm Homeowner Administration loans ($15.8 million), and emergency food stamps ($10.9 million). The efficacy of the federal assistance to Midwestern farmers can be measured, in part, by the financial condition of those in states most negatively impacted by the flood. Examination of farm business records from Iowa and Minnesota revealed farmers experienced a reduction in liquidity (short-term cash availability) during 1993. However, the debt-to-asset ratio (a measure of long-term financial stability) for farmers as a group did not deteriorate significantly (Bennick, 1995; Lazarus, 1995). Obviously, many farmers suffered losses, but in the aggregate, the influx of federal assistance served as a stabilizing influence for farmers in the hardest-hit states.

As a result of the flood's catastrophic impacts and growing dissatisfaction among farmers and insurance companies with the crop insurance program, efforts to reform the crop insurance program were initiated. In addition, several specific provisions of the crop insurance program were changed for 1994, including: (1) provisions preventing planting and late planting, (2) quality adjustment procedures, and (3) special designation of the crop insurance acreage located in the floodplain.

Commodity Market Responses

Responses of the corn and soybean commodity market to the excessive wetness associated with the flood of 1993 were sizable. During each growing season the market is often labeled as "weather-driven," and this was also true in 1993. Figure 7-4 presents day-by-day settlement prices on the Chicago Board of Trade (CBOT) for corn and for soybeans. Settlement prices for the massive drought in 1988 also illustrate that catastrophe's effect on prices.

At the start of the 1993 growing season (May), the harvest contract for (December) corn was trading at about $2.40 per bushel. Even though field and planting conditions were sub-optimal and widely reported, corn prices remained steady and actually trended downward through late June. Possible factors contributing to this price behavior were the high level of beginning corn stocks, and expectations that excessive moisture in June was better for corn than deficit moisture plus an expectation that the rains would cease and everything would get back to "normal." (It is interesting to note that the summer weather prediction

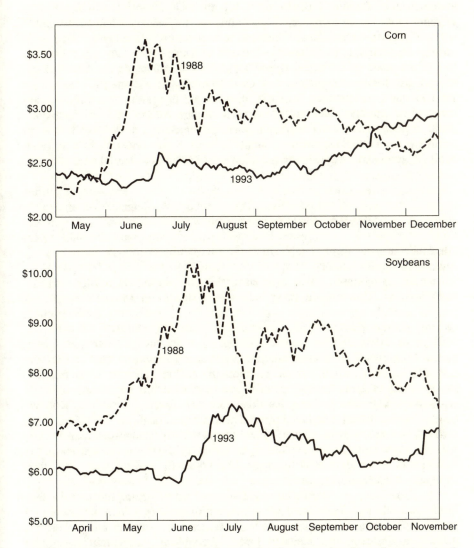

FIGURE 7-4 Fluctuations in the daily settlement prices for corn and soybeans (harvest contract) at the Chicago Board of Trade for 1993 and 1988. The 1993 corn prices jumped in early July and then slowly retreated, rising again during the fall harvest season. Soybean prices increased dramatically from mid-June to mid-July and then slowly descended.

of the National Weather Service (NWS) was for above-average summer rainfall across the Corn Belt, see Chapter 2.) Beginning corn stocks were at approximately 10.5 million bushels, the highest level since before 1988.

In terms of yield expectations being assessed by grain traders, it is interesting to review the 90-day NWS precipitation outlooks, as published in the *Weekly Weather and Crop Bulletin*. The 90-day forecast for January-March 1993 called for slightly drier-than-normal conditions across the Corn Belt, but actual precipitation for this period in the Upper Mississippi basin was near average. The February-April 1993 outlook was for slightly wetter-than-normal conditions, which agreed with what actually occurred. The 90-day outlook for March-May 1993 in the Corn Belt was for drier-than-normal conditions, but precipitation levels were actually in excess of long-term averages. Similarly, the April-June 1993 outlook was for drier-than-normal precipitation levels, again proven incorrect by much-above-normal rainfall for these three months. This poor track record may explain why traders ignored the switch in the outlooks from dry to above normal rainfall for the June-August period.

Review of the price movements (Figure 7-4) and the wet soil conditions suggests that the market "favored" the presence of adequate soil moisture, especially if one expects conditions to dry out (the average condition). In late June and early July, corn prices broke and subsequently maintained the $2.50 threshold through mid- to late August. Wet weather conditions subsided during August, as did corn prices.

It is also important to keep in mind the regional impacts associated with the 1993 season. The western Corn Belt, mainly Iowa and Minnesota, suffered greatly while most of Illinois, Indiana, and Ohio experienced near-optimal growing conditions.

The behavior of the 1993 soybean prices was quite different than that of corn prices (Figure 7-4). Soybean prices remained near $6.00 per bushel through the end of May, moved slightly downward through mid-June, but then began trending steadily upward through early July as crop condition reports indicated substantial replanted acreage and slow crop development. Prices were at or above $7.00 per bushel for most of July, and then trended downward through the remainder of the growing season as weather and crop conditions were expected to stabilize (Taylor, July 27, 1993; and July 28, 1993b). Indeed, the flood had a major impact on the market prices of corn and soybeans, but the effect was much less than experienced during the 1988 drought.

The rapid increase in both corn and soybean prices during early November was most likely attributable to the crop forecast released by USDA's Agricultural Statistics Board on November 9: the corn forecast was at 6.50 billion bushels, down 7 percent from the October 1 forecast. Similarly, the November soybean forecast was down 3 percent from October's forecast, with production at 1.83 billion bushels. Also at this time, the severity of grain quality problems was becoming readily apparent to the market. Several factors such as quality, late development, and shortness of the crop came into play at this time. In terms of the grain processing sector and other agribusiness firms, the impacts of the flood were being realized (in an accounting sense) in late 1994 as these firms conducted their 1994 financial audits.

Production and Acreage Impacts

The ever-worsening weather situation during the growing season ultimately caused crop production forecasts to be continually revised downward during the 1993 season. The USDA's forecasts of corn and soybean production, as issued on August 11, 1993, were at 7.4 billion and 1.9 billion bushels, respectively, down 5 percent from the July forecast (USDA, 1993). On November 9, 1993, the USDA's forecasts of corn and soybean production were at 6.5 and 1.83 billion bushels, respectively. This too was a downward revision of the October forecast (down 7 percent for corn and 3 percent for soybeans). The forecasts during the growing and harvest seasons were too high and never caught up with the decreased yields. The 6.34 billion bushel corn crop for 1993 represents a 15 percent decrease in production compared to an average of 7.47 billion bushels for 1988-1992. The 1993 soybean crop was 1.81 billion bushels compared to the 1988-1992 average of 1.92 billion bushels, a 5.7 percent decrease.

Production losses due to reductions in planted acreage were substantial. In June 1993, the USDA issued estimates of "intended harvested acres" in both crops. The five-state intended acreage was 34.8 billion acres in corn and 29.1 billion acres in soybeans. In August, the USDA issued "projected harvested acreage," and these downward values represented decreases of 14 percent (over the June values) for corn and 13 percent for soybeans. Table 7-4 shows the final harvested acres per state and region, and also shows the differences between intended and projected values and final values. The major decreases occurred in Minnesota, Missouri, and Wisconsin. Final harvested acres were down only slightly from the projected estimates issued by USDA during August. Normally, the USDA estimates about 3.8 percent failed corn and acreage for the region.

Financial Losses and Benefits

Losses to the crop production and livestock sectors led to huge losses across the nine-state flooded region (USDA, 1994). The values of total agricultural losses (IFMR Committee, 1994; Johnson, 1994) were $8.454 billion: Iowa ($1.9 billion), Missouri ($1.79 billion), Minnesota ($1.5 billion), Wisconsin ($0.8 billion), South Dakota ($0.572 billion), Illinois ($0.565 billion), North Dakota ($0.5 billion), Kansas ($0.441 billion), and Nebraska ($0.386 billion). In Iowa, the ripple effect through the state's economy caused by agricultural production losses was calculated as 2.2 times the production value (see Chapter 9). If this index were applicable to the other flooded states, the agricultural loss ($8.454 times 2.2) would result in a total loss in the region's economy of $17.6 billion. Interestingly, this value approximates the current estimate of total losses of $18.1 billion (see Chapter 12). A typical loser was a Minnesota farmer who commented, as he burned 600 acres of wheat too moldy to harvest, "We've never done anything like this before. There is nothing to save." (Kilman, 1993).

TABLE 7-4 Corn and Soybean Acres Harvested in 1993 vs. Intended Acreage Values Issued in June and Projected Acreage Values Issued in August

States	Harvested acres, millions	Difference intended/harvested, %	Difference projected/harvested, %
Corn			
Illinois	10.0	4.8	0.0
Iowa	11.0	9.1	1.0
Minnesota	4.6	27.0	10.9
Missouri	1.9	15.9	2.7
Wisconsin	2.3	36.5	6.4
Totals	29.8	14.4	2.7
Soybeans			
Illinois	8.7	6.5	0.0
Iowa	8.2	6.8	2.4
Minnesota	5.0	15.3	0.0
Missouri	3.5	19.3	1.4
Wisconsin	0.6	14.7	0.0
Totals	26.0	10.5	1.9

Not all impacts from the flood were negative, however. Price increases (Figure 7-4) as a result of the flood were beneficial to farmers (and market speculators) in areas of the Corn Belt (and elsewhere) that had good crops. In particular, farmers in Illinois, Indiana, and Ohio who had high yields were rewarded by the flood-induced higher prices. The sharp contrast between the position of the Minnesota wheat farmer (described above) and that of an Indiana farmer is illustrated by the latter's statement in late September, "This sure is going to be one of our better crops." (Kilman, 1993). The Indiana farmer's soybean yield was 55 bushels per acre, and he indicated he could now afford to go on a winter golfing vacation in Florida, to buy a new tractor, and to give himself a raise in salary. By the end of September, sales in farm equipment in Indiana and Ohio had risen 10 percent over those from the past year. In stark contrast, hard times in a small town in flood-damaged South Dakota led to the closing of a farm equipment dealer and auto sales went down 15 percent during 1993 (Kilman, 1993).

POLICY RESPONSE: A LESSON FINALLY LEARNED

In one sense, the Great Flood of 1993 did not tell agricultural policy makers anything new. The long-raging conflict over federal funding of voluntary crop insurance versus the ever-growing use of ad hoc agricultural disaster relief programs came to a climax as a result of the 1993 flood and the enormous cost of the federal responses, however. The insurance-relief payout inconsistency has been an expensive, confusing, and unwieldy policy. The co-existence of voluntary crop insurance and the "free" disaster program has farmers deciding whether to pay premiums into an insurance pool with low participation (roughly 35 percent), or to rely on Congress to fund ad hoc disaster bills when Mother Nature is unkind to agriculture. *The flood provided the impetus for agricultural policy makers to reform both the funding and management of weather-related disasters in agriculture.*

The pros, cons, benefits, and costs of both policy instruments have long been debated. A definitive government analysis of agricultural disaster relief programs revealed that any federal disaster relief program was flawed and costly, whereas crop insurance appeared to be the most systematic program for dealing with weather-related disasters in U.S. agriculture (GAO, 1989).

Severe agricultural impacts due to the flood and nearly $2 billion in relief payments, along with the pressure of the budget deficit and the ongoing dissatisfaction with the crop insurance/disaster payments situation, culminated in the political will to couple the funding of ad hoc disaster bills with reform of the crop insurance program. USDA Secretary Espy introduced the initial reform legislation in early 1994, and the final bill was signed in October 1994 as Public Law 103-354. There are several essential components of the reform legislation:

- Mandatory participation if farmers are to receive any other USDA subsidies
- A catastrophic coverage policy for farmers
- Analysis and a scoring of disaster spending with crop insurance as the only production agriculture risk management program
- Delivery of catastrophic coverage by both private sector insurance companies and the USDA through its Farm Service Agency
- Legislative constraints limiting Congress' ability to pass future ad hoc disaster payments

Farm-level catastrophic coverage is designed to reimburse farmers at the historic production level received under ad hoc disaster bills. The coverage provides for 50 percent yield coverage with a 60 percent crop price guarantee, as determined by FCIC. Yield coverages are established on the average of farmer-provided production records on Actual Production History (APH). Proxy yields are provided to farmers lacking adequate production records. Each farmer pays a nominal service fee for the coverage, and the fee is based on the number of crops and counties in his/her operation. Higher protection levels of 65 and 75 percent yield coverages are still available under the legislation through private companies. FCIC is also currently evaluating 85 percent coverage as proposed in the legislation.

The reform legislation will be in effect for crop year 1995, the first test of the new program. The USDA, FCIC, private sector insurance providers, and agricultural commodity groups have worked together on the details and implementation of reform throughout much of 1994. Several implementation issues still require resolution and clarification, so it will be interesting to watch the development of crop insurance reform, particularly with a new Farm Bill on the horizon. Historically, Congress has not demonstrated an ability to restrain itself from funding ad hoc disaster programs for agriculture. Congress has also spent a lot of time (in relative terms) attempting to repair and fine-tune the crop insurance program. It will also be interesting to see whether the pressures of the federal budget deficit, coupled with the 1994 election results in the House and Senate, will set a new course for agricultural policy (an issue also raised in Chapters 10 and 11). Will there be a significant increase in the number of farmers obtaining crop insurance? Only the future will reveal if the crop insurance reform legislation proves to be a politically acceptable safety net for U.S. farmers facing extreme weather events such as the Great Flood of 1993.

REFERENCES

Bennick, D., 1995: Personal communication. Iowa Business Association.

Government Accounting Office, September 1989: *Disaster Assistance: Crop Insurance Can Provide Assistance More Effectively Than Other Programs*. Resources, Community, and Economic Development Division, FAO/RCED-89-211, Washington, DC, 345 pp.

Interagency Floodplain Management Review Committee, 1994: *Sharing the Challenge: Floodplain Management into the 21st Century*. Washington, DC, 189 pp.

Johnson, H.M., 1994: *The Floods of 1993: Iowa Flood Disaster Report*. Iowa Flood Recovery Team, Johnson, IA, 35 pp.

Kilman, S., October 21, 1993: Midwest Farmers Reap Their Shrunken Crops, Those Worth Picking. *Wall Street Journal,* p.5.

Lazarus, W., 1995: Personal communication. University of Minnesota.

Long, V.S., September 28, 1993: Harvest Anxiety Pushes Soybean and Grain Futures Down. *Kansas City Star,* p.18.

Taylor, J., July 27, 1993: Soybean Futures Plunge as Weather Prospects Improve for Flooded Farmland of the Midwest. *Wall Street Journal*, p.6.

Taylor, J., July 28, 1993a: Flooded Farmers Ponder the Long and Short of It. *Wall Street Journal,* p.9.

Taylor, J., July 28, 1993b: Wheat Futures Rise on Fears of Rain Damage to Winter and Spring Crops, Chinese Buying. *Wall Street Journal,* p.4.

Taylor, J., October 4, 1993: Grain Futures Prices Decline as Killing Freeze Forecast for Entire Corn Belt Fails to Materialize. *Wall Street Journal*, p. 3.

U.S. Department of Agriculture, August 11, 1993: *Crop Production*. National Agricultural Statistics Service, Washington DC, 39 pp.

U.S. Department of Agriculture, July 8, 1994: *USDA Emergency Assistance Paid to Flood States*. Office of the Chief Economist, Washington, D.C., 34 pp.

U.S. Department of Commerce, and U.S. Department of Agriculture, 1993: *Weekly Weather and Crop Bulletin*. Vol. 80, No. 12 (March 23)- No. 47 (November 23), Washington, DC.

8

Impacts on Transportation Systems: Stalled Barges, Blocked Railroads, and Closed Highways

Stanley A. Changnon

INTRODUCTION

No previous natural disaster in the nation's history has caused more damage to the railroad industry, the barge industry, and to all other forms of surface transportation than the floods of 1993. Losses due to damages and lost revenue to the transportation sector exceeded $1.9 billion.

The flood was concentrated in the center of the nation's rail and highway systems and embraced the heart of the Mississippi Waterway navigation system. Heavy and prolonged summer rains and ensuing floods on the Mississippi and Missouri River systems enveloped a triangle of the nation's three major rail and highway hubs of surface transportation: Chicago, Kansas City, and St. Louis. About 25 percent of all U.S. freight either originates or terminates in the flooded area, and the flood stopped navigation for two months and also produced a huge traffic jam on the region's highways and railroads between June and August 1993.

From April through August 1993, more than 2 feet of rain fell in an enormous area encompassing parts of nine states and centered in Iowa, which experienced rainfall totals of up to 3 feet compared to the state's normal rainfall of 16 inches. The resulting floods were most extreme in western Illinois, throughout Iowa, the northern half of Missouri, and eastern Kansas. These floods broke all-time records for the Mississippi River from Rock Island, IL, south to Cairo, IL, where the Mississippi meets the Ohio, and the floods on the Missouri River broke flood records from St. Louis west to Kansas City and north near Omaha. Numerous major tributaries to these rivers, including the Des Moines, Kansas, Iowa, and Illinois Rivers, also had record floods. The nation's major east-west railroads and highways converge in the three hubs, cross all of these rivers, and the Upper Mississippi, Illinois, and Missouri Rivers are heavily used waterways in the nation's inland commercial navigation system.

The flood was unique for three reasons: (1) it occurred in summer (most Midwestern floods of consequence are due to rapid snowmelt and occur in the spring); (2) it covered 260,000 square miles, an immense area; and (3) it lasted months, not weeks like most floods. These last two factors, the huge area covered and the flood's exceptionally long duration, are what really had severe impacts on the transportation systems and the movement of people and goods, both within and through the huge flooded area.

EFFECTS ON THE BARGE INDUSTRY

The U.S. barge industry hauls 15 percent of all the freight shipped in the nation. Much of this barge traffic uses the Mississippi River system from New Orleans north to Minneapolis-St. Paul, the Ohio River from Cairo east into Pennsylvania, the Illinois River from near St. Louis north to Chicago, and the Missouri River from St. Louis west to Omaha. The barge industry consists of about 800 barge-tow owners (many small businesses with a few tows and a few giant companies), shippers who rely on barges, and ports and terminals where loading and unloading occurs. Along the major rivers of the central United States, barges are used to ship bulk commodities: petroleum products (30 percent of the nation's total), grain (65 percent of the total shipped), coal (25 percent of the total shipped), and wood products (20 percent of the nation's total shipments).

Impacts

In early June 1993, the rapidly rising Mississippi brought water levels well above flood stage. On June 25, the U.S. Army Corps of Engineers stopped all barge and pleasure craft operations for a 215-mile stretch from Clarksville, MO, located just north of St. Louis, north to Rock Island, IL. The problem was two-fold: river levels were too high to allow operation of the locks at Canton, MO, and New Boston, IL, and it was feared that the wakes of barge-tows would damage farm levees.

Closure of the river was extended from Rock Island north to Minneapolis on June 28, a distance of 400 miles. This was not a major shock to navigation interests because the river had been closed because of flooding for 12 days in the spring flood. In fact, on June 28 predictors from the Corps said they weren't sure how long the river would be closed but estimated three days (*St. Louis Post-Dispatch,* June 29). New predictions indicated "it would be two weeks before the barges can move," and a spokesman for the barge industry said, "there would be no long-term impacts from the new flood" (*St. Louis Post-Dispatch,* June 30). Forecasts of the flood ending in a few days or weeks kept shippers from shifting shipments to railroads; they waited for the river to open.

By early July, barge experts said 2,000 barges and 50 towboats were trapped throughout the Midwest (Figure 8-1), and the cost to shut-down industry was $1 million per day, a relatively low loss figure because grain exports happened to be below average. A hint that things were changing came on July 2, when the COE said the Mississippi would remain closed for "at least two weeks."

FIGURE 8-1 On the Mississippi River at Clinton, IA, numerous barges and tows are anchored along both sides of the swollen river as a train slowly crosses the swirling river (Illinois State Geological Survey).

Flooding was present all along the Missouri River west of St. Louis and north to Omaha on July 2. The next day the Corps closed the river to navigation between Jefferson City, MO, and St. Louis, stranding an additional 300 barges. On July 5, the Coast Guard extended the Missouri River closure to Brownsville, NE. The Corps stated on July 6 that the Mississippi River would open to barge traffic on July 25, but then the Mississippi was closed from St. Louis northward on July 7, as were portions of the Illinois River. This error in the forecast was soundly criticized (*Farm Week*, July 19). Distrust in official pronouncements about the flood's status had set in.

Becoming concerned about the prolonged flooding, shippers began seeking other transportation to move their goods during the first week of July (Figure 8-2). River transport managers began planning new routes. There was deep concern at some on-river coal-fired power plants because they had only three weeks of coal supplies by July 9, the day the St. Louis harbor was closed. New estimates of losses to the barge industry were issued on July 12, doubling the earlier figure to $2 million per day due to new and better information on the extent of the troubles along the two rivers. Reports now indicated 2,900 stranded barges, several of which had sunk. Mooring barges alongside the flooded shores was increasingly difficult, and at some locations tows had to be kept running to hold the barges in place against the high flow rates. On July 12, the Coast Guard closed the Mississippi River between Savanna and Cairo, IL (see Chapter 4).

The plight of the barge and tow owners, their crews, and the dock workers had become enormous by late July, a month after the Mississippi had been closed to traffic. Tom Seals, a frustrated St. Louis Port captain for one large barge-tow firm stated, "all we can do is sit and wait." Industry officials reported on July 25 that barge companies were losing $3 million in revenue each day. Seals explained further that, "we only make money when we are moving." Thousands of dock workers were entering their second month without work or pay. In St. Louis, 3,200 dockmen were idle, and one unhappy worker interviewed in a port coffee shop observed, "the damned river has a mind all its own--sometimes the river is calm and sometimes as mean as can be--it can make you rich and it can make you poor too." Companies along the Big River that repair and clean boats and barges were closed for business too. The owner of a St. Louis firm said, "we'll make it, but it's going to hurt like hell. Right now all we can do is drink coffee and wait." Unfortunately, the wait lasted another month.

By July 25, a new industry tally stated that 7,000 barges containing cargoes valued at $1.9 billion were stranded on the two rivers, with admitted losses of $3 to $4 million per day. Unemployment in the St. Louis area included 3,200 workers, who load, unload, and clean barges, and who had been out of work since July 9. A huge flotilla of empty freighters was awaiting shipment at the end of the waterways pipeline in New Orleans. Many of these freighters were anchored in the Gulf of Mexico because of crowded harbor conditions. Barge industry leaders announced that "the economic impact on the barge lines is catastrophic." Shippers also felt negative impacts as some coal producers simply could not get their shipments moved and lost business to other shippers. Delays were also a problem in shipping construction materials (*ENR*, August 30). After the rivers opened and barge shipments could be examined, a major fear was removed: most grain shipments were still in good shape, and the quality had not been harmed after being held on the river in barges for two months.

Total losses of revenues to the navigation industry were assessed at $600 million (IFMR Committee, 1994), easily exceeding the previous record loss to the barge industry ($200 million) during the 1988 drought when barges were stranded due to low river levels. In addition, the Maritime Administration estimated that the closed rivers cost the economies of the flooded states $320 million (*St. Louis Post-Dispatch*, August 18).

Responses

During the flood, shippers who rely on barges turned to the railroads (if they were accessible), to trucks, or both to maintain delivery of either raw materials or processed products. Mounting losses to the barge industry led to price increases. Barge rates had gone up 25 percent by July 10.

Industry representatives, the Coast Guard, and Corps officials established a Center at St. Louis by July 25 to begin planning how to restore the river for navigation and how to restore the barge operations. Being highly independent,

FIGURE 8-2 Freight normally hauled by barges was shifted to the railroads, as on this train departing from Ft. Madison, IA, on July 2. The nearby Mississippi River had already flooded the local railyards (left), and flooding soon ended many train operations here.

the barge industry decided not to seek government aid to meet its huge losses. The industry-government group met on August 10 to discuss opening the harbor at St. Louis and decided to test barge operations when the river fell to 39 feet. The flood crests fell quickly after early August.

After testing operations with a few barges, the Coast Guard opened 830 miles of the Mississippi to limited barge traffic on August 22. The Missouri also opened that day. Full barge operations began on August 28, but shipments were further delayed by the high waters, which kept tow loads below average (12 barges versus the normal 15) to handle difficult navigation in the still-very-swift waters (*Traffic World*, August 30). The following months involved re-charting the river courses, removing sand bars, and putting out new navigation buoys. Nevertheless, the rush was on to get grain south because the harvest had begun and supplies at New Orleans had fallen low. Congestion on the river was prevalent for weeks, and a major bottleneck was created at Cairo in late August because of dangerous navigation conditions between Cairo and St. Louis. Much attention was given to slow speeds and spacing between tows. Use of the river did not return to normal until the late fall of 1993, however.

EFFECTS ON RAILROADS

By late June the flood led the Coast Guard to order stoppage of all barge traffic on the Mississippi and Missouri Rivers. One might initially predict that a severe flood on the big rivers would create a major economic victory for the railroads. The barge industry is a major competitor with the rail industry for hauling bulk commodities including grain, coal, petroleum, and chemical products. These were shipments the railroads gladly would have moved, but once again the flood prevailed.

Impacts

Unfortunately, the flood also halted rail traffic within a few days after all barge traffic had ceased on June 26. The oblate-shaped flood area (with Kansas City at one end and Chicago at the other) occurred over the main lines of the nation's major east-west railroads (Figure 8-3).

Rail troubles began on June 19 when a portion of the Green Bay & Western line in Wisconsin was washed out, and then on June 24 the Canadian Pacific (CP) removed all its cars from the St. Paul rail yards before the flood submerged them (*Pacific Rail News*, August 1993). By early July high waters along the valley of the Mississippi River had inundated low-lying rail lines built parallel to the river valley and the approaches to certain rail bridges across the Mississippi. Bridge problems slowed or stopped trains at seven major crossings (Figure 8-4): (1) the Iowa Interstate bridge at the Quad Cities, (2) Canadian Pacific (CP) at Savanna, IL, (3) Atchison, Topeka & Santa Fe (AT&SF) at Ft. Madison, IA, (4 and 5) Burlington Northern (BN) at Quincy, IL, and at Burlington, IA, (6) Gateway Western (GWWR) at Louisiana, MO, and (7) the Norfolk Southern (NS) Decatur-Kansas City line at Hannibal, MO.

Train stoppages and re-routings were occurring by July 6 on the BN (Figure 8-5), CP, and Southern Pacific (SP). On July 7, the Union Pacific (UP) main line between St. Louis and Kansas City went under water; two days later the NS east-west main line at Hannibal was flooded (see Figure 8-1), and on July 10 the

FIGURE 8-3 A train eases cautiously across the aged Mississippi River bridge at Dubuque, IA, with swirling river just 3 feet below the bridge. A navigation buoy is in the foreground.

AT&SF main line at Ft. Madison was flooded (see Figure 8-2) and a bridge washed out near Marcelline, MO. The UP line between Kansas City and Omaha went out on July 13. The situation had become deadly serious for all railroads in the Midwest.

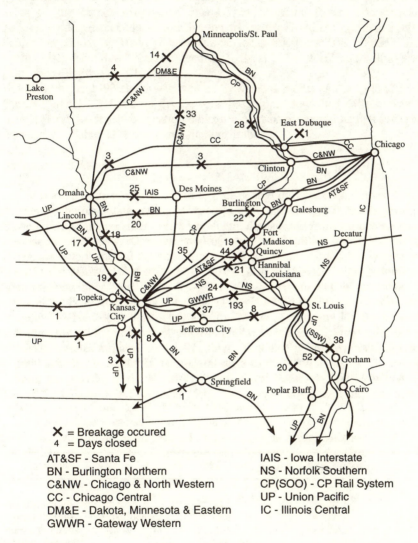

FIGURE 8-4 Rail lines were closed by the flood throughout the Midwest for periods ranging from 1 to 193 days.

FIGURE 8-5 A Burlington Northern coal train, diverted north to Minneapolis because of a bridge closure at Burlington, IA, crawls alongside the flooded Mississippi near Savanna, IL, on July 12. Note the light-colored rock on the track near the water--new gravel brought to protect the track.

Continued record heavy rains in northern Missouri, eastern Kansas, and southern Iowa during mid- to late-July created a series of new flood crests, which resulted in several major washouts and a few "bridge outs" in those three states. One major result was the washout of the Santa Fe bridge near Marcelline, MO, on July 10 (*Traffic World*, July 19). These new floods severed several major lines for periods of two weeks or longer. The massive halting of rail traffic was found on seven main lines crossing the Midwest. These lines included those of six major railroads and they are as follows:

- *the BN's main line between Galesburg, IL, and Kansas City* (across northern Missouri), also home to SP trains operating between Kansas City and Chicago.
- *the BN's double-track main line between Galesburg and Omaha*, NB (across southern Iowa).
- *the AT&SF double-track main line between Ft. Madison, IA, and Kansas City* (across northern Missouri).
- *the NS Decatur, IL-Kansas City main line* (in central Missouri), which remained closed until October, and *the NS St. Louis-Kansas City main line*.
- *the GWWR St. Louis-Kansas City main line* (in north-central Missouri, a line that remained closed until November).

- *the UP main line from St. Louis to Kansas City.*
- *the CP main line between Chicago and Kansas City.*

The impact on the GWWR was severe. In mid-July the Missouri River broke through levees and washed out two segments of track, one 1,000-feet long and another 500-feet long. Then on July 30, the surging new flood crest wiped out the GWWR rail bridge at Glasgow, MO, closing the railroad for many months. When barge operations were allowed to resume in August, and the rivers were still in flood, the GWWR was further damaged when a barge struck its rail bridge across the Mississippi River at Louisiana, MO.

Lines parallel to the big rivers were also closed for prolonged periods. Those included:

- *the UP-Cotton Belt shared railroad line* from East St.Louis south along the Mississippi's east shore to Gorham, IL.
- *the parallel BN river lines* along the Mississippi's west shore north of St. Louis to Burlington and south of St. Louis to Cape Girardeau, MO.
- *the BN and UP lines* along the Missouri River between Kansas City and Omaha.
- *the CP line* along the Mississippi between Dubuque and LaCrosse, WI.

The BN line along the west shore of Mississippi between Burlington and St. Louis was closed on June 30 and not reopened until October. The flooding seriously affected Kansas City where floods closed several rail yards and approaches to the city for two periods in July, altering train movements in and around this key hub, the nation's second busiest rail center just behind Chicago. During July 27-30, most rail traffic was halted at Kansas City. St. Louis was spared flooding of its major yards, as was Chicago.

TABLE 8-1 Financial Outcomes for Individual Railroads (in millions of dollars)

Railroad	*Damages*	*Revenues*
Amtrak	0	-7
Atchison Topeka & Santa Fe	-35	-20
Burlington Northern	-88	-44
Canadian Pacific	-15	-12
Chicago & North Western	-5	-12
Dakota, Minnesota & Eastern	-2	-1
Gateway Western	-10	-7
Illinois Central	0	+18
Iowa Interstate	-4	-3
Norfolk Western	-13	-7
Southern Pacific	-17	-25
Union Pacific	-50	-12

The physical damage to the railroads was massive (Table 8-1). Current estimates indicate losses amounting to $241 million. This figure includes $96 million for damage to track (60 miles were washed out at a replacement cost of $1 million per mile, and 820 miles of track were under water with repair costs at $100,000 per mile). The loss total also includes $15 million for bridge replacement and repair, $14 million for signals, $9 million for train cars and engines, and $55 million for labor and fuel costs associated with train detours.

Revenue losses were quite sizable. For example, the AT&SF estimated a loss of $750,000 per day during the days its trains were blocked and re-routed (*Traffic World*, July 30) for a total loss of $20 million. Delays of one to five days occurred on AT&SF, BN, and SP trains, which created major problems for speed-oriented shippers such as the United Parcel Service. The loss in revenue to BN was $44 million (*Transportation and Distribution*, January 1994). With an estimated $169 million of revenue losses due to delayed trains and shipments lost to other carriers, the actual losses from the flood totaled $410 million, the greatest loss ever experienced by the railroads as a result of a natural disaster in the United States. The amount is more than ten times greater than the previous record loss to railroads: $27 million in losses to six railroads as a result of Hurricane Agnes in 1972.

Responses

Two major responses occurred as the flood developed, persisted, and damages began: plans and action. Affected railroads established "situation rooms" to deal with their emerging problems. By July 11, the "War Room" of the AT&SF was routing 50 trains a day over various other railroad lines to maintain service.

The railroads worked feverishly to raise lines, to rebuild washouts and bridges, and to restore the operations. For example, the NS raised a mile of its threatened track 6 feet with rock in Missouri. During most of July, 500 UP workers labored to keep their Sedalia Subdivision line in Missouri open, and UP crews drawn from all over the nation were still working to restore damaged lines as late as October. To protect its line along the Mississippi's threatened west shore, CP carried 6,000 car loads of rock (see Figure 8-6). Ironically, an abandoned but intact NS rail line across parts of Missouri and Iowa became a highly useful detour when the main lines were flooded (American Railway Engineering Association, January 1994).

Although their lines went out in July, the NS line across Missouri (Decatur-Kansas City) and the GWWR line (East St. Louis-Kansas City) were closed until October to repair damaged bridges, eroded bridge approaches, and major on-line washouts. Of GWWR's 250-person staff, 20 percent were furloughed; and their Missouri bridge that collapsed in July was not rebuilt until February 1994. The NS line across Missouri was the line most damaged during the flood (*Railway Track & Structures*, September 1993).

FIGURE 8-6   A crew rebuilding the right-of-way of the Union Pacific line alongside the Mississippi River near Prairie du Rocher, IL, wait for a freight train to crawl by before resuming their difficult task on October 15, 1993, more than a month after floodwaters drained away.

The Battle of Marcelline.   Leaders of the AT&SF (Santa Fe) railroad, by early July, were fearful of the flood.   They had cars loaded with rock moved to be placed on threatened bridges, hoping these would keep the bridges stable against the force of floodwaters (*Trains,* October 1993).   At a 96-foot long bridge built over a small creek located 17 miles west of Marcelline, MO, two such "ballast cars" sat.   But in the early morning of July 10, an 8-foot wall of water, resulting from a levee break on the nearby Grand River (see Chapter 5) swept away the bridge and the two heavily loaded cars (two weeks later the remnants of the bridge and the two cars had still not been found).

The Santa Fe mobilized to restore the bridge and get its heavily used (40 trains a day) line open.   A new bridge designed to be 280-feet long and built of concrete beams and steel pilings was an enormous logistical challenge for the railroad.   One hundred workers, construction materials scrounged from everywhere possible, and four huge pile drivers were brought to this isolated location, and a command headquarters was established (in a passenger car brought to the scene).   Work began around the clock.   Through rain and sunshine, trucks with rock for fill and other materials and vehicles for the workers, which had to detour 55 miles to reach the bridge site, came and went.   The enormous effort paid off.   At 2 a.m. on July 24, just 14 days after the washout, the new bridge was completed (at a cost of $2 million), and trains were again operating along the Santa Fe's main line.

194

Similar problems were occurring elsewhere on the other railroads. After washouts and destroyed bridges were repaired on the BN Omaha-Galesburg main line, and on four UP lines, all were reopened by late July or in early August. However, the BN Galesburg-Kansas City main line was blocked at West Quincy until late October (see Highway section for an explanation of the West Quincy problem). SP's Chicago-Kansas City trains normally operate on this BN line, but they were either using the CP (Soo) line through Savanna, IL, or the SP line south from Chicago to St. Louis and west over the BN line to Oklahoma at the end of September.

The railroads also helped towns and others fight the flood. For example, in ten days during mid-July, the NS carried 250 carloads of sand (enough to fill 6 million sandbags) and 50 carloads of rock from a quarry to Hannibal to help strengthen a levee. And UP hauled large quantities of drinking water in ten special tanks to Des Moines during the 12 days when its flooded water plant was totally inoperative.

The devotion and heroism of thousands of individual employees of the railroads are evident in their outstanding efforts to quickly rebuild and to maintain a semblance of normal operations. Countless employees worked around the clock, and their story ranks among the finest hours in the history of railroad service.

Train Detours. While the lines were closed, the other major activity was the re-routing of trains, bringing unbelievable changes in train routes. The alternative routes found and taken by the Amtrak passenger trains and the freight

FIGURE 8-7 Amtrak's "Texas Eagle" races north on the Illinois Central from Memphis to Chicago on July 27, having been re-routed by nearly 900 miles to get around the flood.

trains of the AT&SF, BN, NS, SP, and UP were truly amazing. More than 2,870 trains were re-routed during the flood at costs ranging from $9 to $20 per train mile. One train was re-routed 1,000 miles at a cost to the parent railroad of $20,000. The total cost of these re-routings was $55 million (Harper, 1993).

Largely by doing "end runs" around the huge flooded area did the railroads solve their blockage problems (Changnon, 1994). However, a portion of the over-load traffic continued to move across the Mississippi at St. Louis (on a single bridge) and from there westward to Kansas City on the lone, open, direct line, the badly congested UP Sedalia Subdivision line. Some trains were diverted over longer BN alternative lines via Springfield, MO, as shown on Figure 8-4. Various options were used when the flooding hit rail yards at Kansas City.

The various diversions of the high-speed east-west trains of the AT&SF, BN, SP, and Amtrak (Figure 8-7) began with the use of the "north end" alternative. Although the flood was very serious during June in the upper reaches of the Mississippi River basin, it stopped rail traffic only briefly from Savanna, IL, northward to Minneapolis. The Chicago & North Western (C&NW) crosses the Mississippi River at Clinton, IA (see Figure 8-1), and remained open throughout the flood except on two flooded-out days (July 9-10) in central Iowa. Lines of the C&NW became a major thoroughfare for Amtrak trains and the freights of more severely flooded Midwestern railroads. Other railroads crossing the two large river basins and located farther north also remained open: the CP, which crosses the Mississippi at Savanna, the Chicago Central & Pacific at Dubuque, and the BN lines north along the Big River to the Twin Cities (see an example on Figure 8-5). Many diverted BN trains rode the BN rails north around the flood.

After the flood severed its main line on July 10, the AT&SF used every device known to its train dispatchers to move its 50 daily high-speed trains between Chicago and the west coast. Some trains were routed to the SP line from Chicago to St. Louis and then on the BN line to re-join the AT&SF main line in Oklahoma. Other AT&SF trains took the BN line from Chicago north and west through Minneapolis, then on to the West Coast. Others got on the C&NW line at Chicago, went west to Omaha, and wound south to the AT&SF main line or continued west on the UP line. Other AT&SF trains used the Illinois Central (IC) line and went 500 miles south from Chicago to Memphis, then west on BN lines to Oklahoma. By July 13, 25 percent of all rail traffic in the United States was affected, and massive re-routings resulted in 120 trains moving daily across the open bridge at St. Louis. Traffic doubled or tripled during July and much of August on the IC main line, the UP Chicago Subdivision, and the SP main between Chicago and East St. Louis.

Amtrak's trains underwent numerous shifts. The "Texas Eagle" normally operates between several Texas cities and Chicago through St. Louis, but it was re-routed for several weeks. First it crossed the Mississippi at St. Louis and used the UP line south along the Mississippi, crossed back over the Big River at Thebes, and got back to its normal route in Arkansas. When parts of that route were flooded south of St. Louis, the "Texas Eagle" was shifted to another route from Little Rock to Memphis and then north along the IC main line to Chicago (Figure 8-7). The "California Zephyr" normally operates on the BN main line between Chicago and Omaha, but was stopped for a few days in early July, and was re-routed over the C&NW line between Chicago and Omaha for three weeks beginning on July 9. The "Southwest Chief" normally operates on the AT&SF line between Chicago and Los Angeles, but stopped operations between Kansas City and Chicago for several weeks beginning on July 13.

Certain railroads such as the IC benefitted from the flood (*Traffic World*, July 19). Not only did the IC receive revenue from operating 160 AT&SF, SP, and Amtrak trains (see Figure 8-7) for several weeks, but it also got additional grain and coal shipments that could not be handled by the barges moored to the shores of the major rivers for eight weeks. It was the second time in five years that nature provided the IC with such a benefit, the first time being during the great drought of 1988 when the rivers were too low to allow full barge traffic, thus providing the IC with a shipping windfall. Major shippers such as the APL Land Transport Services with standing contracts with the open and operating C&NW line received increased business and revenues because other shippers' major east-west rail lines were blocked (*Traffic World*, July 19).

Government aid to the damaged railroads was relatively small. Of the $21 million allotment, most went to the GWWR and other regional short lines. *The major railroads received no federal or state aid and rebuilt their damaged lines with their own capital.*

IMPACTS TO HIGHWAYS AND VEHICULAR TRAFFIC

The first impacts to the nation's surface transportation systems occurred in late May when roads and highways in southern Minnesota went under water. Flooding of rivers in Minnesota and Wisconsin quickly inundated roads and highways within their floodplains. This early start of highway flooding was just a preview of what would occur in parts of the nine-state flood zone well into October 1993. A major problem developed in the mid-flood period: the widespread closure of bridges of major highways crossing both the Mississippi and Missouri Rivers (Figure 8-8).

Impacts

Several vital highways in Minnesota and Wisconsin were closed due to flooding by mid-June. Flooding problems escalated rapidly in late June, and on June 28, the surging Mississippi flooded Davenport, IA, covering the famed "river road" that runs parallel to the river in that area. By late June, flooding of highways, county roads, and township roads had become prevalent in large parts of Iowa, and in the low-lying portions of Missouri, North Dakota, South Dakota,

FIGURE 8-8 A view of the Quincy bridge on July 3, the only way to get across the Mississippi between St. Louis and Keokuk, IA (a distance of 150 miles). Note the swirling, high-speed water. Twelve days later this bridge was closed too.

Minnesota, and Wisconsin. The Des Peres bridge near St. Louis was closed on July 1, and the Missouri Department of Highways closed Highway 168 in central Missouri and reported that "there was much damage to county roads" (*St. Louis Post-Dispatch*, July 2). Flooded and closed roads were reported in 13 Illinois counties on July 2.

Another major problem facing vehicular traffic was the rash of bridge closures across the Upper Mississippi. The problems of getting across the river increased with the closing of the Mark Twain bridge at Hannibal, MO, on July 2. The only open bridge across the Mississippi River between St. Louis and Keokuk, IA, was that at Quincy, IL (Figure 8-8). When the Illinois Department of Transportation closed the Mississippi River Bridge at Keokuk on July 5, the only highway bridge open between St. Louis and Davenport, a distance of 250 miles, was the one at Quincy. Approaches to the closed bridges had gone under water, and there were also growing fears that the fast-flowing floodwaters were scouring the channels and potentially weakening bridge piers and abutments. The river at St. Louis on July 5 was moving at 5.8 mph, the highest speed ever measured. The ferry across the Mississippi River near St. Louis had closed on July 2, the same date that the ferry across the Illinois River at Grafton had closed, and the ferry at St. Genevieve, MO, was closed on July 6. A major levee break on July 15 closed the Quincy bridge, leaving no way to cross the Mississippi along a 250-mile stretch north of St. Louis.

The closure of the Bayview Bridge at Quincy involved one of the most bizarre and tragic stories of the flood. At 8 p.m. on July 15, floodwaters had overtopped a weak spot in the Fabius Levee just west of Quincy (in Missouri). The rapidly moving floodwaters swept a barge and tow into the breach and these in turn hit the fuel tanks of a filling station, which exploded in a ball of fire. The swirling floodwaters quickly covered five miles of U.S. Highway 36 (the west approach to the Quincy bridge), and spread over 14,000 acres of farmland. The 200 residents of West Quincy were hurriedly evacuated as the flood destroyed many homes and buildings. A man, one James Scott, who claimed to be a flood fighter and eyewitness to the break in the levee, was interviewed on a local TV station. A local sheriff who saw Smith being interviewed recognized Smith as a parolee. After investigation, it was determined that someone had purposefully removed the plastic topping and sandbags, thus sabotaging the levee and causing the breach. Smith, the only one present at the breach at the time, was charged with the act of sabotage on October 1. After a lengthy trial, he was sentenced to life in prison in December 1994 (*USA Today,* December 6, 1994).

Trucks and buses were going around the flood, typically adding 200 to 500 miles to their trips. The Hardin (IL) Bridge across the southern portion of the Illinois River (Figure 8-9) was closed on July 20, effectively isolating three counties.

Problems mounted as the flood enlarged. Wisconsin had more than 100 flooded state roads and 56 damaged bridges (FEMA, 1993a). On July 9, the Nebraska Highway 18 bridge fell into the river, and many state highways were closed (35 in Missouri and 10 in Illinois). Several bridges, highways, and key roads in the St. Louis metropolitan area had been closed by July 11, as depicted in Figure 8-10. These road and bridge closures created mounting problems for commuters and for local and regional trucks and buses.

Estimates of the flood damages to roads and highways began appearing in mid-July. A highway expert in Missouri estimated that damage in that state would amount to $200 million. The Corps estimated on July 14 that repairs to roads damaged in the nine-state area would cost $1 billion. Secretary Pena, head of the federal Department of Transportation, announced on July 20 that the agency would spend $120 million to "restore the Midwest's flood-ravaged transportation network," with $100 million for highways and $20 million for rail lines (*St. Louis*

FIGURE 8-9 Floodwaters cover the approach road (foreground) to the bridge over the flooded Illinois River at East Hardin, IL, (Illinois State Water Survey).

Post-Dispatch, July 21). Angry state officials indicated that $100 million in aid was not nearly enough (*Traffic World*, July 30). At one point in July, Iowa had 45 state highways closed and state road damage estimates were $20 million (Thompson, 1994).

Excessive rainfall and renewed flooding along the Missouri River in late July put more roads in Nebraska, Kansas, and Missouri under water. New crests swamped bridge approaches, and all Missouri River bridges between St. Louis and Kansas City but one were closed by July 30. The McKinley and Lewis and Clark bridges in the St. Louis area remained closed, along with many highways (Figure 8-10). Confusion and congestion were now the norm on the urban transportation scene in Kansas City and at St. Louis. In early August, President Clinton upped the ante for road repairs from $100 million to $175 million (*ENR*,

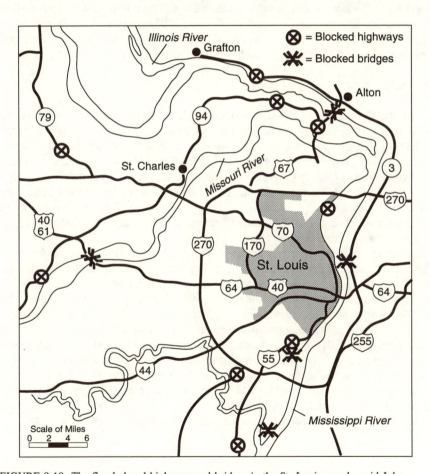

FIGURE 8-10 The flood closed highways and bridges in the St. Louis area by mid-July.

August 9). Initial federal payments for road repairs appeared on August 23: $11 million for Kansas and $28.5 million for Missouri. In late August, Missouri still had 350 miles of roads and highways under water.

Illinois computed its flood-related losses: 121 miles of state highways closed by flooding, 870 miles of county roads closed, 12 state bridges closed and badly damaged, and repair costs of $98 million (FEMA, 1993b). Added to these repair costs were 9,238 jobs lost in 81 communities in which people were unable to get to their jobs. Missouri highway officials stated their damages included 350 miles of inundated state roads and 2,000 miles of flooded rural roads (defined as worse along the Missouri River than along the Mississippi); that 14 miles of state roads had to be totally rebuilt and 100 miles resurfaced; and the repair costs totaled $110 million ($62 million for federal roads and $48 million for nonfederal roads). Road and highway repairs in other states were $122 million (Iowa), $31 million (Minnesota), $22 million (Nebraska) [FEMA, 1993c], $19 million (Wisconsin), $17 million (Kansas)[FEMA, 1993d], and $16 million (North and South Dakota). Repair costs for highways and roads in the nine-state area were $434 million.

Responses

As the floodwaters receded, the damages to roads and highways were found to be much more extensive than had been estimated. Missouri officials declared in late August that it would cost $90 million to fix damaged roads and bridges, but the final figure reached $110 million (IHM Team, 1994). The bridge across the Mississippi at Quincy (Figure 8-8) did not reopen until September 28, 73 days after it was closed. Some commuters used their personal craft to get across the river to jobs in Quincy. Estimated costs in lost revenues for local businesses in Quincy were $30 million. The primary response to flooded roads, highways, and bridges was to detour around them.

Missouri officials reported that many state roads were still not repaired in mid-October. Faced with forecasts of high soil moisture and an above average likelihood for winter-spring flooding in the Mississippi basin, Illinois officials held off making many permanent road repairs during the fall and winter. By mid-1994 most road and highway repairs had been completed in all nine states.

Federal aid for highway and road repairs from FEMA and the Department of Transportation finally amounted to $275 million. An additional $150 million was the estimate for losses due to lost jobs, costs of altered commuting, delayed shipments, costs to re-route shipments and transfer them to other means of transport, and losses of shippers and others awaiting truck-based products or raw materials. Some truck firms benefitted by getting an estimated $13 million in additional business because the stranded barges couldn't transport the cargo.

IMPACTS TO AIRPORTS AND AIR TRAVEL

On July 6, the Smartt Airport near St. Louis was flooded. Creve Coeur Airport at St. Louis became the 13th airport to be flooded and closed on July 20. The Spirit of St. Louis Airport was flooded and closed on July 31. Airports at Jefferson City, MO, St. Joseph, MO, and downtown Kansas City were flooded in July, and the Elwood Airport in Kansas was flooded on August 1.

In all, the flood affected a total of 33 airports including 16 in Missouri (Figure 8-11) and 12 in Iowa, although several of these were small airports. There were no impacts at major highly used urban area airports. The total repair costs were $5.4 million, but some of the smaller airports have not reopened. The only sector of Midwestern travel not affected by the flood was commercial air traffic.

FIGURE 8-11   Floodwaters covered the St. Charles County Airport and invaded the hangars, service buildings, and terminal, as seen here in July 1993 (Illinois State Water Survey).

SUMMARY AND CONCLUSIONS

Flood damages and repair costs, lost revenues, and other losses to the transportation industry, such as unemployment due to the flood, are itemized below.

Flood Damages, Repair Costs, and Other Losses

Railroads

damage repairs and train re-routing	$241 million
lost revenues	$169 million

Navigation

costs to barge industry	$600 million
losses to affected businesses	$320 million

Highways

damage repairs	$434 million
lost revenues to shippers	$150 million

Airports $5 million

Total $1.919 billion

Even though the total damages, repair costs, and other losses amounted to $1.9 billion, there were some benefits in two sectors of the transportation industry: shipments shifted to trucks and railroads created at least $37 million of added income for certain firms.

Long-term effects on the barge industry have developed in the aftermath of the flood. For example, there have been a number of consolidations of barge companies. There is also a continuing concern that the problems due to the flood of 1993 and the problems experienced five years earlier in the 1988 drought will produce lasting negative impacts on the barge business, such as shippers turning to more reliable, but costlier transportation such as the railroads.

Effects of flood costs and losses on the future of the rapidly improving economic status of major railroads such as the BN and AT&SF had largely disappeared by 1995, and effects on the financially struggling SP were not major. The flood kept the railroad industry from achieving the best financial year since World War II (*Traffic World*, January 3, 1994).

A major question about restoration was whether to repair and reopen certain little-used or badly damaged rail lines. The potential of further consolidation of rail operations was under consideration (*Traffic World*, August 23). In contrast, the "thinning out" of the rail lines by extensive abandonments over the past 20 years left few alternatives for detours, suggesting that perhaps railroads should retain these lines as a fall-back strategy.

A series of themes about the flood of 1993 emerges after assessing the impacts and responses to the flood in the transportation sector. A brief description of each theme follows below.

Theme #1: Creative thinking and adaptability were key components of the problem-solving that occurred. This plus system flexibility and cooperation between agencies, companies, and people helped solve many problems. Many adjustments were done quickly, often in unique ways. An excellent example of "real-time" adaptation is the adjustments made by the railroads in re-routing trains on varied lines of other railroads. Flexibility was also found with the railroad systems: the flood proved that certain little-used rail lines in the Midwest, some bordering on abandonment, had value as detour lines and that it was valuable to have competing parallel rail lines.

Theme #2: Had the National Weather Service been able to provide two or three weeks of advance warning about the flood's development, major changes in barge shipments could have saved shippers and barge owners millions of dollars because they could have moved equipment out of harm's reach. Continuing poor estimates of flood crests, flood longevity, and when the rivers would open collectively had major effects on the barge industry and barge shippers. Had the early forecasts been less optimistic, different strategies could have been applied.

Theme #3: Information on the actual amount of damage was inaccurate and slow in coming. For example, consider the shift in the estimated number of stranded barges from a few hundred in early July to 7,000 by July 25. Similarly, many initial estimates of the amount of damages/losses were major underestimates. As the floodwaters receded, surveyors found that damages to fields, roads, bridges, etc. were much worse than predicted.

Theme #4: Flooded and damaged approaches to many critical bridges caused major traffic blockages for weeks. Bridge approaches need to be rebuilt to higher levels. Only then will they be able to survive water levels such as those experienced during the Great Flood of 1993.

REFERENCES

American Railway Engineering Association, January 1994: Railroads vs. 1993 floods, 231-234.

Changnon, S.A., January-February 1994: Trains and water do not mix. *Rail Classics*, 54-64.

ENR, August 9, 1993: Midwest goes into repair mode. p.8-9.

ENR, August 30, 1993: Flood impact felt far afield. p.11.

Farm Week, July 19, 1993: Barge transportation standstill prolonged. p.5.

Federal Emergency Management Agency, 1993a: *Interagency Hazard Mitigation Team Report, Wisconsin*. FEMA-994-DR-WI, Washington, DC, 16 pp.

Federal Emergency Management Agency, 1993b: *Interagency Hazard Mitigation Team Report, Illinois*. FEMA-997-DR-IL, Washington, DC, 58 pp.

Federal Emergency Management Agency, 1993c: *Interagency Hazard Mitigation Team Report, Nebraska*. FEMA-998-NE, Washington, DC, 43 pp.

Federal Emergency Management Agency, 1993d: *Interagency Hazard Mitigation Team Report, Kansas*. FEMA-1000-DR-NE, Washington, DC, 51 pp.

Harper, E.L., 1993: *Testimony of the President of the Association of American Railroads before the Subcommittee on Transportation and Hazardous Materials*. Committee on Energy and Commerce, Washington, DC, 15 pp.

Interagency Hazard Mitigation Team, 1994: *The Floods of '93, State of Missouri. FEMA-989, 995, and 1006*, Washington, DC, 28 pp.

Interagency Floodplain Management Review Committee, 1994: *Sharing the Challenge: Floodplain Management into the 21st Century*.   Report to Floodplain Management Task Force, Washington, DC, 189 pp.

Pacific Rail News, August 1993: Water Water Everywhere. p.5.

Railway Track & Structures, September 1993: Coping with the Midwest Flood, 42-43.

St. Louis Post-Dispatch, June 29, 1993: Flood closes river north of St. Louis. p.1.

St. Louis Post-Dispatch, June 30, 1993: River forecast: It'll be high until mid-July. p. 4a.

St. Louis Post-Dispatch, July 2, 1993: Floods. p. 1.

St. Louis Post-Dispatch, July 21, 1993: Aid promised to get Midwest moving again. p.3.

St. Louis Post-Dispatch, August 18, 1993: Idle barges cost states millions. p.1.

Thompson, H.M., 1994: *The Floods of 1993: Iowa Flood Disaster Report*. Johnston, IA, 35 pp.

Traffic World, July 19, 1993: Flood waters recede in Midwest but rain, delays and detours persist,. pp.15-16.

Traffic World, July 30, 1993: Traffic damage to flooded roads; official coffers won't cover repairs. p.16.

Traffic World, August 23, 1993: As floodwaters recede, railroads take stock of track needs. p.14.

Traffic World, August 30, 1993: Mississippi barge traffic picks up as waters recede. pp.11-12.

Traffic World, January 3, 1994: Railroad's handling of summer floods fuel optimism that '94 will be banner year. pp.15-16.

Trains, October 1993: Santa Fe vs. nature at milepost 364.4. pp.18-19.

Transportation and Distribution, January 1994: Flood means lost income to railroads. Vol.35, p.16.

USA Today, December 6, 1994: Saboteur of levee gets life sentence. p.1.

9

Economic Impacts:
Lost Income, Ripple Effects,
and Recovery

Geoffrey J.D. Hewings
and
Ramamohan Mahidhara

INTRODUCTION

One of the most prominent features of a physical catastrophe is its impact on the economy of the region in which it occurs. Within hours of a major hurricane, flood, earthquake or similar hazard, the news media announces estimates of the economic costs of the disaster. No one is really sure just what process is used to arrive at these numbers; in many cases, they are little more than educated guesses, sometimes based on experiences with prior hazards. Nevertheless, the estimates are produced and reproduced with an air of authenticity that belies their actual formulation; inevitably, the numbers turn out to be wrong, often significantly overestimating the losses.

In an attempt to place the economic impacts of the flood of 1993 in a broad, consistent context, this chapter provides a careful appraisal of the flood's economic consequences through a two-pronged approach: economic consequences for the state and for the nation. Given the existence of an economic model for the state of Iowa, it was possible to undertake a very detailed analysis of the economic impacts of the flood for that particular state. (While nine states were affected by the flood, the level of detail that could be provided was, of necessity, sharply reduced since companion models for individual states other than Iowa have not yet been completed.) National data complement this state perspective by attempting to trace the impacts on major macro-level statistics such as the Gross National Product (GNP). Perspectives on economic conditions in the Midwest are offered in other chapters (see Chapters 7, 8, and 12). Summary comments are offered about the impact at the national level to provide some sense of the degree to which the localized effects on Iowa translated into significant or less significant impacts for the nation as a whole.

IMPACT ANALYSIS OF DISASTERS

One of the major difficulties with impact assessment involves disentangling those consequences that are directly and indirectly associated with a particular disaster: some activities may suffer delayed consequences (albeit with an associated economic cost), while others may be completely destroyed. Furthermore, if major infrastructure (bridges, roads, buildings) is destroyed in the process, its restoration may even generate significant, positive economic impacts: should these be considered as costs or benefits of the disaster? The task at hand is to try to assemble an assessment that handles the impacts in a consistent fashion, and one that avoids double counting and yet tries to place the consequences in the appropriate slot in the accounting framework.

A second important issue concerns the focus of the economic impact analysis. At each spatial level (state, region, or national), it is possible to derive rather different assessment of the effects. In some cases, the impacts outside the immediate state or region in which the flooding occurred may also be negative, while at the national level the effects may actually have had little discernible impact. In fact, the loss of agricultural output in one major region might, through the reduction in goods and supplies, elevate prices for output in the rest of the country, thereby actually yielding a positive net impact on the nation as a whole. This is one of the consequences of the geography of disasters: the grief, suffering, and economic losses are not universally shared across regions.

THE 1993 FLOOD

It was estimated that the 1993 flood's immediate impact was the loss of 52 lives and the temporary or permanent relocation of more than 74,000 people from their homes (Benjamin et al., 1994). A total of 532 counties in the Midwest were declared eligible for individual or community assistance (see Figure 12-6). Although it contains only 10 percent of the U.S. population, the flood-affected area supports nearly 20 percent of all farm employment (Benjamin et al., 1994). Impact assessments published immediately after the flood generally focused only on these impacts, which are usually referred to as the *direct impacts* (see Chapter 1). By the end of summer 1993, it was estimated that total flood losses were somewhere between $12 billion and $20 billion, with $8 billion to $9 billion in crop losses and the remainder from property and nonagricultural income losses, a high cost (Figure 9-1). A few months later, one analysis reduced the total loss to $10 billion (Benjamin et al., 1994). The National Weather Service (1994), in a major report issued several months after the flood, presented an impact analysis revealing that the total damage was as high as $15.7 billion. Now with more data

FIGURE 9-1 The media equated the flood with huge dollar losses (Reprinted with permission of Mike Keefe).

on the secondary and tertiary impacts, the estimate is that the damages and losses amounted to about $18 billion.

How do these impacts compare with other recent disasters? Figure 9-2 shows estimates for property damage resulting from several recent disasters, and three other natural disasters produced more extensive property damage (in dollar terms)

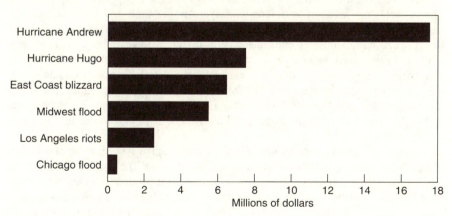

FIGURE 9-2 Estimates of property damage caused by recent natural disasters show the 1993 flood losses ranked fourth (Schnorbus et al., 1993).

than the flood of 1993. However, the population density was much lower in the geographic region affected by the flood, which actually covered a far more extensive area than most of the other disasters. The two large metropolitan areas in the nine-state flood zone, St. Louis and Kansas City, were spared severe flooding of most of their metropolitan areas.

In many ways, it was the sheer size and location of the flooded area that created some of the most difficult problems. Many of the roads, railroads, and bridges along which traffic was interrupted carried only a small portion of the nation's passenger and goods traffic, but they were still important links in the nation's north-south and east-west arteries, and thus disrupted traffic patterns over an even larger area. In fact, the railroads crossing the flooded region carry 25 percent of the nation's freight. From a national perspective, however, the damage was small (i.e., less than 2 percent of the annual expenditure for construction and maintenance of roads and highways in the United States in 1991). However, notwithstanding the spatial range of the impacts, the states of Iowa, Missouri, Minnesota, and Illinois sustained the most damage. Iowa is the primary focus of our investigation of state losses.

THE IOWA IMPACT

Iowa's economy is closely linked with the agricultural sector: the percentage of people employed in agriculture in Iowa is three times that in the United States as a whole, and Iowa has a strong manufacturing base closely linked to agriculture. Figures 9-3 and 9-4 portray the output and employment history for the agricultural sector and the food and kindred products sector in Iowa over the period 1972 through 1990, and their trends are important in assessing the flood losses. Agricultural output has fluctuated more during this period, responding to the vagaries of weather and business cycles; the food and kindred products sector output, on the other hand, has trended upward without major fluctuations. In concert with similar trends elsewhere in the Midwest, both sectors have recorded improved productivity, with more prominent growth in the manu-facturing sector. In fact, employment in the food and kindred products sector (Figure 9-4) is almost the same in 1990 as it was in 1972 but output has grown 28 percent (in constant 1982 dollars). Employment trends in the agricultural sector have been downward sloping, with a loss of 35,000 jobs during the 1972-1990 period.

However, the two sectors are linked in important ways; analysis shows that a $100 change in agricultural output would produce a $20 change in output from food and kindred products. The loss of agricultural production must be viewed within the context of its system-wide impacts, not just losses that occur within the sector itself. Furthermore, many food processing plants are located in agricultural areas to take advantage of each other's geographical proximity, there-

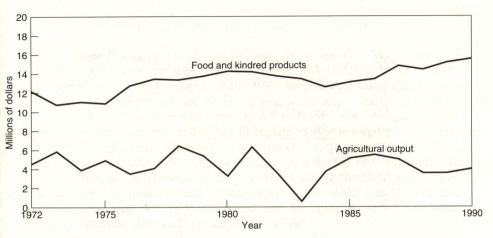

FIGURE 9-3 Outputs of the agricultural sector and the food and kindred products sector in Iowa during 1972-1990 (expressed in 1982 dollars).

by minimizing transportation costs for the relatively lower-value raw products. When the flood disrupted the supply of agricultural inputs into the manufacturing sector, access to alternative sources of supply was difficult because transportation systems were also disrupted. Figure 9-5 summarizes property damage estimates by state as a result of the flood; but how can one add to this the impact of the loss of agricultural production?

To make this assessment, a model developed by the Regional Economics Applications Laboratory (1993) for the state of Iowa, was used. This economic

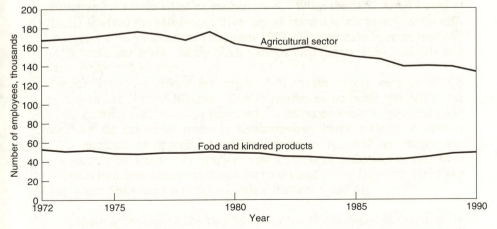

FIGURE 9-4 Employment in the agricultural sector and the food and kindred products sector in Iowa during 1972-1990 (expressed in thousands of jobs).

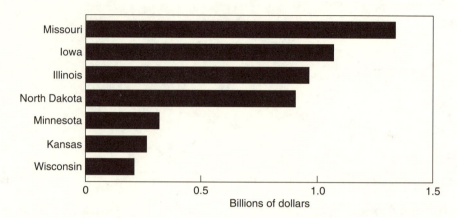

FIGURE 9-5   Estimates of property damages caused by the flood in each state with excessive losses (Schnorbus et al., 1993).

model attempts to mimic the behavior of the economy's markets by capturing supply and demand interactions between all sectors of the economy. This *economic snapshot* enables us to estimate the consequences of actions in one sector on the remaining sectors of the state; furthermore, the snapshot can be redeveloped each year to provide both a historical assessment and forecasts of future activity for the next 25 years.

One of the model's most important features is its ability to capture the *ripple effects* (an apt analogy in this application) of the consequences of change or disruption in one sector on other sectors of the economy. In so doing the model is able to take the *direct effects* of change and estimate the *indirect effects* and thus provide a final assessment of the *total impacts*. Were the issue at hand the impact of opening a new firm or redistributing federal spending from defense to nondefense uses, the problem would be relatively straightforward. In the case of the Iowa flood, the problem is more complicated. What was truly lost, what was merely postponed, and just how were the mitigation expenditures to be judged?

The model mimics chain reactions occurring within the economy as one sector expends, and Table 9-1 provides an example. In this example, it is assumed that the loss in the agricultural sector was $1 billion in 1993. How will this loss ripple throughout the economy?

Initially, the loss of agricultural output will result in lost income to farmers, lost income to the agricultural service sector, lost income to the owners of local businesses that experience decreased sales, and eventually lost income to the agricultural processing sectors. When all the impacts were traced throughout the

TABLE 9-1 Major Sectors Affected by a Change in Agriculture in Iowa

Sector	Output loss ($ million)
Construction	32
Food and Kindred Products	188
Printing & Publishing	26
Chemicals	43
Rubber & Plastic	24
Fabricated Metals	14
Machinery	66
Transportation	44
Communications	12
Utilities	43
Trade	138
Finance & Insurance	60
Real Estate	58
Services	82
Eating & Drinking Establishments	18
Auto Repair	18
Health, Education	58
Total	**2,203**

Note: Table assumes an initial loss of $1 billion. Entries do not comprise the total since only data for selected sectors were shown.

economy, about $2.2 billion of activity were affected: of which $1 billion was the initial loss in agriculture, the remaining $1.1 billion representing the indirect effects. Table 9-1 shows only some of the sectors that would be most affected. The impact on food and kindred products, the largest impact, has already been addressed. Note that the trade sector is the second most affected sector, but the picture that emerges is the degree to which the change has the capacity to influence economic activity in a wide range of sectors, some having little direct connection with agriculture. The rest of this section will attempt to provide a more complete picture of these impacts.

Preliminary estimates (Schnorbus et al., 1993) suggested that crop losses in Iowa due to the flood ranged from $1.2 to $2 billion (recall that the early estimates were $7 billion to $9 billion for the whole flooded area). The state of Iowa (Johnson, 1994) later estimated that the agricultural crop losses were $1.9 billion; hence, there is consistency in the estimates for crop losses. Output was lost because floodwaters resulted in the crop literally rotting in the fields or the fields were so waterlogged or wet that crops could not be planted or harvested, even when the floodwaters receded. Schnorbus et al. (1993) estimated that the reduction in yields was 40 percent per acre for corn and 25 percent per acre for soybeans, but that the impact nationally was not significant.

Using the Iowa model, each loss of $1 in agricultural output generates a system-wide loss of $2.20 in output and $1.87 in income. While this provides some guide as to the potential magnitude of the losses, an alternative method was employed in which the direct losses were represented as the difference between the dollar value of the projected 1993 output against a base case using five-year averages for production and prices. With this approach, direct losses of corn and soybeans were estimated as $380 million and $320 million, respectively. The $700 million total is much lower than the initial estimates of $1.2 to $2 billion, primarily due to the offsets that must be included, such as disaster payments, crop insurance payments, and other assistance. These offsets included $623 million for crop losses by the U.S. Department of Agriculture (USDA) and total federal expenditures for flood-related losses of $1.138 billion (IFMR Committee, 1994). However, not all of the offset funds would necessarily be spent in Iowa. For example, machinery might be purchased from out-of-state suppliers and a great deal of construction material may have been acquired outside the state. Hence, it is difficult to arrive at a consistent set of impact figures since each agency uses a different set of criteria.

While the loss of the actual crops would affect specific industries (through the withdrawal of supplies), the amount of income circulating in the state would not be reduced by a similar amount because of the offsets. However, the offset income would initially affect different sectors than those affected by the loss of agricultural production. For the metropolitan areas of Des Moines and Davenport, where significant disruption was associated with the loss of water treatment capabilities, the losses were apportioned on a daily basis. (A similar strategy was used to estimate the economic impact of the 1992 Chicago flood.) Again, a distinction was made between deferred losses (the costs of disruption) and permanent losses. Taken together, the losses were estimated at $185 million, offset by $44 million through assistance programs that would create a positive stimulus (through post-flood reconstruction, for example).

The crop losses and the urban-based losses were then entered into the Iowa model to derive the system-wide impacts. Gross state product was estimated to decline by about $250 million, personal income by $350 per person, and overall shipments by $1.8 billion. How important are these numbers? Pre-flood estimates of 1993 total output for Iowa were $140 billion, so the value of shipments lost to the state's economy represented up to 1.5 percent of the economy; there was little discernible spillover into 1994, and no trace will be apparent by 1995. As more construction and reconstruction activities are completed, some of the initial losses will be offset by the boosts that these activities will bring to the economy. Table 9-2 summarizes the impacts (Schnorbus et al., 1993). This accounts for damages plus restoration costs for crop losses and rebuilding of the state's infrastructure--a net cost to Iowa.

TABLE 9-2 Summary of Estimates of Direct and Indirect Flood Costs in Iowa (expressed in 1993 dollars in billions)

Effects	$ billion
Wealth effects	1.2
Property Damage	
Output effects	
Agricultural losses	0.9
Nonagricultural losses	0.9
Food processing	0.3
Trade	0.2
Finance, insurance, real estate, services	0.1
Total	$3.6

Earlier it was noted that the food and kindred products sector is closely tied to the agricultural sector: according to Table 9-2, the loss for this sector is estimated at $300 million, of which about $200 million is directly attributable to agricultural losses, and the remainder is due to losses elsewhere in the economy (for example, food and drinking establishments in Des Moines and Davenport that were unable to open and therefore did not purchase supplies). It is not clear just how much substitution occurred in the food and kindred products sector. With significant disruption in major transportation arteries, it may not have been possible to access alternative supplies. When additional transportation costs (and, in all probability, higher product acquisition costs) are included, there would be the additional problem of production costs way out of line with those of other regional and national producers.

Finally, it should be noted Schnorbus et al. (1993) reported evidence that by early fall 1993, there were signs of an upturn in the economy--the effects of delayed purchases, cleanup costs, and expenditures from insurance receipts served to stimulate Iowa's economy. It will be many years before final conclusions can be drawn. However, there is no doubt that even then, no matter what the final assessment, there will have been severe differential impacts by sub-region and sector of the economy.

THE NATIONAL IMPACT

Table 9-3 summarizes the flood's impacts on personal income for the third and fourth quarters of 1993. For the United States as a whole, the net adjustments were approximately $10.6 billion in the third quarter, dropping to $2.7 billion in

TABLE 9-3 Impacts of the Flood on Personal Income in the Third and Fourth Quarters of 1993 (dollars in billions)

State	Third Quarter	Fourth Quarter
Illinois	1.49	0.25
Iowa	2.39	0.63
Kansas	0.89	0.25
Minnesota	1.97	0.64
Missouri	2.27	0.49
Nebraska	0.38	0.11
North Dakota	0.44	0.12
South Dakota	0.28	0.07
Wisconsin	0.49	0.15

Source: Bureau of Economic Analysis, *Survey of Current Business* (April 1994).

the final quarter of 1993. These figures are higher than the ones used in earlier sections since they trace the repercussions of losses in the Midwest on the rest of the country (including the Midwest itself)[1].

Table 9-4 shows the percentage distribution of flood impacts on personal incomes by Midwestern states: the greatest impact occurred in Iowa, closely followed by Missouri, Minnesota, and Illinois (the impact on Missouri would have been even larger had the levee at St. Louis broken and flooded much of that city). When the losses are compared with total personal income in each state, a slightly different picture emerges, however. While Illinois' losses accounted for 14 percent of the Midwest's total, the loss for the state was less than 1 percent; on the other hand, Iowa's losses amounted to almost 5 percent of that state's total. For the Dakotas, especially North Dakota, the losses were far larger in relative terms, accounting for almost 4.5 percent of state income in North Dakota. Hence, states with a strong dependence on agriculture and associated industry suffered more losses in a relative sense than states such as Illinois, which also had a much broader industrial base. The spatial variations of the impacts reveal the importance of focusing attention on those geographical areas smaller than states.

---

[1]Data were generously provided by the Bureau of Economic Analysis or BEA (1994a, 1994b) of the U.S. Department of Commerce; but the interpretations and conclusions drawn should not be ascribed to BEA.

TABLE 9-4 Percentage Distribution of Personal Income Due to Flood Impacts during the Third Quarter of 1993

	Personal income loss ($ billions)	Percentage of Midwest	Total personal income ($ billions)	Loss (percent of total)
Illinois	1.48	14.05	265	0.56
Iowa	2.39	22.59	49	4.88
Kansas	0.89	8.35	50	1.77
Minnesota	1.97	18.58	93	2.10
Missouri	2.27	21.40	101	2.25
Nebraska	0.38	3.58	31	1.23
North Dakota	0.44	4.19	10	4.30
South Dakota	0.27	2.61	12	2.27
Wisconsin	0.49	4.65	100	0.49

Source: Bureau of Economic Analysis, *Survey of Current Business* (April 1994)

EVALUATION

The analysis of the economic impact of the 1993 flood must still be regarded as a preliminary assignment in late 1994 primarily because much of the flood's economic impact was concentrated in activities that have the potential for recovery: some activities were irretrievably lost (for example, crops), but the farmland itself remains. A real issue in any final economic assessment of the flood will center on the degree to which the flood seriously eroded or perhaps enhanced the fertility and productivity of the land, as illustrated in Figure 9-6 (see Chapter 5 for effects due to soil erosion and sand deposition in the floodplains). Additions to the final bill for the flood will include increased insurance premiums, deferred equipment purchases, and the costs of any loans taken out to cover short-term losses. On the other side of the ledger, there needs to be a careful evaluation of the contribution provided to the region by the rebuilt infrastructure, beyond the short-term stimulus provided by construction jobs and the associated ripple effects on the area's economy. Several communities have been abandoned and relocated to safer higher ground; the costs and benefits need to be weighed carefully with a view to the longer-term consideration.

The comments of Schnorbus et al. (1993) provide a sense of the balancing act that analysts must undertake in making assessments of the impacts of unscheduled events: "Within six months to a year after the flood, the bulk of that post-flood

FIGURE 9-6   A huge sand deposit left by the flooding across farmland near Quincy, IL.   The long-term economic impact of the vast amount of soil erosion and deposition of eroded sands and soils on flooded farmlands remained ill-defined a year after the flood (Illinois State Water Survey).

response will have ended.   A real loss in wealth has occurred and that loss can never be made up.   However, in terms of day-to-day economic activity, which can be replaced through overtime and shifting production to other facilities, the net effect may eventually be a boost for the Iowa and the Midwest economy."

Lessons Learned

Impact assessment of unscheduled events is an inexact science; pressure from the news media and television for definitive numbers often results in an escalation of estimates of damage.   There appears to be something magical about providing estimates that hover in the billion dollar range.   They have a cachet of significance that often belies the crudity with which the early estimation process was carried out.   Furthermore, attention is focused almost exclusively on physical damage or losses; little attention is devoted to intangible impacts such as the social losses of a home that has been in the possession of a family for many generations, or the changes in attitudes towards risk that might change the amount and timing of future investment.   There is also a tendency to assume a degree of resilience, the notion underlying the assumption that since an economy can bounce back, so can the lives of the people most significantly affected by the great disaster.

Finally, is the issue of opportunity costs of public (national) funds being used to rebuild communities that were located in high-risk areas. In some cases, these communities have been physically relocated to higher ground, but in other cases, the challenges to conventional wisdom that rebuilding is a right were met with significant opposition. Similar responses were found in the behavior of residents of Atlantic Coast communities subject to periodic hurricane damage or California residents in areas with a high incidence of earthquakes. The final summary of the economic consequences of the 1993 flood will not be written for many more years. For example, the lawsuits stemming from the flood are likely to consume many more millions of dollars before the books are closed. These are the types of economic impacts that are rarely added to the accounting tables.

REFERENCES

Benjamin, G.J., R.H. Mattoon, and W.A. Testa, 1994. Assessing the Midwest flood. *Chicago Fed Letter*, 76.

Bureau of Economic Analysis, 1994a. Total and per capita personal income by state and region. *Survey of Current Business*, 74(4), 117-126.

Bureau of Economic Analysis, 1994b. Unpublished estimate of *Adjustments to Personal Income*.

Interagency Floodplain Management Review Committee, 1994. *Sharing the Challenge: Floodplain Management into the 21st Century*. Administration Floodplain Management Task Force, Washington, DC, 191 pp.

Johnson, H.M., 1994. *The Floods of 1993: Iowa Flood Disaster Report*. Iowa Flood Recovery Coordination Team, Johnston, IA, 35 pp.

National Weather Service, 1994: *The Great Flood of 1993*. National Disaster Survey, National Oceanic and Atmospheric Administration, Washington, DC, 212 pp.

Regional Economic Applications Laboratory, 1993: *Iowa Regional Econometrics Input-Output Model*. Miscellaneous Working Papers, Champaign, IL, 93 pp.

Schnorbus, R, R. Mahidhara, and P. Ballew, 1993: The great flood of 1993 and the Midwest economy. *Midwest Economic Report*, Chicago: Federal Reserve Bank, 1-13.

10

Living with the Flood:
Human and Governmental Responses
to Real and Symbolic Risk

Lee Wilkins

OVERVIEW

While an argument can be made that the Great Flood of 1993 had an impact on the entire nation, it is not possible for this chapter to address the social consequences of this natural disaster entirely from that perspective. Instead, the state of Missouri has been chosen as the focal point in an effort to contextualize and analyze the most significant social impacts of the 1993 flood. However, what happens on a local level, particularly in the disaster arena, can and often does have national significance. Consequently, the central thesis of this chapter is that the severity of the local flood impact in the Midwest has national implications for floodplain management and disaster relief policies. That policy debate, focusing as it does on the interacting roles of federal, state, and local governments with individuals and powerful economic interests, will occur at a time when the nation, particularly the U.S. Congress, is expected to intently examine these issues. In short, how the nation decides to deal with the policy consequences of this disaster will provide scholars from various disciplines with an insight into contemporary thinking on the role of government in a democracy on the edge of the 21st century.

This chapter reviews the most significant social impacts of the 1993 flood, including the impacts on human health and habitation, as well as disruption of economic activity and, in many cases, on patterns of daily living. The role of disaster relief agencies, state and local governments, and informal inter-personal networks in dealing with the flood's onset and recovery are also reviewed. The chapter examines how one particular social institution--the mass media on both the local and national levels--covered the flood onset and immediate post-impact period. While some statistics are included in this review, it is important to note that the social impacts of natural hazards are not easily quantified. The sheer number of federal dollars allocated to the disaster relief effort can provide a framework for understanding the social impact, but individuals and the communities in which they live function by more than total relief allocations. This is why the way one central Missouri community dealt with the flood is explored. Finally, the chapter concludes with a section on lessons learned: the potential directions for national policy making.

For those readers not intimately familiar with the Midwest, what follows is a brief introduction to the "Show Me" state and its neighboring states, which were flooded. In many ways, Missouri is typical of the nine Midwestern states that were inundated in the late spring and early summer of 1993. Much of Missouri's economy is tied to the Missouri and the Mississippi Rivers, which run through the entire region, thereby placing more than 40 percent of Missouri's land area within a 100-year floodplain. In the summer of 1993, all but three Missouri counties were declared national disaster areas in the wake of what many hydrologic experts have categorized as a 500-year event (see Chapter 4). Only one state was more severely impacted, Iowa, in which all 99 counties were designated federal disaster areas.

In other ways, however, Missouri is atypical. First, its geography meant that the floodwaters had an enormous impact on urban areas, the largest concentrations of people affected by the 1993 flood, although Des Moines, IA, as a single community, was more severely affected at the apex of the flood. Metropolitan St. Louis and Kansas City each dealt with the rising waters for several months (see Chapters 1 and 4). At one point, only one bridge connecting St. Louis and East St. Louis, IL, remained open to automobile traffic. Rail traffic was equally curtailed in and around these urban areas (see Chapter 8). This disruption of the transportation system represented many similar events throughout the Midwest as rising waters cut off routes to work, normal methods of moving raw materials and manufactured goods, and provided "instant" tourist attractions.

Second, Missouri was the only state in which the capital, Jefferson City, was inundated. Indeed, floodwaters came within a few blocks of the capitol building itself--a situation that was not overlooked by elected officials. Third, before the flood of 1993 the state could not be characterized as among those political entities in the forefront of floodplain management. Thus, the flood provided Missouri with a significant opportunity to evaluate its political response to the event. Finally, Missouri was one of three Midwestern states in which the state government, in conjunction with academic institutions, undertook a systematic study of the social impact of the flood with some emphasis on the physical and mental health of individuals affected. The results of that work (conducted by the Center for Advanced Social Research at the University of Missouri) provide some insight into the consequences of the flood many months after the event officially ended.

THE HISTORICAL VIEW

The social impact of the Great Flood of 1993 has its roots in the history of human habitation of the Mississippi and Missouri River basins. How people have chosen to use this land, and the environmental impacts of those choices, laid the groundwork for much of what occurred in spring and summer 1993.

Long before Europeans settled the area, Native Americans had congregated along the Mississippi River basin. One study noted that the native people "built their houses on the high land, and where there is none, they raise mounds by hand and here they take refuge from the great flood"(Clark, 1982).

There was an intuitive wisdom in that approach to rising waters that the burgeoning economic development of the 19th century United States would forget. As early as 1849, the U.S. Congress granted funds to the U.S. Army Corps of Engineers to conduct a study of flood control possibilities along the Lower Mississippi. There was economic motivation for that work. St. Louis was engaged in competition with other Midwestern cities, particularly Chicago, for economic dominance of the region. St. Louis' economic future was clearly tied to the river and to the link it provided with the port of New Orleans. The Civil War and the emergence of the railroad as the least expensive way to transport goods great distances ultimately determined that Chicago would win this economic contest, but St. Louis' reliance on the economic and physical power of the river was established in the first half of the century (Cronon, 1991).

The first river flood control study in the 1850s provided the template for much of what was to come in the ensuing 150 years. The initial study of 1849 concluded that the river should be controlled with a "levees-only" policy, a refuge in technology that was supplemented after the massive 1927 flood (see Chapter 11) by other structural measures such as reservoirs, fuse-plug levees, floodways, and channel improvements. Well before the flood of 1993, this reliance on technology and physical structures had resulted in an extensive network of federally constructed levees augmented by thousands of agricultural levees built to much less exacting standards, a riverbed that had been dredged and channeled for many years, and, within the confines of St. Louis itself, a river wall 49 feet above normal river flood levels through the downtown corridor that would come within a few inches of being topped by the overflowing Mississippi during the flood of 1993. While there is still enormous technical dispute on precisely how much impact this reliance on technological control had on mitigating and exacerbating the consequences of "a lot of rain," there is little dispute that Missouri provides a microcosm through which to study the convergence of historic, economic, and social conditions in conjunction with a natural disaster of historic proportions.

LIVING WITH RISING WATERS

The Mississippi is not a commonplace river. Considering the Missouri, its main branch, it is the longest river in the world--four thousand, three hundred miles....It discharges three times as much water as the St. Lawrence, twenty-five times as much as the Rhine, and three hundred and thirty-eight times as much as the Thames. No other river has so vast a drainage basin; it draws its water supply from twenty-eight States and Territories; from Delaware, on the Atlantic seaboard, and from all the country between that and Idaho on the Pacific slope--a spread of fourth degrees of longitude. The area of its drainage basin is as great as the combined areas of England, Wales, Scotland, Ireland, France, Spain, Portugal, Germany, Austria, Italy, and Turkey (Mark Twain, 1883).

To understand the impact of the 1993 flood, it is necessary to briefly review its precursor, the 1927 flood. Hazards scholars agree that this event was of somewhat greater magnitude than the 1993 event. This calculation focuses on the amount of water carried down the river during that period, the loss of life due to the flood, and the total number of people affected. Total dollar estimates of damages, of course, were much higher in 1993 than 66 years earlier, even after adjustment of the 1927 losses to 1993 dollar values. The 1927 flood occurred in the Lower Mississippi basin.

In the 1927 flood, the official death toll was 246, but it may have been as high as 500. Before 1927, local governments had paid a total of about $292 million in flood protection works for the lower Mississippi. After that flood, Congress authorized expenditures of $325 million. Between 1930 and 1950, there were extensive modifications to the rivers in the basin, and cities such as St. Louis, Kansas City, and Minneapolis-St. Paul developed urban business and industrial centers along the rivers.

Within this context, the 1993 flood may be viewed as anywhere from a 50-year to 500-year event, depending on geographical location (see Chapter 4). In Missouri, where both the Mississippi and Missouri Rivers reached record levels, statistics collected by the U.S. Geological Survey indicate the 1993 flood should be defined as a 500-year event.

Flooding caused significant damage in nine states: Illinois, Iowa, Kansas, Minnesota, Missouri, North and South Dakota, Nebraska, and Wisconsin. All counties in Iowa were declared disaster areas. More than 1,000 levees stretching nearly 6,000 miles were breached or overtopped. Many others sustained significant damage. A total of 532 counties were included in the presidential disaster declarations.

Fifty-two deaths were attributed to the flood, including six drownings in metropolitan St. Louis where rising waters trapped children on an outing with a clergyman in a cave. However, the flood's death total remains uncertain. The state of Missouri, for example, suggests that 50 Missourians died as a result of the flood, 30 of them in flash floods that were ancillary to the flooding on the Mississippi and Missouri. There are similar debates over death and injury tolls in other states.

Estimates for damages from the flood also vary widely. Figures of $12-$16 billion were commonly cited at the time of the flood, with more than half of those losses sustained by agriculture. In August 1993 the *New York Times* published a damage estimate of $12 billion based on information provided by state and federal sources, and the National Weather Service (1994) estimated total damages at $15.7 billion (IFMR Committee, 1994).

It is also important to note that the nation's investment in flood protection projects paid off. It is estimated that reservoirs and levees built by the U.S. Army Corps of Engineers prevented more than $19 billion in potential damages (IFMRC, 1994). Large areas of Kansas City and St. Louis were protected by both private and public levee systems, although several suburbs suffered extensive damage.

The total number of people touched by the flood will never be known. However, the American Red Cross estimated that 56,295 family dwellings were affected in some way. The Red Cross spent more than $30 million in flood relief efforts, sheltered 14,502 people in 145 shelters in the region, and served more than 2.5 million meals. Surveys by Red Cross workers immediately after the flood identified more than 55,000 flooded residences, an estimate later updated to 70,545 by the Federal Emergency Management Agency (FEMA). As of April 1994, the federal government had received 167,224 requests for individual assistance and 112,042 applications for the Disaster Housing Program, of which 89,734 had been approved. The Disaster Housing program data indicate that more than 100,000 residences were flooded.

Contrary to popular belief, considerable damage from the flood did not occur within the floodplain itself but resulted from the heavy rains falling on already saturated soils. In Cook County, IL, many homes on Chicago's south and west sides sustained flooded basements due to stormwater and sewer backup from a three-day rainstorm. Ultimately Cook County was added to the Illinois disaster declaration.

Property damage has been estimated as high as $12 billion, and Congress allocated $6.2 billion for disaster relief. FEMA covered about $650 million for public assistance. No overall damage estimates for businesses are available, but Small Business Association loans after the flood exceeded $334 million for physical damage and economic injury (IFMRC, 1994). Much of this damage occurred in Kansas City and St. Louis where both private and publicly built levees were overtopped. For example, an American Cyanamid Plant near Hannibal, MO, was protected by its own levee and escaped damage from floodwaters, but the plant was shut down for nearly three months because its access road was flooded when an agricultural levee failed. In aggregate, at least 30,000 jobs were disrupted by the flood.

Flooding that wiped out access roads, and sometimes major arteries, added hours to the time it took to get to work and resulted in much lost business (see Chapter 8). Many of the region's water treatment plants, which are often located at lowest possible sites, also sustained damage. The Environmental Protection Agency has identified 200 water treatment plants affected by the flood, the most well-known being the Des Moines Water Works, which remained out of operation for 12 days and could not produce potable water for 19 days. Other large communities with flooded water treatment plants and prolonged outages were Alton, IL (Figure 10-1), and St. Joseph, MO. Damages to public buildings exceeded $27 million. Water control facilities sustained more than $20 million in damages, and parks and other recreational facilities recorded more than $22 million in damages (IFMRC, 1994).

Superfund sites were flooded and huge volumes of farm chemicals and raw sewage were flushed into the rivers (White and Myers, 1994). More than 100 towns have taken steps to partially or completely relocate, with a potential cost of $500 million.

The Federal Crop Insurance Corporation estimated that 57 percent of the flooded acreage was insured; those claims are expected to top $600 million. Officials with the Department of Agriculture predicted perhaps 400,000 acres in floodplains would remain covered with sand (much of which was eroded from breached levees). In Missouri alone, 455,000 acres (60 percent of the cropland in the Missouri River floodplain) were damaged by sand deposits and scouring. Of that, 77,500 acres were covered with up to 24 inches of sand, and 59,000 acres were covered by more than two feet of sand.

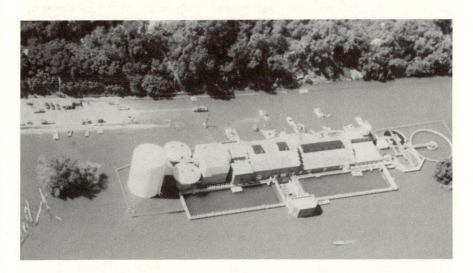

FIGURE 10-1 The flooded water treatment plant at Alton, IL, left 77,000 residents without potable water (Illinois State Water Survey).

While these various statistics are staggering, it is essential to note that these impacts were not uniform throughout the population. A generalized statement about risk applied to the 1993 flood: the riskiest thing to be was poor. Flooded neighborhoods tended to be lower income, with a high percentage of rental properties generally housing more elderly residents, more young families, and more people on assistance. Homes in the floodplain often had market values of less than $25,000 (IFMRC, 1994). Thus, the Great Flood of 1993, widely regarded as the third most costly domestic disaster in U.S. history (see Chapter 11), affected certain portions of the population much more severely than others. Those who were among the least able to cope economically often bore the largest social costs.

MEDIA COVERAGE OF THE FLOOD: FROM DOMESTIC AFGHANISTANISM TO SOLIDARITY

> The usual conception of floods is of raging waters, like a dam bursting. But really big floods, like on the Mississippi, are far more insidious. The damage doesn't come from roaring walls of water, it comes from quiet backwaters that spread amoebae-like, creeping higher and higher ever so gently--gently and inexorably. Sometimes nature is terrifying in its fury, sometimes in its relentlessness. (*Des Moines Register*, July 3, 1993).

While Midwest residents often viewed the flood firsthand, most of the nation learned about the flood from the news media, particularly the American television networks and national newspapers such as the *New York Times* and newsmagazines such as *Newsweek* and *Time*. This mediated vision of the flood is important for several reasons.

First, journalists covering the disaster managed to transform a 500-year event into what sociologist Gay Tuchman (1973) has called a "routinization of the unexpected." This activity--taking a disaster and making it into a manageable problem--mirrors the activities of other organizations involved in flood work, from the Red Cross to state and federal institutions such as FEMA. In each case, institutions followed well-developed patterns to cope with warning, onset, and recovery.

Second, the patterns of journalistic coverage also reflected some cultural understandings of the flood itself and of human relationships to the natural events. In fact, the concept of the flood as an event is in itself significant in media coverage, for while it provided journalists with topics for their news stories, it also allowed journalists to ignore some of the deeper contributors to the flood's magnitude and impact. Mass communication scholars refer to this phenomenon as "decontextualization" (Altheide, 1976) or the notion that typical journalistic coverage of many types of news stories, including disasters and hazards, allows journalists and their audiences to focus on the event rather than on underlying causes and potential solutions and mitigation strategies

(Wilkins, 1987). This emphasis on the event, when it reaches the audience, also has an important subtle effect (Iyengar, 1994). By focusing on the event itself instead of framing the story as a problem with potential solutions (Jamieson, 1992), the audience comes to believe that there is little they can do, either as individuals or as members of larger political and social communities, to cope with and ultimately solve the problems presented by the flood. This mediated reality is, in some important ways, distinct from the reality of the actual events of the flood, and of human response to those events.

Third, journalistic coverage of the flood was perhaps most important for what it omitted. With the exception of the *St. Louis Post-Dispatch*, most news organizations covering the flood ended their systematic and sustained coverage when the waters receded. This central omission, particularly on the part of the national news media, has important implications for the political process, particularly as the national debate about appropriate flood mitigation strategies is joined.

Coming from the tradition of hermeneutics (the study of news accounts in totality), Ana C. Garner, who lived through the flood from the vantage point of Milwaukee, WI, conducted a content analysis of two national news magazines, the *New York Times* and the *Des Moines Register*. Garner (1994) notes that "media discourse can be conceived as a set of interpretive packages that give meaning to an issue." Each package has an internal structure with a central organizing idea, or frame, for making sense of relevant events, suggesting what is at issue (Gamson and Modigliani, 1989). Discourse can also be visual, a particularly important finding for disaster researchers who note that television often arrives on the scene and begins broadcasting before print reporters are able to file their first stories (Smith, 1992). The visual images broadcast on television, in turn, often frame the disaster reality for the print reporters who follow.

Garner's study (1994) found that the national news media covered the flood in a framework that has been referred to as "domestic Afghanistanism" (Hungerford and Lemert, 1973), or an event that has little relation to faraway audience members. As will be illustrated below, the national media's discourse was primarily framed in billions of dollars, thousands of acres, and the U.S. economy; all of which are certainly the facts, but none of which the average citizen can relate to on a personal level (Garner, 1994). Further, an underlying theme in much national news coverage was a human battle against "Mother Nature"--a battle humans fought but ultimately lost, as revealed by the headlines in Figure 10-2. *Time* called the flood a "Season in Hell' (July 19), while *Newsweek* noted "The Great Flood of '93 rolled inexorably down the Mississippi, teaching everyone--even television anchormen--never to underestimate nature," (July 26). The *New York Times* noted that "there is nothing anyone can do...people sandbagged like crazy and they still lost the war" (July 11). Garner summarized:

...Readers of only the national media could [wind] up believing that only those communities along the Mississippi were affected, that most flood victims were unable to deal with the disaster (emotionally or physically) and that the disaster didn't ultimately affect anyone beyond the Mississippi River. (Garner, 1994).

In an often unacknowledged contrast to the theme of human helplessness against nature, Garner also found that news accounts framed the flood in terms of national economic costs--and sometimes double-edged views. While stories printed at the height of the disaster tended to focus on total dollar losses (for example, $1.2 billion pledged in emergency funds, $1 billion in property damage, $2.5 billion in aid, and $12 billion in farm and property losses), even early stories indicated that the dollar damage might not be as substantial an initial reports indicated. (In fact, this view turned out to be somewhat accurate. For example, while corn crops losses were originally listed for all the states involved in the flooding, Illinois produced a 1993 yield higher than its five-year average. See Chapter 7.

The theme that economic losses might not be as catastrophic as originally projected became particularly strong as the floodwaters receded, and the print media reminded their audiences that televised images of destruction did not convey the entire story (Figure 10-2). *Newsweek*, for example, noted, "you saw it on TV [Davenport, Iowa, under water]--but you didn't see the 97 percent of Davenport's 72 square miles that almost completely escaped the flood's vengeance. Of some 35,000 homes in the city, only one percent were evacuated, and just 200 of the 3,700 businesses were swamped" (*Newsweek*, August 9). The news media also noted that flood victims would eventually purchase replacement goods and services, thus boosting local economies.

Framing the story in economic terms provided the news media with an opportunity to escape the "event" frame of news coverage and investigate, instead, the underlying policy issues. And, to a limited extent, that happened. For example, *Newsweek* noted on July 19:

..In the current catastrophe, two Iowa cities demonstrate the two approaches-- we pay or they pay--with the pungency of a parable. After the terrible flood of 1965, Dubuque decided to contribute its share ($1 million) of the $12 million necessary to build a flood wall. In 1984, nearby Davenport rejected a proposed $65 million flood wall because it neither wanted to pay its third of the cost nor mar the look of its historic riverfront. Today, Dubuque is sitting pretty--and downtown Davenport is underwater...

Newsweek also reported that flood insurance was easy to obtain, even until the last minute. The magazine quoted St. Charles County, MO, building commissioner Tom Szilaszi saying, "Taxpayers have bought some of these people refrigerators and chain saws 10 times over" (August 2, 1993).

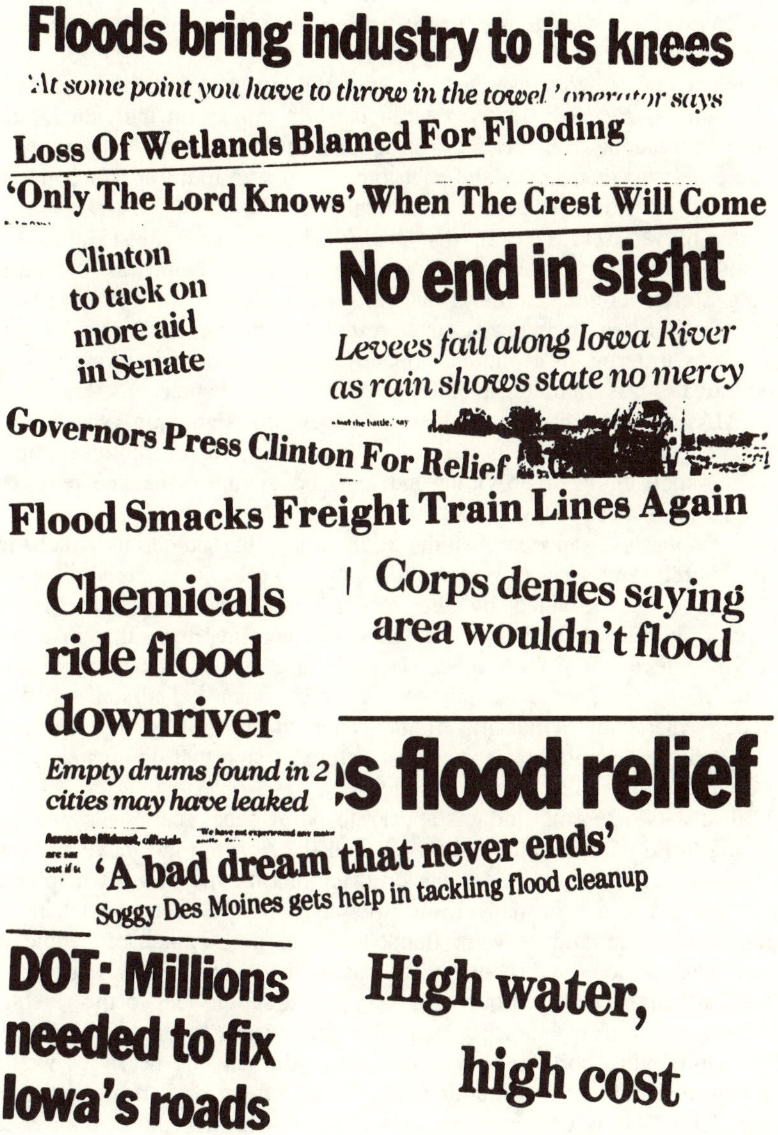

Floods bring industry to its knees

'At some point you have to throw in the towel,' operator says

Loss Of Wetlands Blamed For Flooding

'Only The Lord Knows' When The Crest Will Come

Clinton to tack on more aid in Senate

No end in sight

Levees fail along Iowa River as rain shows state no mercy

Governors Press Clinton For Relief

Flood Smacks Freight Train Lines Again

Chemicals ride flood downriver

Corps denies saying area wouldn't flood

Empty drums found in 2 cities may have leaked

s flood relief

'A bad dream that never ends'
Soggy Des Moines gets help in tackling flood cleanup

DOT: Millions needed to fix Iowa's roads

High water, high cost

FIGURE 10-2   A sample of the news headlines from various sources during the peak of the flood in mid-July.

But these stories were seldom followed up, nor were the issues they raised linked to the larger national flood policy debate. The event-centered focus of national media accounts, a mechanism that accommodates the way journalists normally do their work, prevented linking the flood impact with larger, conceptual issues.

However, media coverage was not monolithic. Local media, particularly the *Des Moines Register*, linked the flood to its impact on individuals and to provided its readers with specific instructions on how to cope. This coverage of people helping themselves and each other also was found in a second study that focused on Missouri media, specifically the *St. Louis Post-Dispatch* and the Columbia *Missourian*. In that study, Thorson and Meeds (1994) also examined news story frames, albeit from a more empirical perspective. Warning stories dominated news accounts early during the flood and again before the Mississippi and Missouri crested for the second time. Framing flood stories in terms of economic impact--although seldom in terms of impact on individuals--was common in flood coverage (see Chapter 1). And the two major Missouri newspapers studied also devoted significant space to the development of community as a result of the flood; for example, community efforts at sandbagging or providing aid to flood victims, what the researchers characterized as a solidarity frame.

This emphasis on people helping each other, the numerous sandbagging efforts, church- and service organization-related work, etc., was similar to the sort of coverage provided by the *Des Moines Register*. Furthermore, it supports a significant finding of the wider disaster literature: that in times of disaster people do help each other (Drabek, 1986). In this framing, media accounts portrayed people as able to help each other. Thorson and Meeds concluded that the solidarity frame adopted by Missouri newspapers contradicted the "people helpless against nature" frame that dominated national news coverage.

While the two sets of findings appear to be at odds, reality may have had something to do with how journalists covered the story. First, coverage by the *Des Moines Register* would be expected to emphasize the view of helplessness against nature because in many Iowa cities that was precisely what happened. Levees broke, communities were flooded, and large numbers of people were without water, food, and housing for many days during the summer. In contrast, although rural Missouri was very much subservient to the rivers, the city of St. Louis itself escaped a major disaster thanks to the downtown flood wall. Communities north and south of the city did not fare nearly as well, but for many residents of metropolitan St. Louis, the story truly was one of helping flood victims who were far less fortunate. Furthermore, almost half--48 percent--of the stories analyzed in the Missouri content analysis appeared to employ no dominant frame. Many of these stories were stories of predictions and warnings, and they were extremely important to Missouri residents, who made daily decisions based on their accuracy.

However, the most important finding to arise from the content analyses is one of omission. News outlets, whether national or more local, gave scant attention to the policy issues raised by the flood. Similar findings have been noted in other studies of media coverage of hazards and disasters (Wilkins, 1987). Coverage of those issues, for example, the regulations governing the federal flood insurance program or the decision to buyout various communities, was treated in an episodic and event-centered manner. Policy choices on the individual or community level were not linked with national policy choices--at least in the news media.

> Compassion plays a major role in the way people respond to disasters and rush to provide disaster relief. ... As for the 1993 floods, the nation can remember pictures carried by CNN of the house being swept away when a levee was breached. Viewers were left wondering how this could happen rather than why the house was there in the first place....Human compassion and the way news is reported influences how Congress and the nation respond to disasters. A great push arose to replace levees along the Missouri River, many of which should not be replaced without careful design and engineering considerations. If federal response to disaster relief is driven by the immediacy of an event, rather than by rational decision making, the effort to put everything back to the way it was may increase future risk rather than reaching long-term solutions to risk reduction. In the haste of some disaster relief and under the pressure of the media effect, the nation may have subsidized some bad decisions and penalized some good ones, forgoing opportunities for change. (IFRMC, 1994).

At a time when people were prepared to pay serious attention to such issues, the news coverage failed to follow suit.

INDIVIDUAL RESPONSES TO RISING WATER AND CONFLICTING ADVICE

Social scientists have often studied human response to disasters through quick response research: arriving in the field as soon as possible after the disaster starts and collecting data from people at specific locales. This type of research has yielded somewhat consistent findings. For example, hazards scholars know that disasters create some psychological problems for a subset of the population. Further, the economic dislocation caused by disasters will also indirectly contribute to such human problems as increased drug usage, domestic abuse, etc. Individual daily routines are often disrupted, and in the early days of disaster onset and recovery, people spend a lot of time trying to reconstruct their lives by fulfilling immediate needs for medical care, food, and shelter, as well as more long-term needs for rebuilding and reconstruction.

However, social scientists seldom have the luxury of asking people how they have been affected long after a disaster ends. There has been a paucity of studies evaluating human experiences after the recovery period is well underway when both time and distance may have allowed those individuals most affected to be somewhat more reflective.

Missouri residents have had such a chance to reflect. During March and April 1994--about seven months after the "official" end of the event--about 1,988 Missouri residents were surveyed regarding various issues raised by the flood[1]. Some of the questions dealt with specific actions taken by residents during the height of the disaster, such as boiling water or seeking certain sorts of information in making daily decisions. Other questions asked residents to evaluate the response of local, state, and federal officials to the flood. And others attempted to determine some of the longer-term flood impacts, for example, by asking residents what they "worried" about six months after the event. The public's oft warped views of the risks of natural hazards were a media theme during and after the flood, as illustrated in Figure 10-3.

Residents of every county in the state were surveyed, and rural respondents equaled the percentage of rural residents in the state. About 53 percent of the respondents were male, slightly higher that the state's population, and about 9 percent of the respondents were people of color, less than the 13 percent of the state's population listed as African-American. About 65 percent of those responding said they had been born in the state; more than 89 percent had lived in Missouri for at least ten years. The statistical results are considered accurate within three percent.

In many ways, previous social science research would have predicted Missourians' long-term response to the flood. For example, even after the event, Missourians were relatively poorly informed about their level of risk due to flooding. Almost 88 percent of the respondents said they did not live in a floodplain, and about 16 percent said they carried flood insurance. However, 40 percent of Missouri's total land area is within a 100-year floodplain. Similarly, Missouri residents were vague about specific facts linked to reducing their risk of illness and injury during a flood. Whether the issue was how to decontaminate well water, food safety after exposure to floodwaters, period of time necessary to boil water (if informed that a water source had been contaminated), or how to decontaminate yourself if exposed to floodwater, the majority of respondents could be viewed as a potential public health problem. Missouri residents either did not know the correct answers or were positive that doing the wrong thing was appropriate. Not surprisingly, among the better educated, there was a higher likelihood of correct answers to

---

[1]The survey was conducted by telephone, and the methodology used allowed the interviewers to speak with those having unlisted and new phone numbers. The statewide survey was funded by the Missouri Department of Health and conducted by the University of Missouri's Center for Advanced Social Research.

FIGURE 10-3   This cartoon captures the all-too-common theme of "it can't happen to me" expressed by those in high risk areas (Reprinted with permission of Copley News Service).

such questions. Women also were somewhat more likely to know the correct answers to questions about how to appropriately handle contaminated or potentially contaminated food than were men.

At another level, however, social science research also would predict that knowledge of specific facts would evaporate rather rapidly (pun intended) after having served its apparent usefulness. And, at a deeper level, the Missourians sampled indicated in a variety of ways that the flood had significant and long-term impacts.

For example, when asked, "what is it that you worry about," one-third of the respondents said "nothing" and an additional 18 percent listed crime. These responses are predictable, particularly because of the high crime rates in the metropolitan Kansas City and St. Louis areas. However, 17 percent of the respondents said they worried about environmental issues, among them flooding, rain, etc. More than twice as many people said they worried about the environment as about health or the economy. Upon further questioning, about 15 percent of the respondents listed the environment, ranking it fourth behind "miscellaneous" concerns, the economy, and health.

When respondents were asked to change their focus from general concerns to concerns specifically about "the weather or climate in Missouri," more than 18 percent listed flooding as their top concern. Worry about tornadoes/storms and cold and ice was the top concern for 19 percent of the sample. Additional worries connected to weather and climate revealed flooding as the top category listed by more than 19 percent of those responding. This worry outranked concern about tornadoes by more than four percent. (Missouri is one of the Midwestern states considered part of the northern hemisphere's tornado alley.) Thus, more than six months after the flood, the disaster was still very much on residents' minds.

Survey respondents also indicated that the flood had been very important to them--what social scientists call salient--in a variety of ways. For example, more than 70 percent of the respondents said they had followed "what was going on with the flood" most of the time. And they indicated they had done much of this "following" through the mass media, specifically television.

The broadcast media, primarily television and radio, were named as the "primary source of information about the '93 flood" by more than 86 percent of those surveyed. Furthermore, what Missourians expected to find in media accounts was what disaster researchers would describe as information about the quick onset and recovery phases of the event. People relied on the broadcast media for information about local flood crests (85 percent); weather forecasts (96 percent); bridge, highway, and street closings (89 percent); and information about "what to do if you were exposed to flood water" (79 percent). After being asked to rank the importance of certain kinds of flood news, respondents said they wanted news stories about "how to remain healthy and safe" (60 percent), how to protect yourself (59 percent), how and where to get help (53 percent), pictures of flood damage (46 percent), and the rainfall predictions (45 percent).

While Missourians were in clear consensus that such news stories were important, what they apparently learned from "following what was going on with the flood" was more problematic. About 60 percent of the respondents agreed that Missouri received about the same amount of flooding as other states and sustained about the same number of deaths. And yet, Missouri was among the hardest hit states by the 1993 flood.

A second category of news account, information on long-term recovery and mitigation issues, was less sought after but still considered important by a significant minority (34 percent) of those surveyed. People said they wanted news about the economic impact of the flood (32 percent), information about what government is doing (28 percent) and about interagency conflicts (27 percent), and information about who to blame for the disaster (12 percent). This less-sustained interest in the deeper causes of the flood was also reflected in responses. When asked about flood prevention measures, 60 percent of the respondents agreed with the statement that "once it starts raining, there's little you can do to prevent a flood," while 65 percent said they believe "there is no way to avoid the possibility of another great flood."

Missourians also thought that both the state and federal government had done a good job of dealing with the crisis, although that evaluation appeared somewhat equivocal. About 73 percent of the respondents said they believed the federal government had been helpful during the flood. And fully 90 percent said their state and local governments had been helpful. More than 53 percent disagreed with the statement that "there would have been less death and injury due to the flood if the federal government had done a better job;" 45 percent of the respondents disagreed with the same statement about state and local governments.

The media emphasis on a solidarity frame noted by one group of scholars who studied media coverage of the event also appears to be right on target. Of those who responded to the survey, more than 88 percent said they had talked to people about the flood, and 64 percent said they had visited a flooded area. Almost half (48 percent) said they had volunteered in some way to help with flood relief, 13.5 percent as sandbaggers and 37.4 percent helped in other capacities. Other scholars have noted a similar trend throughout the Midwest.

> Thousands filled and stacked sandbags to hold weakening levees; others worked day after day to help clean the homes and business of people they had never met. Dry communities adopted those in need....Those who were recipients of this assistance will never forget this demonstration of true caring. (IFRMC, 1994).

Flood relief work, particularly work as a sandbagger (see Figure 10-4), also was the strongest predictor of knowledge about how to handle risks associated with floodwaters, including the appropriate ways to deal with contaminated foodstuffs and with personal hygiene. And, in a finding that may be linked to the number of deaths in the state associated with flash floods, more than 45 percent of the respondents said they had driven on flooded streets at least once during the disaster.

The vast majority of those responding characterized their mental health as good six months after the flood. Seventy-three percent said the flood had no impact on their psychological or physical health, and 92 percent reported no curtailment of their current daily activities. Fewer than 100 of the 1,988 surveyed indicated that the flood had made it impossible for them to reach their homes; 29 respondents said they had to move because of the flood, and 27 reported that their homes had been flooded. While these figures are heartening, it is important to note the psychological stress due to the flood was widely reported at the time of the event, and that the state and federal governments established counseling centers and other facilities to help people cope with psychological problems. Most of these problems focused on what the disaster research literature has termed post-traumatic stress.

While people said they were relatively unscathed psychologically by the event, responses to another set of questions seemed to indicate that the flood reminded many of potential dangers in an environment they normally consider benign. For example, almost 60 percent of those surveyed said they lived near creeks, streams, and rivers. Of those who did, two-thirds said they did not regard those creeks, streams, and rivers as dangerous before the 1993 flood.

FIGURE 10-4   Well after the floodwaters receded, millions of used sandbags awaited removal, evidence of the flood-fight and the huge recovery effort that lasted for months.

After the event, opinion shifted dramatically, with 63 percent now asserting that those same geographic features were dangerous, but three percent reported that their children had played near floodwaters.

While it would be inaccurate to suggest that Missourians' responses to such questions would duplicate those of all other Midwestern residents flooded in the summer of 1993, there are some trends worth noting:

Trend #1 The flood event appears to have heightened and generalized the concern about the weather, climate and geography in the state. In terms of mitigation, this heightened awareness means that government entities "have the attention" of residents about these issues.

Trend #2   People relied heavily on the mass media--particularly on television--for onset and coping information in times of crisis and disaster. While this finding is well accepted in the scholarship of mass communication, hazards scholars and government officials whose work is recovery and mitigation have traditionally been much less concerned with mass communication. Clearly, a shift in communications practices, particularly toward the broadcast media, is suggested. Just as important, the media are only as accurate as their sources. When government officials learn that huge majorities of the public are turning to the broadcast media for weather reports and crest predictions, the accuracy of those predictions becomes paramount for public safety. Since the accuracy of river crest predictions during the 1993 flood has been questioned, understanding how those predictions were portrayed and perceived should become a high priority for a variety of government agencies and scholars.

Trend #3 In times of crisis, Missouri residents at least perceived that government at both the federal and local levels is helpful. At a time when generalized trust in government is not high, working through the problems associated with the flood may be one place to help rebuild the government-citizen relationship.

Trend #4 A sense of community grew out of the flood. Providing flood assistance, particularly as a sandbagger, was linked with more knowledge about the flood. As mitigation strategies are developed, their link to the work of such communities may further the goals of risk communication about long-term preparedness and mitigation.

CEDAR CITY: A TALE OF ONE CITY

The total amounts of damage caused by the flood are staggering and in most cases impersonal. Americans outside the Midwest understood the reality of the flood through the mass media. Images of houses being washed away, of people traveling to their homes by boat, and the "floating McDonald's" near St. Louis's famous Mississippi River arch, all became part of the national visual memory of the event. But such an understanding is one of aggregates, not specifics. In an attempt to put the flood on a more human, and hence individual scale, what follows is the story of one city in central Missouri that received little national news attention but whose flood response mirrors the social costs--and the policy questions--raised by the Great Flood of 1993.

It actually began raining often in January, but not until late spring did most Missouri residents really begin to take notice. According to the poll of Missouri residents conducted six months after the flood, only 30 percent of the respondents recalled becoming concerned about the weather before March, and another 30 percent recalled becoming concerned during April and May (when spring flooding occurred on the Mississippi--see Chapter 4).

The residents of Cedar City, a suburban community of about 110 middle- and working-class homes located outside the state's capital of Jefferson City, were no exception. Heavy rains early in June occurred in the Upper Missouri River basin, but these rains were far from the central Missouri community (see Figure 3-4a). By late June the Missouri River on the edge of town began a calamitous rise.

On July 3, the bulging river was closed to barge and boat traffic. About 380 prisoners were evacuated from the Renz Correctional Center west of town as a precaution. Two days later the river apparently crested more than two feet lower than the originally projected value of 29.8 feet in Boonville, an historic Missouri River community located about 50 miles downstream from Cedar City. Heavy rains on July 7 drenched mid-Missouri (see Figure 3-6). More than seven inches fell in a 24-hour period in nearby Jefferson City. The ground in central Missouri was already saturated, and evacuations began in McBaine, a 300-person community that is also the home of the water treatment plant for Cedar City, Columbia, and several other communities. Government workers in Jefferson City briefly evacuated state buildings after a flood-induced electrical short circuit on July 7.

On July 8, floodwaters inundated Cedar City. Many residents abandoned their cars and trucks and traveled by boat in attempts to rescue valuables from their homes. The state highway patrol reported that more than 30 roads in central Missouri were closed, including major roads to many small communities. Roads leading to central Missouri's major cities, including Columbia and Jefferson City, appeared threatened. On July 9, newly-elected Missouri Governor Mel Carnahan, a Democrat, cut his European vacation short after only one day to return to his soggy state and declared all 114 Missouri counties as state disaster areas. One man drowned in the floodwaters at nearby McBaine.

Even though Governor Carnahan returned from his vacation, Missouri residents by the hundreds decided that the rising floodwaters provided an ideal tourist opportunity. Sightseers traveled to the central Missouri river towns, interfering with relief workers who were sandbagging in preparation for what they were told would be a record river crest. The same phenomenon occurred in the St. Louis area, which had also been hit by the rising Mississippi River.

By July 12, several roads in suburban Columbia were closed due to flooding; the next day the floodwaters breached the levee near Hartsburg. Rising waters in residential basements in the region became epidemic.

On July 14, the flood washed out about 1,000 feet of railroad track atop a levee at the central Missouri community of Glasgow. Residents fled Franklin and New Franklin, communities about 25 miles downstream. The Salvation Army, which was already providing assistance to Cedar City residents, began to help residents of the newly flooded communities of Hartsburg and New Franklin. The rising water came within 14 inches of the water treatment plant at McBaine. Columbia residents were asked to conserve water for essential uses, and aerial photographs of the plant published in local newspapers show an island of sandbags surrounded by a muddy, swollen river.

One day later, the flood closed U.S. 63 near Jefferson City, the major north-south access route to the capitol. From that point until floodwaters began to recede, state workers who commuted by automobile or bus took lengthy, tortuous routes to work. Relief workers, including sandbaggers who reported to affected communities by the hundreds before the waters receded, also traveled by bus. The next day rising waters threatened to cover U.S. 54 into Cedar City, blocking the only remaining land access to the community.

On July 16, the Missouri River crested at 34.8 feet in Jefferson City, breaking the 1951 record of 34.2 feet. The next day, fundraising events began for the flood victims. On July 18, one side of U.S. 63 reopened, providing limited access to the state capitol. FEMA was not far behind, opening a disaster relief office three days later in Columbia. Initial estimates of property damage in Missouri due to the flooding topped the $3 billion mark. But the wet weather was not finished. On July 22, more heavy rain fell in northwestern Missouri, Kansas, Nebraska, and Iowa (see Chapter 3). Three days later, residents began repacking belongings and rebuilding sandbag walls as forecasters projected new crests of between 37 and 38 feet on the Missouri. Columbia residents were again urged to curtail water use should the sandbagging at the McBaine plant fail to hold for the second time. Twenty-four hours later, U.S. 63 was again closed by flooding near the state capitol at Jefferson City.

As Cedar City residents prepared for this new river crest in late July, U.S. Representative Harold Volkmer, a conservative Democrat representing the area for more than a decade, toured the flooded town and asked residents if they would consider permanently moving away from the Missouri River bottomlands. While Volkmer's visit was similar to visits conducted by many elected officials during the flood (see Chapter 1), it also had national significance. The Congressman, who had previously supported more traditional disaster mitigation efforts, particularly those that relied on increased river infrastructure, changed his mind about the appropriate course of mitigation. His insights could well leave a mark on legislation in what some will call the Volkmer bill: government allocations for the relocation of entire communities from their historic floodplain sites. His future Congressional efforts in this area will likely become central to the national policy debate over flood mitigation. At the time of this initial visit on July 25, Cedar City resident Terry Smith responded to Volkmer's questions with, "But I don't know how much it would cost to relocate." Shirley Love, owner of the Cedar City Coffee Cup Cafe, vowed to return. "We'll be getting an apartment Monday. We're going to stay there until we can remodel our house and get back into it."

In the small nearby community of Rocheport, known for its bed and breakfasts and an excellent local winery, nestled on the rocky bluffs above the Missouri River, possible water contamination led government officials to issue a boil order on July 27. A small distance downstream, the rising river came within inches of closing Interstate 70, the major highway artery crossing the state and the only road across the Missouri that remained open (see Chapter 8). Traffic was eventually constricted to one lane in each direction. Hundreds of volunteers traveled on the I-70 bridge from the nearby cities to sandbag in the small communities of Rocheport, Hartsburg, and McBaine. Those approaching the river were greeted, at the top of the bluffs on the eastern side of the bridge, with a view of a huge expanse of water with farmhouse roofs barely perceptible above the water line, railroad tracks leading into the water, roadside billboards almost completely covered by floodwaters, and a channelless river the locals dubbed "Lake Missouri." Residents took thousands of pictures with cameras and camcorders. Most major employers in communities like Columbia shifted to use of skeleton staffs so that interested citizens could sandbag or provide other forms of assistance. Traffic on the remaining lanes of the interstate backed up for miles, and travelers were told to expect four-hour delays.

On Saturday July 27, the Salvation Army served about 200 meals in Cedar City. But within 48 hours, most residents had left the community. Police were stationed 24 hours a day to protect against looting. On July 28, U.S. 63 just north of Cedar City was closed by the floodwaters. State transportation workers set up barricades in an attempt to prevent a similar fate for U.S. 54. Although Cedar City itself had been flooded for more than two weeks, residents continued to move appliances and other items from their homes. The next day, three propane tanks owned by MFA Oil and Propane broke away from their foundations near Cedar City. Two tanks were secured before they could rupture, but a third tank lodged against the guardrail near U.S. 54 spewing flammable gas into the air. The remaining residents were evacuated and the highway closed until already busy state officials could secure the situation. By this time, national news (formal communication channels) and churches and other community organizations (informal channels) had focused outside attention on Cedar City. People from other parts of the nation, such as Delores Steca of Nashville, TN, arrived to aid Cedar City's flood victims. The next day floodwaters swept over U.S. 54.

By July 30, the flood had washed away large chunks of pavement on U.S. 54 and U.S. 63. (It was mid-1994 before both roads could be completely repaired.) Repairs on the I-70 bridge across the Missouri, which was never completely closed to traffic, would take longer still, and one worker would fall to his death more than a year after the flood in a construction accident.

Also on July 30, thousands of Jefferson City residents lost gas service as floodwaters cracked pipes buried beneath the river near the capitol. The river crested at 38.6 feet in Jefferson City, shattering the previously existing two-week-old record. The next day, the waters finally began to recede. Within a week, two lanes of U.S. 54 were reopened, the state-issued boil order was lifted in Rocheport, and the water conservation advisory in Columbia ended.

Meanwhile, Cedar City residents continued to fight the flooding. Employees at the ABB Power Transmission & Distribution Company pumped water out of their building until only a few inches remained. On August 3, the U.S. Army Corps of Engineers announced it was studying the possibility of building another levee or evacuating the floodplain to better protect U.S. 63 and U.S. 54, the community of Cedar City, and the Jefferson City Airport, which had spent most of the past month with runways either threatened or inundated by the flood. The existing privately built levee at Cedar City was "built primarily as an agricultural levee," said Jim Beck, president of the Capitol View Levee District, the landowner group that had privately funded the work. "It was never meant to be anything more. In the process, it protected Cedar City."

But conditions in Cedar City remained too dangerous for residents to return. On August 5, police videotaped the town and showed the tape to homeowners at the Red Cross center in the First Baptist Church in Jefferson City. Residents hoped to receive word on when they could return at a homeowners meeting scheduled for the same day. However, at that meeting, Congressman Volkmer told residents that while farming the rich Missouri bottomlands would remain economically worth the risk of flooding, he questioned the logic of allowing permanent residents in the floodplain. "I think we should have a program allowing them to relocate off the floodplain and not allow any new people to move in there," Volkmer said. Jim Beck, who owned land in the floodplain, said that sometimes emotional bonds prevent people from making the exclusively rational decision to move. "Part of it is that the floods themselves create a common bond in that community. In a sense, what should be driving them away is keeping them here."

On August 6, more than 250 Cedar City residents met to hear and discuss a proposal to have Jefferson City buy out Cedar City residents and other landowners in the bottomland. These meetings continued for months and provided a forum for intense community debate on flood mitigation questions and on issues of individual and governmental responsibility for mitigation. Many Cedar City residents were interested in the buyout plan, which would turn Missouri River bottomland into nonprofit uses, such as parks or playgrounds, and forbid the construction of permanent structures. Specific plan details remained vague, as did the dollar allocations and the method for determining those allocations, for residents interested in participating in the buyout program.

On August 8, Darrell Byers became the first person in mid-Missouri to receive a Family Assistance Grant from the American Red Cross. The $450 grant was welcome relief for Byers, his wife, and their four children. But the impact of some of his decisions was not lost on the Cedar City man. "You can't really expect much when you don't have flood insurance, so I'll just take what I can get and appreciate it." Officials continued to bar Cedar City residents from their homes, but three area motorists disregarded warnings about driving through floodwaters and had to be rescued from their stalled vehicles. In addition, official house-to-house investigations brought preliminary word that only four houses appeared salvageable--the rest would require major repairs before their owners could return to live.

Residents were allowed to return to their homes the next day even though the floodwaters were too shallow in some areas for boats, yet too high for land vehicles. Residents were asked to sign in at a police mobile station on U.S. 54 before entering the city. Travel remained hazardous due to power lines and other hidden obstacles under the water. In the ensuing week, residents continued to sift through their belongings while they tried to decide whether they would remain. For many, there were strong psychological ties. "This here's a jelly cabinet that my brother made for me," explained Dorothy "Dot" Boss as she looked for valuables in her water-soaked home. "He gave it to me just two days before he died. I'm going to try my best to save it, but I don't think it's possible."

As August unfolded, the Cedar City buyout plan occupied a seemingly permanent place on the Jefferson City Council agenda. Conflicting emotions, among both Cedar City and Jefferson City residents and elected officials, often broke through formal meetings. Some residents disliked the buyout plan being offered by Jefferson City officials and said the $1 million price tag and the prices being offered for individual properties were too low. Some residents also asserted the city merely wanted their property so it could establish riverboat gambling casinos at their former homesites, a rumor Jefferson City Mayor Louise Gardner vehemently denied.

One month later on September 29, officials from the Environmental Protection Agency arrived at Cedar City to collect hazardous materials, including containers that once held gasoline, pesticides, and propane. By early October, most of the community's 110 homeowners/residents had decided that they did not want to return. Volkmer and Jefferson City officials begin working to get more federal funds injected into what had been, until this point, a locally funded buyout plan.

In a lengthy and emotional meeting on October 5, attended by many Cedar City residents, the Jefferson City Council, in a five-to-four vote, rejected the buyout plan. Homeowners now believed that the federal government would provide their best hope for financial compensation for flood damage and relocation efforts. About two weeks later, on October 18, Jefferson City authorities mailed notices to all Cedar City property owners stating that buildings more than 50 percent damaged by the flood were to be demolished and hauled away within 30 days. Those not complying with the demolition order would be fined. At the end of the month on October 31, a local televangelist offered displaced Cedar City residents land south of New Bloomfield, an evangelistic community the minister had founded. He offered Cedar City residents one-third acre plots, and the total value of the offer was estimated to exceed $100,000. About 12 former Cedar City residents accepted. "There's nothing to go back to," said former resident Marlee Green. "You've got to do what you've got to do."

During the remaining months of 1993 and into early 1994, Cedar City's fate was decided in Washington. Intense lobbying over disaster relief legislation and agency policy decisions about how federal money could be spent to encourage residents along the Mississippi and Missouri to move permanently from the floodplain yielded results. On February 22, 1994, FEMA announced it would provide $1.5 million to buy out Cedar City property owners. Those funds were to be supplemented by federal funds passed through Jefferson City in the form of $1.1 million in community development block grants, plus an additional $300,000 in purely local funds to help with the buyout. Some former residents continued to protest, but the overwhelming majority agreed to the new federal-local partnership. Seven months later, on September 23, 1994, bulldozers began razing what was left of the Cedar City homes. Some residents had already completed the buyout process, and others were in the midst of the final paperwork. Plans call for the cleared land to become a park, a public garden, and, perhaps, an entrance to central Missouri's popular nature walk, the Katy Trail. In December 1994, citing a lack of funds, the state and federal government closed the Jefferson City flood relief office, which had provided mental health counseling to flood victims.

CONCLUSIONS: LESSONS WE *MAY* LEARN

One set of lessons taught by the flood of 1993 is truly local in character. They mirror the findings of hazards scholars from various disciplines. *In a disaster of such magnitude, local officials need to be prepared to handle the event and a variety of related events that might not normally be associated with the major event itself.*

Take, for example, the state of Missouri. If the state's records are accepted as accurate, then most of the Missourians who died did so in flash floods that were causes of the major event, the large river flooding. Floating propane tanks provide another example, as do the numbers of people who reported driving on flooded streets and visiting flooded areas as sightseers of unusual conditions. Local and state officials need to anticipate such companion hazards, and also help the public understand and anticipate them. *The mass media, particularly the broadcast media, can be used as one element in a risk communication campaign aimed at increasing public awareness of such potential risks.* Further, the flood itself seems to have grabbed the attention of many Midwesterners, indicating that any information campaign may be perceived as salient by at least some audience members.

If mitigation strategies are to develop at the local level, then the flood itself seems to have encouraged a feeling of community and participation among substantial numbers of residents. Local officials who want to implement mitigation strategies might be well advised to contact those who were willing to sandbag to help them with other grassroots efforts. Churches and civic organizations could also be enlisted in such an effort as could residents of communities such as Cedar City which, once relocated, could serve as demonstration projects about the results of mitigation efforts. *Listening to your friends and neighbors, and observing the results of a mitigation strategy on a local level, will do much to ease fears about the impact of mitigation proposals on dearly held ways of life and relationships.*

But, while many of the lessons from the flood of 1993 are local, there is one national lesson that supersedes them. Soon after the flood officially ended, a federal task force headed by General Gerald Galloway was asked to examine both the scientific and social impacts of the flood. In June 1994, the Interagency Floodplain Management Review Committee delivered its report calling for a fundamental change in the country's flood management policies (IFMRC, 1994). In essence, the report proposed that the country adopt a strategy designed to mitigate the inevitable rise and fall of the nation's rivers. This strategy included reliance on traditional methods, such as channeling and levees where appropriate, but acknowledged that such technological answers could no longer be expected to halt the ever-increasing costs of flood damage.

The report proposed that the country invest in reclaiming wetlands along portions of the Mississippi and Missouri Rivers, to act as natural sponges that would soak up some floodwaters. It also proposed adoption of a variety of plans to encourage, and in some cases require, people to move from the floodplains, which would be returned to recreational, ecological, and agricultural uses. While the initial costs for this movement of people and property would be substantial, it would be a one-time-only payment. People and their communities, once moved, would never be returned to the floodplain. And the taxpayers would never again have to pay to literally bail them out of a problem that had been anticipated.

The Committee's report has gone to the U.S. Congress, which must ultimately adapt its proposals through legislation at a pivotal time in U.S. political history. For the first time in more than 40 years, Republicans control Congress with an explicit promise to cut back on government. Simultaneously, government at the federal, state, and local levels is being asked to intervene in people's lives to mitigate future hazards losses presently borne both by individuals and by the taxpayers of the entire nation. Further, if results from the Missouri survey, along with responses of other disaster victims in Florida and California, can be taken as an indication of national opinion, then U.S. citizens believe that disaster relief, recovery, and mitigation is an appropriate role for government at all levels, including the federal government.

The issue to be decided is relatively straightforward, although by no means easy. *In an era when reducing government seems to be the voter demand as prudent fiscal policy, are the cutbacks going to include investing in mitigation measures that may save the country substantial sums in the longer term?*

Resolution of this issue will not depend on the lessons learned from the flood of 1993 in a social and scientific sense, but rather on political will. That debate will ask some entrenched interest groups, for example, the U.S. Army Corps of Engineers, to develop new roles for themselves. Environmental organizations may have to form alliances with nontraditional partners, for example, many Republican legislators, if mitigation strategies become the new national flood control policy. At the center of this debate will certainly be newly-elected House Majority Leader Newt Gingrich, whose home state of Georgia was drenched by flooding in 1994, and Senate Majority Leader Robert Dole, whose home state of Kansas was among those severely flooded in 1993. Both have Presidential aspirations, both have promised to place more responsibility for a variety of programs in the hands of the private sector, and both face first-hand demands from constituents that government get involved in the disaster relief, recovery, and mitigation process. How these sometimes conflicting constituencies will resolve the issue will make a fine story for journalists and hazards scholars alike. *In short, the central lesson taught by the Great Flood of 1993 is a political one. It remains to be seen whether the state, local, and federal government and the general populace have learned and will act upon what they have learned.*

REFERENCES

Altheide, D. L., 1976: *Creating Reality: How TV News Distorts Events*. Sage,Beverly Hills, CA, 86 pp.

Clark, C., 1982: *Planet Earth, Flood*. Time-Life Books, New York, 334 pp.

Cronon, W., 1991: *Nature's Metropolis: Chicago and the Great West*. W.W. Norton & Co, New York, 267 pp.

Des Moines Register, July 3, 1993, p. 6A.

Drabek, T., 1986: *Human System Responses to Disasters: An Inventory of Sociological Findings*. Springer-Verlag, NY, 332 pp.

Gamson, W.A., and A. Modigliani, 1989: Media discourse and public opinion: A constructionist approach. *American Journal of Sociology*, July 1989, 1-37.

Garner, A.C., 1994:"The cost of fighting Mother Nature: News coverage of the 1993 Midwest floods," a paper presented to the Association for Education in Journalism and Mass Communication, August 1994.

Hungerford, S., and J.B. Lemert, 1973: Covering the environment: A new Afghanistanism, *Journalism Quarterly,* 50(3), 475-481, 508F.

Interagency Floodplain Management Review Committee, 1994: *Sharing the Challenge Floodplain Management into the 21st Century*. Washington, DC, 191 pp.

Iyengar, S., 1994: *Is Anyone Responsible: How Television Frames Political Issues*. University of Chicago Press, Chicago, 208 pp.

Jamieson, K.H., 1992: *Dirty Politics: Deception, Distraction and Democracy*.Oxford University Press, Portsmouth, NH, 139 pp.

Myers, M.F., and G.F. White, 1994: The challenge of the 1993 Mississippi flood. *Environment*, 35(10), 7-35.

National Weather Service, 1994: *The Great Flood of 1993*. Natural Disaster Survey Report, National Oceanic and Atmospheric Administration, Washington, DC, 220 pp.

Newsweek, July 19, 1993, p. 23.

Newsweek, July 26, 1993, p. 21.

Newsweek, August 2, 1993, p. 24.

Newsweek, August 9, 1993, p. 40.

New York Times, July 11, 1993, p. 18A.

Smith, C., 1992: *Media and Apocalypse: News Coverage of the Yellowstone Forest Fires, Exxon Valdez Oil Spill, and Loma Prieta Earthquake.* Greenwood Press, Westport, CT, 89 pp.

Time, July 19, 1993.

Thorson, E., and R. Meeds, 1994: "The Framing of newspaper stories about the Great Flood of '93," a paper presented to the Association for Education in Journalism and Mass Communication, August 1994.

Tuchman, G., 1973: "Making news by doing work: Routinizing the unexpected." *American Journal of Sociology,* 79(1), 110-131.

Twain, M., 1883: *Life on the Mississippi.* Harper, New York, 104 pp.

White, G.F., and M.F. Myers (eds.), 1994: Coping with the flood: The Next Phase, *Water Resources Update,* 94-95.

Wilkins, L., 1987: *Shared Vulnerability: The Media and American Perception of the Bhopal Disaster.* Greenwood Press, Westport, CT, 233 pp.

11

Effects of the Flood on National Policy: Some Achievements, Major Challenges Remain

James M. Wright

The year or two that is ahead is likely to be extremely important because of the recent conjunction of major disasters, and public rethinking about the environmental, social, and relief aspects of response to natural disasters. Some highly significant changes in public policy may be in prospect. *Gilbert F. White,* statement at the Annual Hazards Research & Applications Workshop, University of Colorado, Boulder, July 18, 1994.

INTRODUCTION

In the aftermath of the 1993 Midwest flood, the Executive Office of the President (Administration Floodplain Management Task Force) in January 1994 assigned to an Interagency Floodplain Management Review Committee the mission to delineate the major causes and consequences of the Midwest flooding, and to evaluate the performance of existing floodplain management and related watershed management programs. The Review Committee was also to recommend changes in current policies, programs, and activities of the federal government that most effectively would achieve risk reduction, economic efficiency, and environmental enhancement in the floodplain and watersheds.

In its final report, issued in June 1994, the Review Committee stated,

As we review the Great Flood of 1993 and our policies for managing this nation's floodplains, there is a call for a new approach to their management and their related watersheds. This approach involves a shared challenge. The situation that exists on floodplains today is the result of past federal policy decisions that were successful in achieving past national goals. Over recent decades, as social preferences shifted, national goals changed. In evaluating ongoing and future floodplain management, the nation must recognize not only that these shifts and changes have occurred but that no action taken today should reduce the opportunity for future adjustments in national goals and purposes. Government at all levels and individuals must share the responsibility of appropriately managing land and water resources to reduce the nation's vulnerability to flood disasters. Coordination of environmental, social, and economic planning is essential to maximize efficiency, equitably share burdens, economic planning is responsibility. (Executive Office of the President, 1994).

245

The current state of the nation's floodplains reflects in part a succession of political decisions made at the national level over the past 150 years. Approaches to dealing with floods in the United States and federal government involvement in solutions to their consequences have changed dramatically during this century.

Flood mitigation initially centered on structural measures to modify flooding. In response to changing situations, needs, values, and priorities, broader approaches were studied and applied to adjust future floodplain development and use to be appropriate for the flood risk. The environmental values of floodplains received growing recognition and support. During the past 25 years, the nation has made significant progress in applying and gaining acceptance of various mitigation measures as a principal means of reducing economic and environmental losses to acceptable levels.

The 1993 flood and other severe storm events concentrated in recent years (Changnon and Changnon, 1993) have been sobering reminders of work yet to be done to further reduce the nation's vulnerability to extreme natural events. In a year of hard lessons, the Great Flood of 1993 heightened awareness, interest, and debate regarding appropriate uses of vulnerable areas: whether governmental programs (particularly federal) reward inappropriate behavior, and whether those who choose to stay where natural disasters are predictable and recur frequently should pay the full price for any damage incurred.

The nation is entering a new era in hazards and emergency management--one in which a comprehensive multi-hazard approach, a strong emphasis on mitigation, and use of technological advances will play leading roles. This will require further changes in approaches to managing the nation's floodplains, to redefine national policies, and to adjust existing programs.

In studying the historical record, floods along the Mississippi River and its two major tributaries, the Missouri and Ohio Rivers, have been significant in the evolution of U.S. policies to deal with these dramatic natural events. And history will likely demonstrate that the Great Flood of 1993 will also have an effect on flood policy. To lay the framework for assessing the 1993 flood, this chapter examines the forces and events that have shaped the evolution of floodplain management in the United States. This evolution has come as a result of the gradual merger of flood control, disaster assistance, and resource protection. A number of recent assessments of the nation's floodplains have provided important findings that should further help shape policy changes that are also discussed. Finally, the flood taught us many lessons, including opportunities and outlook for fundamental changes in policies on disaster response, recovery, and mitigation, and for long-term management of the nation's floodplains.

THE EVOLUTION OF POLICIES

Policies dealing with floods in the United States have changed significantly since the first efforts to direct the paths of floodwaters in the early 1800s. These changes have been largely *event driven*.

Flood Control

Flood mitigation initially centered on structural measures to modify flooding, principally through the use of flood protection levees. Levees were in particular favor along the Lower Mississippi River to overcome the river's propensity to overflow the vast and rich alluvial valley, which it had created. By the 1840s, after more than a century of individual, group, and state efforts to confine the mighty Mississippi, inhabitants of the area realized that this task would require the help of the entire nation.

Aware of the large costs of flood control, Congress was not yet ready to enter the battle against floods, but large floods in the lower delta in both 1849 and 1850 changed that. Congress recognized that some action was required and granted funds for the Corps of Engineers to conduct an extensive study of flood control possibilities on the Lower Mississippi. The study took more than a decade and proposed completing the existing levee system but excluded consideration of alternative flood control plans. Adopted in 1861, the "levees-only" policy of flood control on the Lower Mississippi would persist well into the 20th century. The effect of this policy would be pernicious beyond belief.

Recurrent flooding in the Mississippi Valley heightened public interest in a comprehensive solution to the problem, and in 1879 Congress created the Mississippi River Commission with the authority to survey the Mississippi and its tributaries, formulate plans for navigation and flood control, and report on the practicality and costs of various alternative courses of action. The Commission agreed on the levees-only approach to control flooding on the Lower Mississippi. Some felt that 1879 marked the policy turning point in the long battle. From that time forward, Congress gradually became reconciled to the idea that the federal government had some degree of responsibility to control floodwaters.

Even as the levee system expanded, floods continued without letup either in frequency or fury. Under continual public and political pressure from the beleaguered states of the Lower Mississippi, the federal government was inexorably drawn into greater participation in flood control. The Flood Control Act of 1917 authorized the Commission to spend $45 million for cost-sharing with local levee districts.

Throughout this period the Corps remained committed to the "levees-only" policy. The Mississippi River Commission proclaimed in 1927 that the levee system "is now in condition to prevent the disastrous effects of floods" (Clark, 1982). Even as this Commission spoke, conditions were developing that would forever change the nature of flood control on the Mississippi River and its tributaries, and extend the degree of federal participation on a national scope.

Until 1927, no levee built to the standards adopted by the Mississippi River Commission had failed. The Great Flood of 1927 demonstrated the fallacy of the levees-only policy, however. Much of the levee system along the Lower Mississippi failed, and the flood torrent fanned out over the flat delta. At its highest point, the river spread out 50 to 100 miles wide in a yellow sea stretching a thousand miles from Cairo, IL, at its confluence with the Ohio River, to the Gulf. The official death toll was 246, but it may have been as high as 500. More than 700,000 people were made homeless by the flood. In excess of 325,000 refugees were cared for during a period of several months in more than 150 Red Cross camps. Approximately 137,000 buildings and homes were damaged or destroyed, and property damage exceeded $236 million, an enormous figure even in those pre-Depression years. Nearly 13 million acres of land was flooded (Moore and Moore, 1989). *This flood event was arguably the greatest natural disaster to befall this nation in terms of total human misery and suffering.* The Great Flood of 1927 demonstrated that levees alone were an inadequate solution to flood problems, and the nation began to consider other approaches.

Several major floods during the 1930s resulted in legislative measures providing for increasing federal assumption of the costs for flood control projects. With the Flood Control Act of 1936, Congress formally recognized that floods were a menace to national welfare, declared flood control a proper federal responsibility, and articulated national policy regarding the control of floodwaters. With the Flood Control Act of 1938, Congress changed its cost-sharing provisions, providing for federal assumption of the entire cost of reservoir and channel modification projects. Between 1936 and 1952, Congress spent more than $11 billion for flood control projects, primarily to store floodwaters. This massive construction program subsequently prevented substantial flood damages.

Federal involvement in flood control to include flood protection structures in *upstream* watersheds began nationally in 1944 with passage of Public Law (P.L.) 78-534 authorizing installation of upland treatment and flood damage reduction works in selected watersheds. This policy was expanded to the entire nation when Congress enacted the Watershed Protection and Flood Prevention Act (P.L. 566) in 1954. This act authorized the Soil Conservation Service to participate in comprehensive watershed management projects in cooperation with states and their local governments.

Even as recently enacted federal policies on flood control were being implemented, there were those who began to question the wisdom of overreliance on structural measures to control the paths of floodwaters. Among the prominent voices was that of Gilbert White, who characterized the prevailing national policy as "essentially one of protecting the occupants of floodplains against floods, of aiding them when they suffer flood losses, and of encouraging more intensive use of floodplains" (White, 1942). He instead advocated "adjusting human occupancy to the floodplain environment so as to utilize most effectively the natural resources of the floodplain, and simultaneously applying practicable measures to minimize the detrimental impacts of floods." Many people were convinced that White's concepts offered a real alternative to existing flood control practices and helped set the course for the emergence and evolution of broader approaches to flood problems.

Disturbing trends developed by the mid-1950s. Both the potential nationwide damage from flooding and the costs of providing protection were rising. Rapidly increasing urban population and affluence were at the heart of the problem. The national flood damage potential was increasing at a faster rate than it could be controlled under existing flood protection construction programs. Wise land use management practices within flood-prone areas seemed to be a neglected alternative to these programs.

Alternatives to controlling flood damages through structural measures to control the paths of floodwaters were first applied on a broad scale by the Tennessee Valley Authority (TVA), a federal regional agency created by Congress in 1933. Working with state and local planners, TVA water resources engineers in 1953 embarked on a pioneering cooperative program to tackle local flood problems. Under this program, flood damage prevention was considered a matter of adjusting the use of the land to the flood risk. Reports identifying local flood hazards were prepared by TVA to provide a sound technical basis for flood damage prevention planning.

After only a few years of experience with the program, TVA was convinced that this floodplain management assistance program had real merit and was suitable for national application. A report was submitted to Congress in 1959 proposing *A Program for Reducing the National Flood Damage Potential* (Committee on Public Works, 1959), and TVA staff freely shared expertise and carried out extensive promotional efforts of this management concept nationally.

The Corps was authorized in the Flood Control Act of 1960 to provide technical services and planning assistance to communities for wise use of the floodplain. Instrumental in bringing about this authorization were two reports (White, 1958), and the Senate's review of the 1959 TVA report. The Corps subsequently prepared local floodplain information reports patterned after the TVA experience. The Soil Conservation Service and the U.S. Geological Survey were also conducting local floodplain mapping efforts and providing floodplain management assistance during the early 1960s.

The most significant step toward a more unified federal policy for managing floodplains came in 1965 with the establishment of the Bureau of the Budget Task Force on Federal Flood Control Policy under the leadership of Gilbert White. The Task Force's key report, House Document 465, was published in 1966 (Task Force FFCP, 1966). Citing numerous problems, such as mounting flood losses and inadvertent encouragement of floodplain encroachments, the report advocated a broader perspective on flood control within the context of floodplain development and use.

While House Document 465 provided the groundwork for redirecting the federal involvement from structural control to a more comprehensive approach for floodplain management, two major legislative items were also significant: establishment of the National Flood Insurance Program (NFIP) and passage of the National Environmental Policy Act (NEPA). At the same time the Bureau of the Budget was evaluating federal flood control policy, the Department of Housing and Urban Development was studying the feasibility of a national flood insurance program. (Congress had established a National Crop Insurance Program in 1938, employing the principle of insurance in order to lessen the cost, both financial and human, of future crop disasters.)

The program that finally emerged was built upon the recommendations of the Task Force on Federal Flood Control Policy. A sequence of hurricane-induced disasters in the early 1960s revived interest in providing some form of insurance. Congress created the NFIP in 1968 in response to mounting flood losses and escalating costs to the general taxpayer for disaster relief. The NFIP provided relief from the impacts of flood damages in the form of federally subsidized flood insurance to participating communities, contingent on flood loss reduction measures embodied in local floodplain management regulations.

Passage of the NFIP marked an important change in federal flood control policy. Primary responsibility for managing the floodplains still remained with local government, but now development was to be consistent with the flood risk. The act sought to return to the landowner the cost for his/her locational decision, and thereby shift the burden from the taxpayer. With more than 18,000 of 22,000 identified flood-prone communities currently participating, this program has had a profound effect on floodplain management activities over the past 25 years. Unfortunately, the program has fallen short of achieving its objective of shifting the burden of flood losses from the taxpayer.

Resource Protection

Changes in federal flood control policies occurred simultaneously with the growing interest in the environment. Although a number of single-purpose federal laws and programs were established to protect various natural resources, it was not until passage of the National Environmental Policy Act (NEPA) in 1969 that the natural resources of floodplains and other natural systems were formally recognized and incorporated in the federal decision-making process. This act declared environmental quality to be a national goal and established a procedure for assessing the impact of proposed federal projects and programs that could significantly affect the environment. Thus, a foundation was laid to assess the environmental resources associated with river corridors and coastal zones.

The goal of protecting and enhancing environmental quality was emphasized in other important legislation enacted over the two decades following NEPA, including the Wild and Scenic Rivers Act of 1968, the Coastal Zone Management Act of 1972, the Endangered Species Act of 1973, the Clean Water Acts of 1972 and 1977, the Coastal Barrier Resources Act of 1982, and the Water Quality Act of 1987. Section 404 of the Clean Water Act of 1972 supplemented the existing Corps permitting program by requiring permits for the discharge of dredged or fill materials into all waters of the United States. This has been interpreted to include most of the nation's wetlands and has therefore become an important wetland protection measure. Most of the nontidal wetlands are located within riverine floodplains.

Over the past few decades, better methodologies have been developed to identify and quantify the natural resources contained in relatively undisturbed floodplains and the beneficial functions they perform (Figure 11-1). There is a growing interest and experience in incorporating measures to protect, and in some instances to restore, the floodplain environment as part of broader floodplain management goals and policies.

Disaster Assistance

Parallel with these efforts to redirect federal policy in dealing with economic and environmental losses was a growing federal role in disaster response and recovery. Until 1950, Congress periodically enacted relief bills to aid victims of specific disasters, dating from the 1815 New Madrid earthquake (Mittler, 1992). In legislation enacted in 1950, the president was authorized to define what constituted a major disaster and, after making this declaration, to direct federal agencies to provide aid to the victims. This law formally took notice that natural disaster relief was a local responsibility, but the severity of some disasters would put relief and rehabilitation efforts beyond the financial capabilities of state and local governments.

Following the 1964 "Good Friday" earthquake in Alaska, Congress ushered in the direct subsidy or grant as a federal disaster relief policy. Thereafter, some form of grant provision has been included in virtually every disaster relief act.

The Robert T. Stafford Disaster Relief and Emergency Assistance Amendments of 1988 made important changes to existing disaster relief programs in an attempt to increase post-disaster mitigation measures and reduce vulnerability to damages from future disasters. Hazard mitigation is stressed, including funding for acquiring destroyed or damaged properties, not rebuilding, rebuilding in the nonhazardous areas, and reducing the exposure to flood risks in reconstruction.

The historical record demonstrates that disaster relief policies and programs are fluid, being subject to public sentiment for the disaster "victims," often strong political pressure "to do something," and resultant legislative changes--often more liberalized assistance through federal grants. The flood control construction program of the 1930-1950 era now seems to have been replaced by an equally massive federal relief and recovery assistance program for flood disasters in the present era.

WATER RESOURCES
Natural Flood & Erosion Control
- Provide flood storage and conveyance
- Reduce flood velocities
- Reduce flood peaks
- Reduce sedimentation

Water Quality Maintenance
- Filter nutrients and impurities from runoff
- Process organic wastes
- Moderate temperature fluctuations

Groundwater Recharge
- Promote infiltrations and aquifer recharge
- Reduce frequency and duration of low surface flows

BIOLOGICAL RESOURCES
Biological Productivity
- Support high rate of plant growth
- Maintain biodiversity
- Maintain integrity of ecosystem

Fish and Wildlife Habitats
- Provide breeding and feeding grounds
- Create and enhance waterfowl habitat
- Protect habitats for rare and endangered species

SOCIETAL RESOURCES
Harvest of Wild & Cultivated Products
- Enhance agricultural lands
- Provide sites for aquaculture
- Restore and enhance forest lands

Recreational Opportunities
- Provide areas for active and passive uses
- Provide open space
- Provide aesthetic pleasure

Areas for Scientific Study and Outdoor Education
- Contain cultural resources (historic and archaeological sites)
- Provide opportunities for environmental and other studies

FIGURE 11-1 Natural resources of floodplains (Source: A Unified National Program for Floodplain Management, 1994).

THE GREAT FLOOD OF 1993

An Historical Perspective of the Flood

The Great Flood of 1993 lasted from late May through mid-September in the basins of the Upper Mississippi and Lower Missouri Rivers and provided sobering evidence that the nation has yet to resolve Nature's periodic need to occupy her floodplains and prevent human occupancy and use of these same floodplains. The flood reached record levels at many locations within these basins (see Figure 1-1, Chapter 1).

Although the 1993 flood was labeled by various media as the "Flood of the Century," the 1927 flood on the Lower Mississippi, described earlier, was the greatest flood disaster in our nation's history in terms of overall human suffering and misery. Table 11-1 compares the two floods.

Response and Recovery

The flood's large areal extent led to presidential disaster declarations for 532 counties in the nine-state region affected (see Figure 12-6). These declarations allowed the designated areas to receive federal disaster aid from various agencies. On August 12, 1993, Congress appropriated $1.7 billion in funds for the Emergency Supplemental Appropriations for Relief from the Major, Widespread Flood in the Midwest Act of 1993 (P.L. 103-75) to provide initial federal aid. Then in September, the White House issued a statement that described the president's "Cost-Share Adjustment for Midwest Flood Recovery." It stated that the unprecedented degree of damage to the Midwest economy led the president to change the reimbursement of eligible public assistance disaster costs for the Midwestern states affected by the flooding. This change was from the previous 75 percent federal/25 percent nonfederal ratio to 90/10.

With the passage of the Hazard Mitigation and Relocation Assistance Act of 1993 (P.L. 103-181) in December 1993, there was a significant increase in both

TABLE 11-1 Comparison of the 1993 and 1927 Floods on the Mississippi River

Conditions	1927 flood	1993 flood
Area flooded, millions of acres	12.8	20.1
Property damage, billions of dollars	12.3[1]	12.7
Number of deaths	246	52
Buildings damaged	137,000	70,000
Number of people made homeless	700,000	74,000

[1] Adjusted to 1993 dollars, $0.65 billion in 1927 dollars.

cost-sharing and funding for hazard mitigation, authorized by Section 404 of the Robert T. Stafford Disaster Relief and Emergency Assistance Act of 1988 (P.L. 93-288, as amended). Under the new legislation, the federal government can fund up to 75 percent of the eligible costs of a project, a change from the previous 50-50 cost-share formula. The amount of funds made available was increased from 10 to 15 percent of the total amount spent on all public and individual assistance. Hazard mitigation refers to measures enacted to protect lives and property from repeated damages caused by natural disasters.

The funds made available were used almost entirely for buyouts of flood-damaged homes and businesses from willing sellers. The act also clarified the conditions under which such buyouts were acceptable; essentially they must represent the complete removal of flood-prone structures and the dedication of the purchased land "in perpetuity for a use that is compatible with open space, recreational, or wetlands management practices."

In February 1994, President Clinton signed into law the Emergency Supplemental Appropriations Act of 1994 (P.L. 103-211), which was principally designed to provide relief for victims of the January 1994 Northridge earthquake in California. The act also made an additional $685 million available to Midwest flood victims. The total federal funds ultimately awarded for flood relief were $6.2 billion.

ISSUES ARISING FROM THE 1993 FLOOD

Shortly after the floodwaters subsided, intensive debates surfaced regarding the range of alternative uses of the floodplain to be considered in the flood recovery effort. Four broad issues were discussed and debated: (1) whether to repair the hundreds of damaged levees and if so, who pays for permitted repairs, (2) whether to permit the repair or rebuilding of thousands of substantially damaged structures for future inhabitation, (3) the amount of community planning and financial assistance to develop alternative mitigation strategies to the typical repair/rebuild scenario, and (4) the experience of risk insurance as a mitigation tool.

Levees

By some counts, more than 8,000 miles of levees of various descriptions exist in the Upper Mississippi River basin. Many were part of the public "experience" of the 1993 flood. The news media widely reported massive and heroic local flood-fighting efforts principally through the construction of emergency levees or the reinforcement and/or raising of existing levees, and some subsequent spec-tacular failures.

Approximately 1,600 levees (of which 1,400 were nonfederal) were damaged enough to require some form of rehabilitation or repair. Fewer than 500 of these levees were under the Corps emergency flood control repair program (P.L. 84-99). (Eligibility for inclusion in the Corps program requires that a levee be a primary one that provides an adequate level of protection, that it be sponsored by a public entity, that the sponsor maintain the levee to a standard established by the Corps, and that the cost of any levee repair be shared: 20 percent by the local sponsor and 80 percent by federal government.)

Given the gravity of this situation and because less than 15 percent of the nonfederal levees that were damaged qualified for repair consideration under the Corps program, the Clinton Administration and Congress provided supplemental funding for levee repair. To receive this federal funding, it was stipulated that levee districts or sponsors would have to agree to join the Corps program. According to information provided, about three dozen districts or sponsors have agreed to take this action (Zwickl, 1994).

Under the authority of P.L. 84-99, the Corps plans to rehabilitate 201 levees that were already eligible under its program. As of November 1994, repairs to 145 levees were complete, repairs to 54 levees were in process, and repairs to two levees were not started. The estimated cost is approximately $250 million (Peterson, 1994b).

Significant *land use issues* were involved in the levee repair debate. Some of the nation's most productive farmland was flooded, and in some instances heavily damaged by deposition of sand and other sediment or by erosion from water flow over the land. Many officials and environmentalists saw the opportunity to restore lost or impaired natural resources, including converting agricultural fields back to wetlands.

Recovery from the 1993 flood was, in some instances, dramatic. In 1994 most farmers throughout the Midwest reaped the benefits of the best soybean and corn crops in history. Missouri, hit hard by flooding, had a stunning agricultural recovery. Although officials had predicted a bad year because sand deposits from flooding had ruined floodplain fields, farmers removed the sand over the winter, leveled the land, and planted crops on all but 27,000 sand-buried acres.

Substantially Damaged Buildings

The extent of the area inundated by floodwaters affected an estimated 149,000 households, although the estimates vary widely. Whole communities were flooded. The depth and duration of flooding and other factors resulted in substantial damages to several thousand residences and other structures.

Where repair or rebuilding was permitted, local codes of communities participating in the NFIP required structures damaged beyond 50 percent of their value to be rebuilt in compliance with certain minimum standards. These standards require that the lowest floor must be at or above the level of a flood that has a one percent chance of occurrence in any given year. This requirement is intended to reduce future exposure to flood risk through elevation of the structure in place or relocation outside the regulatory floodplain. In a post-flood situation this often presents an overwhelming economic burden on those who have to replace or repair their property and also elevate or relocate their homes or businesses. Because of the widespread nature of the flood and the large number of properties affected, it has been difficult to document what has happened to the substantially damaged structures. No reliable data have been gathered, although such information would be helpful to policy makers. A number of structures have been elevated, acquired, or relocated using flood recovery funds. Others, undoubtedly, have been brought into compliance with local codes using owner funds. Still others (perhaps most not using recovery funds) have been reoccupied, circumventing local codes that likely have not been rigorously enforced. And finally, a number of structures were just abandoned.

Alternative Mitigation Measures

Many individuals and communities affected by the Great Flood of 1993 had never before dealt with floods and their consequences. Because of their lack of experiences they did not know what to do after the flood. There seemed to be a consensus from many sources that rebuilding or restoring to pre-flood conditions was not an acceptable policy position.

Federal funds made available for the disaster response and recovery effort were earmarked for about three dozen programs administered by various agencies. The Administration established buyouts of flood-damaged properties as the first priority for mitigation funds available for the Midwest flood. As of October 1994 (Erat, 1994), the federal government had approved 160 projects for elevation, acquisition, or relocation of 7,500 buildings. It is anticipated that as many as 8,000 buildings in 140 different communities will eventually be elevated, acquired, or relocated. Projects range in size and complexity from elevations of one or two homes in a neighborhood to whole communities relocating to new locations (Valmeyer and Grafton, IL, and Rhineland and Pattonsburg, MO). This initiative represents a turning point in flood recovery policy; *it is the first time that buyouts have been attempted on such a large scale.*

Buyouts are viewed by many as an appropriate governmental response to the 1993 flood and future floods like it. Under the right circumstances, buyouts will not only reduce flood damages and protect people and property, but will also achieve other objectives, such as improving the quality of affordable housing, increasing recreational opportunities and wildlife values, and general betterment of the community.

Insurance as a Mitigation Tool

In enacting the Federal Crop Insurance Act (P.L. 75-430) in 1938 and the National Flood Insurance Act (P.L. 90-448) in 1968, and in subsequent acts, Congress recognized disaster insurance to be a more fiscally prudent public policy than relief and other forms of federal assistance.

Despite several important successes, such as identification of hazard areas and increased controls over inappropriate use of floodplain lands, neither the crop insurance or flood insurance programs have met the Congressional intent of transferring the cost of floodplain occupancy and use from the taxpayer to the individual. The Federal Crop Insurance Corporation estimated that slightly more than 50 percent of the insurable crop acres in the states affected by the 1993 flood were insured against losses. Crop insurance payments totaled about $1 billion. The Floodplain Management Review Committee noted that although policy holders filed 16,167 flood insurance claims, the Federal Emergency Management Agency (FEMA) approved 89,734 applications for the Disaster Housing Program, and 38,423 applications for Individual and Family Grants. The Small Business Administration approved 20,285 loans for individuals and businesses.

Admittedly, many of these applications, or loan approvals, were for persons outside of identified flood hazard areas or for renters who do not normally purchase flood insurance. Still, the numbers are disturbing. *In the counties and communities affected, it is estimated that no more than 10 percent of insurable properties had flood insurance coverage.* Flood insurance claims payments for the 1993 Midwest flood totaled $251 million, a very small percentage of the $6.2 billion federal response and recovery costs for the flood (Pollnow, 1994). The insurance problems led to action: the NFIP was modified in September 1994 by P.L. 103-235, and the Federal Crop Insurance Program was modified by legislation (P.L. 103-354) enacted in October 1994 (see Chapter 7).

CALLS FOR SOUNDER NATIONAL POLICIES

The continuing search for a sound, workable program to ensure wise use of the nation's floodplains transcends the 1993 event. The search was ongoing when the flood occurred and involves broader policy issues than those arising from the flood. A number of studies have been carried out over the past decade, and these are examined in this section.

Towards a Unified National Program for Floodplain Management

In creating the National Flood Insurance Program in 1968, Congress stated in Section 1302(c) of the act that "the objectives of a flood insurance program should be integrally related to a unified national program for floodplain management and directed that....the President should transmit to Congress for its consideration any further proposals for such a unified program." A report was prepared and issued in 1976 that provided a conceptual framework of general and working principles and set forth management "strategies" and "tools" to guide federal, state, and local decision makers in implementing a unified national program for floodplain management. The report was updated in 1979 and again in 1986 by a Federal Interagency Floodplain Management Task Force.

The 1986 report, which built on earlier reports, subsequent legislation, directives, and activities, set forth two broad goals for floodplain management: to reduce loss of life and property from flooding, and to reduce losses of natural and beneficial resources from unwise land use. It brought together concerns for mounting flood losses with increasing interests in maintaining important natural functions of floodplains and wetlands. Four primary strategies were presented to achieve the two floodplain management goals. Specific tools were identified under each strategy (Figure 11-2). These strategies and tools are described in detail in the Unified National Program documents.

The National Assessment

One of the recommendations in the 1986 report was to "provide evaluation of floodplain management activities with periodic reporting to the public and to the Congress on progress toward implementation of a unified national program

---

Strategy: Modify Susceptibility to Flood Damage and Disruption
1. Floodplain regulations
2. Development and redevelopment policies
3. Disaster preparedness
4. Disaster assistance
5. Floodproofing
6. Flood forecasting and warning systems and emergency plans

Strategy: Modify Flooding
1. Dams and reservoirs
2. Dikes, levees, and floodwalls
3. Channel alterations
4. High flow diversions
5. Land treatment measures
6. On-site detention measures

Strategy: Modify the Impact of Flooding on Individuals and the Community
1. Information and education
2. Flood insurance
3. Tax adjustments
4. Flood emergency measures
5. Post-flood recovery

Strategy: Restore and Preserve the Natural and Cultural Resources of Floodplains
1. Floodplain, wetland, coastal barrier resources regulations
2. Development and redevelopment policies
3. Information and education
4. Tax adjustments

FIGURE 11-2   Strategies and tools for floodplain management   (Source: A Unified National Program for Floodplain Management, 1994).

for floodplain management." To follow up on this recommendation, the Task Force in 1987 initiated an assessment of the nation's program for floodplain management. The professional judgments and views of many individuals and groups actively involved with or affected by floodplain management activities were sought. A special National Review Committee, composed of prominent floodplain and natural resource management professionals, was assembled to assist in an evaluation of the effectiveness of floodplain management. Its report to the Task Force significantly aided in carrying out the assessment (National Review Committee, 1992).

The Task Force's work was published in 1992 in two reports (FIFM Task Force, 1992). There were a number of key findings of the study, as follows:

- *Individual Risk Awareness.* Although substantial progress has been made in increasing institutional awareness of flood risk, individual awareness falls far short of what is needed, resulting in unwise use and development of flood hazard areas.

- *Migration to Water.* People are attracted to riverine and coastal environments but not usually due to economic necessity. In recent decades, the annual growth rate in these areas has greatly exceeded that of the nation as a whole.

- *Floodplain Losses.* Despite attempts to cope with the problem, the large-scale development and modification of riverine and coastal floodplains has resulted in increasing damages and loss of floodplain resources.

- *Short-term Economic Returns.* In many instances, private interests develop land to maximize economic return without regard to long-term economic and natural resource losses. This increases public expenditures for relief, recovery, and corrective actions.

- *Enhanced Knowledge and Technology.* Institutions and individuals that deal with floodplain problems require a broad range of information, a variety of technologies to deal with emerging problems, and standards to which they can refer for guidance. Research enhances our knowledge about these areas.

- *National Flood Protection Standard.* Protection from the effects of greater, less frequent flooding is still needed in areas where such flooding will cause unacceptable or catastrophic damages.

- *Limited Governmental Capabilities.* Many states and most communities lack the full resources necessary to bring about comprehensive local action to mitigate flood problems without federal support. Local governments invariably misjudge their ability to deal with severe flood events. However, they are necessary partners to any successful solution.

- *Need for Interdisciplinary Approaches.* Plans to solve flood problems have to encompass the entire hydrologic unit and be part of a broader water resources management program. Training in a variety of disciplines is required to devise and carry out mitigation strategies.

- *Application of Measures.* Measures implemented locally typically involve only floodplain regulations (to meet the requirements of NFIP and state programs) and eligibility for the individuals to purchase insurance. Communities typically have not implemented other floodplain management measures (see Figure 11-3).

- *Effectiveness of Mitigation Measures.* Structural flood control measures have been effective in reducing economic losses. The application of additional structural measures is limited because of economic and environmental considerations. Land use regulations required by some federal programs and implemented by state and local governments have reduced the rate of floodplain development. Compliance with regulatory controls is a significant problem. New technologies and techniques associated with risk assessment, forecasting, warning, and construction practices have substantially improved these activities. The potential of NFIP has not been realized: less than 20 percent of floodplain residents have insurance.

- *Role of Disaster Assistance.* Liberal federal assistance in post-flood relief and recovery has reinforced expectations of government aid when flood disasters occur. This view has resulted in limited mitigation planning and actions by communities and individuals.

- *National Goals and Resources.* Despite significant progress, the United States still lacks a truly unified national program for floodplain management. Ambiguity in national goals has hindered the effective employment of limited financial and human resources.

Followup to the National Assessment

Further proposals for A Unified National Program for Floodplain Management were developed by the Federal Interagency Floodplain Management Task Force in 1993 to reflect trends affecting floodplain management and the findings and conclusions of the assessment of the nation's program. The work of the Task Force was essentially completed before the 1993 Midwest flood. The report sets out intermediate- and long-term goals that would bring the nation closer to using its floodplains wisely. These goals are based in part on the opportunities identified in the national assessment (FIFM Task Force, 1992) and in other documents and forums, and in part on national and global trends. The report was prepared prior to and independent of the subsequent report of the Clinton Administration's Floodplain Management Review Committee.

Four broad goals are recommended for the Unified National Program. Objectives necessary to achieving each goal were identified and a target date was set for completing them, and these are shown on Figure 11-3. The goals and objectives are phrased to set an "action agenda" and to make estimates of progress feasible. Further refinement of the various objectives, precise definition of their components, and methods for measuring progress will need to be addressed as the program proceeds.

The report of the Task Force (FIFM, 1994) was submitted to President Clinton at the end of 1994. This document represents just one of many reports prepared by the Task Force over nearly two decades. *However, no entity exists to act upon the report's recommendations and those of the previous national assessment.*

The Unified National Program for Floodplain Management has suffered from lack of high-level attention from past administrations. To meet its goals, this program must be recognized by the Administration and given all the attention it rightfully deserves.

Interagency Floodplain Management Review Committee Report

As stated earlier, the Executive Office of the President in January 1994 assigned to a federal Interagency Floodplain Management Review Committee the mission of delineating major causes and consequences of the 1993 Midwest flooding and evaluating the performance of existing floodplain management and related watershed management programs. The report issued by the committee (Executive Office of the President, 1994) was based on its research and interactions with federal, state, and local officials, businesses, interest groups, and individuals in and outside the Mississippi River basin. Taken with the assessment of the nation's program for floodplain management (FIFM Task Force, 1992) and the revised proposals for A Unified National Program for Floodplain Management (FIFM, 1994), it should provide "a blueprint for change" in the nation's programs and policies affecting its coastal and riverine floodplains.

Some of the report's more salient statements include:

- *The goals for floodplain management are clear.* The means to carry out effective floodplain management exist today but need improvement and refocusing. It is time to share responsibility and accountability for accomplishing floodplain management among all levels of government and with citizens of the nation.

- *Full disaster support for those in the floodplain [should be] contingent on their participation in self-help mitigation programs such as flood insurance.* Measures that internalize risks reduce the moral hazard associated with full government support.

- *State and local governments must have a fiscal stake in floodplain management.* Without this stake, few incentives exist for them to be fully involved in floodplain management.

- *People and property remain at risk throughout the nation.* Many of those at risk neither fully understand the nature and the potential consequences of that risk nor share fully in the fiscal implications of bearing that risk.

- *The lessons of the flood of 1993 are clear.* The nation should not carry the burden of massive federal flood disaster relief costs that current policies generate each time a major flood occurs.

- *The dominant federal role in funding flood damage reduction and recovery activities limits the incentive for many state and local governments, businesses, and private citizens to share responsibility for making wise decisions concerning floodplain activity.*

- *Increased state involvement will require greater state technical capabilities in floodplain management.* Few incentives exist for the state to build this expertise.

Objective	Completion Date

Goal-Setting and Monitoring
a. Devise a mechanism for setting, monitoring, and revising national goals. ... 1995
b. Hold a national forum on "Floodplain Management for the First Quarter
   of the 21st Century," to discuss and modify the mechanism as needed ... 1996
c. Institutionalize the mechanism through legal, legislative,
   or administrative measures. ... 1997

Mitigation of Risk
a. For all metropolitan floodplains, complete an inventory of
   - all existing structures ... 1996
   - all natural resources ... 2000
b. For all nonmetropolitan floodplains,
   - inventory existing structures ... 2000
   - identify areas with high potential for development ... 2000
   - inventory all natural resources ... 2005
c. Mitigate the risk of flood damage for at least half the nation's
   highest-risk floodplain structures. ... 2020
d. Reduce, by at least half, the risk of degradation of the most important
   natural resources of the nation's floodplains. ... 2020

Public Awareness
a. Develop a simple concept and definition of floodplain management
   that improve public understanding and support. ... 1996
b. Lay out a leadership strategy to encourage initiative and
   acceptance of responsibility. ... 1996
c. Establish new incentives that give credit for integrating
   different floodplain management programs, strategies, and tools. ... 1996
d. Devise a national strategy to foster public understanding that mitigating action
   is required when floodplain development potentially damages public or
   private property or natural resources. ... 1997

Professional Capability
a. Make available enhanced training, especially that which takes
   a comprehensive view of floodplain management. ... 1996
b. Establish in-house, professional floodplain management capability
   in all states and metropolitan areas. ... 1998
c. Provide professional floodplain management services to nonmetropolitan areas. ... 2000
d. Establish professional standards for floodplain management expertise. ... 2000

FIGURE 11-3   The action agenda for a Unified National Program for Floodplain Management for 1995-2025 (Source: A Unified National Program for Floodplain Management, 1994).

The committee was charged with making recommendations to the Clinton Administration's Floodplain Management Task Force on changes in current policies, programs, and activities of the federal government that, in their view, would most effectively achieve risk reduction, economic efficiency, and governmental enhancement in the floodplain and related watersheds. Its report contains 89 recommendations in "a blueprint for the future," and many of these recommendations are significant.

To ensure a long-term, nationwide approach to floodplain management, the committee proposed legislation to develop and fund a national floodplain management program with principal responsibility and accountability at the state level. It also proposes revitalization of the federal Water Resources Council to better coordinate and direct federal activities for water management, limited restoration of some river basin commissions for basin-wide planning, and issuance of a Presidential Executive Order requiring federal agencies to follow floodplain management principles in the execution of their programs. This report was well received by the Clinton Administration and may become the catalyst for change in existing policies for managing floodplains.

Other Views Concerning the Nation's Response to the 1993 Flood

As a result of the severe and long-lasting flooding in 1993, one would expect that the experience and the subsequent response and recovery efforts would result in numerous calls for changes in the way the nation responds to flood disasters and manages its floodplains. In the aftermath of the flood, the editorial page of *USA Today* was particularly active. This newspaper kept the flood and its consequences in the public eye for nearly eight months. Numerous articles and editorials in local, regional, and other national newspapers and magazines also attempted to shape public opinion (see Chapter 10).

Several national experts on the present use of rivers and adjacent lands, and representing the nonfederal sector, were invited to prepare articles for publication in special reports on the flood or for special sections of magazines devoted to this topic. Much of what they say echoes other calls for sounder policies. Among the views presented was a broader consideration of utilizing the natural function of floodplains (to temporarily store floodwater to decrease downstream peaks) in conjunction with engineering works such as levees and dams (Leopold, 1994). Leopold thinks that this theory has not been put in use in flood control policy.

Other experts believe the opportunity is now at hand to reverse current watershed management and restore some of the natural conditions that made the Mississippi River an unusually rich ecosystem. One authority states that the federal government should expand the Wetland Reserve Program, created by the 1990 Farm Act, in the Mississippi basin (Tripp, 1994). He contends "the nation could finance the conversion of one million acres of floodplain wetlands for less than $1 billion, a large sum, but only about one-fifth the amount the federal government appropriated for disaster relief in the Upper Mississippi basin."

Other authorities view the Hazard Mitigation and Relocation Assistance Act of 1993, cited earlier, as having failed to address more fundamental flaws in the nation's flood control and floodplain management policies (Faber and Hunt, 1994). They go on to state that "the Midwest floods of 1993 may have shaken people's faith in levees, but the vast majority of federal and state relief dollars will be spent to rebuild and put people in harm's way. Perhaps $500 million will be spent to help relocate river towns. In contrast, $2.35 billion will be delivered in the form of one-time crop-loss payments to farmers. *If we are to avoid disaster bills of this magnitude in the future, our funding priorities must change"* [emphasis added].

Shabman (1994) presents a compelling argument for a new public policy goal: restoring the landscape. He wrote, "Clearly, how to minimize damages should not be the question of concern in public policy debate. Public policy should be concerned with achieving the best uses of floodplains and wetlands, however difficult it may be to define 'best' use. This means that the evaluation of any restoration must compare the net benefits to a landowner from a particular parcel's land use with the benefits to the larger society."

Others note that "although floodplain agriculture may be profitable from an individual farmer's point of view, no one really knows whether it is sustainable and cost-efficient from a national perspective. This is because the economic analyses do not count the full costs of subsidies, opportunities foregone, and environmental effects" (Sparks and Sparks, 1994).

And still others believe that generous disaster assistance creates negative incentives for the purchase of flood insurance. As a result of this and other reasons, the National Flood Insurance Program has not achieved the 1968 Congressional goal of reducing escalating costs to the general taxpayer for disaster relief. In examining ways to improve the Program, two national experts note that "there has been a distinct shift in public attitude toward disasters in recent years," and everyone is now expecting federal aid (Kunreuther and White, 1994). They go on to state that in enacting policies that provide uninsured disaster victims with liberal relief, Congress determines that this special group should be aided at the expense of all taxpayers.

Platt, in discussing a recent U.S. Supreme Court decision in an Oregon property rights case, observes that "ironically, with a growing property owner's rights movement, demands for federal bailout of communities and property owners stricken by foreseeable natural disasters have never been so intense. Approximately $27.6 billion was spent on disaster assistance from FY 1989-1993, as compared to $6.7 billion between 1965-89 (not corrected for inflation). And the proportion of federal to nonfederal cost sharing has increased from 75-25 to 90-10 for three recent disasters (Hurricane Andrew, Midwest flood, Northridge earthquake). This level of federal largesse is unjustified if local governments and private owners do not mitigate hazards within their control. *If private owners are unwilling to accept limits on unsafe building practices in known hazardous areas, why should the nation hold them harmless from the results of their 'own free choice'"* (Platt, 1994) [emphasis added].

RECENT AND ONGOING ACTIVITIES AND STUDIES

Amendments to the National Flood Insurance Program

For several years prior to the 1993 flood, Congress had considered changes to the National Flood Insurance Program. These changes would have, in all likelihood, been made, but may have received renewed attention because of the Great Flood. They are contained in the Riegle Community Development and Regulatory Improvement Act of 1994 (P.L. 103-325) and the National Flood Insurance Reform Act of 1994.

The legislation should improve compliance with the mandatory requirements of the program involving those individuals who have mortgaged homes or businesses in flood hazard areas, but have not purchased or maintained flood insurance coverage. It creates a supplementary mitigation insurance program to provide expanded coverage to rebuild repetitive and substantial loss properties to current building code standards. It also creates mitigation assistance grants for activities that are technically feasible and cost-beneficial.

The legislation prohibits the nonwaiver of flood insurance purchase requirements of recipients of federal disaster assistance to repair or to rebuild structures damaged by floods. The legislation decrees that agricultural structures are no longer eligible for federal disaster assistance and prohibits such assistance to anyone if the previous recipient let a flood insurance policy lapse. As the historical record indicates, these provisions could easily be waived by future post-flood response and recovery legislation.

Amendments to the Federal Crop Insurance Program

On October 13, 1994, Congress enacted legislation to reform the Federal Crop Insurance Program (P.L. 103-354). As a condition for receiving support payments for 1995 and subsequent crops, or for obtaining a direct loan or loan guarantee, a producer must obtain catastrophic risk protection insurance coverage (Hammond, 1994). It will be interesting if these reforms result in a significant increase in individuals obtaining crop insurance coverage. Previous program reforms have not produced the desired results in coverage.

Congressional Directed Assessment of the 1993 Flooded Areas

There were several calls for a broader review of post-flood recovery alternatives--one that examines the entire Upper Mississippi and Lower Missouri

266

watersheds. Long-term solutions must be based on a comprehensive watershed approach to planning and action. This would involve determining and quantifying causal factors and developing mitigation measures meeting multi-objective goals and enjoying strong public and political support, particularly at the local and regional level.

The ensuing public discussions generated Congressional authorization and appropriations for the Corps to conduct comprehensive, systemwide studies to evaluate the floodplain management needs in the areas that were flooded in 1993. The assessment is to be accomplished over an 18-month period, starting in January 1994 (Figure 11-4). According to the Corps, a systems approach to floodplain management will be used, recognizing and complementing the efforts of the Clinton Administration's Floodplain Management Task Force (Peterson, 1994a). A draft report is projected to be completed by the end of March 1995, with a final report by June 1995.

Congressional Task Forces

The Emergency Supplemental Appropriations Act of 1994 included a provision for establishment of a Bipartisan Task Force on Funding Disaster Relief. Both the House and Senate have subsequently established such task forces to seek more

FIGURE 11-4   A breach in a levee near Quincy, IL. The vast damages to over 1,000 levees and the ensuing flooding formed the basis of major policy issues facing the nation in the aftermath of the 1993 flood (Illinois State Water Survey).

effective ways to confront natural disasters and mitigate their impacts on the federal budget. The task forces will recommend methods to improve disaster relief, enhance coordination between all levels of government, and lessen the budgetary impact of federal disaster relief. The House task force met during the 103rd Session of the Congress, and it is expected that the issue will come up again in the 104th Session.

Action on the Report of the Administration's Interagency Floodplain Management Review Committee

Shortly after issuance of the report in mid-1994, two multiagency work groups were established by the Administration's Floodplain Management Task Force to determine how to implement its recommendations. It is expected that the White House will issue a floodplain management "action plan" by mid-1995. The action plan will consist of those recommendations that the Task Force wishes to implement and identify those agencies responsible for implementing each recommendation (McShane, 1994).

All-Hazards Management

There is growing interest in integrating flood loss reduction strategies and measures with those for other natural hazards such as land subsidence, earthquakes, dam failures, hurricanes, and other high winds. Periodically, the nation has had to deal with simultaneous hazards in post-recovery efforts. The federal government seems to be moving in this direction.

As evidence, the Federal Emergency Management Agency has begun designing a new "National Mitigation Strategy." (There is now a fairly well-established consensus that the disaster cycle of preparedness, response, and recovery must include the fourth component of mitigation.) The agency envisions that such a strategy will offer innovative approaches for combining funds and coordinating activities between the private sector and citizens. Both the federal government and private sector would provide leadership, coordination, and research support, including financial incentives to communities, businesses, and individuals for mitigation activities. This strategy would emphasize building safer communities now and, after a disaster, using safe building practices in recovery measures and implementing wiser land use decisions.

SUMMARY AND RECOMMENDATIONS

Much Remains to be Accomplished

Present Situation. The typical "flood scene" over the last two years has included the Midwest, the Florida-Georgia area, and Texas and is all-too familiar.

The typical story begins with widespread flooding in a portion of a state, sometimes even encompassing several states. The situation is instantly reported by the media. Within a day or so, the affected localities request, through their governor, a presidential disaster declaration. (Federal aid may already be on the way, often before it is requested.) It is unusual for a declaration not to be readily issued, given the political ramifications.

Assistance is offered through several dozen federal programs. Then a post-flood damage assessment reveals that only a few homeowners and businesses, out of the hundreds or thousands affected, had flood insurance coverage to indemnify themselves from flood losses. Public facilities equally suffer from the lack of insurance coverage.

Massive amounts of federal disaster assistance are required to recover from the flood disaster. In the absence of a previously prepared post-flood mitigation plan to guide redevelopment of the affected area, consistent with the flood risk and the "window of opportunity" to meet other community goals, recovery typically involves restoring the area to pre-flood conditions, to await the next flood event, to repeat the cycle.

In all likelihood, some of the measures already taken to recover from the Great Flood of 1993 may have a significant impact on future policies. The historical record of response to catastrophes provides both encouragement for needed changes and caution about becoming overly optimistic.

Natural catastrophes provide a mixed bag: an incentive to reconsider policy and a social climate anxious to return to normalcy. The 1993 event certainly heightened public and political interest and awareness and instituted a louder debate concerning the occupancy and use of the nation's floodplains and who should pay the price that nature capriciously exacts from time to time in an erratic and merciless manner.

The need for certain changes, such as modifications to the National Flood Insurance Program and to the Federal Crop Insurance Program, received attention because of the 1993 flood. The work of the Federal Interagency Floodplain Management Task Force has greatly assisted in identifying future directions for floodplain management. The flood led President Clinton to establish the Interagency Floodplain Management Review Committee, and its report (Executive Office of the President, 1994) provides a blueprint for changes in management of floodplains through sharing of responsibility among federal, state, tribal, and local governments, businesses, and citizens. Detailed findings and recommendations for changes in existing policies and programs are presented. *Taken together, the reports of the task force and the review committee have provided the basis for an informed decision-making process in any further efforts to shape sounder national policies.* Their findings also identify those attitudes, conditions, and situations that can be viewed as "barriers" that would have to be overcome to realize any truly meaningful changes in policies and programs, particularly at the federal level.

A Vision for the 21st Century: Recommendations. The report of the Interagency Floodplain Management Review Committee (1994) presents a vision for sharing the challenge for floodplain management into the 21st century. This author would like to help sharpen that vision with a series of recommendations. Any vision on how the nation should manage its floodplains should start with the premise that *individuals, not government, must begin to take responsibility.* This responsibility should extend to the community and state level where each should be held accountable for its actions and decisions affecting floodplain occupancy and use, and the consequences thereof. However, at present there are few *real incentives* for any of the above to take more responsibility, given the present level and types of federal involvement.

To be fair, most floodplain occupants are likely unaware of their flood risk. They typically first learn of that risk when a property is offered for sale (disclosure is rare at this point), when a property loan has to be secured by a flood insurance policy, when they apply for a permit involving land modification or development, when they apply for a permit (usually local) to alter an existing structure, or when they experience an actual flood event. Even then the risk may be explained to them in very general terms, or worse, trivialized. *Truly concerted efforts are needed to make individual property owners aware of the degree of flood risk they face, in terms they understand.*

Changes are also needed in the provision of floodplain management assistance and other services to flood-prone localities. The state is the appropriate governmental level for the delivery of such services. But, as already demonstrated, there are few present incentives for states to become involved. Again, concerted efforts are needed to devise incentives to achieve state involvement. Both the Federal Interagency Floodplain Management Task Force and the Interagency Floodplain Management Review Committee have emphasized the importance of developing enhanced floodplain management capabilities at the state and community levels. This capability can be developed by making available enhanced training, especially that which takes a *comprehensive* view of the management of floodplains.

The private sector has an important role and responsibility in hazard mitigation. For example, many experts believe the *real estate professional* should investigate and disclose flood risks when properties are *initially* offered for sale and that *lending institutions* should also provide such disclosures at the time of *loan application*, not at loan closing when irrevocable decisions may have already been made. Experts also believe that the *insurance companies* could do more to assure the hazard-resistant quality of homes they insure. This could be accomplished by asking specific construction questions on insurance forms, through site inspections, and by creating ratings and adjustments to premiums based on the existence or employment of certain mitigation measures. Market forces and factors that determine if insurance should be available and that establish premiums reflecting actual risk could be important in the many decisions about locations and construction, *if* federal and state governments allowed them to act and without any form of intervention.

Finally, floodplain management can greatly benefit from a broadened mission. Full integration of environmental protection measures with existing (and more widely applied) flood loss reduction strategies will increase overall interest and support for floodplain management. This support can be realized from all governmental levels and from nongovernmental sources, including concerned citizens and special interest groups.

Prospects for Further Change

The floods of 1993 on the Upper Mississippi and Lower Missouri Rivers have brought into sharp focus the many conflicting goals, objectives, and views we as a nation have in managing our water and related land resources. They show once again how difficult it is to balance the economic, social and political interests of those in the basin and of the citizens of the United States as a whole. They illustrate a number of policy problems discussed in this chapter.

To harken back to the words of Gilbert White, quoted at the beginning of this chapter, the recent conjunction of events and the rethinking of what should be our public policies regarding planning for and responding to natural disaster suggest the best prospects for meaningful policy changes since those changes result from the recommendations of the 1966 Task Force on Federal Flood Control Policy. In its report, the Floodplain Management Review Committee noted that "the time is ripe for serious attention to be paid to how this nation responds to the threat of floods" (Executive Office of the President, 1994).

Additional policy changes may result from further consideration and action on the recommendations of the Interagency Floodplain Management Review Committee, the Federal Interagency Floodplain Management Task Force's revised proposals for A Unified National Program for Floodplain Management, and the Congressional directed assessment of the 1993 flooded areas (a report is due by mid-1995). The extent and the real long-term significance of possible policy changes remain a matter of conjecture at this time.

Several matters of concern emerged from the Midwest floods and deserve continuing attention in the policy arena. These include problems related to disaster relief and subsidy programs, the lack of viable alternatives to structural flood control projects, the need for restoration of natural systems and functions, the question of how individuals and their local communities perceive and deal with their flood risk and management programs, overreliance on insurance as a mitigation and loss reduction approach, and the lack of accurate knowledge of the full costs and benefits of occupying floodplains. *Until and unless these matters are adequately dealt with, including their underlying causes, there is little prospect for meaningful changes, no matter how well intentioned the motives of the policy makers.*

Recent trends in disaster response and recovery are particularly disturbing. The federal government is becoming the first respondent in regional and local disasters, supplanting, not supplementing, local and state efforts. By rushing to pay for such predictable events, state and local fiscal responsibility are rendered irrational. As a result, such federal efforts are rewarding local and state lack of preparedness for emergencies.

In addition, recent policy changes seem to be moving federal policies in the opposite direction from which many feel they should go. They were the consequence of a number of disasters affecting large populations (Hurricane Andrew, the 1993 Midwest flooding, and the Northridge earthquake). Non-federal cost-share requirements were decreased to respond to state and local financial constraints. In its report, the Clinton Administration's Floodplain Management Review Committee (Executive Office of the President, 1994) expressed concern that disaster-specific changes in federal/nonfederal cost-share percentages for FEMA disaster assistance programs may have an adverse effect on floodplain management. (The original 75/25 federal/nonfederal cost-share was adjusted to 90/10 for all three disasters.)

The Review Committee cautions that these cost-share changes have two potentially significant consequences. *First*, they set up an expectation of similar treatment in subsequent disasters and increase political pressure to provide a lower nonfederal share. This perpetuates the dominant federal role in recovery and increases federal costs, a situation that the task force suggests throughout its report should be reversed. *Second*, they argue that these changes may defeat the fundamental purpose behind cost-sharing, which is to increase the amount of local involvement, responsibility, and accountability. They go on to point out that by lessening the nonfederal investment, state and local governments have less at stake and, therefore, may have a lower incentive to develop and adopt sound floodplain management policies and practices.

Regarding prospects for restoration of lost or diminished natural resources and functions within floodplains, it will be difficult to obtain appropriations for this specific purpose, regardless of the demonstrated benefits. It will also be difficult to achieve acceptance that protection of floodplain resources is a goal that is just as important as the goal of flood loss reduction in floodplain management policies and programs. Instead, any long-term progress in restoring or protecting floodplain resources will likely come from programs or policies that have not been developed specifically for floodplain application, but apply to resources found outside the floodplain as well. *Buyouts of flood-damaged properties in the Midwest, with the goal of restoring the land to open space, is an encouraging shift in the use of post-flood recovery funds.*

Generous disaster assistance creates negative incentives for the purchase of flood or crop insurance. Provision of such assistance to those individuals without insurance creates a perception among many floodplain residents that purchase of hazard insurance is not a worthwhile investment.

In summary, given the wide differences in existing views on these issues, resolutions will not emerge easily. Significant changes in federal policy will likely be based on compromise. There is a danger that a strong special-interest group or coalition will dominate the decision process. If that is the case, it is unlikely that any progress will be made in improving use of the floodplains (see Figure 11-6). The final outcome also will be driven by constraints imposed by the budget deficit. Nevertheless, a change in national policies and the public response to living and investing in flood-prone areas is necessary (Kitch, 1994).

Lessons Learned

Flood mitigation in the United States has undergone some dramatic changes over the past 150 years. Changes in national policies to deal with the most pervasive of our natural hazards have been largely event driven. The Great Flood of 1993 may prove to be no exception.

This massive event demonstrated that much work remains to bring into better balance the flood risk society incurs from use of floodplain lands.

A key action needed is the assumption of responsibility by individuals for their locational decisions. There are also challenges and opportunities for integrating programs and measures for achieving flood loss reduction with those for protecting the natural and beneficial resources and important functions of floodplains. There are additional opportunities to further broaden the scope of measures to encompass other water resource management activities and to integrate flood-related strategies and measures with those designed to mitigate other natural hazards.

Our policy philosophy must change: the nation needs to move beyond reliance on political responses and solutions to inappropriate uses of its floodplains. For the federal government to change ingrained public expectations of copious amounts of aid when calamity strikes, and instead expect individuals to pay for the risk they assume, will require consistent, supportive behavior through a reform in federal policy. (In addressing this and other policy issues, the present interdependency of flood control, disaster assistance, and resource protection will have to be taken into account.)

Many observers believe that some "bold new approaches" are warranted to achieve this goal. One approach might include a significant shift in present government programs that assist individuals, perhaps totally eliminating some forms of disaster assistance. Instead, they might provide a better service through a "contract with all Americans." Such a "contract" entails a number of steps:

1. An inventory of all properties located in known flood hazard areas.
2. Full disclosure of flood risk to individuals, through personal contacts, in terms and ways that they could understand (e.g., expected depths of floodwaters on properties or around or in structures, and the expected frequency and duration of these depths).

3. Provision of information on options that individuals should consider to to reduce their exposure to flood risk (e.g., structural modification), or reduce their losses when a flood did occur (e.g., flood insurance).
4. Further disclosure to individuals (perhaps included in the third step) that most forms of existing disaster assistance (particularly grants) will be eliminated.

This contract would, ideally, send a loud, clear message that hereafter individuals, not government, will be held responsible for their decisions regarding occupancy or use of flood hazard areas and lack of action to reduce their existing exposure or potential economic losses.

Admittedly, this would involve a massive undertaking with involvement of all governmental levels and the commitment of significant resources. The resources required would probably be less, on an annual basis, than the average expenditures for federal disaster assistance under present policies, however. A very strong case would have to be built for the plausibility of what many of our poli-

FIGURE 11-5   The key policy question illustrated by this cartoon is whether the effects of the 1993 flood on federal policy will compete favorably against all the other issues facing President Clinton and the Congress (Reprinted by permission: Tribune Media Services).

ticians would view as a profound change in present policies. Arguments based on spending today to avoid future costs have not been well received in recent federal budgeting.

Enactment of significant changes in public policies, and consistent long-term support of such changes, will require *real* political courage and discipline. Too often the Clinton Administration and Congress have not demonstrated such courage and discipline. The American public seemingly wants less government, but in the aftermath of flood events, those affected won't want less federal assistance.

REFERENCES

Clark, C., 1982: *Planet Earth, FLOOD*. Time-Life Books, 176 pp.

Changnon, S. A. and J. M. Changnon, 1993: Storm catastrophes in the United States. *Natural Hazards,* 2, 612-616.

Committee on Public Works, 1959: *A Program for Reducing the National Flood Damage Potential*. U.S. Senate, 86th Congress, 1st Session, 70 pp.

Erat, D.M., 1994: Personal communication, September 29, 1994. Federal Emergency Management Agency, Washington, DC.

Executive Office of the President, 1994: *Sharing the Challenge: Floodplain Management Into the 21st Century*. Report of the Interagency Floodplain Management Review Committee, U.S. Government Printing Office, Washington, DC, 189 pp.

Faber, S., and C. Hunt, 1994: "River management post-1993: The choice is ours". *Coping with the Flood: The Next Phase, Water Resources Update*, Issue No. 95, The Universities Council on Water Resources, Southern Illinois University, Carbondale, IL, 21-25.

Federal Interagency Floodplain Management Task Force, 1994: *A Unified National Program for Floodplain Management*. FEMA 248, U.S. Government Printing Office, Washington, DC, 43 pp.

Federal Interagency Floodplain Management Task Force, 1992: *Floodplain Management in the United States: An Assessment Report*. Volume 1, Summary Report, 70 pp., Volume 2, Full Report, U.S.Government Printing Office, Washington, DC, 600 pp.

Hammond, M., 1994: Personal correspondence, December 2, 1994. U.S.Department of Agriculture, Washington, DC.

Kitch, H.E., 1994: Limiting the impact of future floods. America Under Water. *USA Today,* Valley Stream, NY, 36-39.

Kunreuther, H.C., and G.F. White, 1994: The role of the National Flood Insurance Program in reducing losses and promoting wise use of floodplains. *Coping with the Flood: The Next Phase, Water Resources Update*, Issue No. 95, The Universities Council on Water Resources, Southern Illinois University, Carbondale, IL, 31-35.

Leopold, L.B., 1994: Flood hydrology and the floodplain. *Coping with the Flood: The Next Phase. Water Resources Update,* Issue No. 95, The Universities Council on Water Resources, Southern Illinois University, Carbondale, IL, 11-14.

McShane, J., 1994: Personal communication, December 5, 1994. Federal Emergency Management Agency, Washington, DC.

Mittler, E., 1992: *A Fiscal Responsibility Analysis of a National Earthquake Insurance Program*. The Earthquake Project of the National Committee on Property Insurance, Washington, DC, 54 pp.

Moore, J.W., and D.P. Moore, 1989: *The Army Corps of Engineers and the Evolution of Federal Floodplain Management Policy*. Special Publication No. 20, Natural Hazards Research and Applications Information Center, Institute of Behavioral Science University of Colorado, Boulder, 184 pp.

National Review Committee, 1992: *Action Agenda for Managing the Nation's Floodplains*. Special Publication No. 25, Natural Hazards Research and Applications Information Center, Institute of Behavioral Science, University of Colorado, Boulder, 17 pp.

Peterson, J.Q., 1994a: Personal correspondence, December 6, 1994. U.S. Army Corps of Engineers, Washington, DC.

Peterson, J.Q., 1994b: Personal correspondence, October 21, 1994. U.S. Army Corps of Engineers, Washington, DC.

Platt, R.H., 1994: The Supreme Court and *Dolan v. City of Tagard*. *Natural Hazards Observer*, September 1994, 11-12.

Pollnow, C., 1994: Personal communication, December 5, 1994. Federal Emergency Management Agency, Washington, DC.

Shabman, L., 1994: Responding to the 1993 flood: The restoration option. America Under Water, *USA Today,* Valley Stream, NY, 26-30.

Sparks, R.E., and R. Sparks, 1994: After floods: Restoring ecosystems. America Under Water, *USA Today*, Valley Stream, NY, 40-42.

Task Force on Federal Flood Control Policy, 1966: *A Unified National Program for Managing Flood Losses*. House Document 465, 89th Congress, 2d Session, 47 pp.

Tripp, J.T.B., 1994: Flooding: Who is to blame. America Under Water, *USA Today,* Valley Stream, NY, 30-32.

White, G.F., 1942: *Human Adjustment to Floods, A Geographic Approach to the Flood Problem in the United States*. University of Chicago, Department of Geography, 225 pp.

White, G.F., 1958: *Changes in Urban Occupance of Flood Plains in the United States*. Research Paper No. 57, Department of Geography, University of Chicago, 235 pp.

White, G.F., 1994: *Statement*. Natural Hazards Research & Applications Workshop, Boulder, CO.

Zwickl, K., 1994: Personal communication, November 29, 1994. U.S. Army Corps of Engineers, Washington, DC.

12

Losers and Winners:
A Summary of the Flood's Impacts

Stanley A. Changnon

INTRODUCTION

The record Midwestern flood of 1993 inundated 10,300 square miles in nine states, thereby creating a multitude of environmental effects and immeasurable social and economic impacts. As the 1993 flood developed, the considerable uncertainty over whether it qualified as a 50-year, 100-year, or 500-year event helps reveal that floods, like droughts, are defined not just by their geophysical dimensions, but by the damages they ultimately inflict. That the flood of 1993 qualified as a record flood by the damages it created is not open to question: it was the record-setting flood of all time in the Upper Mississippi River basin.

This chapter summarizes the varied impacts, describes a few of them in detail, and then quantifies the magnitude of the impacts (number of items damaged, persons displaced or killed, or dollars lost) based on existing and sometimes conflicting values. The primary source is the material in the preceding chapters, although other important sources of information are also referenced.

The flood of 1993 produced major impacts within four broad sectors: (1) environmental effects, (2) economic impacts, (3) impacts to and responses by government at the local, state, and federal levels, and (4) social disruption. Each of these four areas is discussed.

ENVIRONMENTAL EFFECTS

Many of the flood's impacts on the environment were difficult to measure, some are still unmeasured, and many are tertiary and will take years to become fully evident. The flood sizably altered the natural ecosystem of the Upper Mississippi and Missouri Rivers and their floodplains, changing many environmental conditions forever. Along with the flooding and related excessive erosion came further erosion and extensive silting of the floodplains and their wetlands. Although the flood damaged some trees and plants, it generally provided a windfall for most plant and animal species, especially fish populations. However, alterations in river flow and river water quality were detrimental to much of the riverine environment. Prolonged immersion of the nonfarmed portions of the floodplains had deleterious effects on certain trees. When levee breaks suddenly inundated vast areas, some wildlife already isolated by the flood drowned. Populations of certain insect pests were altered, at least on a one-year time scale. The full extent of the effects of various eroded and spilled chemicals on the delicate ecosystem of the Gulf of Mexico still remains to be seen.

Soils

Wet soil conditions were the most immediate environmental effects of near continuous Midwestern rains from late May to late August 1993. During June-August, 77 large rain areas including 175 flash flood storms (Richards et al., 1994) fell on already soaked soils (Kunkel et al., 1994). Such an abnormally large number of heavy rains created two major impacts. First, they kept the soils saturated at a time when evapotranspiration usually is high. As a result, soil moisture levels remained high throughout the spring and summer, leaving the vast area soaked and vulnerable to fall, winter, and spring floods if heavy precipitation occurred. Evaporation from the continuously wet soils also helped enhance the summer rainfall.

Second, the heavy rains produced enormous amounts of erosion from upland soils, river bluffs, and floodplains, making the flood a "geologic event" as it forever altered the Midwest landscape. Erosion was classed as severe (greater than 20 tons/acre) on seven percent of Wisconsin's cropland and on 2.4 million acres in Iowa (Thompson, 1994). It will take many years to replace the soil lost. Remaining soils lost some of their fertility, many flooded soils were compacted, and some soils even experienced further erosion after floodwaters receded and winds blew over fractured soils that had little remaining plant growth to protect them (Siemens and Hoeft, 1994). Abnormally large amounts of agricultural chemicals were also eroded and captured by the floodwaters, partly because of the delayed applications due to the late 1993 planting season as a result of the wet spring soil conditions.

The resulting waterborne silt, plus the agricultural herbicides, pesticides, and fertilizers eroded from farmed soils throughout the Midwest, were rapidly transported into stream and river systems. Along the levee-confined Upper Mississippi and Lower Missouri, the large volume of water reached record heights, producing high river speeds (from 5 to 15 mph). This too eroded the river channels, as well as the inundated floodplains, causing further erosion of sands and silts in the river courses. High-velocity flows also scoured the riverbanks. Bank erosion in 1993 was severe, not only for the Mississippi and the Missouri, but for many of their tributaries also at flood stages. These factors (erosion, high water speeds, and an enormous volume of moving water) help explain the large amount of silt, sands, and agricultural chemicals deposited in the flooded bottomlands. Several river bottoms were severely scoured, whereas other sections received major depositions of sediments, necessitating major dredging of the navigation channels in the Mississippi and the Missouri Rivers.

Sediment

The Great Flood of 1993 carried a substantial amount of sediment, both as suspended load and as bed load. It is estimated that the Mississippi and the Missouri Rivers carried 60 to 70 percent of their annual sediment load during the 1993 summer flood (Bhowmik, 1994). During the last major flood on the Mississippi River in 1973, the gates on all locks on the Upper Mississippi were open, as they were in 1993, clearing all sediment accumulated in the pools. Approximately 30 to 40 feet of sediment deposited upstream of the locks since 1973 were scoured away from all river pools during the 1993 flood.

With more than 1,000 levees failing in the Midwest, turbid and sediment-laden water moved out of the river into the newly opened floodplains. Sediment and sand were moved and deposited in massive quantities and more than 500 scour holes were created. As the waters receded, substantial dunes were found within many floodplains along with thick layers of sand, particularly in Missouri River bottomlands. Even before the 1993 flood, many backwater lakes along the Mississippi and the Missouri Rivers had already lost between 70 and 100 percent of their capacities, and they lost substantially more volume after receiving sizable quantities of sediment during the 1993 flood. This excess of silt and sand in the floodplains smothered vegetation and compromised large areas of the nation's most productive farmland.

Water Quality

Floodwaters with high flow rates resulted in much-above-normal amounts of eroded sediments and agricultural chemicals in the rivers, and these sizably impacted water quality. In-stream measurements in the main rivers and tributaries revealed large quantities of herbicides and fertilizers (Goolsby et al., 1993). The in-river concentration of atrazine serves as a good indicator of pesticide runoff because it is the most common chemical used in Midwestern watersheds. The concentration during August 1993 near Cairo, IL, was between 2 and 3 parts per billion (ppb), not significantly higher than that during lesser floods, such as in 1991. However, the total amount by weight was high because of the large flow rate: the daily load of atrazine passing in the Mississippi River near Cairo was 12,000 pounds per day, four times higher than during any previous year. Extraordinarily large amounts of other chemicals such as nitrates were also flushed into the rivers. Although there was some early expectation that concentrations of farm chemicals in river waters would be lower during an extreme flood because they would be diluted by record-high flows, herbicide and pesticide concentrations were well above the previous maximum concentrations (USGS, 1994).

Record flood flows for the summer season occurred at the mouth of the Mississippi near New Orleans, entering the Gulf of Mexico at a time when flows are usually low, which had a major impact on the ecosystem of the Gulf shore area.   This unexpected large volume of freshwater depleted oxygen in the Louisiana and Texas coastal waters. A large percentage of the eroded herbicides and nitrates entering the Midwestern rivers were carried into the Gulf. The vast quantity of freshwater entering the Gulf mixed slowly with the salt water and remained a huge mass of low salinity water.   As shown in Figure 12-1, anomalous winds in July-August moved this vast volume of freshwater across the Gulf via the Loop Current. It then passed through the Straits of Florida in late August, entered the Atlantic Ocean, and moved north in the Gulf Stream past Cape Hatteras by late September (Coastal Ocean Office, 1994).

Another water quality problem along the Mississippi and the Missouri Rivers was a result of the large amounts of raw sewage, bacteria, viruses, and parasites carried by the floodwaters. Raw sewage was discharged into the river and its tributaries from more than 120 overflowing wastewater treatment plants and numerous failed septic systems.   Health officials were concerned that the organisms in the water could cause hepatitis, cholera, typhoid, or gastrointestinal illnesses, and warned people against ingesting floodwaters. Exposure to the open

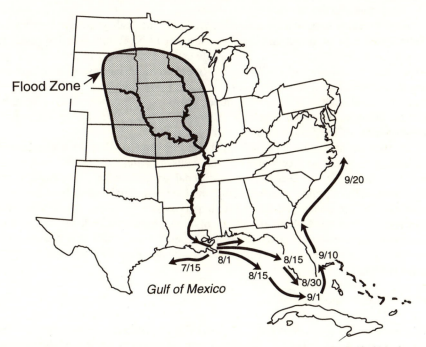

FIGURE 12-1   The flood's enormous volume of freshwater moved across the Gulf of Mexico and into the Atlantic Ocean on the dates shown.

wastes could lead to tetanus, hepatitis, or dysentery. During the flood, thousands of persons living and working along the river were inoculated to prevent disease outbreaks, and, fortunately, waterborne diseases were minimal.

Ground-Water Conditions

The 1993 flooding caused major effects on the quality and quantity of ground water in and along the floodplains. Impacts included bacterial contamination of wells and contamination of aquifer systems from nitrates, pesticides, herbicides, and other hazardous materials (J.K. Johnson, 1993). Infiltration induced by the high surface waters caused major rises in shallow ground-water levels, which undermined many levees, damaged buried utility systems, and flooded basements. Extensive flooding occurred in one area along the Illinois River when water from saturated aquifers caused artesian flows.

Sandbagging to contain floodwater helped keep surface water from overtopping the levees, but it damaged the levees' structural integrity so that they could no longer control the hydraulic pressure from ground water. When ground water seeped through and/or beneath the levees, "sand boils" formed and the levees collapsed. Some levee districts constructed relief wells so ground water freely discharged into drainage ditches along the levee and then was pumped back over the levee and into the river.

Several cities experienced sewer failures due to high ground-water levels. Sewers broke in 14 floodplain communities east of St. Louis, leaving residents without service for many days. Permeable sands and gravels in the bottomlands adjacent to the Mississippi and Missouri Rivers provided large supplies of ground water for domestic, municipal, and industrial development. Ground-water recharge continued throughout summer 1993, a very abnormal condition. Record-high ground-water levels persisted from April 1993 through December 1994 in most of the floodplains.

Bacterial contamination of individual domestic and municipal wells became a problem as flooded surface water entered wells, making chlorination of the well and plumbing systems necessary. Additional ground-water contamination occurred when floodwaters entering wells contained materials washed from landfills, road salt storage areas, and hazardous materials storage sites. There were still concerns in late 1994 about the effect of high ground-water levels on already contaminated areas because above-normal ground-water levels have the potential to shift ground-water flow patterns, thus changing plumes of below-ground contamination.

Fish, Wildlife, and Vegetation

The ecosystems in and around the flooded rivers derived overall benefits from the flood of 1993. Large river-floodplain ecosystems in the Midwest have adapted to exploit seasonal flooding. Even the few species that appear to have been harmed by the flood may ultimately benefit. Any damage incurred may have been due primarily to human factors such as the failures of many levees, erosion of stored hazardous materials on the floodplains, and dispersal of introduced pests, rather than the flood itself.

At least 36 species of fish from seven families, including important commercial species and sport fish, used the inundated floodplains and the expanded backwaters for spawning areas and nurseries. Nutrients and organic matter were released from newly flooded soils in inundated floodplains, stimulating microbial activity and the production of microcrustaceans and aquatic insects, just as they were required as food by larval fishes. Some of the fish produced grew to edible size and were eaten by predatory fish and birds. This benefitted not only the predators, but also the prey by preventing overpopulation and the stunting that sometimes occurs in ponds and backwater lakes with relatively constant water levels. The overwinter survival rate of the fish produced during the flood of 1993 was high. With water levels remaining high, fish had access to backwater wintering areas at depths too deep to freeze, and the winter 1993-1994 temperatures were not below normal. These fish will now grow and survive for many years, increasing sport and commercial catches.

Some of the beneficial effects of a natural flood pulse did not occur when the levees failed and water suddenly surged into the floodplains. A slow, natural rise allows terrestrial animals to evacuate to higher ground, creating a moving littoral zone that advances across a floodplain. The annual migration of waterfowl along the famed Mississippi flyway was also changed during 1993-1994 as the flood destroyed traditional feeding grounds and created new ones. For example, the 275-mile-long Mark Twain National Wildlife Refuge was submerged by the flood.

The flood was a boon to several pest species, including some mosquitoes that are vectors of human disease and the newly-introduced zebra mussel. Larvae of several species of mosquitoes did well in temporary flood pools that their predators (primarily other insects and fish) could not enter or survive.

Zebra mussels were inadvertently introduced to North America in 1986 in ballast water taken on by ships in European rivers and then subsequently discharged in the Great Lakes. Industries and municipalities of the Great Lakes region have already paid a hefty price to treat, kill, and remove the mussels from water intakes, piping, and equipment within water treatment plants. The mussels entered the Illinois River from Lake Michigan via the canal system at Chicago in 1991-1992 and established themselves in the middle and upper Illinois River during 1991-1993. These mussels released their larvae as the 1993 flood was occurring, and the floodwaters transported the larvae into the lower Illinois River at densities ranging from 28,000 to 94,000 mussels per square meter. Larvae were also carried downstream into the Mississippi, laterally into many floodplain lakes and up many tributaries, and into industrial and municipal treatment plants. Although highly unwelcome, the zebra mussel will prosper in its newly-colonized habitats, adding greatly to the cost of water treatment and plant maintenance, jeopardizing the survival of native mollusks, and perhaps even altering river food webs by filtering detritus, suspended sediment, and the contaminants associated with these particles. Zebra mussels also literally smothered all 12 species of native mussels that once occurred in the western basin of Lake Erie. Hence, the prognosis for the 22 species of native mussels in the Illinois River and the 37 species in the Upper Mississippi River is not good. This spread of the zebra mussels is truly an "environmental disaster." This and other undesirable flood effects on the ecosystem were all due to human actions over previous years.

The protracted flood temporarily eliminated the understory of floodplain forests. Gaps have opened in the canopy of the bottomlands as tree varieties not adapted to floodplains (such as oaks and pines) succumbed to suffocation from high waters, insects, or disease (Hopp, 1994). The absence of shading and other competition, however, will enable cottonwoods and other adaptable species to germinate and grow, thereby rejuvenating mature plant communities. In some places along the Missouri River, the river itself was rejuvenated where it broke levees that will probably not be rebuilt (at least not in the same place), and it scoured new basins and channels to replace those lost to sediment accretion.

The Hydrologic Aftermath

Going into the fall of 1993 the Upper Mississippi River basin had the highest soil moisture level on record. Ground-water levels in the floodplains and upland prairies also stood at record levels as winter approached. Shallow wells in Illinois and Missouri showed ground-water levels 3 to 9 feet above average at the end of October, and water was flowing from newly-created artesian wells in certain lowlands along the rivers.

A soil moisture model and historical precipitation data were used to estimate future moisture conditions in the region (Kunkel, 1993) and showed high probabilities for above-normal soil moisture levels in excess of 90 percent throughout the Upper Mississippi basin throughout the fall and winter of 1993-1994. An analysis of excess water in the basin also revealed a 65 percent chance that the amount of excess water would be more than 5 inches by May 1994, strongly suggesting the potential for spring flooding. The highest amount ever experienced in the past 44 years was 5.3 inches. This critical outlook indicated a high likelihood of flooding during fall 1993, winter 1993-1994, and spring 1994. This outlook was true for November 1993 and again during March-April 1994 when heavy precipitation produced flooding in Illinois and Missouri.

ECONOMIC IMPACTS

Total Losses and a National Perspective

The economic impacts of the floods of 1993 involved losses to individuals in and near flooded communities, to floodplain farmers, and to Midwest businesses and industries. Business losses affected regional sales, agricultural production, utilities, manufacturing, transportation, tourism, and recreation. However, the flood also produced some major winners in the agriculture, business, and transportation sectors.

Various state and federal agencies assessed the damages, and many firms and business associations reported losses. Initial estimates of total flood losses varied from $12 billion to $15.7 billion (IFMR Committee, 1994). Actual losses to the transportation systems and the region's economy exceeded the estimates made during the flood. Current estimates of damages and revenue losses in the affected states are $16.8 billion: $6 billion (Iowa), $5 billion (Missouri), $1.4 billion (Illinois), $1.1 billion (Minnesota), $1 billion (Wisconsin), $0.8 billion (South Dakota), $0.6 billion (Kansas), $0.5 billion (North Dakota), and $0.4 billion (Nebraska). When the railroad and barge losses of $1.3 billion are added, the total is $18.1 billion. And when the yet-to-be-quantified losses due to pollutants released by the flood, soil losses, ground-water damages, and environmental changes are known, the grand total may eventually climb above $20 billion and challenge Hurricane Andrew as the nation's single worst weather-created disaster.

Although the regional losses over the nine-state area were extreme, the flood had little impact on the nation's economy as a whole. Economic impact analyses used to predict 1994 conditions, done with and without the flood for 1993, revealed several interesting speculations. The flood did not change the nation's gross domestic product (GDP) in 1993, but it was expected to increase the GDP by 0.01 percent in 1994 due to expenditures for flood repairs. Employment was unchanged nationally in 1993, although a loss of 20,000 jobs occurred in the third quarter, and employment recovered in 1994 with a gain of 0.01 percent due to flood-related restoration jobs. The 3.3 percent rate of inflation in 1993 was unchanged by the flood, but the rate increased from 3.5 to 3.6 percent in 1994 as corn and soybean losses in 1993 caused wholesale farm prices to rise 6 percent. Corporate profits in 1993 dropped by 0.01 percent due to the flood losses and insurance costs, but profits increased by 0.8 percent in 1994 due to rebuilding and cleanup efforts.

Agriculture

The flood inundated 10,300 square miles, much of it valuable farmland representing about 4 percent of the Corn Belt's planted acreage (Figure 12-2). Lands lost to crop production due to flooding included 5.1 million acres of corn and 3.1 million acres of soybeans, plus some losses of farm animals. Continuation of wet conditions into the fall and winter of 1993-1994 greatly limited field work, and wet conditions in spring 1994 limited planting of 1994 crops in several floodplains. Damaged levees had a severe impact on drainage districts that had built drainage systems and levees to protect croplands. The intrusion of floodwaters in the high-quality floodplain soils brought mud and sands that hurt existing soils and limited farming in 1994. Many farmers lost homes,

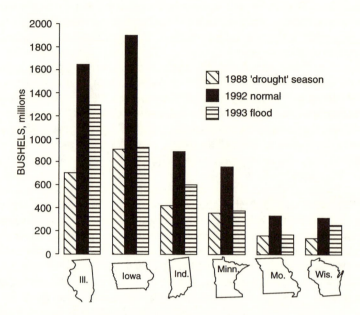

FIGURE 12-2   Corn production in major Corn Belt states for 1993, 1992, and 1988, a drought year, indicates that values in Iowa, Minnesota, and Missouri were down 50 percent in 1993 over 1992 values but not quite as low as 1988 values.

buildings, and farm equipment. Agricultural losses amounted to $8.9 billion with $2 billion in Iowa (Thompson, 1994), which exceeded losses of all other sectors.

National corn production for 1993 was 31 percent less than for 1992, largely due to the flood, compounded by an early October frost and late-maturing crops in the Corn Belt (due to a cool, wet spring). The 1993 corn production for each flooded state is shown in Figure 12-2. The 1993 values were much less than those in 1992, but not quite as low as those caused by the severe 1988 drought. The waterlogged Iowa value was 918 million bushels, nearly a billion bushels below that in 1992. Iowa's average corn yield was 80 bushels per acre (bu/acre), less than that after the 1988 drought. Soybean production nationally was down 16 percent, the lowest since the 1988 drought. The Iowa bean yield was 31 bu/acre as compared to 44 bu/acre in 1992. Although crops on Illinois floodplain farms (4 percent of the farmland in Illinois) were wiped out, the wet summer produced near-average corn yields of 129 bu/acre for the state, and the state's 1993 soybean yield was 44 bu/acre, a near-record high.

Many nonflooded Midwestern farmers came out "winners" as the flood caused grain prices to rise. The highly weather-sensitive market price for corn on June 10 (before the flood because serious) was $2.25 per bushel, but by July 15 (mid-flood), it had risen to $2.55 per bushel. Soybean prices also jumped from $5.85 per bushel on June 10 to $7.30 per bushel on July 15 (Chapter 7).

Weeds flourished in the wet weather and caused problems. Many broadleaf and grassy weed seeds were spread by floodwaters and deposited on flooded lands, and the fresh silt provided an excellent seedbed for weed seed germination. In addition, crop stands thinned by flooding provided little competition for weed seedlings. One result was that Midwestern farmers ordered record amounts of herbicides and fertilizers in the spring of 1994 to replace the farm chemicals eroded by the heavy rains in 1993. Farmers planted large crops in 1994 and good weather brought high yields and a major financial rebound for area farmers.

Once the floodwaters receded from pastures, livestock producers were concerned about potential hazards from toxic plant regrowth and disease problems. Stress from displacement, changes in management schemes, confinement, and feed changes affected livestock. Humidity and standing water increased mosquitoes and other disease-transmitting insect populations. As floodwaters receded, a variety of weeds sprouted quickly, particularly cocklebur and pigweed, which are potentially toxic to livestock. Livestock-related losses in the Midwest due to the flood were $0.3 billion.

Transportation

One of the greatest flood problems was the curtailment of transportation as a result of excessive damage to surface transportation systems. The flood became an absolute barrier to cross-river train and vehicular traffic, paralyzing transportation along 500 miles of the Mississippi River for up to six weeks. River-based barges were halted for nearly two months with nearly 1,000 miles of navigable rivers closed to navigation, and 33 general aviation airports were closed. With losses in excess of $1.9 billion, damages to the region's surface transportation systems were the worst in history.

By June 25, high waters had halted all barge movement on the Upper Mississippi. As the flood crest moved south in July, the river was closed to navigation from St. Louis to Cairo, preventing any barge or pleasure craft movement on 550 miles of the river, and the Missouri and Illinois Rivers were also closed in early July. Of 7,000 barges stalled on the rivers, many were heavily loaded with grain, coal, and other bulk commodities. As the flood continued, estimates of losses to barge companies rose from $1 million to $4 million a day, with an ultimate total of $600 million. Revenues lost by navigation interests during the two-month shutdown amounted to $320 million, of which the greatest loss was in Illinois with shipping losses of $185 million. Many barge-dependent shippers shifted their cargoes to trains and trucks. Although the rivers opened to navigation in late August, barge movement was reduced for several weeks due to dangerous navigation conditions and adjustments to allow for the altered river courses. It took three to nine months after the flood for the stocks of most of the barge-dependent shippers and receivers to return to normal.

The nation's major east-west railroads interconnect the top three rail hubs at Chicago, Kansas City, and St. Louis, but unfortunately cross through the badly flooded areas of Missouri, Iowa, and Illinois. Several major railroads suffered severe impacts, including the Atchison, Topeka & Santa Fe, Burlington Northern, Canadian Pacific (Soo), Norfolk Southern, Southern Pacific, and Union Pacific, which all had major washouts of track and bridge closings. Eighteen short-line railroads largely used to haul grain also experienced damages ranging between $0.3 and $0.5 billion each, but the Gateway Western lost $17 billion. Total damages for the railroads amounted to $240 million, which included $55 million in costs to operate detoured trains. Nearly 3,000 long-distance trains had to be re-routed on longer, circuitous routes around the flood zone, as illustrated in Figure 12-3. Because most east-west trains were delayed by one to four days for more than a month, the railroads lost revenues of $169 million. Shipment delays and losses had a major ripple effect, hurting those industries dependent on reliable scheduled rail shipments of grains, coal, and auto parts. A few railroads such as the Illinois Central benefitted by hauling shipments originally destined for barges and by accommodating many re-routed trains on their tracks. *The damages and losses suffered by Midwest railroads ranked the 1993 flood as the worst natural disaster ever experienced by the U.S. railroad industry.* However, the railroad industry had largely recovered by late 1994, ever-expanding just as it was when the flood occurred.

FIGURE 12-3   For the first time in history a Santa Fe freight train highballs southward along the Illinois Central's main line near Champaign, IL, on July 25. The train had been re-routed nearly 1,200 miles around the flood, heading from Chicago to Memphis, where it crossed the Mississippi River and headed west to find its main line in Oklahoma to its destination, Los Angeles.

The public sector of surface transportation was also heavily damaged. Approaches to 20 highway bridges across the Mississippi River were flooded and damaged. During some portions of the flood, several bridges were closed for several weeks: nine across the Mississippi River, eight across the Missouri River, and two across the Illinois River. For five weeks all bridges between St. Louis and Rock Island (a distance of 250 miles) were closed, and many did not reopen until late August and September. Many bridges sustained damage due to erosion around piers and washouts of their approach roads. As a result of the bridge closings, cross-country truck traffic had to be drastically re-routed, a very costly outcome. This also adversely affected thousands of commuters who normally used the bridges to reach shopping or their jobs.

Road and highway closings during the flood were mainly concentrated along the major rivers. In mid-July, 3,200 miles of roads were closed, and travel along the Mississippi and Missouri Rivers was effectively halted from four to six weeks (Figure 12-4). Severe erosion and washouts affected state and interstate highways and hundreds of county roads, damages that have required rebuilding road foundations as well as their surfaces. Damages to highways, roads, and bridges amounted to $434 million. Revenues lost from shipping delays and curtailment of commuting were $150 million.

Business and Industry

Several floodplain businesses and industries were flooded, or their operations were severely curtailed (Figure 12-5). Facilities were damaged, and production either stopped or slowed down greatly. Severe limitations on transportation systems interrupted incoming and outgoing raw materials and manufactured pro-

FIGURE 12-4 A classic symbol of the flood's effect on road transportation is this sign on a highway near flooded Grafton, IL, in late July (Illinois State Water Survey).

ducts, producing loss of revenue and work stoppages. Many perishable goods in stores and warehouses were a total loss. Farm losses meant that farmers were unable to repay bank loans, a problem that continued into 1994, but banks were active in loaning businesses money for flood repairs. Claims for flood losses to the private insurance industry from the nine-state region amounted to $655 million (B.D. Johnson, 1993).

Most of the industrial and commercial flood impacts were associated with lost income opportunities. For example, more than a third of the local commerce in river cities depends upon traffic crossing the rivers, but because bridges were blocked in Quincy for six weeks, that city lost $30 million in sales. Overall reductions in commercial sales were between 15 and 50 percent along the flood area, totaling an estimated $0.9 million.

About 1,900 businesses reported closings due to flooding, and most of these businesses incurred flood damage. As a result of the closures and commuting problems, about 20,000 persons became unemployed. Payments for unemployment insurance cost these businesses an additional $60 million. Property insurance companies were busy adjusting losses. Several industries were also inundated or had partial damage due to the flood, and many suffered reductions or closures in operations. Agribusinesses along the river were particularly severely hurt by the flooding. When floodgates were closed in East St. Louis, access to the large concentration of the riverfront industries was entirely blocked,

FIGURE 12-5 Many businesses rallied to help flood victims, as illustrated by these clippings from Midwestern newspapers during late July.

effectively forcing them to shut down operations. Lost opportunities due to flood-related business closures provided benefits to competitors operating in other areas of the nation. Along the large rivers in Illinois and Missouri, several power plants that depend on barge-supplied coal had to switch to more expensive fuels as their coal supplies dwindled (B.D. Johnson, 1993).

The barge and rail problems also affected industries awaiting bulk commodities such as coal for utilities, grain for mills, and petroleum products for refineries. Power plants dependent on coal either shifted to expensive truck deliveries or to equally expensive gas-coal fuel mixes. Many grain companies normally ship by barge but were forced to ship summer grain supplies by rail and trucks instead.

Flood losses and the extensive media coverage scared many potential tourists away from riverside recreation areas. Estimates for business losses to tourism ranged from 15 to 34 percent, and the recreation business along the Upper Mississippi River is valued at $1.2 billion annually. The flood also halted recreational boating on the Mississippi River and flooded a 75-mile hiking and biking trail along the Missouri River. Several museums were destroyed, and 71 archaeological sites were badly damaged by flooding and erosion (Green and Lillie, 1994). Many recreational activities were simply not conducted during summer 1993.

GOVERNMENT

Government entities at all levels from local to federal experienced severe impacts due to the flooding. Many government activities fell within the broad definition of "responses," but many others were more clearly "impacts." Within the nine-state region, 532 counties were identified as federal disaster areas, including all in Iowa and most of those in Missouri (Figure 12-6). Sizable government relief in the form of services and payments was necessary to offset the enormous personal and business losses.

Federal Government

The federal government ultimately paid $6.2 billion for flood aid, insurance, and loans, which did not include the direct losses to various federal agencies that lost facilities and the costs of many extra services, for an estimated $43 million (Figure 12-7). Most of the federal payments were made during the November 1993-June 1994 period. Payments made by 12 federal agencies amounted to $4.3 billion in direct expenditures, $1.3 billion in federal insurance (crop and flood programs), and $0.6 billion in loans (IFMR Committee, 1994). As one of the most damaged states, Iowa had received $1.2 billion ($150 million to individual assistance, $919 million to small businesses and farm assistance, and $100 million in public assistance) by June 1994 (Thompson, 1994). Other states

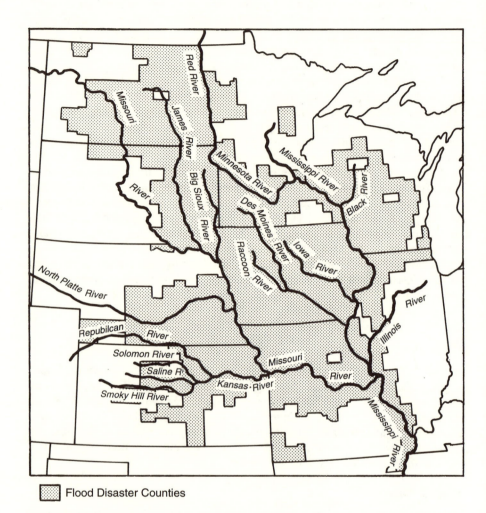

☐ Flood Disaster Counties

FIGURE 12-6   Federal disaster areas were declared in 532 counties in the nine-state region, with severe flooding leading to declarations for all Iowa counties.

with large federal flood payments were Missouri ($1.37 billion), Minnesota ($0.96 billion), and Illinois ($0.63 billion).   And it is the taxpayers who are footing the bill for the relief payments and the hundreds of other governmental costs to rebuild the regional infrastructure.

Several weather and water operational agencies were significantly affected by the flood because they had to greatly increase their activities, including the National Weather Service (for forecasts), the Corps of Engineers (measurements,

FIGURE 12-7   The high cost of the flood became the subject of several cartoons (Copyright 1995, Des Moines Register and Tribune Company, reprinted with permission).

system operations, and repairs of flood control structures), the U.S. Geological Survey (monitoring), and the Coast Guard (river protection). Hundreds of staff gallantly worked thousands of extra hours to warn and protect the citizenry along the rivers. Flood-fighting efforts by the Corps of Engineers cost more than $13.5 million (NWS, 1994). The NWS issued 16,000 special forecasts during the flood. The flood's long duration, typically two months at most locations, coupled with the loss of many flood-monitoring facilities, made it extremely difficult to forecast and monitor river conditions. One of the major problems was the failure of the NWS flood forecast system to correctly anticipate the flood heights. This failure was primarily due to an antiquated hydrologic modeling system that was unable to incorporate future rainfall data (NWS, 1994).

Many federal agencies also had flooded facilities with $32 million in damages. Top-level officials toured the flooded areas, and President Clinton convened a special regional summit conference with the governors in July to seek solutions to the complex flood problems.   Federal Emergency Management Agency (FEMA) staff were quickly on the flood scene, assessing the losses and providing assistance. Federal and state agencies plus volunteers filled and distributed more than 30 million sandbags along the rivers.

State Government

Certain state agencies were heavily involved in flood and water monitoring, in emergency services, levee repair (National Guard units), water quality assessments, and in measuring the losses. There were diverse and often extensive special demands on state agencies for added services such as counseling of flood victims and the issuance of rules for clean-up procedures. The need to raise millions of dollars to match federal relief funds had a severe impact on state budgets, and the flooded states spent an estimated $1 billion on aid and on the costs to rebuild infrastructure.

Local Government

Hundreds of communities along the rivers experienced profound impacts. More than 80 small towns were totally flooded, and 55 small towns were largely destroyed. When three major cities (Des Moines, IA, Alton, IL, and St. Joseph, MO) lost their water treatment plants for two to three weeks, it was extremely difficult and expensive to provide potable waters. More than 40 communities had severe or total losses at their sewage treatment plants, and high ground-water levels damaged thousands of sewage lines in floodplain communities. Mud-covered, flooded streets and city facilities required costly clean-up efforts. The net result of the urban impacts left many communities broke. Flood-fighting efforts at mid-sized river communities such as Quincy, IL, cost each city about $0.5 million. Estimated local costs for flood-fighting and post-flood restoration were $83 million. By the end of the flood many towns were considering relocation, many severely flooded small towns would never be rebuilt, and four small communities opted to totally rebuild on higher ground.

Levees and Federal Flood Policies

Excessive levee damages affected various governmental bodies. The first levee breached was in Wisconsin on June 20, and levee failures and repairs continued throughout 1994. A constant levee watch and repair operation was conducted along hundreds of miles of riverfront from mid-June until mid-September 1993. The levee system along the flooded rivers included 229 federal levees (39 damaged), 268 nonfederal levees (164 damaged), and 1,079 private levees (879 damaged). These levees, most built and reinforced during the past 70 years, protected urban areas or agricultural farmland developed in the floodplains. The losses to these levees represent substantial costs, depending on which ones are rebuilt, to the federal government, to state governments, and to numerous local flood-protection districts that constructed private levees that failed to withstand the 1993 flood levels. More than 200 pumping stations were disabled by the flood. In sum, the damages to flood protection works along the

Mississippi, the Missouri, the Kansas, the Iowa, the Des Moines, and the Illinois Rivers were profound.

The flood's magnitude and damages raised fundamental questions about the nation's floodplain management approach and the utility of the flood insurance program. Many questions about restoring the area centered on the future land use in the floodplains and the flood control system (Figure 12-8). Severely questioned were the benefits and effects of the development of the lock and dam system by the Corps of Engineers and the levee system. Construction of levees along the Mississippi by farmer groups began in the 1850s, and then levees along the river were enhanced by federal levee programs in 1917 and again in the late 1920s. Environmental interests claimed the widespread development of levees by the Corps had been a "military campaign against nature," and they argued for different land management practices and the return of some floodplains to natural wetlands (Faber and Hunt, 1994). In the post-flood debates, others argued for a fiscal approach involving a mix of levees and wetlands, depending on the best economic solution (Shabman, 1994).

The Corps of Engineers calculated that the flood-protection works (reservoirs and levees) on the Upper Mississippi had actually prevented an additional $19.1 billion in damages (IFMRC, 1994). Environmentalists countered, arguing that had the floodplains largely been left in their natural state, the 1993 flood would have been of lesser magnitude and the damages due to unwise occupancy of the floodplains would have been negligible. In the last 200 years, 57 percent of all the wetlands in the nine states with flooding have been destroyed.

Even though we cannot "turn back the clock," it is interesting to reflect on how the Native Americans who originally occupied the area behaved more than 1,000 years ago, thriving in a culture centered on floodplain residence and use. They farmed in the floodplains, fished the rivers, hunted bison, and built earthen mounds in the floodplains for their homes, for their food storage buildings (to keep their corn and dried meats when floods occurred), and to bury their dead (Stout, 1994). They had adapted to floodplain living with its intermittent flooding. And within a few decades after the Native Americans had been driven from the Mississippi-Illinois River floodplains, the white man's levees, dams, and drainage systems had changed the river and its floodplains forever.

SOCIAL DISRUPTION

Deaths and Illness

The descriptions of the environmental effects, the sizable and pervasive economic impacts, and the complex maze of governmental actions due to the 1993 flood all lead to the same obvious conclusion: there were considerable impacts on society in the flooded areas. Fatalities in the floods of November 1993 raised the death total to 52 lives, a relatively small number considering the magnitude of

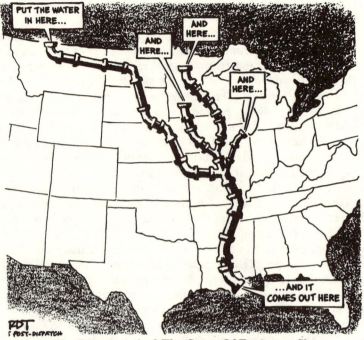

**The Public, Congress, And The Corps Of Engineers Show
The Ideal Plan For The Midwest River Basin System**

FIGURE 12-8   One of many critical commentaries on the drainage system developed on the Mississippi   (Copyrighted 1993 Engelhardt in the *St. Louis Post-Dispatch*/reprinted with permission).

the flood.   There were great fears that the polluted river waters would create outbreaks of waterborne diseases, leading to massive inoculations for tetanus and hepatitis in riverside areas.   The relatively low loss of life and the lack of major disease outbreaks are a tribute to the flood forecasting, monitoring, and prompt actions by government and private health agencies to warn the populace and provide massive inoculations.

Flood-Fighting

"Fighting the flood" was one of the major efforts of the flood.   The massive, multi-month effort involved thousands of persons residing in the threatened floodplains, volunteers who came from throughout the Midwest, and thousands of National Guard troops.   Because of the prolonged nature of the flood, a massive number of flood-fighters often worked endless weeks of exhausting 12-

hour days. No one knows precisely how many people and millions of man-hours were involved; suffice it to say, the numbers are staggering. An estimate in mid-July 1993 indicated that 70,000 persons had been involved in fighting the flood across nine states: loading sandbags, hauling bags, and placing them on dangerous levees in hot, humid weather. The constant threat of possible levee breaks kept everyone involved under stress.

Reacting to Flood Damages

Losses to flooded homes, as shown in Figure 12-9, included most or all family possessions, including clothing, furniture, vehicles, and family mementos. Blocked bridges over 200 miles along the Mississippi and along the Missouri River between St. Louis and Kansas City either halted commuters or made getting to work incredibly time-consuming. And then there were all those canceled vacations for residents along the rivers. Flood-damaged schools could not open on time in August and instead started a month or two late. Countless students and teachers were late to school due to flooded areas. Hundreds of caskets were unearthed from flooded cemeteries. After fighting the flood for weeks, those in the flood zone faced flood cleanup and then the extensive rebuilding efforts that lasted for months.

FIGURE 12-9 Floodwaters swirl around a rural home in a floodplain along the Mississippi River near Miller City, IL, a location where the river tried to develop new cutoff channel (Illinois State Water Survey).

Most of the property damage occurred in towns located within inundated levee districts, although considerable damage also occurred to riverside towns. For example, Keithsburg, IL, a community of 750, was evacuated on July 7 when a levee gave way, and two-thirds of the town was inundated in less than two hours. Two thousand people were evacuated from the Columbia and Harrisonville levee districts in Illinois on July 31, and their levees broke on August 2. When Valmeyer, an Illinois town of 900, was inundated, all but four of the town's 350 homes were damaged, and 75 percent of them sustained damages in excess of 50 percent of their value. Valmeyer is one of the communities that decided to rebuild on higher ground.

Responding to Damages

Post-flood cleanup required enormous efforts, including shoveling mud out of structures and then painstakingly cleaning muddy surfaces with water and detergents. Typical damages to buildings during the flood included warped walls and floors, collapsed or weakened structures, damaged equipment and appliances, ruined furniture, and water stains. One Illinois agency used an industrial shredder to chop up damaged furniture, wallboard, and other debris. During the cleanup, landfills typically had a 50 percent increase in deliveries, and in many cases, waived limitations on the type of material that they would accept.

Anxiety among flood victims was high for long periods due to the initial fear of being flooded, the actual flooding and damages to personal property, and finally the exhaustive clean-up and restoration process (Mairson, 1994). Loss of residence, or fear of its loss, was a primary cause of stress. Another source was the loss of primary services, including protracted outages of power, water, and sewage treatment in communities and farms along the flooded rivers. A major personal problem for thousands was where to get assistance, how to get assistance, and when to get assistance. Most relied on TV for information. FEMA was frequently cited as having a good record under difficult circumstances: reportedly 149,000 families received some form of government assistance, and FEMA spent $50 million in housing and rental assistance. Home buyout qualifications remained confusing, delaying the process into the winter of 1993-1994.

Major volunteer assistance agencies such as the Red Cross and the Salvation Army were profoundly impacted, and their assistance efforts were very costly. For example, the Red Cross reported that their expenses by the end of August were $25 million.

Social disruption from the flood is most startling in the following numbers: of 94,000 persons evacuated from their residences, 45,000 were homeless at the end of November 1993, and 3,000 were still homeless in June 1994. Further, more than 100,000 homes were seriously damaged, of which 60 percent were a total loss. In Missouri 15,000 homes were damaged, and 10,000 were condemned. At least 20,000 persons in the Midwest lost their jobs and income due to flooded factories and businesses and because many were unable to commute to jobs across flood-closed arteries.

SUMMARY

The flood of 1993 had five major impacts. In assessing these it is important to appreciate that some impacts are poorly defined as yet. The major impacts centered around the uniqueness of the extreme rainfall and the high waters. From a hydrometeorological perspective, the flood was unique with respect to its occurrence during summer, its long duration, and the large area it covered, ranking it among the nation's three worst weather-created disasters and the worst flood ever on the Upper Mississippi River system.

• *Environmental effects* related to erosion and siltation, including waterborne chemicals, were very severe. *The landscape was changed forever.* Effects on flora and fauna were mixed: there were general benefits in the river floodplain ecosystems. The rapid spread of the destructive zebra mussels during the flood has been classed an "environmental catastrophe." There are also deep concerns over the long-term effects of the eroded soils and the riverborne chemicals on the ecosystem of the Gulf of Mexico.

• *Economic impacts* were the greatest on record for any flood ($18 billion), but the flood had very little effect on the nation's economy. Greatest damages occurred in agriculture, transportation, and the commerce and industry along the major rivers. There were winners among nonflooded farmers and businesses.

• *Impacts on government entities* were extensive, requiring massive efforts to predict, monitor and warn of the flooding, to fight the flood, and subsequently to bring aid to individuals affected and to rebuild the region's infrastructure. The federal flood-related payouts were $6.2 billion, and those by the states and local agencies were $1 billion.

• *Social impacts* were regionally pervasive, but the flood produced relatively low loss of life and no major widespread disease. Extensive regional losses of homes and jobs created great stress, anxiety, and insecurity, which lasted for several months after the flood ended.

• *Policies* were affected, and the flood 1993 raised major policy questions about how the nation should manage floodplains and handle flood and crop insurance. These included:

1. How inadequate are the flood control structures?
2. How do we change the lack of use of floodplain insurance?
3. How can the nation's crop insurance program be altered effectively?
4. How should government programs for buyouts of floodplain property be handled?
5. How should a shift to environmentally-appropriate uses of flood-prone lands be accomplished?

298

6. How do we prevent further environmental problems like the zebra
   mussel invasion?

Interestingly, 15 months after the flood's end and as a result of the flood, we
have partial answers to some of the above questions.   New laws address
deficiencies in the crop and floodplain insurance programs and allow for buyouts
(and relocation) of flooded homes, businesses, and entire communities.   The
terror and destruction experienced by hundreds of thousands of people during the
flood, and the raging debates about what to do with the mighty Mississippi River
bring to mind the words of a well-known river sage, Mark Twain.   In his *Life on
the Mississippi,* published in 1896, Twain wrote:

> Ten thousand river commissions, with the minds of the world at their back,
> cannot tame that lawless stream, cannot curb it or confine it, cannot say to it,
> 'Go here,' or 'Go there,' and make it obey; cannot save a shore which it has
> sentenced; cannot bar its path with an obstruction which it will not tear down,
> dance over, and laugh at.

REFERENCES

Bhowmik, N.G. (ed.), 1994: *The 1993 Flood on the Mississippi in Illinois*. Miscellaneous Report 151, Illinois Water Survey, Champaign, IL, 149 pp.

Coastal Ocean Office, 1994: *Coastal Oceanographic Effects of Summer 1993 Mississippi River Flooding*. National Oceanic and Atmospheric Administration, Washington, DC., 77 pp.

Faber, S., and C. Hunt, 1994: River management post-1993: The choice is ours. *Water Resources Update,* 95, 21-25.

Goolsby, D.A., W.A. Battaglin, and E. M. Thurman, 1993: *Occurrence and Transport of Agricultural Chemicals in the Mississippi River Basin, July through August 1993*. Circular 1120-C, U.S. Geological Survey, Washington, DC., 22 pp.

Green, W., and R. Lillie, 1994: *Archaeology and the Great Midwestern Floods of 1993*. Research papers, Volume 19, University of Iowa, Iowa City, IA, 197 pp.

Hopp, M.W., 1994: Go with the flow: legacy of the '93 flood. *Urban Forests*, 11, 8-11.

Interagency Floodplain Management Review Committee, 1994: *Sharing the Challenge: Floodplain Management into the 21st Century*. Washington, D.C., 191 pp.

Johnson, B.D., 1993: Down the drain. *Illinois Issues,* 12, 22-25.

Johnson, J.K., 1993: Water quality. *Proceedings Farm Flood Response Workshop,* University of Iowa, Iowa City, IA, 8-9.

Kunkel, K.E., 1993: *Soil Moisture Conditions in the Midwest on September 15, 1993*. Midwest Climate Center, Champaign, IL, 6 pp.

Kunkel, K. E., S. A. Changnon, and J. Angel, 1994: Climatic aspects of the 1993 Upper Mississippi River flood. *Bulletin American Meteorological Society*, 75, 811-822.

Mairson, A., 1994: The great flood of '93. *National Geographic,* 85, 42-87.

National Weather Service, 1994: *The Great Flood of 1993*. National Disaster Survey Report, National Oceanic and Atmospheric Administration, Washington, DC., 195 pp.

Richards, F., D.A. Miskus, and S.A. Changnon, 1994: Hydrometeorological setting. *Coastal Oceanographic Effects of Summer 1993 Mississippi River Flooding*, National Oceanic and Atmospheric Administration, Washington, DC., 3-25.

Shabman, L., 1994: Responding to the 1993 flood: the restoration option. *Water Resources Update*, 95, 26-30.

Siemens, J.C., and R.G. Hoeft, 1994: Effects of the flood on soil conditions. *Today*, 27, 16-18.

Stout, C., 1994: The first Illinoisans. *Early American Museum Newsletter*, 1, 1-3.

Thompson, H. M., 1994: *The Flood of 1993: Iowa Flood Disaster Report*. Johnston, IA, 35 pp.

U.S. Geological Survey, 1994: *USGS Yearbook Fiscal Year 1993*. Washington, DC., 124 pp.

13

The Lessons from the Flood

Stanley A. Changnon

The flood was the nation's major news story of 1993 (Figure 13-1) and one of the worst weather-related disasters in American history. Based on economic losses, it became the worst flood on record and rated as a once-in-500-year event on rivers draining thousands of square miles. The flood's physical dimensions were unusual in three respects: it occurred in summer when major Midwestern floods seldom occur; it covered an immense area (large parts of nine states); and it lasted a very long time (three months).

The final tally of major losses due to the flood included: 52 deaths, the highest death toll in an American flood since the floods of 1951; 56,000 homes and 2,900 businesses severely damaged; 8.5 million farm acres either unplanted or unharvested; and more than $1.9 billion in losses to transportation systems, including $920 million by the barge industry, which lost 20 percent of the year's revenue. Although the total amounted to an estimated $18 billion, the flood's impact on the nation's economy was negligible.

What was the "bill" to the taxpayer? Congress ultimately authorized $6.2 billion in flood aid (over the past five years the United States has spent $34 billion in relief of natural hazard losses). Insured crop losses totalled $1.6 billion, and the federal government paid out $301 million in flood insurance payments. Nine state governments spent an estimated $1 billion in flood-related costs.

Top 5 stories of 1993

1. **The Flood of '93**
2. **Fire ends standoff in Waco, Texas**
3. **Clinton's freshman year activities**
4. **World Trade Center bombing**
5. **Somalia's mercy mission turned violent**

FIGURE 13-1 The top five news stories of 1993, as voted by 300 news executives in a survey by the Associated Press.

Reflecting on the flood a year later reveals several important outcomes. Summer rainfall in 1994 across the region flooded during 1993 was near normal and quite timely for Midwestern crops, which produced record yields. The transportation network had been fully restored. By September 1994, everyone displaced by the flood had finally moved into permanent housing. Rebuilding of damaged roads was still under way. Levee rebuilding has been delayed principally because of uncertainties as to who is going to pay the costs to rebuild, but by November 1994, 145 of the 201 damaged federal levees had been repaired. Flood-related laws have been passed or amended, studies have been launched, and the regional restoration is well under way.

This assessment of impacts and responses one year after the flood has afforded the authors the opportunity to reflect on the data and to identify the lessons taught by a great teacher, the flood itself. But have American society and government really learned the lessons and acted accordingly? We hope so, but it is still too early to know for sure.

The author of each chapter has attempted to identify the "lessons learned" within the framework of topics investigated: the weather factors causing the extreme rains; the climatic and hydrologic aspects of the flood; the environmental consequences; the impacts on agriculture, transportation, the economy, and society; and past, present, and future policies relating to floods. These lessons have been reviewed, interpreted, and summarized *as a series of seven major over-arching lessons, each based on several specific lessons identified in the various chapters.*

Lesson 1: Unique flooding defies past experience and design extremes
Lesson 2: The flooding had significant, unexpected impacts
Lesson 3: Many systems for monitoring and predicting flood conditions were inadequate
Lesson 4: Incomplete or incorrect information was released during the flood
Lesson 5: Many past approaches to mitigate losses failed
Lesson 6: The flood produced major benefits
Lesson 7: Flood outcomes reaffirmed old lessons

It is anticipated that the lessons identified will be helpful to those attempting to deal with future floods--for they certainly will come again. This chapter concludes with a description of three areas in which many key issues raised by the flood remain unresolved: flood policy, the environment, and human reactions. These are issue areas for which only future actions will show whether the lessons taught by the 1993 flood have been learned.

LESSON ONE:
UNIQUE FLOODING DEFIES PAST
EXPERIENCE AND DESIGN EXTREMES

The flood occurred after a period of prolonged above-normal precipitation across the Midwest that began in mid-1992 and continued through 1993. In that sense, the prolonged flood was a "climate aberration," much like a drought in both persistence and size, and as some claimed, "an act of God." The 1993 flood left estimated losses of $18 billion and struck the Midwest just five years after the severe drought of 1988, an event that created losses of $39 billion across 75 percent of the nation.

What made the flood meteorologically unusual was uniquely persistent atmospheric circulation pattern that created a prolonged series of heavy rains across the central United States (Chapter 2). Rains fell daily during 2.5 months across large portions of the Upper Mississippi River basin, a huge region of 300,000 square miles. Nowhere in the basin was rain below average (Chapter 3), and the basin received 20 inches of rain during June-August 1993, a value two-and-one-half times the average. Each summer, the Midwest normally experiences a few extreme heavy rain events, but never until 1993 had the area experienced so many (77) large, all-encompassing events. The previous record three-month rainfall in the basin (set in 1915) was 25 percent less than that in 1993, an enormous difference in climatic terms.

The hydrologic assessment of the 1993 flood revealed the event was "unprecedented in modern history" (Chapter 4). A series of Midwestern floods occurred in 1993: one in the spring, the prolonged summer flood, and then two floods in the fall. The massive summer flood developed in the north (Minnesota and Wisconsin) and gradually migrated south to Iowa, Kansas, Missouri, and Illinois as the summer wore on. All this culminated in a unique hydrologic event that had never occurred before--the simultaneous arrival of twin flood peaks, one on the Missouri River and one on the Mississippi River, at their confluence near St. Louis on August 1. The floodwaters broke all-time flow records on 1,800 river miles in eight states, and the highest flows ever seen on 200 miles of the Missouri River were equivalent to 500-year extremes. More than 500 scour holes were created on the Missouri River along with 14 channel changes (Chapter 5).

Lessons: When such extreme events occur, there are seldom-seen effects on riverine systems, extreme damage to "containment" structures, unexpected social and economic impacts, and assessments of the "cause" of the event come under scrutiny. Many system failures due to the 1993 flood were no one's fault--the design values were simply exceeded by conditions never experienced since river records have been kept.

A series of necessary scientific and technical actions will improve understanding, mitigation, and response to exceptionally extreme flooding. These actions include:
- *development of plans for data collection during and after floods,*
- *development and installation of better instruments to measure floods and river flows,*
- *development of new hydrologic models for floods, and the*
- *collection of unique 1993 flood data before it disappears.*

We need to make the financial investment necessary to support these actions.

LESSON TWO:
THE FLOODING HAD SIGNIFICANT
AND UNEXPECTED IMPACTS

A record flood such as that in 1993 produced several largely unexpected impacts and a few responses that experts would have been hard pressed to imagine before the event. The authors identified five such areas of unexpected outcomes and consider each of these to be "lessons learned."

#1: Unique Impacts on All Forms of Transportation.   Among the most spectacular and unexpected flood damages were those to transportation systems, along with the ensuing problems for shippers and recipients of goods. Because the heart of the flood centered on the nation's major rail and highway networks and embraced the heavily used navigable waterways of the central United States, one-third of the nation's freight movement was paralyzed, halting the east-west and north-south flow of goods hauled between the Midwest's major transportation hubs and coastal ports (Chapter 8). Drastic delays prevailed, commutes across the rivers were halted for weeks by closed bridge systems along hundreds of river miles, and the losses ultimately rose to $1.9 billion. And, despite only minimal government aid, the barge, trucking, and railroad industries rallied.

In responding to the flood, transportation employees revealed considerable inventive genius, allowing rapid solutions to problems, often based on existing flexibility in many systems and on cooperation among agencies, companies, and persons collectively acting together to solve problems. Many adjustments were done quickly and often in unique ways. Sudden re-routings of 3,000 trains on lines of other railroads served as an excellent example of such "real-time" adjustment. The flood proved that in the Midwest certain little-used rail lines, some bordering on abandonment, had enormous value for train detours and thus still served a useful purpose.

Lesson: The nation's surface transportation systems, particularly the railroads and highway systems, have considerable flexibility to adjust to blockages and outages caused by floods. Redundant routes should be retained to ensure transportation between hubs.

Continuing poor estimates of flood crests, flood longevity, and when the rivers would open to navigation collectively had major effects on the barge industry and on shippers who rely on barges (Chapter 1). Had warnings been issued two or three weeks before the flood's development, major changes in barge shipments could have been made and shippers and barge owners could have moved equipment and supplies beyond harm's way, thereby saving millions of dollars. Furthermore, once the flood started, the strategies could have been different had the projected dates for the end of the flood (issued in the early stages) been less optimistic.

Approaches to many important highway and rail bridges were flooded, leading to prolonged closures and major costly re-routing of trains, trucks, and autos.

Lessons: The barge industry and shippers depending on commercial navigation should seek improved river forecasting models and flood-monitoring systems.

If critical bridges are to survive 100-year to 500-year flood levels, approaches to the bridges must be rebuilt to higher levels.

#2: Structural Damage Exceeded Expectations. More than 1,000 levees were damaged or destroyed, leading to the massive flooding of farmland, communities, and transportation systems. This sizable damage to levees was unexpected, yet this is predictable (by hydrologists) as an outcome from a massive flood (Chapter 5). Levees failed for several reasons, but failure was frequent where levees were built on old active channels and at flanks where levees tie into bluffs. When the floodwaters receded, flood damages (types and extent) to various structures were often found to be more severe than estimated during the flood (Chapter 1). Much of the structural damage to bridge piers, flooded buildings and homes, inundated highways, etc., was much greater than past experience would have predicted, likely due to record fast flood flows and prolonged submersion (Chapter 4).

Lessons: The record flood conditions offer data and information for engineers and structural experts about how to more effectively design structures to withstand flood extremes. Data on types of structural damages should be collected. Because current damage estimation techniques are inadequate, data from the 1993 flood should be used to develop better guidelines for estimating flood damage based on river currents, depth of water, and time under water.

A river will reclaim its floodplains in extreme floods. When deciding where and how to build levees, it is wise to work with the river, not against it. Old meanders are not suitable sites for levees, and flanking sections require higher specifications.

#3: River-Floodplain Ecosystems Came Out Winners. River ecologists already understood that floods are an essential and helpful part of riverine ecosystems. Given the magnitude of the 1993 flood and the many changes as a result of human intervention on the floodplains of the major Midwestern rivers, the likely ecosystem outcomes from a major flood event were not clear. However, most components of the river-floodplain ecosystem responded favorably to the flood (Chapter 6). Nutrients released from soils stimulated the food chain, submersed aquatic plants disappeared in some areas during 1993 but regrew in 1994, 52 fish species spawned in the floodplains during the flood and became abundant, and floodplain forests are regenerating despite the loss of some tree species. Tree death was up to 35 percent near St. Louis in the areas of worst flooding, but even there seedlings appeared in 1994.

Lesson: Regardless of the human alterations to the floodplains, major floods maintain and even rejuvenate river-floodplain ecosystems.

#4: Major, Unexpected Environmental Problems. Human actions combined with the flood to create several unanticipated environmental problems, for example, the first big "population explosion" of zebra mussels in the Midwestern river system (Chapter 6). Introduced into the Great Lakes in 1986, large numbers of these pests were moved by floodwaters down the Illinois River and into tributaries. The flood also caused the accidental release of imported Asian black carp, which consume native clams and mussels. Levees broke and some terrestrial animals were killed or washed away. When the U.S. Army Corps of Engineers lowered the Mississippi River below normal levels to help drain still-flooded areas during November-December 1993, fish may have been trapped and killed in backwater lakes. Many black willows died during 1994, possibly due to river-transported atrazine.

Serious long-term effects are expected from the severe damage to the ecosystem of the Gulf of Mexico. Due to riverborne nutrients released in the Gulf, the existing dead zone was increased. It makes no sense economically and ecologically for the major rivers to simultaneously carry millions of tons of valuable nutrients in opposite directions (upstream on fertilizer barges and downstream in the water). In addition, vast amounts of herbicides eroded from Midwestern farmland were carried into the Gulf along with a huge volume of low salinity water that spread into the Atlantic (Chapters 5 and 6).

Lessons: Human activities have hurt river ecosystems in many ways, and floods can facilitate pest invasions and help create environmental disasters. Future use of the Midwestern floodplains requires a careful balance between controlling natural variations in waterflow for navigation and flood protection purposes and allowing some variation for benefits to the ecosystem. There should be a national ecosystem management plan for river-floodplain ecosystems. The long-term effects of the flood on the Mississippi and its tributaries, and on the Gulf of Mexico, should be monitored to improve river science and management, but adequate collection of ecosystem data requires planning prior to the next flood event.

#5: Unusual and Unplanned Adjustments and Responses. Plugging unexpected levee breaches, escaping threatening flood situations, and addressing a myriad of human needs for assistance (Chapter 10) all required many unplanned responses. Among these were the quick and effective handling of sudden loss of water supplies due to inundated water plants at large cities such as those at Des Moines, IA, St. Joseph, MO, and Alton, IL. These responses demonstrated capabilities to solve new and unexpected problems at the local and state levels.

Lesson: Some existing governmental systems can respond quickly and effectively to unexpected major impacts from extreme events. Ingenuity and resources appear to be the key here.

LESSON THREE:
MANY SYSTEMS FOR MONITORING AND
PREDICTING FLOOD CONDITIONS
WERE INADEQUATE

The assessment of the flood's chronology (Chapter 1) revealed that information issued on the flood's current conditions was often incorrect or unavailable (see lesson #4). The National Weather Service (NWS) study of the flood revealed that many flow-measuring systems were damaged, destroyed, or unable to function during the flood. Basin hydrologic models were incapable of generating reasonable outcomes partly because of inadequate monitoring of flows (Chapter 4).

Precipitation measurements were seldom adequate for detecting and measuring flash-flood rain events, although there were notable exceptions. The few new radars of the NWS operating in 1993 proved invaluable for measuring heavy local rains. Most lives lost were the result of flash floods. A major loss of life was prevented in Wisconsin due to the automatic flood detection system and the alert actions of NWS flood forecasters (Chapter 2). NWS basin runoff models are "antiques" incapable of handling effects of levee breaks or forecasted precipitation. The models also do not reflect the many changes to the basins as a result of human intervention. A major flaw in the design frequencies of extreme rainfalls and floods for many areas is that they have not been updated over the last several decades.

> *Lessons: Existing systems for flood monitoring and flood forecasting are inadequate. The NWS needs to implement its new radar network and flash-flood warning techniques.*
>
> *The inadequacy and loss of river monitoring equipment offers an opportunity to make major improvements. Collection of post-flood flow data is required to fully understand the record flood flows. Updated frequency studies of extreme hydroclimatic events are also necessary.*
>
> *The basin hydrologic models require major revisions. For example, there is a need for a layered Geographical Information System for every river mile to allow better damage estimates as floods develop. Improved communications would enhance decisions by thousands of flood-affected officials at the county, state, and regional levels during floods.*

LESSON FOUR:
INCOMPLETE OR INCORRECT INFORMATION
WAS RELEASED DURING THE FLOOD

Assessments of impacts and responses to the flood revealed that much of the information made available was incorrect (often based on erroneous estimates) or was incomplete and failed to present all aspects of an issue. Much of this "misinformation" came from government agencies, the media (newspapers and television), and experts at universities and other institutions. Regardless of the source, this situation created undue confusion, bad choices of actions taken, and debates that delayed responses and hampered proper policy development. Five informational problems were found, each with a lesson.

#1: Misinformation: Loss Values. Several major themes were evident from the chronology of the 1993 flood (Chapter 1). One theme was the *continuing escalation of all parameters*: in the forecasts of the flood's magnitude, the continuing extension of the predicted dates of flood crests, and in the ever-continuing increases found in (1) the assessments of flood damages (in each impacted sector and as a total event), (2) political attention, and (3) the dimensions of federal and state relief aid.

One would expect ever-increasing loss values since the flood was an ever-expanding event from late May through late July. However, one is impressed by the sheer magnitude of the errors in the damage estimates (Chapter 9). The economic assessments pointed to major early errors in the economic impacts values, some too large, others too small. The problem was compounded because many losses were not covered by insurance, thus making their quantification more difficult than in many disasters.

Past studies of other major natural hazards have shown early estimates typically inflate the losses (Chapter 9), but the assessment of the 1993 flood reveals the opposite: most were underestimates of the losses and hence in the aid required during the flood. These underestimates were due to poor data and inadequate collection of information. For example, information on the actual amount of damage was slow in developing. Consider the figures on stranded barges: reliable sources claimed only a few hundred barges were stranded during the first two weeks that the Mississippi River was closed, but this number changed to 7,000 stranded barges just three weeks later (Chapter 8).

Important loss values also shifted rapidly. Estimates of losses to the barge industry, to agriculture, and to the entire economy resulting from the flood began to appear on or shortly after July 1, as shown in Table 13-1. The daily loss to the barge industry was estimated at $1 million on July 1, rising to $2 million per day on July 12, then to $3 million on July 23, and finally to $4 million per day by July 27. All other critical loss values also changed rapidly, as shown by the ever-larger numbers in Table 13-1.

> *Lesson: During a major flood, data on flood conditions and losses are typically poor and generally inaccurate (on the low side in 1993), and estimates remain highly inaccurate for months after the event. Means for obtaining more accurate near real-time data on conditions and losses should be developed to improve planning for in-flood adjustments and for relief and restoration activities.*

TABLE 13-1 Time Line of Shifting Values on the Dates They Appeared during July-August

| | *July* | | | | | | | *August* | | | | *Total* |
	1	*5*	*10*	*15*	*20*	*25*	*30*	*1*	*5*	*10*	*15*	*losses*
Barge industry losses per day, millions	$1		$2		$3	$4						$600
Crop losses total, billions	$.1	$.3	$1	$2	$2.5		$3.5		$4.5			$8.9
Flood losses total, billions		$2	$5	$10	$15	$25	$15-20			$13		$18
Federal aid, billions	$0.8	$1.2	$2.5		$3.6	$4.3	$4.7		$5.8			$6.2

#2: Misinformation: Poor Forecasts by Government Agencies. The flood condition pronouncements of the National Weather Service (NWS) and those of the Corps of Engineers for the St. Louis area were often inaccurate and sometimes controversial (Chapter 1). Flood predictions, often sizable underestimates of future river levels and/or dates when the crests would occur, and the optimistic statements that the flood would end soon, helped lead to early underestimates of flood damages. These incorrect predictions of an early end to the flood had detrimental effects on the decision-making of those industries seriously affected by the flood, including the barge industry. The forecasts certainly affected strategies used to fight the flood and to seek alternatives in shipping and other endeavors affected by the flood. A key problem was the use of antiquated hydrologic models that did not address levee failures or integrate future precipitation predictions. Added to this was the loss of flood-measuring equipment washed away by the flood. Another problem concerned the fact that federal officials at St. Louis and Des Moines issued several flood forecasts and status statements during July that disagreed, thereby confusing the general public (Chapter 10) as well as flood-fighting efforts.

Assessment of the crop forecasts issued by the U.S. Department of Agriculture (USDA) revealed continuing in-season overestimates of final outcomes (Chapter 7). The process of collecting data and estimating agricultural outcomes, including effects of the wet weather and flooding on harvested acreage estimates (issued during the summer of 1993) and on outlooks for the production of corn and soybeans (as issued throughout the late summer and fall), were consistently wrong and by sizable percentages. The July forecast for national corn production was 7.8 billion bushels, decreasing to 7.4 billion in the August forecast, with an ultimate value of 6.34 billion bushels, 23 percent less than estimated in July 1993. A similar estimation problem was noted during the 1988 drought.

Lessons: The hydrologic models used by the NWS for flood predictions on all time scales need major improvements as described (lesson 3). Interactions between NWS forecasters and the Corps hydrologists require improved clarification of responsibilities.

Methods used to estimate regional and national effects of large-scale wet and dry weather conditions on crop outcomes are capable of making sizable errors and need improvement.

#3: Misinformation: Effects on Government Relief. A related finding concerns "political attention" to the flood and how it shifted over time. As the flood evolved in June and early July, the frequency and stature of government visitors to flooded areas increased: the first visits were by governors of the affected states and then a few members of Congress to flooded areas, followed by heads of federal agencies, Vice President Gore, and President Clinton, who ultimately made four visits to the flooded areas (Figure 13-2).

THE PRESIDENT TOURS FLOOD DAMAGED IOWA

FIGURE 13-2   The frequent visits of President Clinton and other government officials to the flooded area received considerable attention and became the subject of political pundits (Copyright 1995, Des Moines Register and Tribune Company, reprinted with permission).

This upward trend in the stature of political visitors, and the ever-upward spiral in estimates of the flood's losses, reflected considerable uncertainty in the validity of the estimates at any given time. As shown in Table 13-1, federal aid values escalated from an initial value of $850 million on July 1 to $5.8 billion on August 7. The final figure was $6.2 billion. One result of the ever-changing and increasing relief requests (and then payments) was considerable Congressional debate over the amounts of aid needed and the source of funds. These aid adjustments, like the weather and flood forecasts, didn't catch up with the magnitude of the flood and its impacts until well after the fact. The seemingly never-ending adjustments in relief aid created unnecessary confusion and political controversy. This process delayed achieving realistic and timely amounts of aid needed. The decision-making process was further impeded by various agencies with overlapping responsibilities, and it was not clear which agency was responsible.

Lessons: Near real-time estimates of flood losses and predictions of the flood's size, both physical and economic, were underestimates.   They reflect the lack of real-time information about the magnitude of the flood and its impacts, plus poor forecasting of the growth of damages.   The government should improve its means for acquiring information on impacts and work to remove or clarify overlapping responsibilities between agencies

*for handling relief aid for problem areas like home reconstruction
and levee rebuilding.*

#4: Misinformation: Public Understanding of Floods. For several weeks
(June and early July 1993) everyone was operating with the belief that the flood
in any given area would end in a matter of days. Weather experts also attempted
to explain the causes for the record-breaking, long-lasting heavy rains. Every
possible meteorological cause was offered and a lack of agreement among several
independent experts was present, further muddying the issue (Chapter 2).

Another area of considerable scientific-public confusion related to the
magnitude of the flood. This was compounded by several "expert" pronouncements indicating the 1993 flood would be either the greatest on record or
more or less than the 1973 flood, or some other past flood (Chapter 1). Another
aspect of this confusion was the general public's misunderstanding of what a
"100-year flood" event means. Many such terms are confusing to the public
(Chapter 11).

Studies in Missouri of public responses to the flood revealed that most citizens
got their information from the print and television media (Chapter 10). They
found that the public came away from the flood with a greater interest and
concern about weather and climate issues.

*Lessons: There is widespread misunderstanding about floods
and their frequency. The merits of a flood-related educational
program include increased understanding of forecasts, warnings,
and terms used by scientists and engineers, plus clearer
recognition of the risks related to living and farming in floodplains.*

*Government officials need to use the broadcast media more
effectively to disseminate information during and after a disaster.*

#5: Media Focus on the Event, Not Causes and Solutions. Assessment of the
presentation of the flood news by the media (Chapter 10) found most of the media
reports "routinized" the unexpected flood; focused on the event rather than on its
causes or solutions; quit presenting useful news and information immediately after
the flood ended; and made the event seem distant, dehumanized, and a battle
fought and lost. However, certain regional newspapers presented accounts with
much information on underlying causes of the flood as well as how to get help.
The media's key omission was information on the policy issues at a time when
people were ready to pay attention.

*Lesson: The mass media have become the major source of
information for disaster victims and others interested in a natural
hazard. Experts and government agencies providing information
to the media should work to get the media to address causes,
solutions, and policy issues underlying such events.*

LESSON FIVE:
MANY PAST APPROACHES TO
MITIGATE FLOOD LOSSES FAILED

Flood Mitigation Policies Have Not Succeeded. As the severity of the flood grew, and the damages spread, there was widespread concern over the underlying causes of the flood losses and what to do about future flooding. The issues centered on (1) failure of the levee systems, (2) interrelated questions of wise land use in the floodplains, including the issue of returning floodplains to their natural state, (3) failure of the flood insurance program, and (4) confusion over the nation's flood aid programs being handled by a myriad of federal and state agencies. Major national newspapers ran editorials about these issues, and the titles of these editorials offer valuable clues as to the policy issues faced by the nation and the region (Table 13-2).

Members of the U.S. Congress from the flooded states began calling for special flood studies during the flood, various interest groups put forth widely different views in Congressional hearings, and bills were offered to correct various ills of the nation's flood mitigation program. The traditional approach to flood control involving 8,000 miles of levees in the Upper Mississippi basin failed, with 1,067 levees breached and damaged. Statistics relating to the nonstructural approach to flood mitigation showed failure too: only 10 percent of those persons with flood damage had floodplain insurance, and less than 50 percent of all farms with damaged crops had federally backed crop insurance. In essence, thoughtful past recommendations of how to attain flood mitigation had never been adequately implemented.

TABLE 13-2   Titles of Selected Editorials during the Flood

"Putting the River in a Straitjacket Backfired" *(USA Today,* July 14)
"U.S. Should Acquire Floodplains" *(St. Louis Post-Dispatch,* July 27)
"Don't Remove Farms From River Valleys" *(St. Louis Post-Dispatch,* July 29)
"Levees and Dams Form the Basis for Civilization" *(Washington Post,* August 9)
"As the Floodwaters Recede" *(Chicago Tribune,* August 12)
"Flood Relief: Restored Wetlands" *(St. Louis Post-Dispatch,* August 12)
"Flood Recovery Offers Opportunities" *(St. Louis Post-Dispatch,* August 27)
"The Flood Next Time" *(Chicago Tribune,* August 25)
"The New Course for Flood Control?" *(St. Louis Post-Dispatch,* September 2)
"Uncle Sam Shouldn't Pay to Move Flood Victims" *(USA Today,* November 11)

Lessons: Many structural and nonstructural approaches to flood mitigation have not worked, and many past efforts to improve U.S. flood policies have not succeeded.   The flood of 1993 reinforced the need to improve floodplain use policies and to improve the federal insurance programs, with important changes already being made in the crop and floodplain insurance programs. However, flood insurance is not the total answer; other mitigation approaches need to be considered and implemented.

Not all levees, particularly agricultural-protection levees, can be built cost effectively to withstand record floods. If these levees are rebuilt, it should be with the clear recognition by those supporting the costs and thus choosing the design levels of these levees that occasional floods will overtop them.

In essence, the nation's policy philosophy about flood mitigation must change: the nation needs to move beyond reliance on political responses and solutions to inappropriate uses of floodplains. Individuals, not the government, must assume responsibility for their locational decisions, and future government policies must stand firm over time to seek such an approach.

Successes in Flood Control Efforts. Although the 1993 flood caused massive damages, Corps of Engineers studies found major benefits from existing flood control structures (Chapter 4). Reservoir management reduced the magnitude of the flooding. Federal levees prevented major flooding of two threatened major cities, St. Louis and Kansas City. Federal efforts to thwart new and damaging cutoffs in the main channels of the Mississippi and Missouri Rivers also were effective. The Corps estimated the flood control structures saved $19 billion in flood losses, a figure that nearly matches the estimated total losses of $18 billion.

Lesson: Many past investments in flood control structures were wise.

LESSON SIX:
THE FLOOD PRODUCED MAJOR BENEFITS

Although the major theme of the 1993 flood was the extensive damage, there was also an interesting set of benefits or positive outcomes of the flood. There has been regional and national utility (value) in the record event because it:

- focused attention on inadequate national policies (Chapters 7, 10, and 11)
- improved river-floodplain ecosystems (Chapter 6)
- led agencies to install new measurement instruments, to assemble data, and to develop updated weather and river models (Chapters 2 and 4)
- provided useful data and information for scientific purposes (Chapters 2, 3, 4, 5, and 6)
- led to rebuilding of outmoded infrastructure (Chapters 1, 8, 9, and 10)
- focused public awareness on key environmental issues (Chapters 5 and 6)

- instilled a new sense of community (Chapter 10)
- produced winners in agriculture and business (Chapters 1, 7, 8, and 9)
- developed a positive view towards government (Chapter 10).

Government Policies. Long-standing needs for improvements in natural hazard and flood-related policies were clearly illuminated and brought to national attention. Although there is skepticism about what might really be achieved as a result of the flood (Chapter 10), many major changes in flood policy have already been made in the 15 months since the flood ended (Chapter 11). In many respects, the flood of 1993 was the "icing on the cake." That is, the magnitude of the cost of relief assistance to the federal government, coupled with the high costs of other recent severe natural disasters such as Hurricane Andrew, caused the Clinton Administration and Congress to seriously address management of major rivers such as the Mississippi as well as how to make other changes affecting the cost of relief due to natural hazards. At a time when the public is suspicious of government, the flood helped created a sense of public trust in government for its role in flood relief.

The Interagency Floodplain Management Review Committee, a powerful committee established by the Clinton Administration, made an excellent assessment and issued a highly credible report in June 1994. Its recommendations are expected to become a "national action plan" by 1995. Congress in 1993 mandated an assessment (by the Corps) of the flooded areas leading to an ongoing evaluation of floodplain management needs. A bipartisan task force on funding disaster relief was established by law in 1994 to seek more effective ways to confront natural disasters and mitigate their impact.

The issue of moving people out of the floodplains and restoring portions of the floodplains to natural wetlands was debated in the media and in Washington during and after the flood. The Hazard Mitigation and Relocation Act passed in December 1993 created an important change in federal-state-local cost-sharing, allowing federal funding of up to 75 percent of eligible costs. These funds have been largely used for buyouts of flooded homes and businesses, a major accomplishment. By October 1994, 160 buyout projects had been approved to elevate 7,500 buildings and four entire communities to higher ground (Chapter 10). The Federal Emergency Management Agency (FEMA) has begun designing a new national mitigation strategy for all natural hazards.

Several new laws and improvements in policies tied to the flood have already occurred. Necessary changes in the National Flood Insurance Program Act were enacted in 1994 (Chapter 11). Necessary revisions in the Federal Crop Insurance Program were made in 1994 (Chapter 7), also largely a result of the flood's impetus. Continuing activities in Congress (early 1995) suggest other major changes will occur in how Congress handles future disaster payments in order to get better control of the budget, to address more effectively the economic dislocation of disasters such as the flood, and to help the private insurance industry in handling such catastrophic losses. These future actions could include requiring a three-fifths Congressional majority for emergency appropriations, cutting spending in other areas to fund disaster payments, or establishing a rainy day fund (as some states do). The December 1994 report of the House Task Force on Natural Disasters has led to drafting a bill that would reduce federal disaster expenses through a program of loss mitigation, private insurance, and a federal backstop for natural disaster reinsurance (possibly by establishing a private corporation to provide this reinsurance).

River Ecosystem Benefits. The flood of 1993 was an economic disaster, but it was a boon to many plants and animals in and near the Missouri, the Illinois, and the Mississippi Rivers. Even the few species that appear to have been harmed may benefit in the long run. Every component of the river-floodplain ecosystem, from the bottom to the top of the food chain, responded to the exceptional 1993 flood (Chapter 6).

Improved Measurements, Models, and Data Bases. The flood wiped out many river-measuring installations and revealed that certain older forms of measurement were inadequate (Chapter 4). These missing and inferior instruments will be replaced by newer, better ones. The flood also showed that remote flood-detection warning systems located in critical areas were of great value for flash-flood alerts, and the potential value of the new NWS weather radars for flash-flood detection was demonstrated (Chapters 1 and 2). The failure of the existing NWS hydrologic models to accurately predict flood conditions is resulting in long-needed improvements in models and computer capabilities at NWS river forecast centers.

The myriad of problems during and immediately after the flood led federal policy makers to identify causes of the problems and to seek ways to improve how the nation handles flood losses and mitigation (Chapter 11). Their efforts were frustrated because detailed spatial data on physical characteristics (such as which acres were flooded and types of levees breached) and on socioeconomic conditions (such as where did crop insurance coverage exist and when was flood insurance purchased) were not readily available in comparative formats. This led to the formation of an interagency group, the Scientific Assessment and Strategy Team (SAST), which developed a massive detailed digitized data base for the Upper Mississippi River basin. The team's data bases and recommendations were important input to the meaningful report of the Interagency Floodplain Management Review Committee, and its information has been valuable to the sound reformulation of the flood insurance and crop insurance programs. This highly successful effort now stands as a prototype for preparing physical and economic data bases for other parts of the nation.

Scientific Findings. The flood as an extreme event provided unique data that allow testing and confirmation of various scientific theories and concepts: new studies of river-floodplain relationships, flood and ground-water relationships, and river behavior, plus a test of the theory on the role of disturbances in maintaining the biodiversity of floodplains (Chapter 6). The flood also showed scientists how to sample floods and revealed needs for new measuring techniques, as well as plans for collecting environmental data during floods.

Rebuilding Infrastructure. The flood damaged bridges, highways, buildings, water and sewage treatment plants, and numerous other structures, many of which were old and in need of repairs, poorly located, or built with inadequate designs. The replacement of these structures and facilities with more effective designs and modern construction methods represents a major improvement in the region's complex infrastructure.

Enhanced Awareness of Environmental Problems. Three growing environmental problems were exacerbated by the 1993 flood: (1) zebra mussels, (2) the detrimental effects of nitrates and herbicides in the Gulf of Mexico, and (3) herbicides in the rivers and floodplain ecosystems (Chapter 6). There were major news stories about these problems, bringing them to the attention of the public, which is exactly what is needed to get governmental action.

A Sense of Community. Studies revealed that the voluntary provision of flood assistance and working together to fight the flood and to restore homes and towns after the flood created a sense of community across the region (Chapter 10). A common bond of understanding prevailed, linking the value of individual assistance to the good of the group.

Financial Winners. The detrimental impacts of the flood created many losers, but in the process also created many winners, a fact that lessened the national economic impact of the flood (Chapter 9). Railroads hauled increased tonnage that could not move on flood-stalled barges (Chapter 8), and food-producing firms in nonflooded areas of the Midwest reaped benefits because their competitors in flooded Iowa could not function for months (Chapter 9). The wet, but not too wet, weather in the eastern Corn Belt (most of Illinois, Indiana, and Ohio) led to high corn and soybean yields. When the flood caused grain prices to escalate, Corn Belt farmers with good crops reaped large financial benefits (Chapter 7). Rebuilding thousands of flood-damaged or destroyed structures in the Midwest became a financial bonanza for the construction industry (Chapter 9).

Positive Attitudes about Government. During the flood, regional residents viewed the government, at both the federal and state levels, as helpful (Chapter 10). This occurred at a time when trust in government was low. Working together through the post-flood problems offers an opportunity to help rebuild the government-citizen relationship.

Lessons: Most weather events, including climatic extremes such as droughts and floods, produce winners as well as losers. The 1993 flood was no exception. Scientists and engineers have the benefit of new knowledge about floods; certain environmental problems are receiving needed attention; most aspects of the river-floodplain ecosystem benefitted; inadequate federal policies were brought to public and political attention, resulting in improved policies; damaged, aged, or inadequate facilities and

*equipment are being replaced with better ones; and many farmers
and businesses profited financially.*

LESSON SEVEN:
FLOOD OUTCOMES REAFFIRMED
OLD LESSONS

Many of the impacts caused by the major summer flood of 1993 in the Midwest were not unexpected, and some were quite predictable. Among these were excessive losses to the agricultural sector (Chapter 7). The flood-related wetness in farmed uplands and the drowning of crops in floodplains led to losses estimated at $8.9 billion, but these were not as high as losses experienced in the Midwestern drought in 1988. Relief aid covered most of the agricultural losses.

Flood losses in the floodplains were excessive, a highly predictable outcome. Nearly 100,000 persons were displaced by the flood, 20,000 lost their jobs, and flood-related anxiety was pervasive and persistent in the flooded zones across nine states (Chapter 10). The federal and state governments ultimately provided $7.2 billion in relief aid to farmers, communities, displaced persons, and for repairs to the region's damaged infrastructure.

It was no surprise to discover that floodplains act as "capacitors" to handle flood flows and that rivers reclaim their floodplains in extreme floods (Chapter 5). The reaffirmed lesson is: "it is better to work with a river than against it." The flood again illustrated several other hydrologic truths; that is, extreme floods (1) initiate new meanders and cutoffs, (2) produce major scouring and deposition in riverbeds, and (3) affect both ground-water quantities and quality of aquifers in the floodplains.

Enormous volunteer responses occurred, including sizable financial aid, widespread volunteer efforts to help flood-fighting (like the filling and placing of sandbags), and contributions of materials and facilities from individuals and communities across the nation (Chapter 10). These are typical of responses that have occurred after other natural hazards.

The flood also reaffirmed an old lesson: major floods occur and thus will occur again in the future. We must not lose sight of the fact that future flooding in the Midwest, California, and elsewhere in the nation is inevitable.

UNRESOLVED KEY ISSUES

Government Policies

A major issue emanating from the flood concerns future governmental responses in the flooded area, and particularly changes in the nation's flood mitigation policies. The 1994 report by the special federal study committee established by the White House called for sweeping and revolutionary changes in national flood activities and policies. Will these turn into an action plan that is adopted and funded?

Many groups have called for further governmental monitoring of the flood's impacts on the environment, as well as the rebuilding of the systems to monitor river flow and flooding. There is a great need to develop more sophisticated river basin models that allow drastically improved flood forecasts. The SAST data base for the basin will need monitoring and constant updating if it is to remain valuable. Will federal and state agencies interact to adequately fund and address these needs involving flood data collection, data assembly and inter- pretation, and forecasting?

Debates over what to do with the "big rivers" continue, and many issues remain to be resolved in the political arena, although major changes to correct some of the problems could be resolved by federal agencies. Do we nationally continue to subsidize agriculture in former lakes and floodplains? There are alternatives. Effective policy-related strategies have been offered, but there are conflicting and entrenched interest groups, and the outcome will ultimately be resolved in Washington. Only the future can provide answers to these major policy questions.

Human-Induced Problems in the Ecosystem

Three emerging environmental problems were made worse by the flood and remain to be resolved. Human activities abetted all the major environmental impacts credited to the flood, which will require considerable attention over time to resolve. These are (1) the introduction of zebra mussels and other pests; (2) excessive nutrient loading in Midwestern rivers, which is seriously affecting the ecosystem in the Gulf of Mexico; and (3) excessive herbicide concentrations in rivers and the Gulf of Mexico. Chapter 6 presents a series of recommendations for specific government actions to halt the spread of zebra mussels, to stop future pest invasions, to reduce leaching of nutrients, and to protect ecosystems against modern herbicides.

Reactions of the Public Affected

Will the new laws relating to flood insurance and crop insurance attract public participation, or will the farmers and floodplain residents continue to rely on "relief" as their "insurance" against floods and other hazards (as they have in the past)? Future participation by the population at risk will determine whether another flood (certain to occur) will be as damaging.

Will citizens assume more responsibility for their actions? Will changing government policies for reducing federal expenditures and giving more responsibility to the states and private sector help or hurt?

In an era when cutting back on government seems to be the voter demand as prudent fiscal policy, are the cutbacks going to include investments in flood mitigation measures that may save the country substantial sums in the long term? Resolution of this issue depends on public involvement and political will and wisdom. Sustainable development of the nation also depends on adoption of effective approaches for mitigating impacts of natural hazards. It remains to be seen whether government and the general populace have learned and will act upon lessons taught by the Great Flood of 1993.

FIGURE 13-3   A fitting end to the story of the Great Flood of 1993. This photograph captures a late summer sunset along the flooded Mississippi River (Illinois State Water Survey).

About the Book

The flood that affected a third of the United States during the summer of 1993 was the nation's worst, ranking as a once-in-300-years event. It severely tested national, state, and local systems for managing natural resources and for handling emergencies, illuminating both the strengths and weaknesses in existing methods of preparing for and dealing with massive prolonged flooding.

Through detailed case studies, this volume diagnoses the social and economic impacts of the disaster, assessing how resource managers, flood forecasters, public institutions, the private sector, and millions of volunteers responded to it. The first comprehensive evaluation of the 1993 flood, this book examines the way in which floods are forecast and monitored, the effectiveness of existing recovery processes, and how the nation manages its floodplains. The volume concludes with recommendations for the future, in hope of better preparing the country for the next flood or other comparable disaster.